I0820446
Ultimate
ORIGAMI
INSTRUCTIONS
OVER 30 PROJECTS
hinkler

Published by Hinkler Pty Ltd
45–55 Fairchild Street
Heatherton Victoria 3202 Australia
www.hinkler.com

Author: Dr Matthew Gardiner
Contributor: Darren Scott (origami artist)
Cover design: Hinkler Studio
Photography: Ned Meldrum
Internal design: Hinkler Studio

ISBN: 978 1 4889 7498 4

Printed and bound in China

CONTENTS

ABOUT ORIGAMI

WHAT IS ORIGAMI?

Origami is the ancient art of paper folding. Origami is a curious sounding word because it is not English, but Japanese in origin. Ori, from the root verb oru, means "to fold" and kami is one of the many terms for paper. In the purest renditions, origami creates an intended shape from a single sheet of paper with no cutting, gluing, taping, or any other fastening device allowed. To create less rigid versions one may make small cuts as in kirigami (cut paper) or long slits as in senbazuru — where a single sheet is effectively divided into a number of smaller, still-connected squares. This book focuses on the action of folding paper and the manifestations from this action.

ABOUT THE AUTHOR

Dr Matthew Gardiner is an artist who works with origami and technology, as exemplified by oribotics, which is a combination of robotics and origami (see www.matthewgardiner.net).

Matthew's simple geometric origami designs often have a touch of utility and his diagramming style aims to be detailed and easy to follow.

THE ORIGIN OF ORIGAMI

No-one really knows when origami was invented. We do know that paper had to be invented first, so we can safely say that it is less than 2000 years old, but an exact date, even to the nearest century, cannot be authentically established. Despite its Japanese name, some claim that origami is Chinese in origin; this cannot be entirely discounted, since many art forms now claimed by others can be traced back to mainland China. We will accept that this art activity has been around for a long time.

One reason for origami's hazy history is that for many centuries there was almost no documentation on how to do it. The oldest book known to contain origami-like instructions, the Kanamodo, is from the 17th century, yet older woodblock prints show paper folding. The oldest origami book for amusement in the world is the Hiden Senbazuru Orikata from 1797. The title roughly translated means "the secret technique of folding one thousand cranes". There are around one hundred designs known as "traditional origami", that were passed from hand to hand in Japanese culture: typically a mother showing a child, or children sharing among themselves. In fact, until the middle of the 20th century, origami was thought of as something that women did as decorations for weddings, funerals and other ceremonial occasions, or something that young children did as a recreational pursuit.

After World War II, people from around the world started to visit Japan in greater numbers, and Japanese citizens increased their travel to other countries. Through this exposure, origami started to spread across the globe, especially in the hands of exchange students—those young ambassadors of Japanese culture. The form began to spread across genders and cultures. Today, a finished model can be made and displayed for your own pleasure, or given as a gift, cementing a friendship through paper folding.

THE ULTIMATE ORIGAMI BOOK

Greetings Origami Artist! You've picked up this book because you love origami and want to refine your paper-folding skills.

Origami is generally understood as a purist art form. All you need is paper and your hands (or feet!) to fold paper into new artistic creations. However, like many forms of craft, origami is also the result of technology and tools and you can use these to make your origami folds easier and cleaner.

Paper is an important technology, developed over centuries. Paper-making processes are still refined today, by both industry and artisans, transforming wood and plant pulp into thin, durable and flexible sheets. Origami artists are often connoisseurs of paper; they develop a keen eye for high-quality paper, learning to select for strength, foldability, and appearance. Origamists study, often as a result of experimentation as they create their origami, how different types of paper fold. Some paper is tough and can withstand being folded many times over. Other paper is delicate and needs to be handled gently. Each paper type has an application.

Because of the wide variety of paper types, origami artists sometimes choose to use hand tools to help with folding. The following sections introduce some commonly used tools and their suggested applications to help enhance your origami experience.

FOLDING BONES

A folding bone is the origamist's first choice all-rounder tool. It has long flat edges and a curved surface that is useful for making strong creases in all types of paper. Strong creases are formed by rubbing the flat edge along the line of the crease. The pointed end is useful for flattening folds in tight corners. A folding bone can be held in many ways, so practice on different types of paper with both bone shapes and get a feel for how each flattens out folds. Compare your hand-folded creases with the creases created by the folding bone. Generally, bone-folded creases are sharper and a raised edge will become clearly visible on the mountain side of the fold.

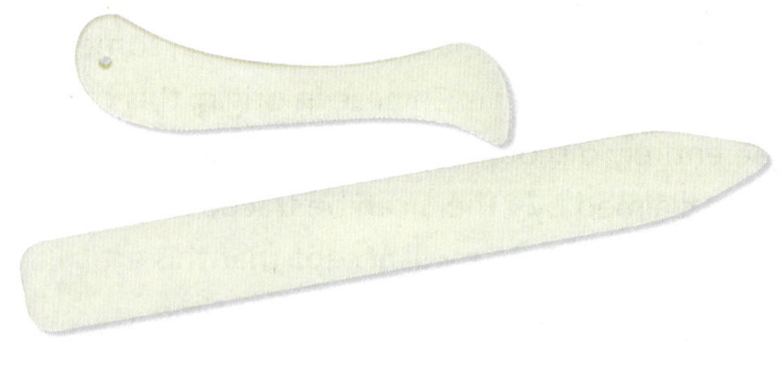

SCORING TOOL

I love my scoring tool. A "score" is a line that is marked to become a crease but has not yet been folded. It is so useful for teaching the paper where you want to place creases. When you fold a scored line, it folds easily and cleanly. Scoring tools are especially helpful for thicker materials, or complex crease patterns. Use your scoring tool with a ruler for the neatest results. Hold the scorer like a pen, press down firmly, and use it to draw along the ruler's edge. The scoring tool has two sized balls at each end, a large and a small end. Use the small ball on paper and light card and the large ball on thicker materials.

TWEEZERS

Paper can be folded into very tiny shapes, and not everyone has tiny, agile fingers to get into those tight spots. Tweezers are useful for gently pushing and pulling the paper into shape. Paper can be delicate, so don't use too much force.

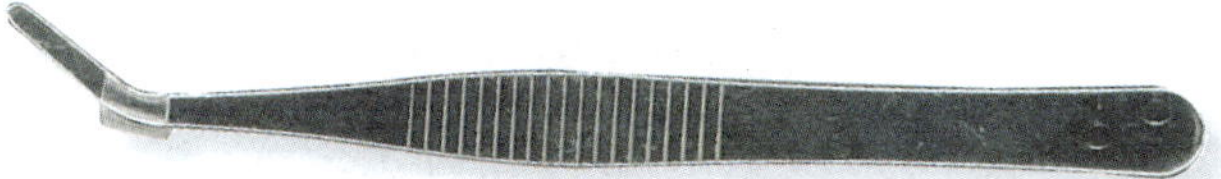

HOW TO FOLD

| BY: MATTHEW GARDINER

The art of origami begins with simple folds. Many beginners rush through their first folds, not paying attention to accuracy. The key to high quality origami is the quality of each fold. There are many kinds of folds, but the principles described below can be applied to most folds. Origami paper has a colored side and a white side. When diagrams refer to the colored side, it is to indicate which color will be the dominant color in the final model.

Good origami is patient origami.

1

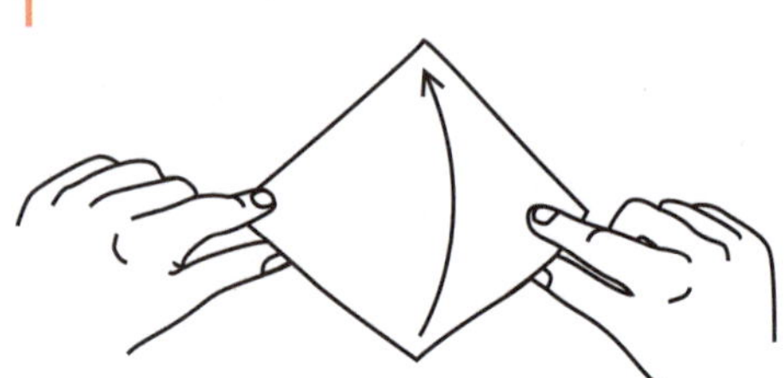

Gently lift the bottom corner to the top corner. Don't crease yet, just hold the paper in position.

2

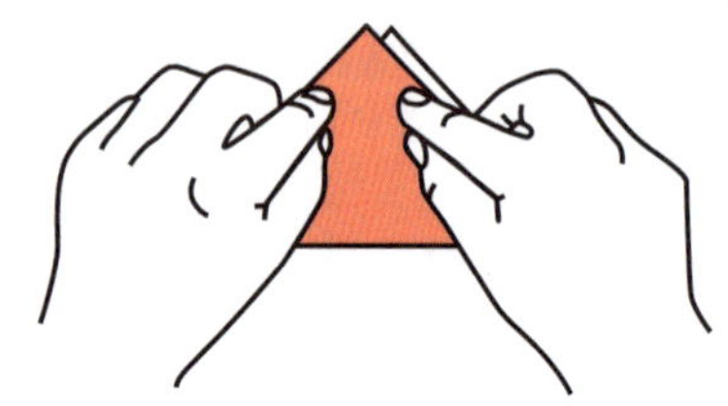

Line up the corners exactly. The image above is not aligned correctly.

3

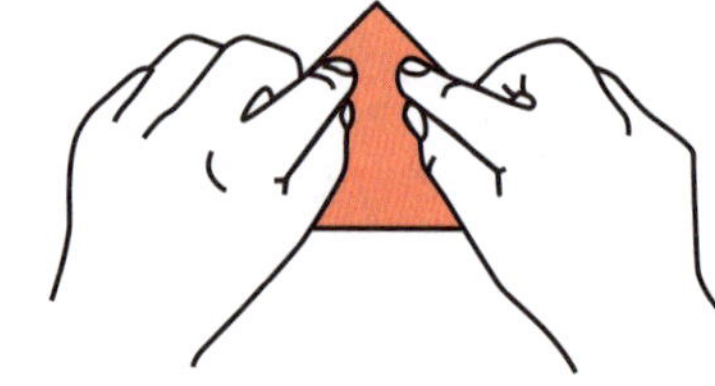

The corners are exactly aligned; there is no visible difference.

4

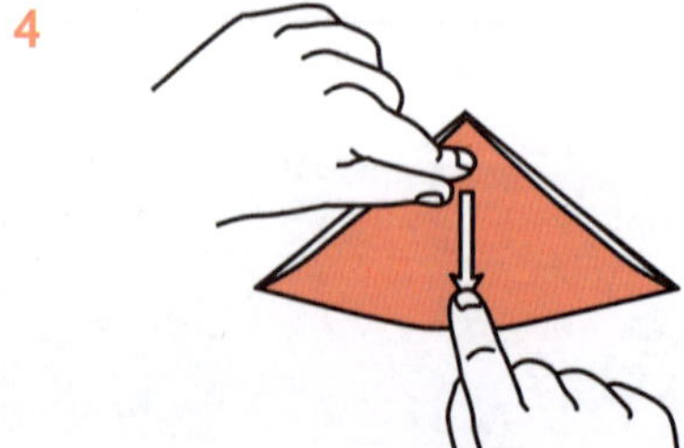

Hold the corner with one hand, and slide the forefinger of the other hand down to the bottom.

5

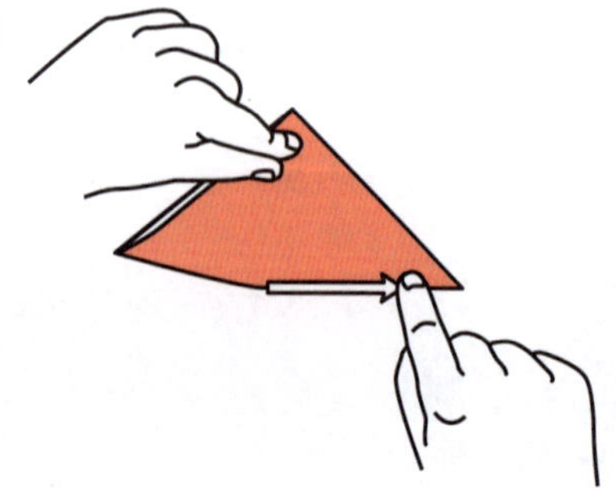

Crease from the center to the edge. Check that the crease goes exactly through the corner.

6

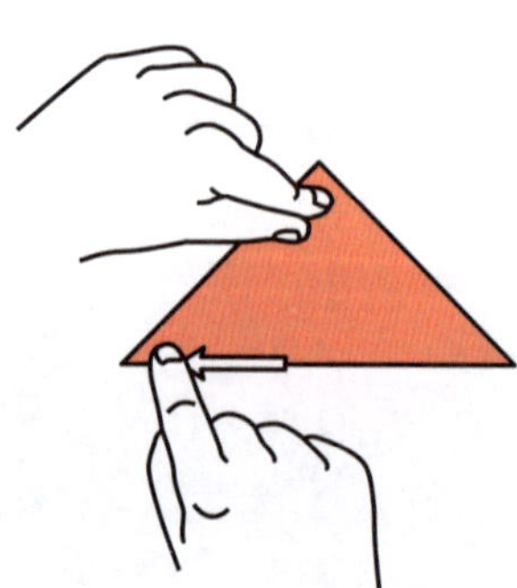

Crease from the center to the edge on the other side to complete the fold.

Like the diagonal fold the book fold is very simple. The best way to make both folds is to check twice (or more) and fold once. In origami, to check is to use other parts of the paper as references to make sure your crease is accurate. In these two introductory folds, the edges and corners are the references. In origami you will use existing creases, corners, edges, intersections of creases, and points to help make sure your fold is accurate.

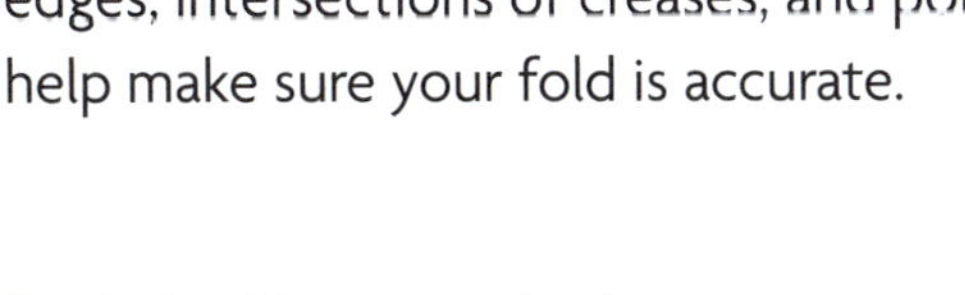

Good origami is accurate origami.

1

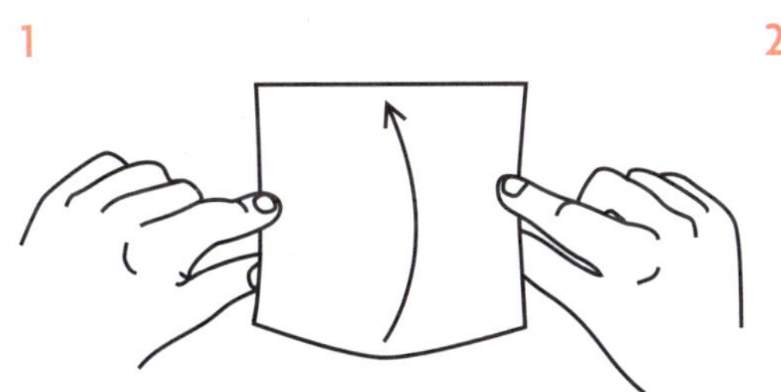

Lift the bottom edge to the top edge.

2

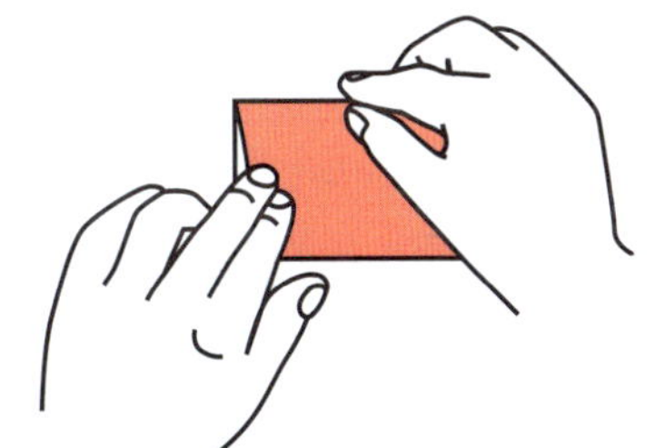

Align the corners and then align the edges, and the edges on one side.

3

Align the opposite corner and edges so that both sides are perfectly aligned.

4

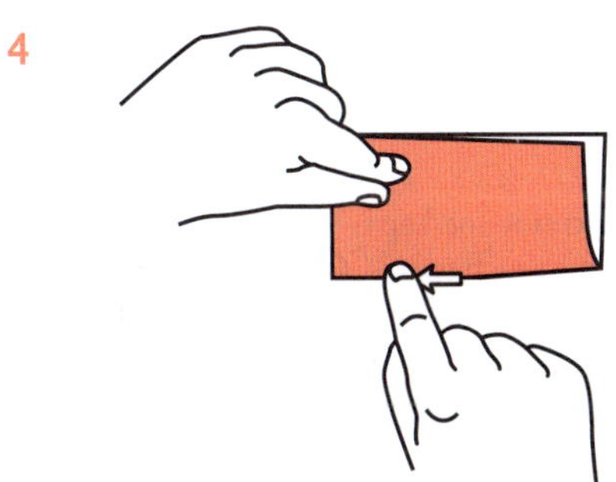

Hold one corner and crease from the center to the edge.

5

Crease from the center to the other edge to complete the fold. All corners and edges should be aligned.

SYMBOLS

BY: MATTHEW GARDINER

LINES

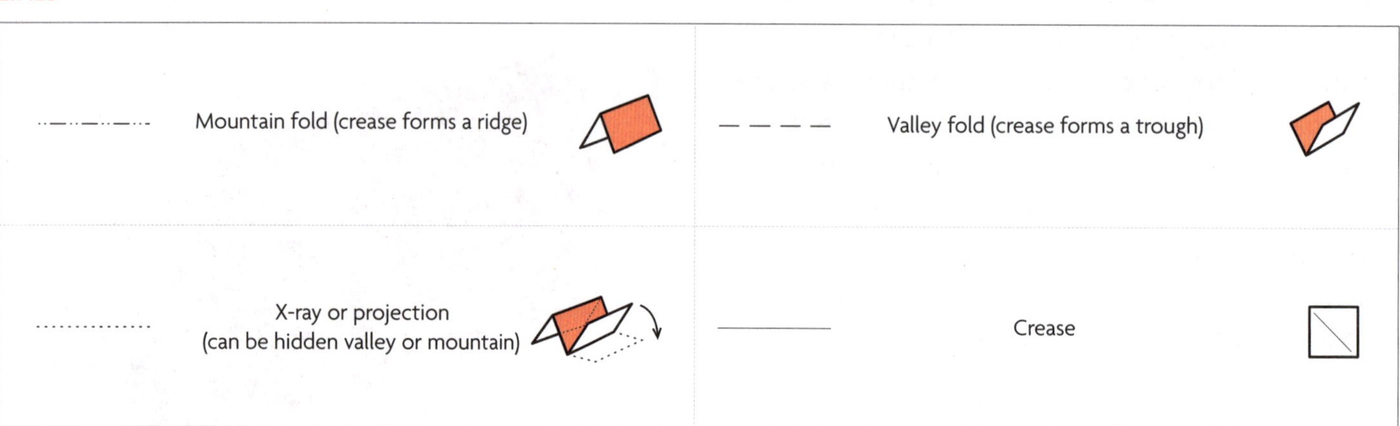

ARROWS

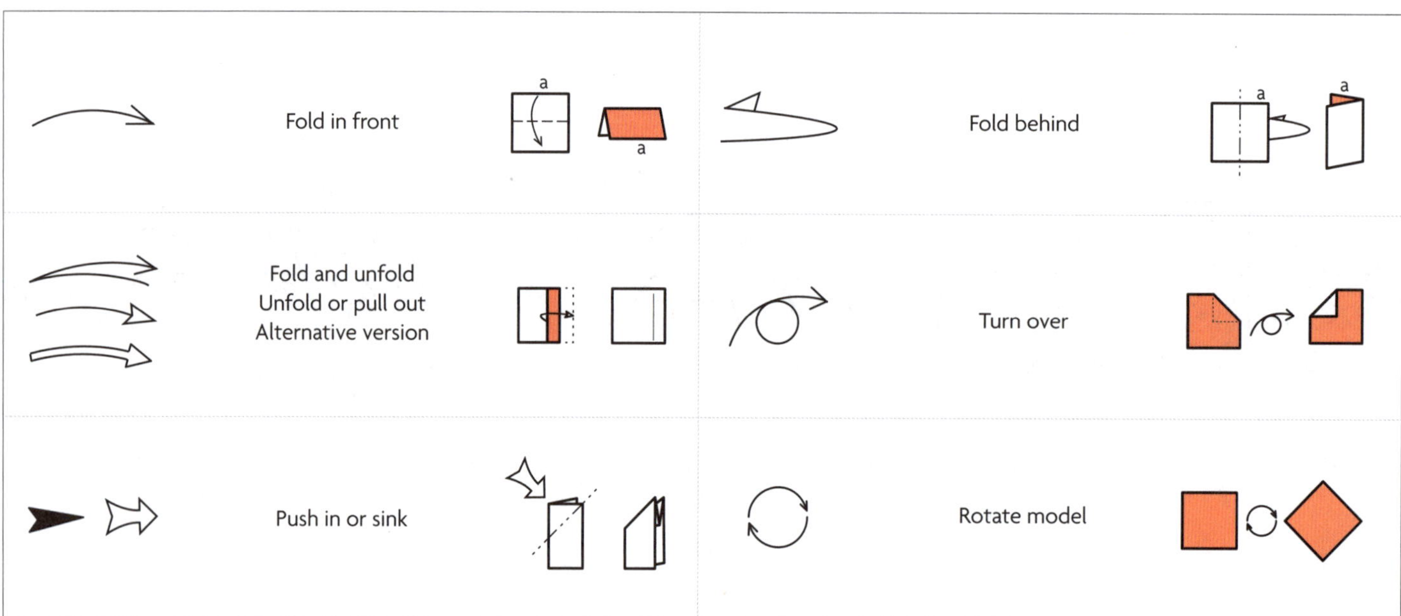

EXTRAS

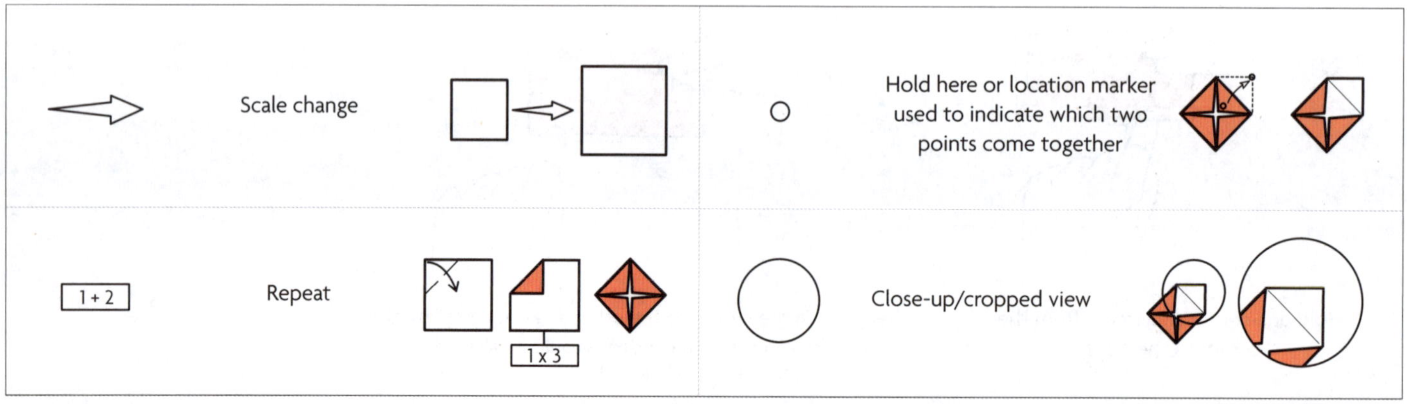

TYPES OF FOLDS

BY: MATTHEW GARDINER

BOOK FOLD

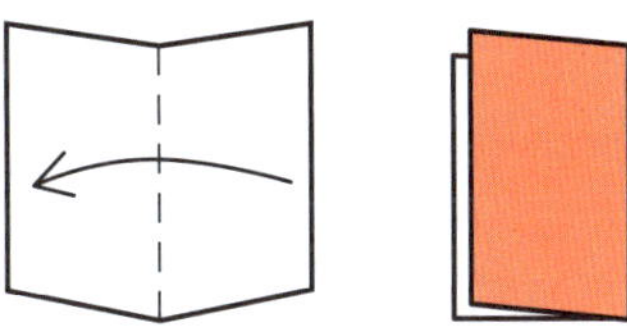

Valley fold one edge to another, like closing a book.

CUPBOARD FOLD

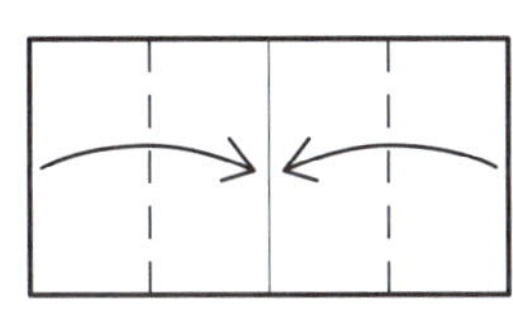

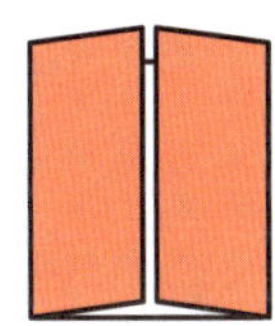

Fold both edges to the middle crease, like closing two cupboard doors.

BLINTZ

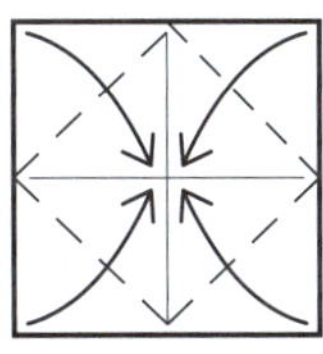

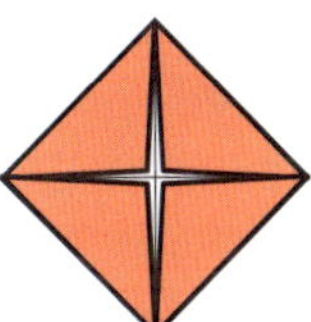

Fold all corners to the middle. This was named after a style of pastry called a blintz.

PLEAT

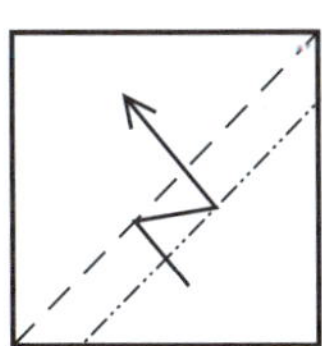

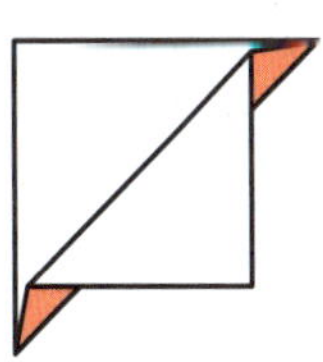

A mountain and valley fold combination.

BISECT - DIVIDE A POINT IN TWO

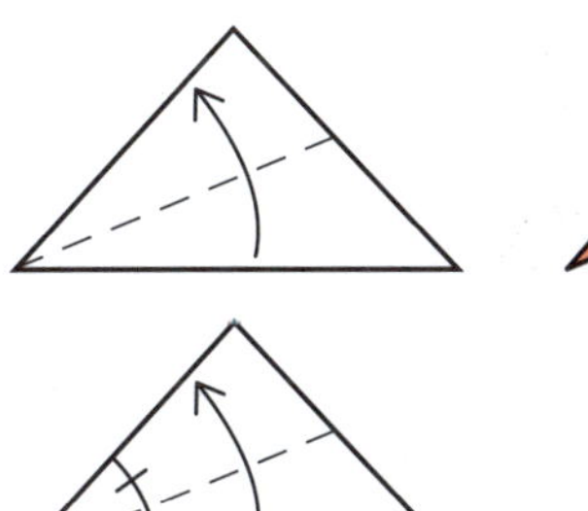

Many folds use a corner and two edges to position the fold line. The most common is a bisection, or division of an angle in two.

Fold one edge to meet the other, making sure the crease goes through the corner.

INSIDE REVERSE FOLD

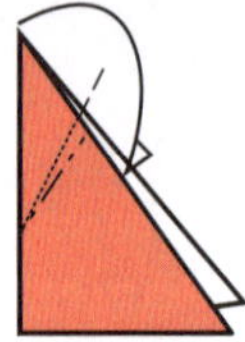

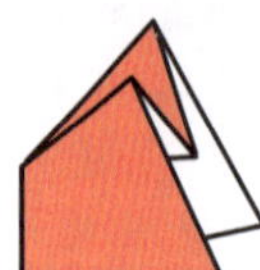

The spine of the existing fold is reversed and pushed inside.

OUTSIDE REVERSE FOLD

The spine of the existing fold is reversed and wrapped outside.

DOUBLE REVERSE

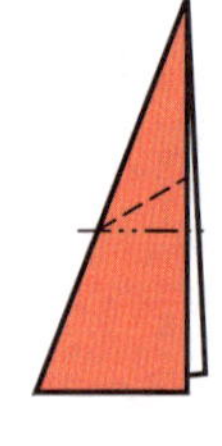
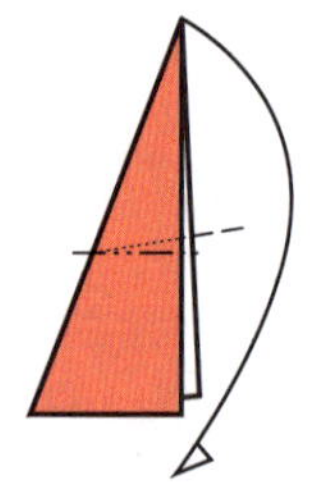
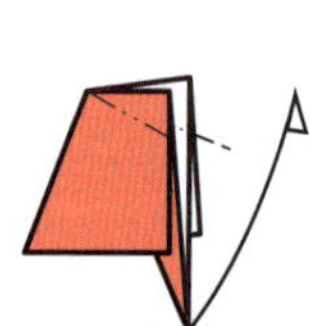

A double reverse fold is two reverse folds made in sequence on the same point.

The last diagram shows the paper slightly unfolded, to illustrate the folds that are made.

INSIDE CRIMP

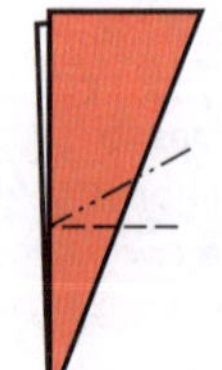
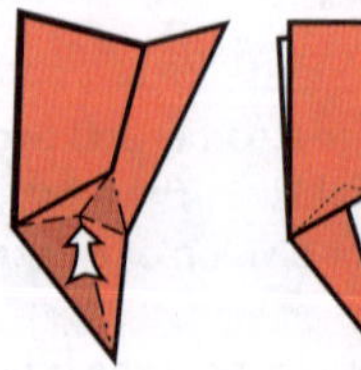
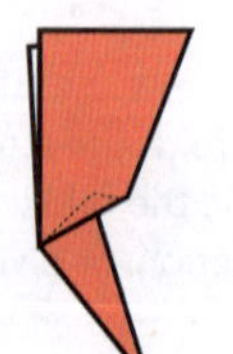

OUTSIDE CRIMP

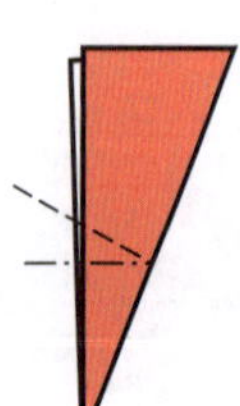
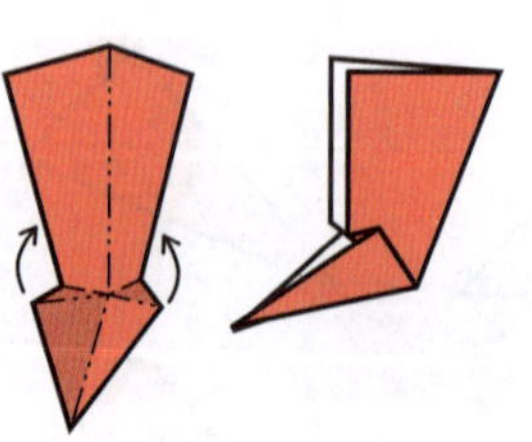

Crimps are often used for making feet or shaping legs. They can be thought of as a pleat mirrored on both sides of the point.

An inside crimp tucks the pleat on the inside of the point.

An outside crimp wraps the pleat over the outside of the point.

PETAL FOLD The petal fold is found in the bird and lily base.

1

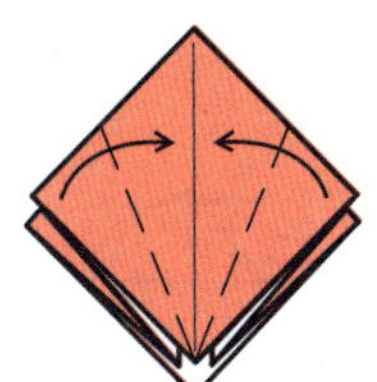

Fold top layer to the center crease.

2

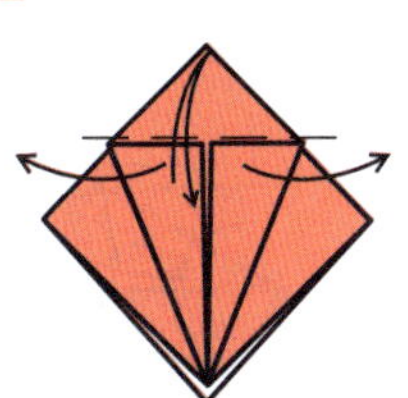

Fold and unfold the top triangle down. Unfold flaps.

3

Lift the top layer upward.

4

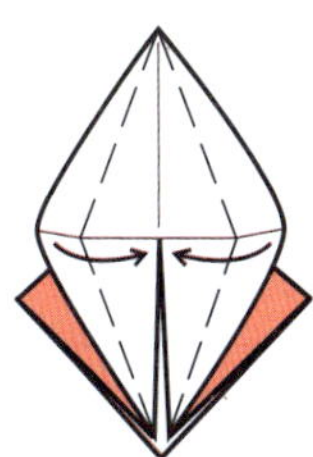

Step 3 in progress, the model is 3D. Fold the top layer inward on existing creases.

5

Completed petal fold.

SQUASH A squash fold is the symmetrical flattening of a point. The flattening movement is known as squashing the point.

1

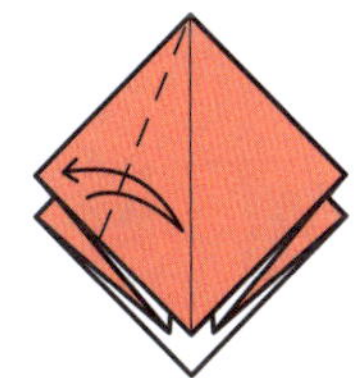

Pre-crease on the line for the squash fold.

2

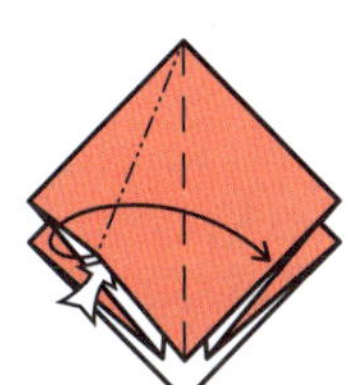

Open up the paper by inserting your finger. Fold the paper across.

3

As you put the paper in place, gently squash the point into a symmetrical shape.

4

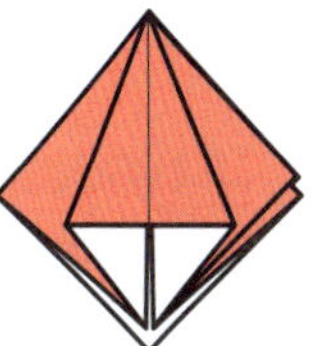

Completed squash fold.

OPEN SINK

1

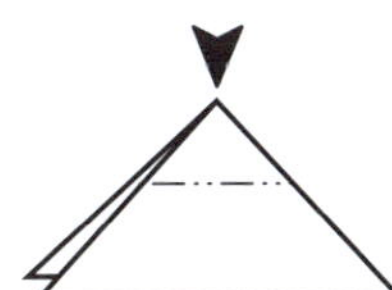

Pre-crease through all layers along the sink line. It's best to make a mountain and a valley fold on this line.

2

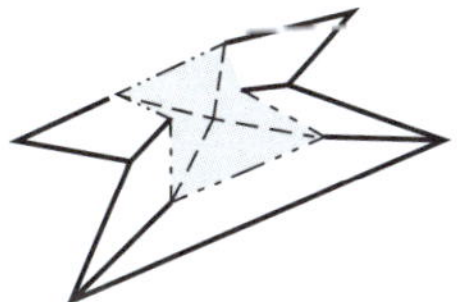

Open out the point, and push the point into the paper. Take care to reverse folds as shown. The sink should squash flat.

3

Completed sink.

RABBIT EAR | The rabbit ear fold is named after a most useful shape—that of a rabbit ear. It is used to make a new point.

1

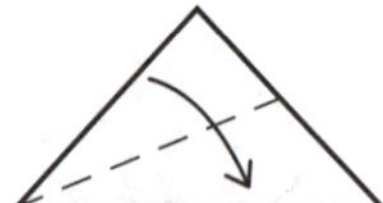

2

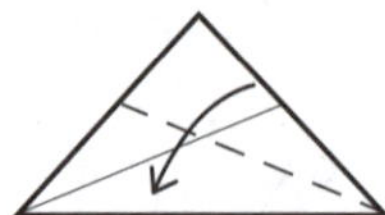

3

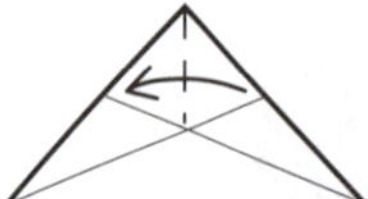

1- 3 | Divide each corner of the triangle with valley folds.

4

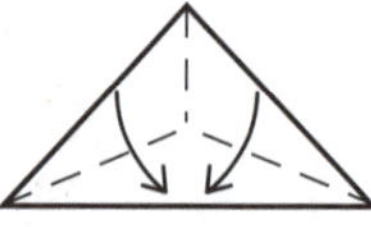

Fold top edges to the bottom, the middle crease will form a point.

5

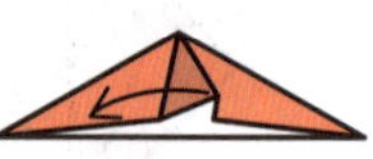

Fold the point to one side.

6

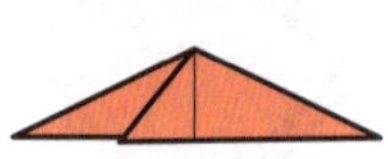

Completed rabbit ear.

DOUBLE RABBIT EAR | The double rabbit ear is a rabbit ear fold that is mirrored on both sides of the point.

1

Make a rabbit ear fold on the point.

2

Unfold the rabbit ear.

3

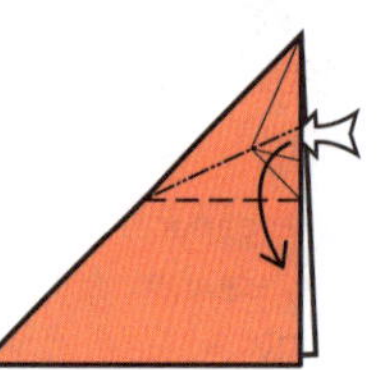

Squash fold the point.

4

Inside reverse fold the two points.

5

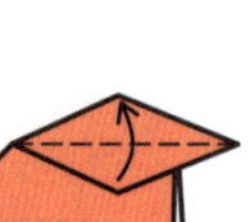

Valley fold point upward.

6

Completed double rabbit ear.

SWIVEL FOLD | A swivel fold is often made on a pleat. It narrows its two points, and the excess paper swivels under one of the points.

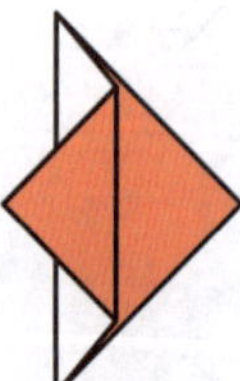

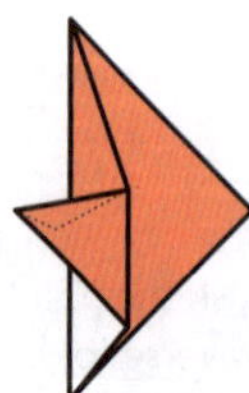

WATERBOMB BASE

BY: MATTHEW GARDINER

Origami has standard shapes often repeated because they are very useful. The original use of this base form was to make the waterbomb model, but its five points make a versatile shape for many designs.

1

Begin colored side up.
Book fold and unfold. Turn over.

2

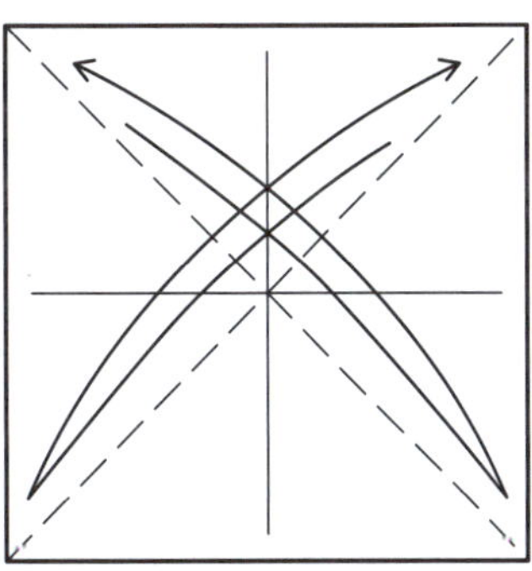

Fold and unfold diagonals.

3

Collapse on existing creases.

4

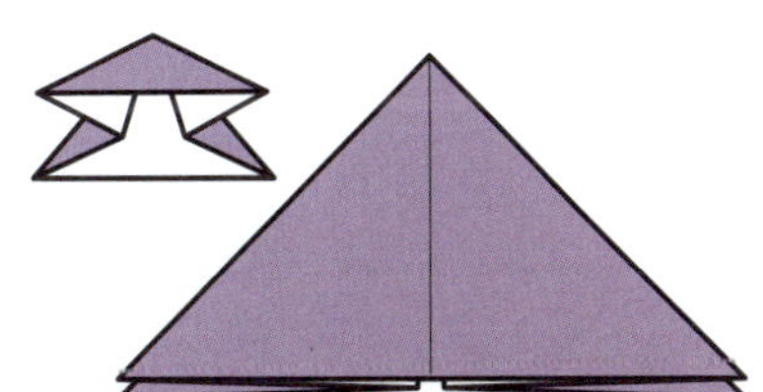

Completed waterbomb base.

PRELIMINARY BASE

BY: MATTHEW GARDINER

The preliminary base is the starting point for the bird base and the frog/lily base. It is a very common origami base. Interestingly, the preliminary base is an inside-out waterbomb base. Try making a waterbomb base using the same creases in the preliminary base. Hint: unfold the base and turn the paper over.

1

Start colored side up.
Fold and unfold diagonals.

2

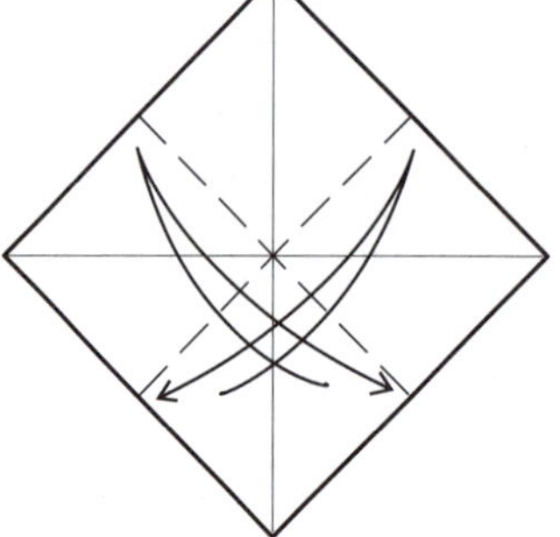

Turn over, book fold and unfold.

3

Bring three corners down to meet bottom corner. Start with corners 1 and 2 together followed by corner 3.

4

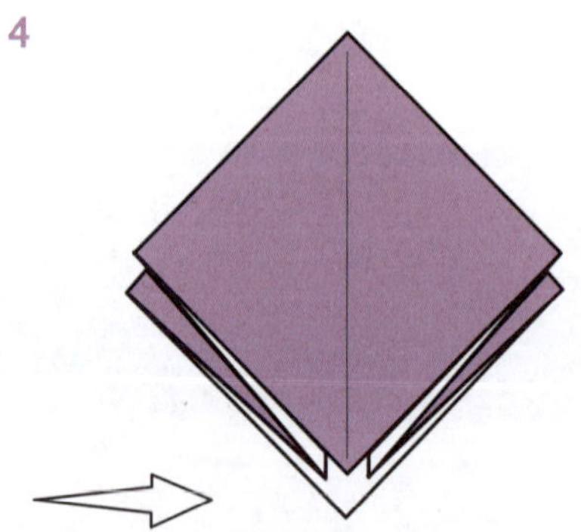

Completed preliminary base.

FROG/LILY BASE

BY: MATTHEW GARDINER

The frog base is also called lily base, because of its use in both the traditional lily and frog. It begins with a preliminary base.

1

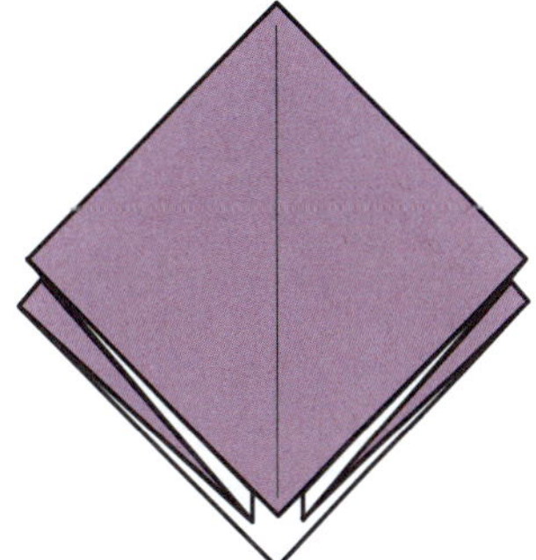

Start from the preliminary base. Rotate 180º.

2

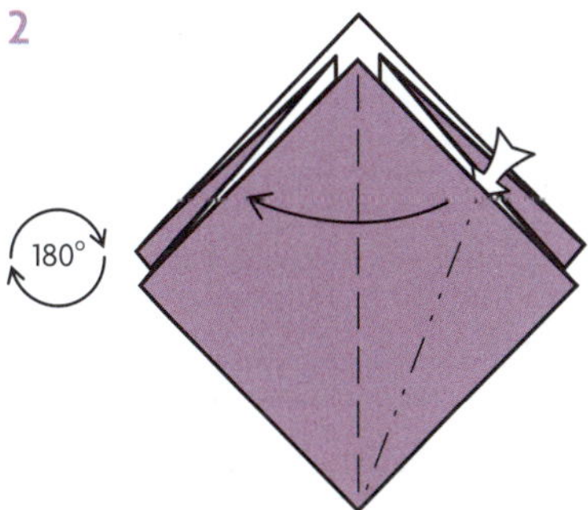

Check that the open points are at the top. Pre-crease then squash fold the top layer on one side.

3

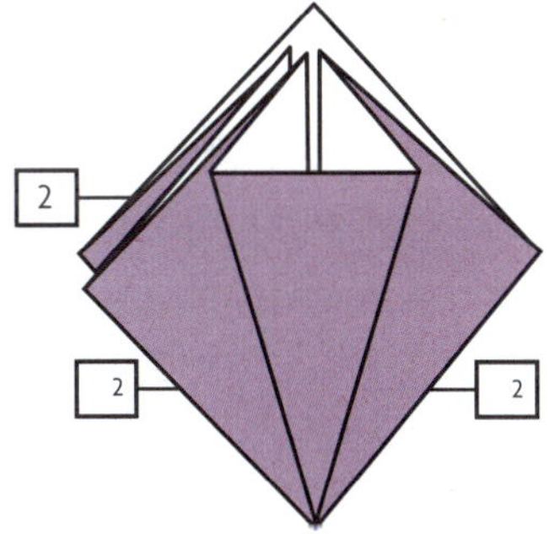

Repeat step 2 on the other three points.

4

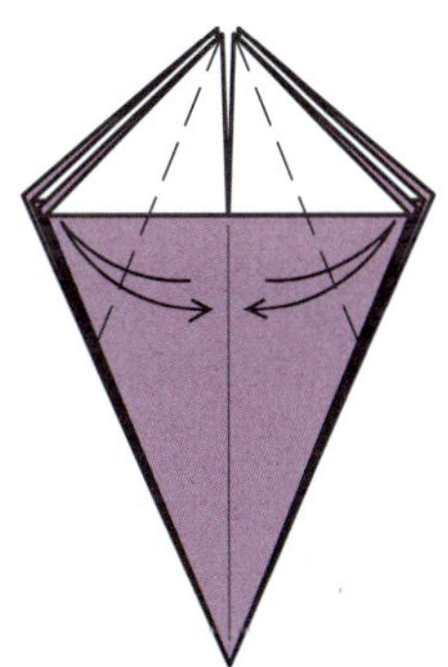

Fold the top layer only to the center crease.

5

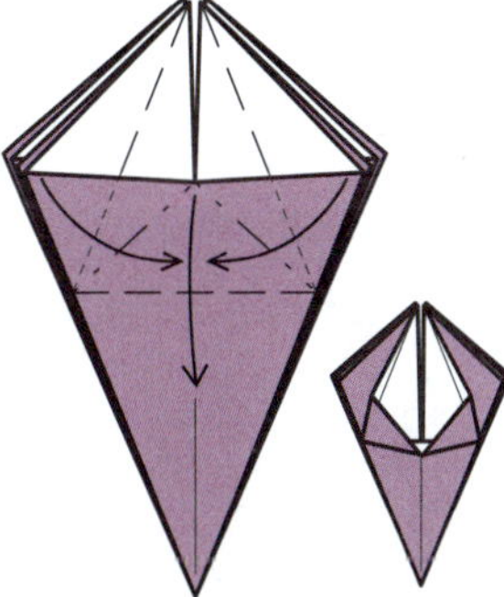

Petal fold: pull down the top layer, and fold the sides to the middle. Lastly make the mountain folds.

6

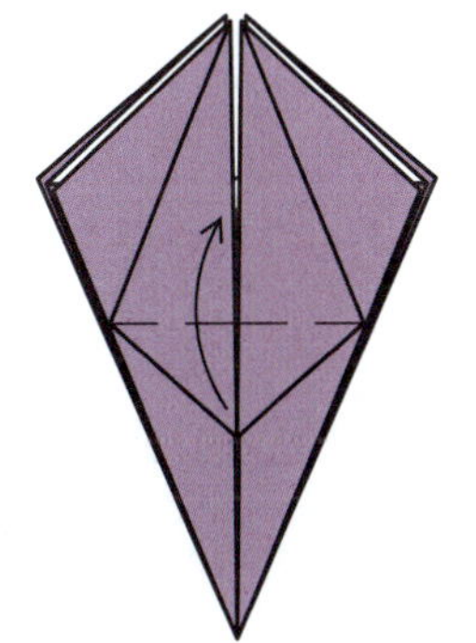

Completed petal fold. Valley fold the triangle flap upwardv.

7

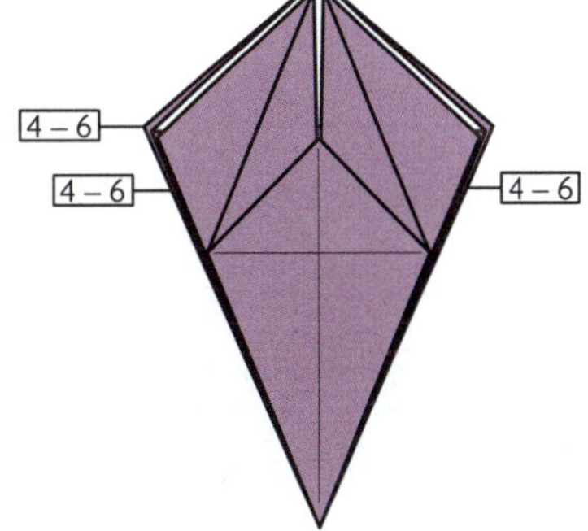

Repeat steps 4 to 6 on the three remaining sides.

8

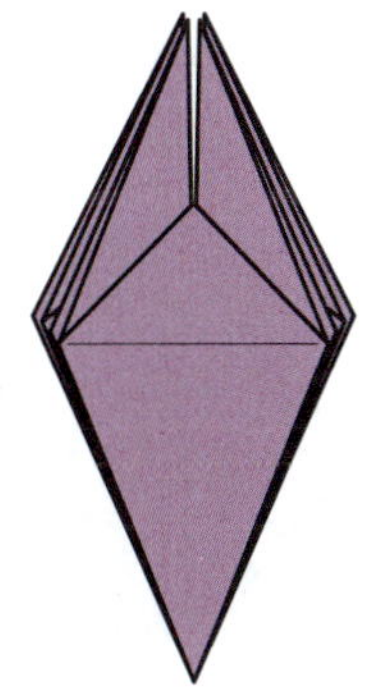

Completed frog/lily base.

BIRD BASE

BY: MATTHEW GARDINER

The bird base is the start of the classic origami crane. It is also useful for creating a wide variety of birds and other animals.

1

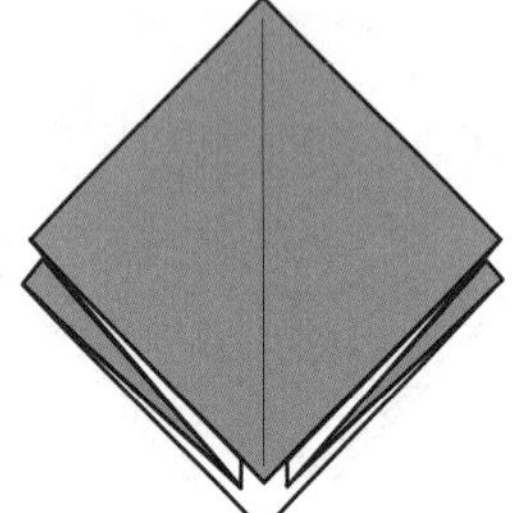

Start from the preliminary base.

2

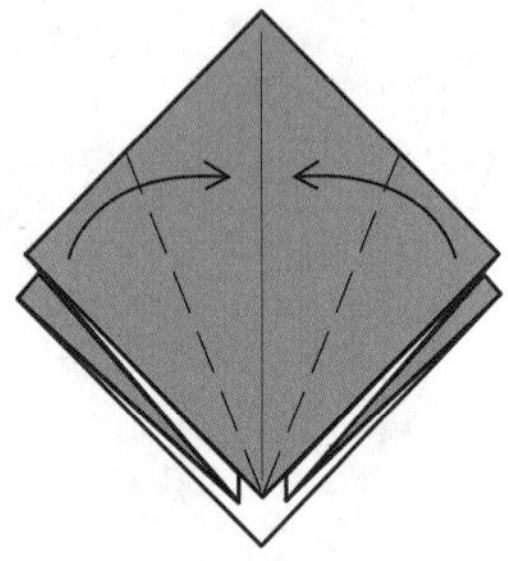

Fold top layer to the center crease.

3

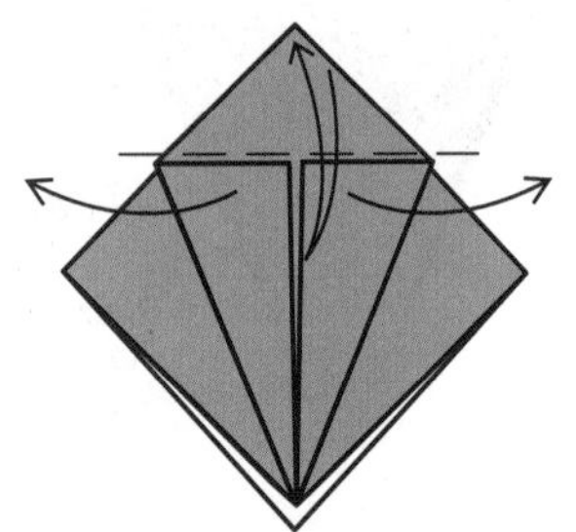

Fold and unfold the top triangle down. Unfold flaps.

4

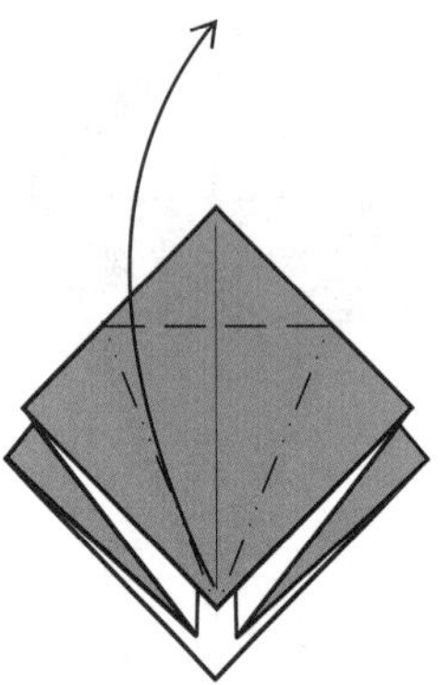

Lift the top layer upward.

5

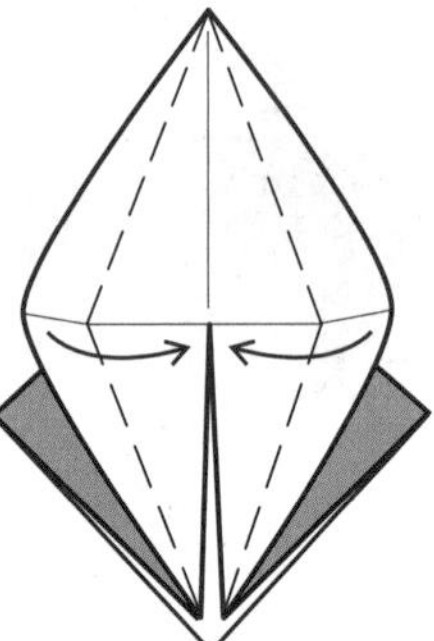

Step 4 in progress, the model is 3D. Fold the top layer inward on existing creases.

6

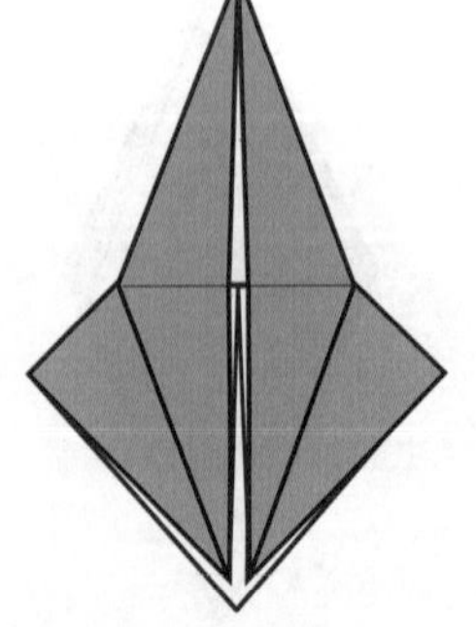

Step 4 completed, the model will be flat. Turn over.

7

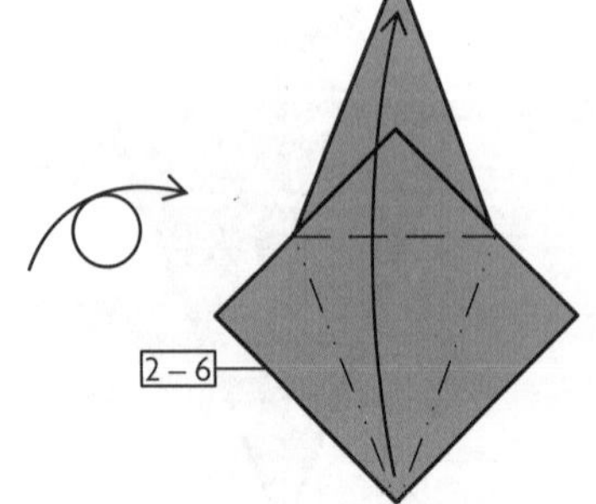

Repeat steps 2—6 on this side.

8

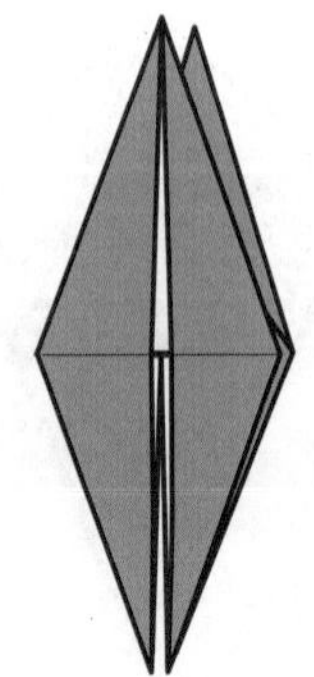

Completed bird base.

FISH BASE

BY: MATTHEW GARDINER

The fish base is used to make the traditional fish, but can also be used as a starting point for more complex models.

1

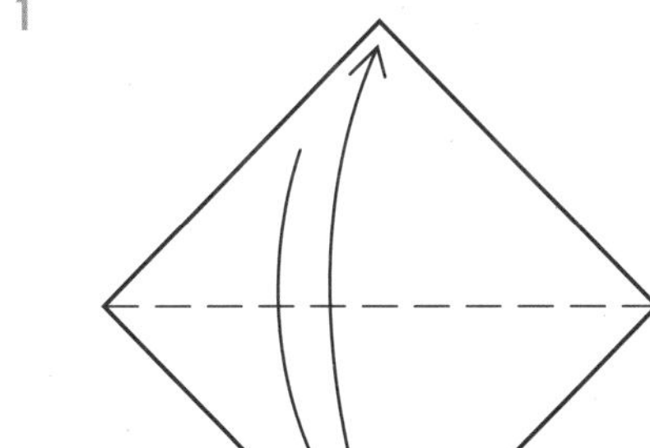

Start with white side up. Fold and unfold diagonal.

2

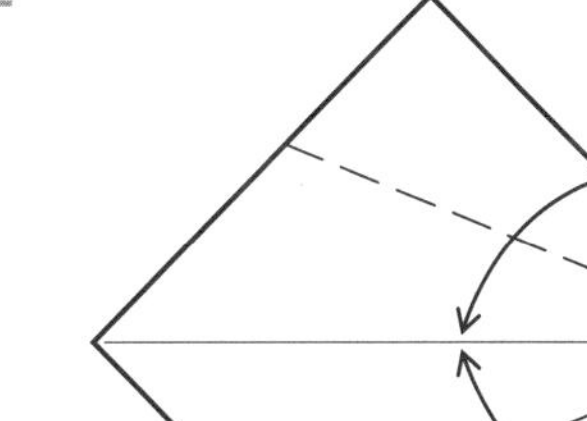

Fold both sides to the middle.

3

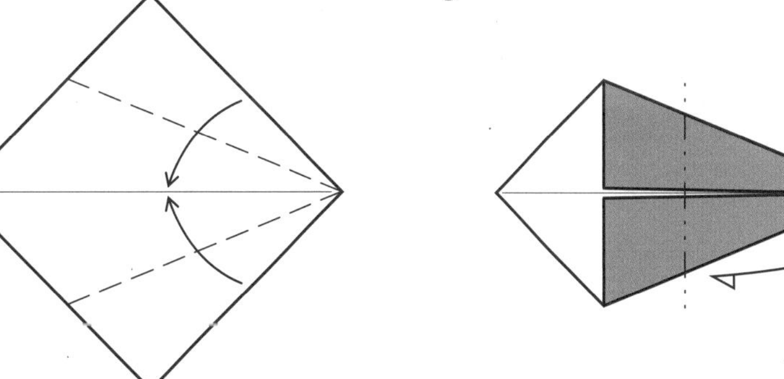

Mountain fold in half behind.

4

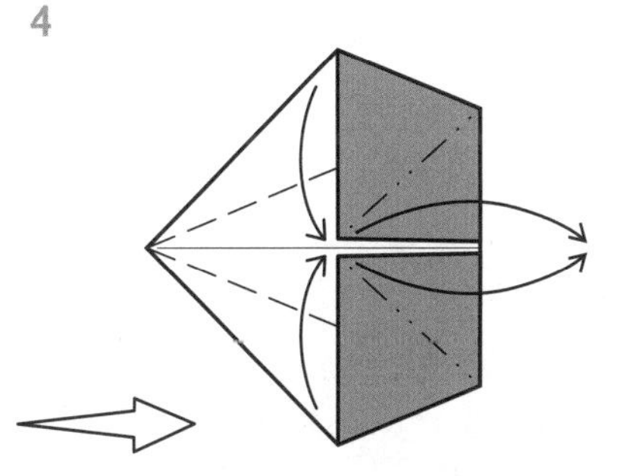

Squash fold both sides.

5

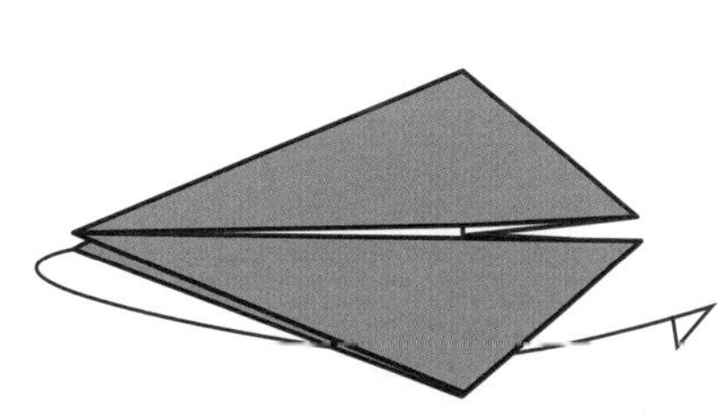

Mountain fold the back layer behind.

6

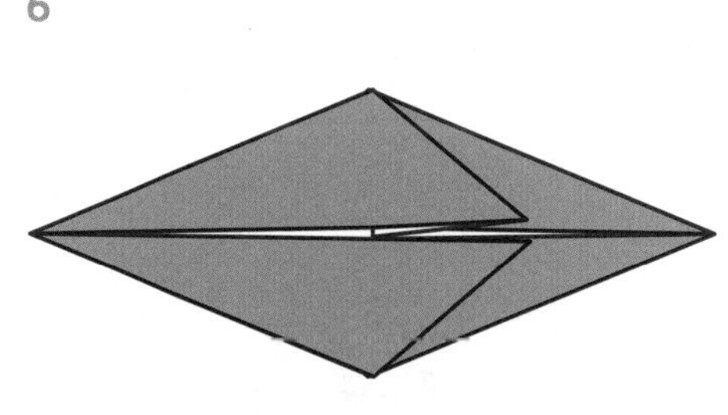

Completed fish base.

SIMPLE PROJECTS

BOAT

MODEL: TRADITIONAL, JAPAN
DIAGRAM: MATTHEW GARDINER

The boat is a fantastic origami model. At step 9 the model forms a hat and by step 14 you have an origami model that actually floats. For longer floating time, use a greaseproof paper, or better yet, modern technology has produced synthetic paper that won't soak up water, so your boat won't sink.

A German artist named Frank Bölter has used this origami design, with special paper and lots of help, to actually sail down rivers in Europe!

1

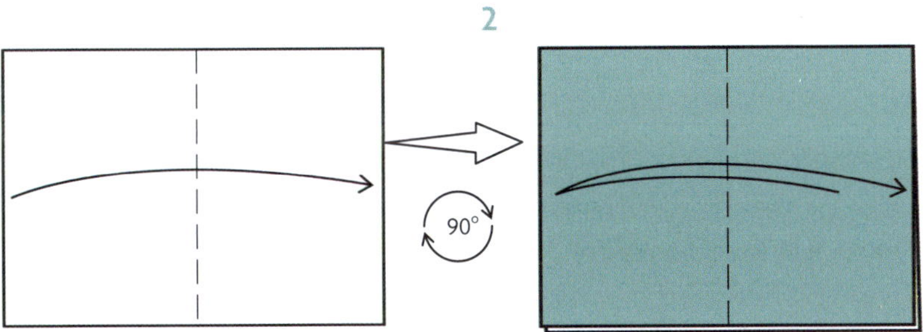

Start with a rectangle. Letter (8.5 x 11in) is a good size—use a sheet of newspaper for a wearable hat. Book fold.

Turn 90º and book fold and unfold again.

3

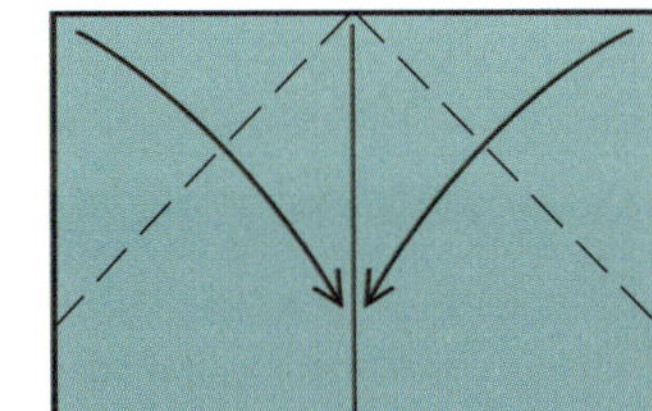

Fold corners down.

4

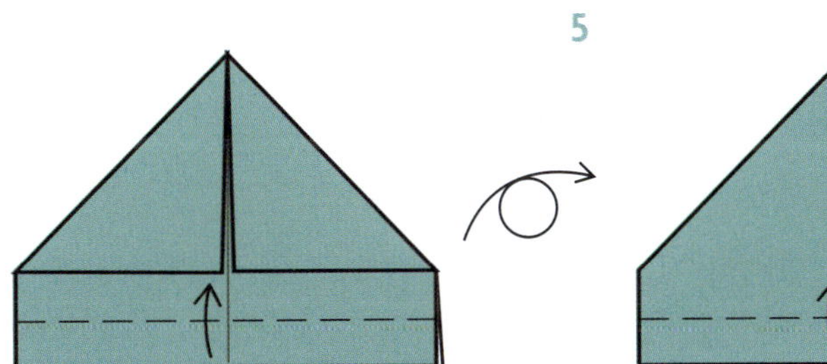

Fold up to the bottom of the triangles. Turn over.

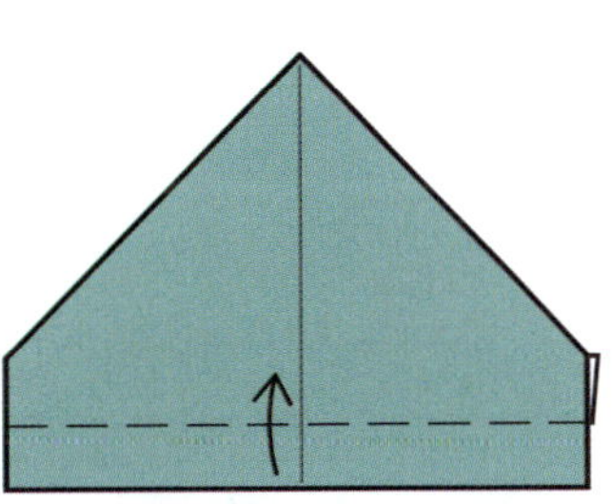

Fold up to match the fold in step 4.

6

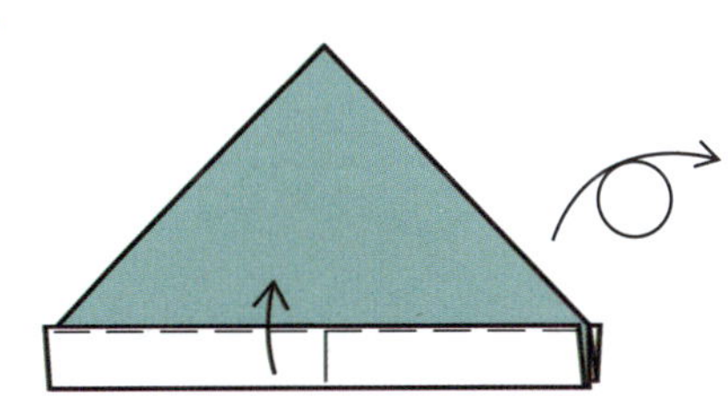

Fold up over the bottom of the triangle. Turn over.

7

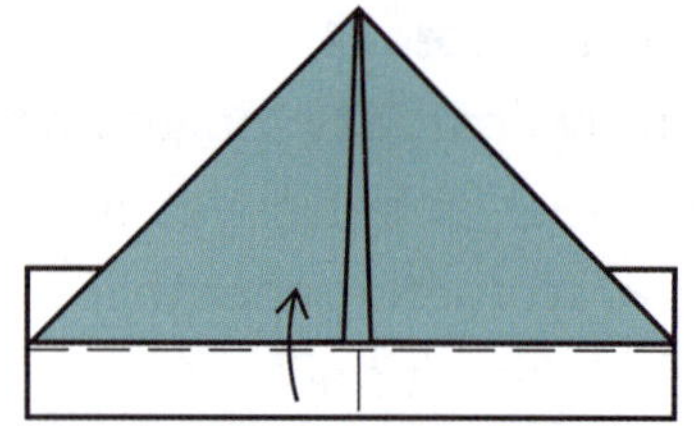

Repeat step 6.

8

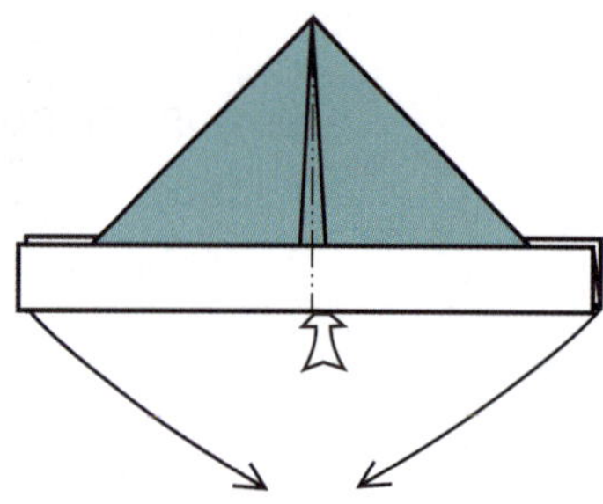

Lift the middle and push both points together, to make a squash fold.

9

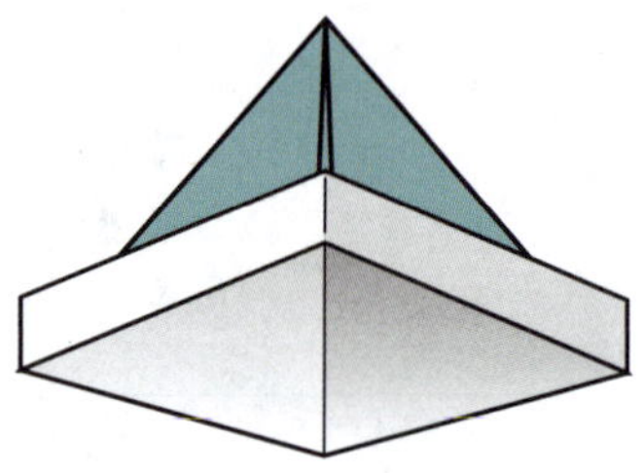

Squash fold in progress. This stage can also be used as a hat.

10

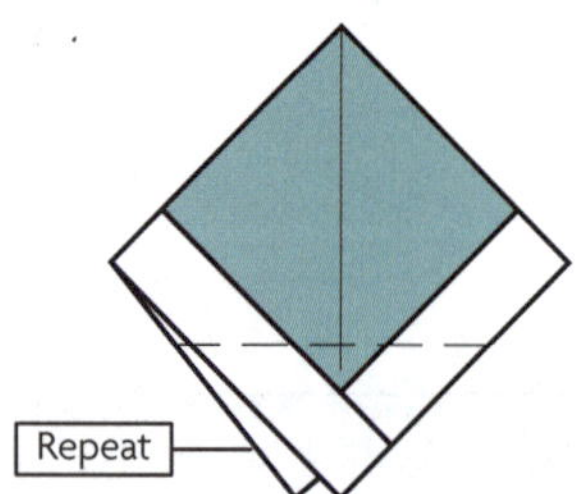

Fold bottom point about one third. Repeat behind.

11

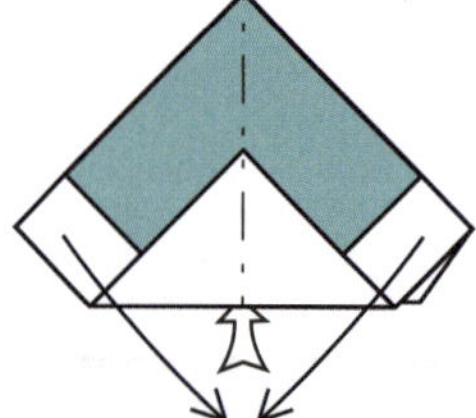

Squash fold, lifting the middle, similar to step 8.

12

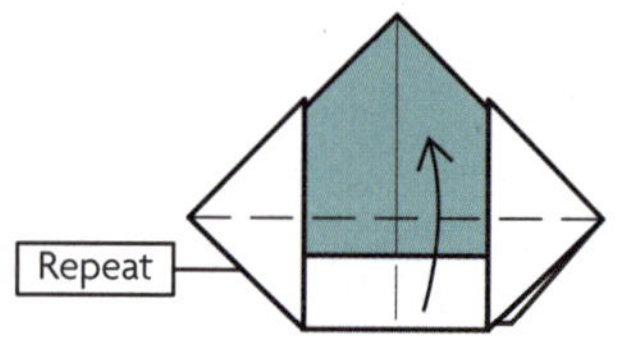

Fold up. Repeat behind.

13

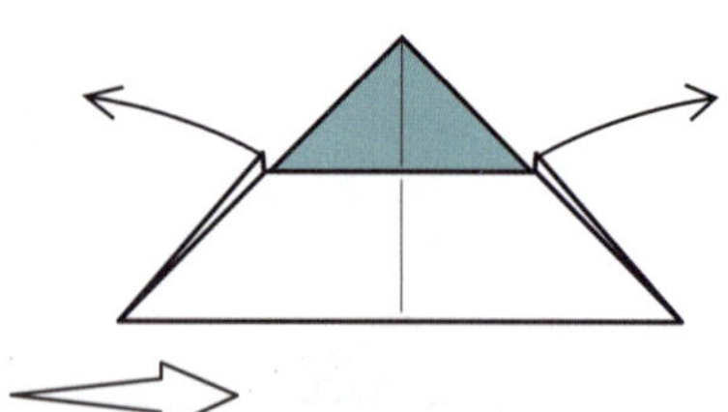

Pull the points out to shape the boat. The boat will become 3D.

14

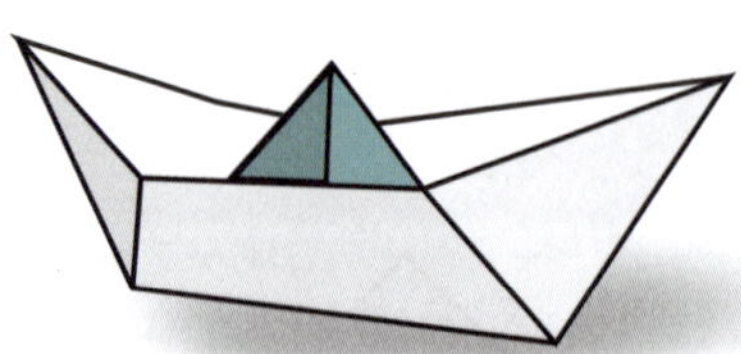

Completed boat.

WATER BOMB

MODEL: TRADITIONAL, JAPAN
DIAGRAM: MATTHEW GARDINER

The water bomb is a classic because in the last move you actually get to inflate it! The model forms a box that can hold a liquid. Ironically, the water bomb when made from paper, does not actually hold water for very long. Use plastic or greaseproof paper to keep the water a little longer.

Australian composer David Young wrote "16 Boxes," a musical piece for percussion with origami accompaniment. To perform this, the artist must fold 16 origami boxes (waterbombs) in 12 minutes: that's 45 seconds each.

1

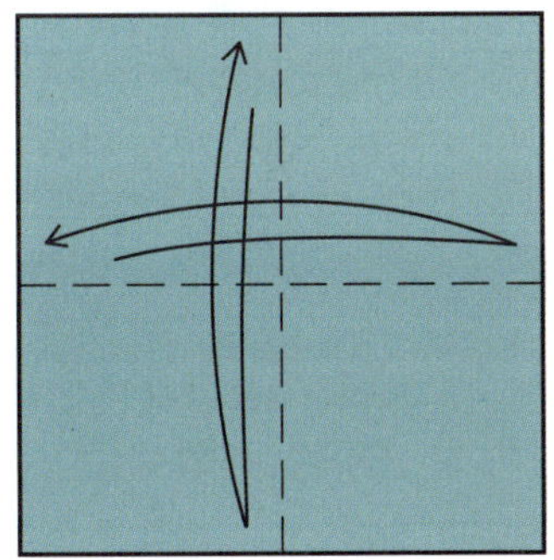

Begin colored side up.
Book fold and unfold. Turn over.

2

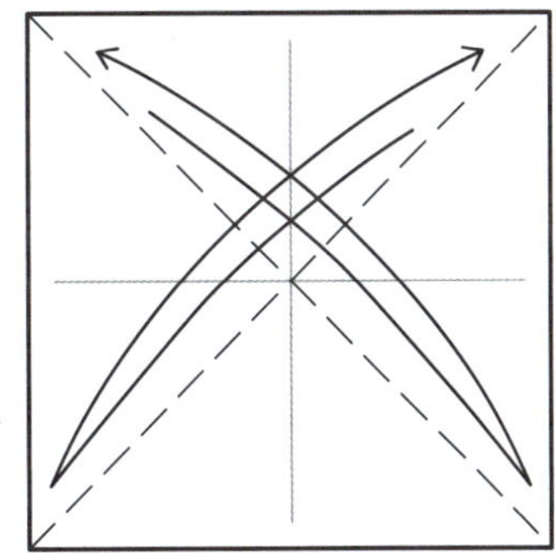

Fold and unfold diagonals.

3

Collapse on existing creases.

4

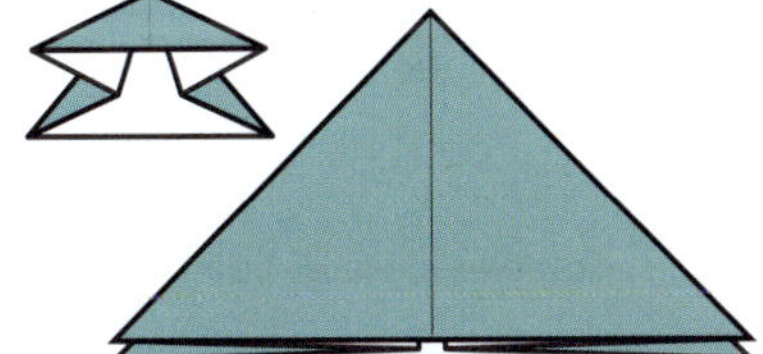

The waterbomb base.

5

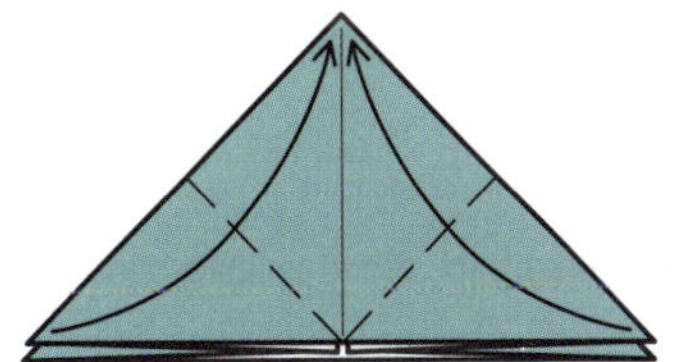

Fold corners up. Turn over.

6

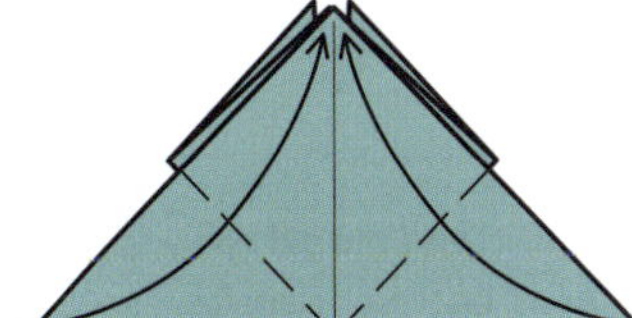

Repeat step 5.

7

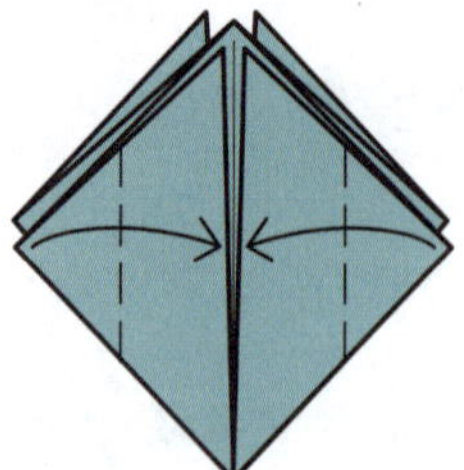

Fold corners of top layer to the middle.

8

Fold top two flaps down.

9

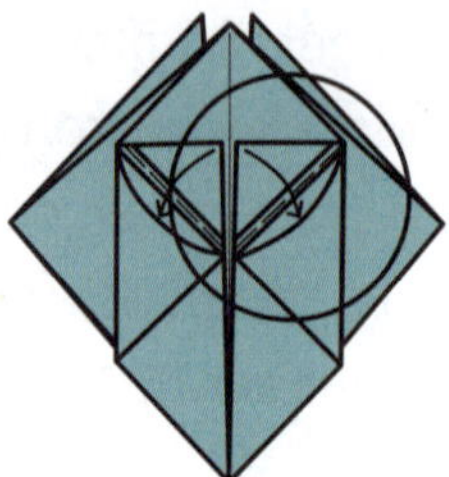

Pre-crease the triangles, and then tuck them into the pockets.

10

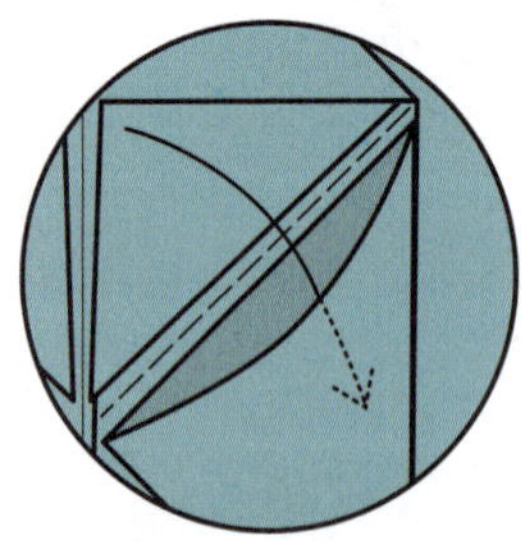

Detail of step 9, showing how to insert the triangle into the pocket.

11

Step 9 completed. Turn over.

12

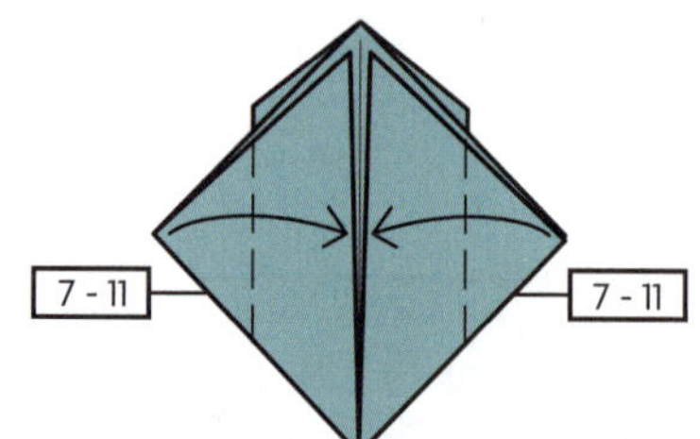

Repeat steps 7-11 on both sides.

13

Fold and unfold top and bottom triangles.

14

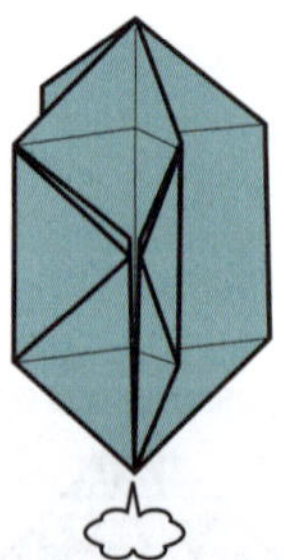

Pull flaps apart. Blow air into the hole in the bottom and shape into 3D cube.

15

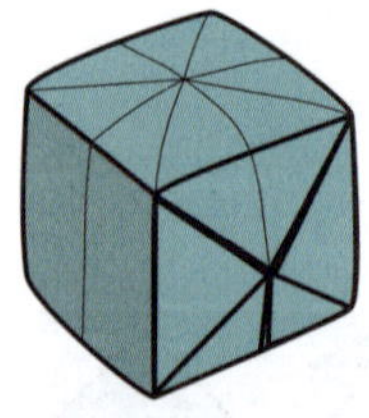

Completed water bomb.

PUFFY STAR

MODEL: TRADITIONAL
DIAGRAM: MATTHEW GARDINER

The puffy star is a traditional form popular in Asian countries. It is often made for new year celebrations for good luck. They can be strung together with a needle and thread to make hanging decorations. You will need strips of paper about 0.6in x 12in (1.5cm x 30cm).

Knotology, a term coined by Heinz Strobl, is the art of folding strips of paper. Many geometric forms can be made from making the pentagon as shown below.

1

Cut 0.6in (1.5cm from) a letter (8.5 x 11in) sheet of paper.

2

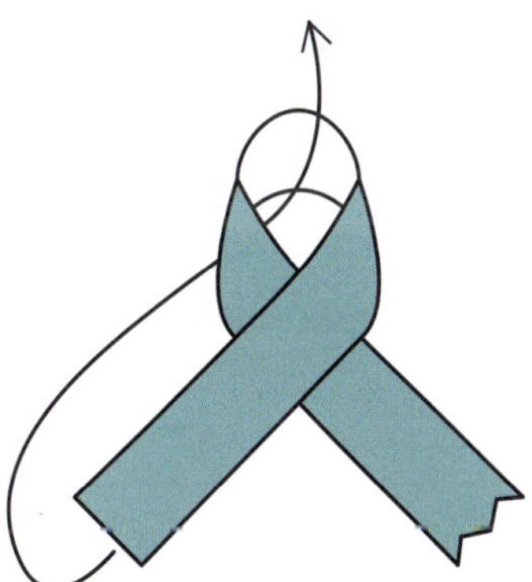

At one end of the strip, make a knot as shown.

3

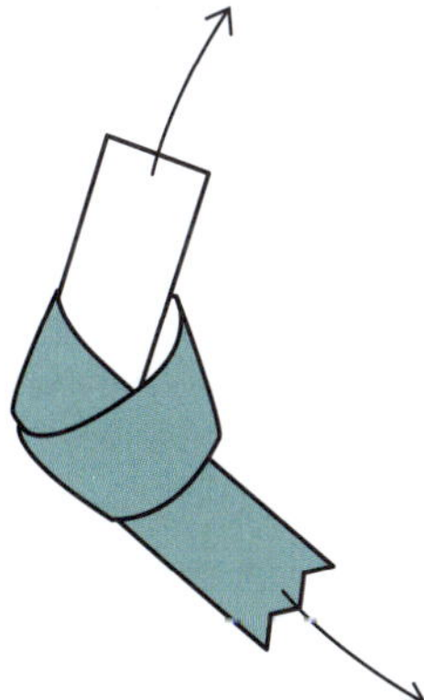

Gently pull both ends until the pentagonal shape is clearly formed.

4

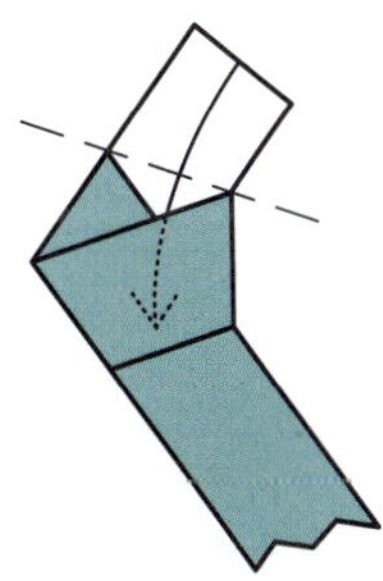

Fold the end of the strip over and tuck under the layer.

5

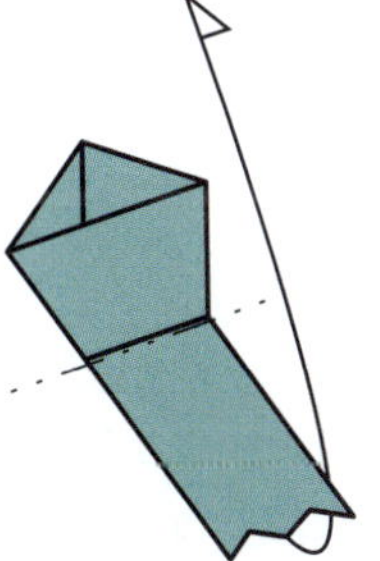

The next steps follow the pentagon shape, wrapping up the puffy star.

6

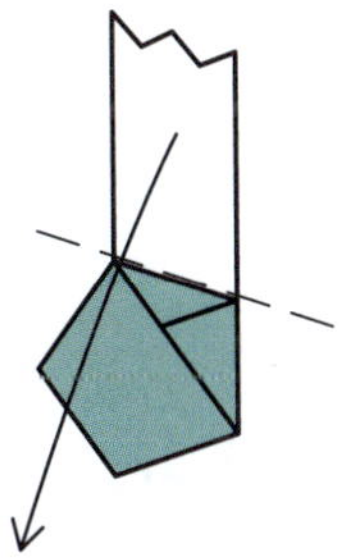

Valley fold.

7

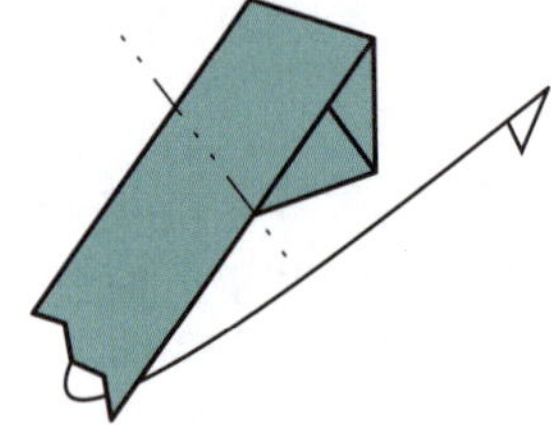

Mountain fold.

8

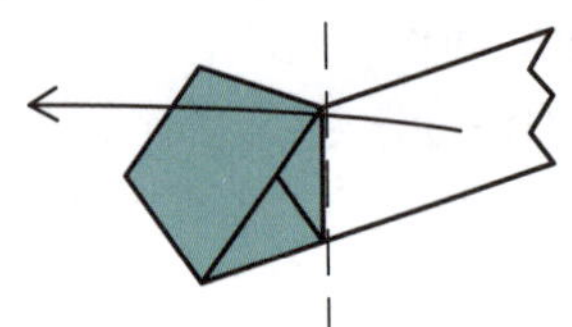

Valley fold.

9

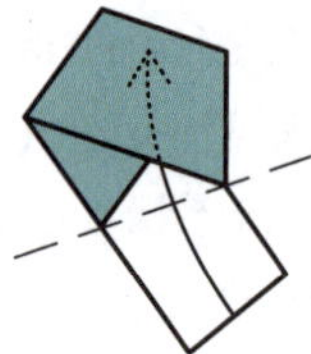

Keep wrapping until you end up with a small stub. Tuck the stub under the next layer.

10

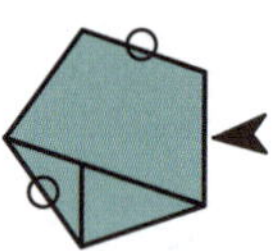

Hold at the circles and use the back of your nail to push in the side of the star.

11

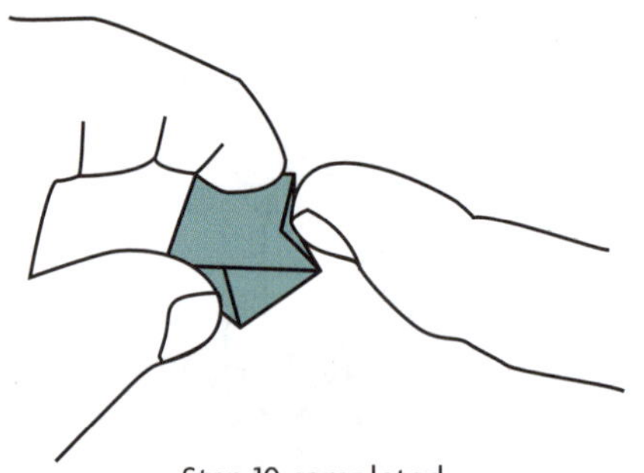

Step 10 completed.

12

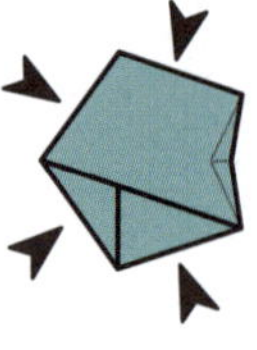

Push in the wall of the star on the remaining sides.

13

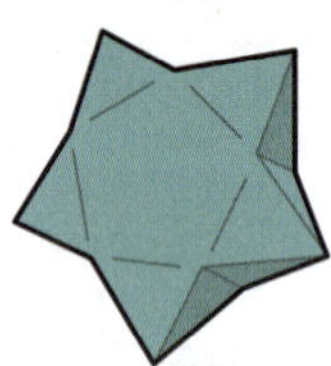

Completed puffy star.

BUTTERFLY

MODEL: TRADITIONAL, JAPAN
DIAGRAM: MATTHEW GARDINER

Butterflies capture the imagination of children and adults alike. Their delicate shape is perfect for hanging decorations. Try using a patterned sheet of origami paper.

This butterfly is a traditional fold from Japan.

1

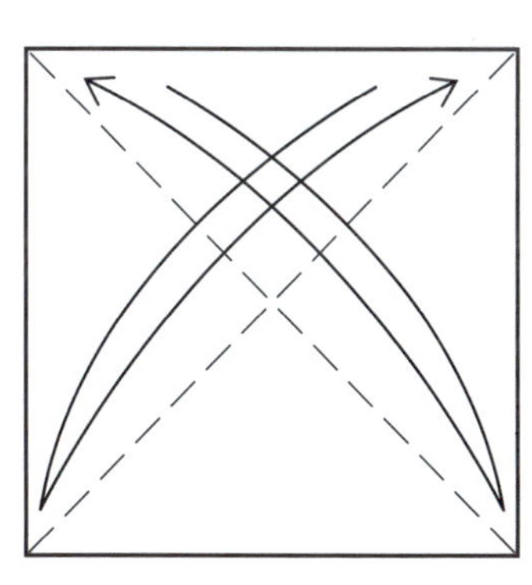

Fold and unfold diagonals.

2

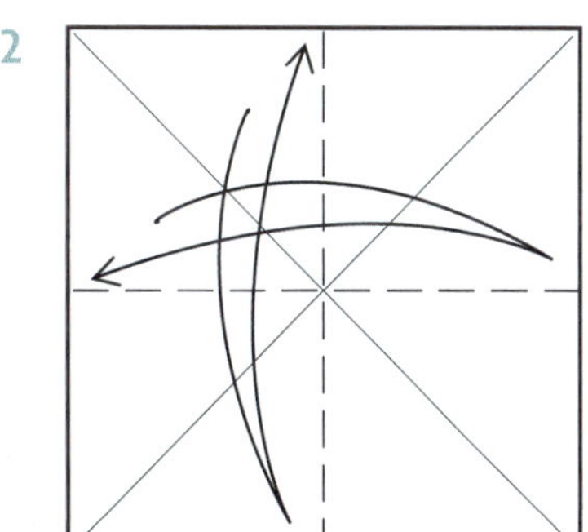

Book fold.

3

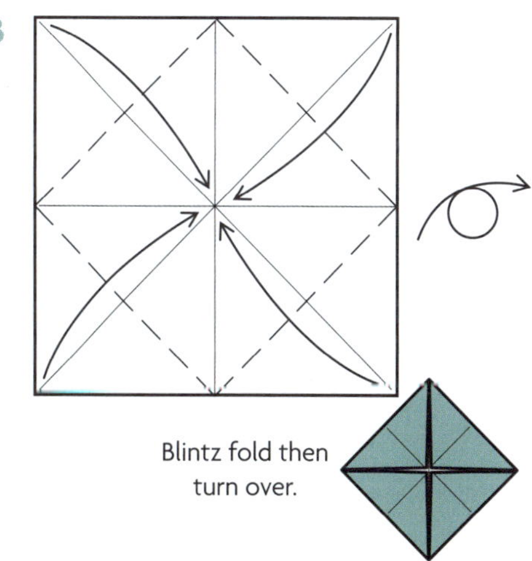

Blintz fold then turn over.

4

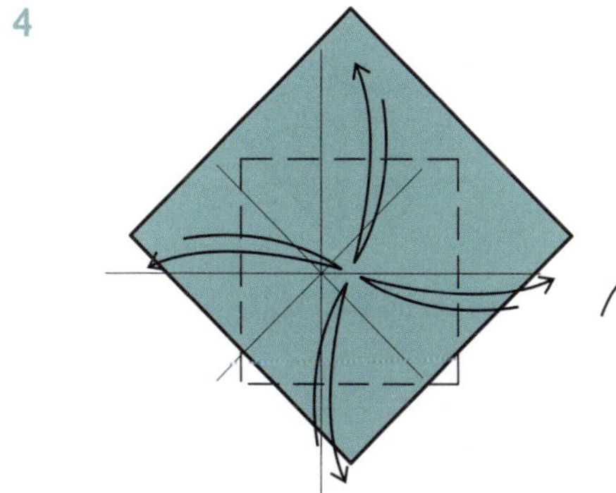

Blintz fold then turn over.

5

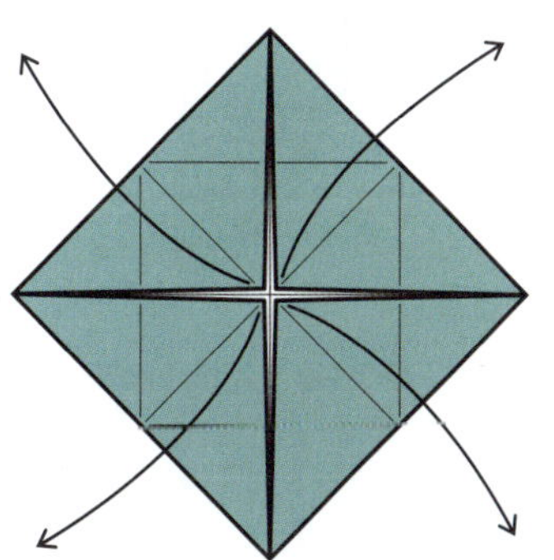

Completely unfold out to a flat sheet.

6

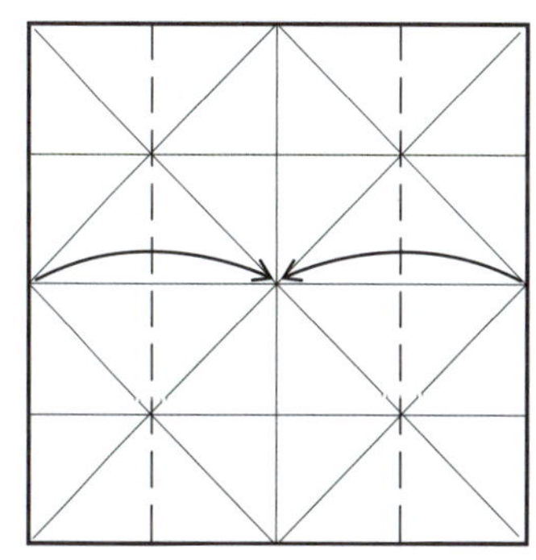

Fold sides to the middle.

7

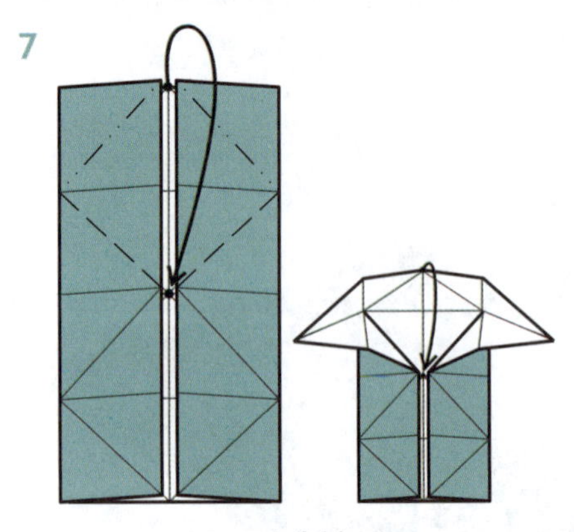

Squash fold using existing creases.

8

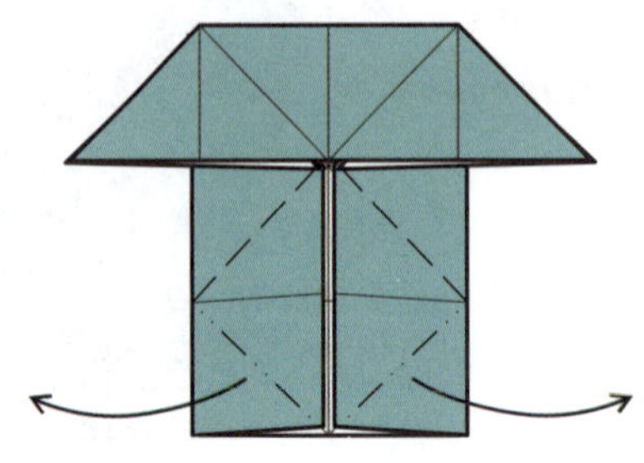

Repeat step 7 on the bottom.

9

Mountain fold in half.

10

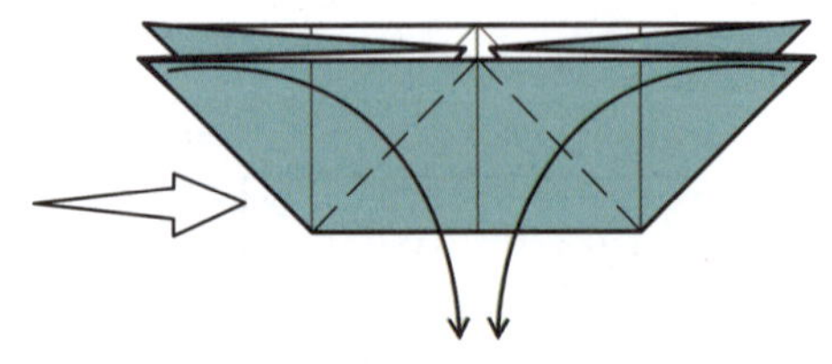

Fold points on the top layer down.

11

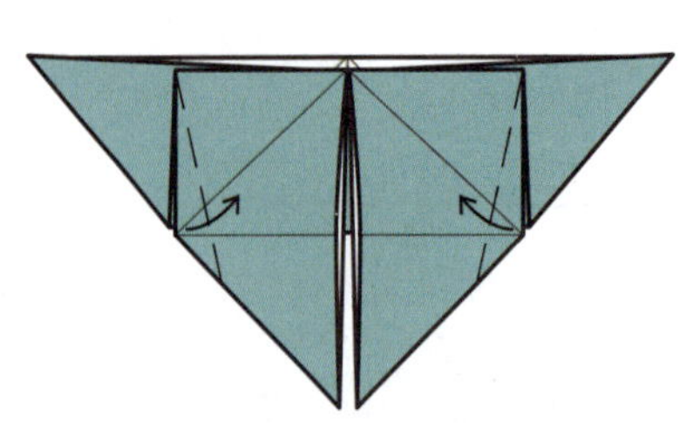

Fold sides in.

12

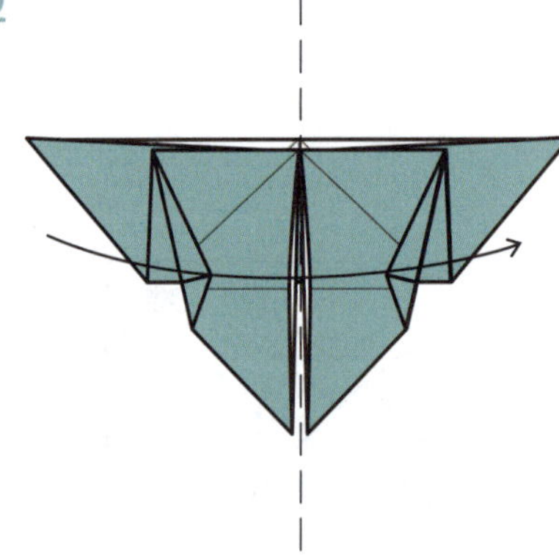

Fold in half.

13

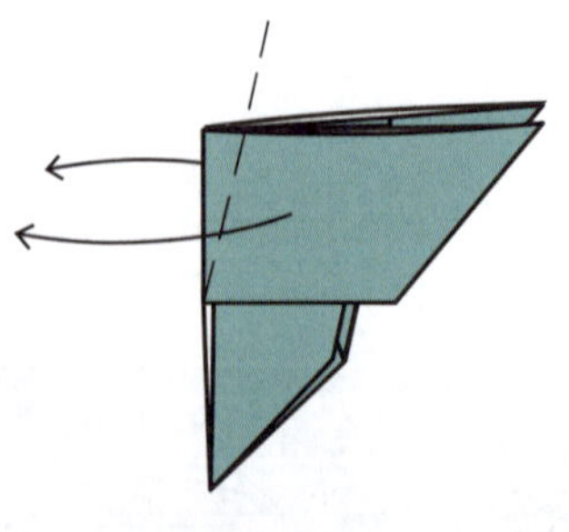

Fold both wings.

14

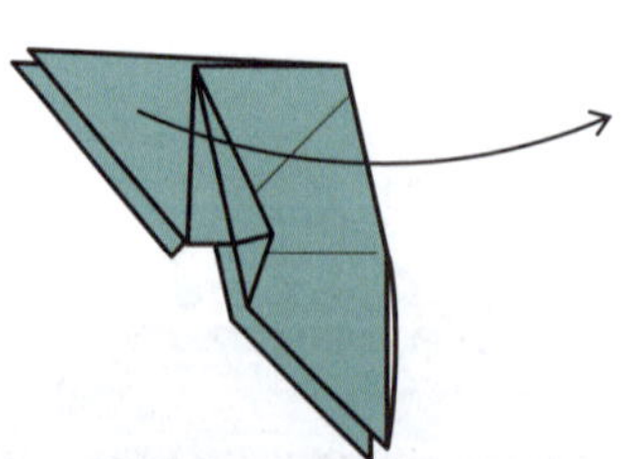

Fold one wing back.

15

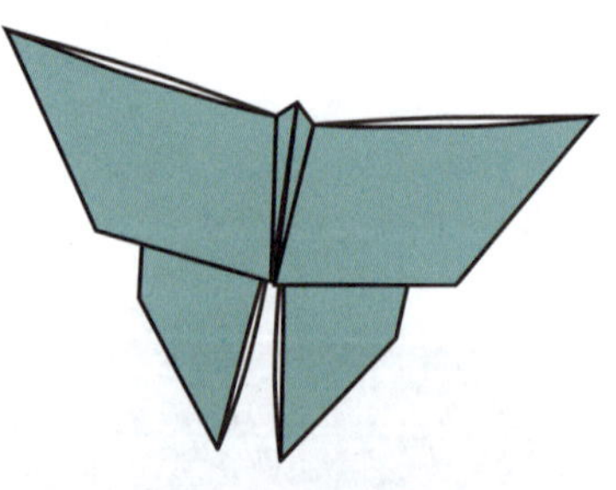

Completed butterfly.

WHALE

MODEL: TRADITIONAL, JAPAN
DIAGRAM: MATTHEW GARDINER

Fish are adored by the Japanese, both as a food and as a symbol of health, vitality and energy. A Japanese annual festival for boys uses the highly spirited carp (koi) as a symbol for energy and power. Look above the rooftops in late April to early May in Japan and you will see paper and cloth fish flying high. One fish per boy in the household is flown. Use a bright color for this origami fish.

1

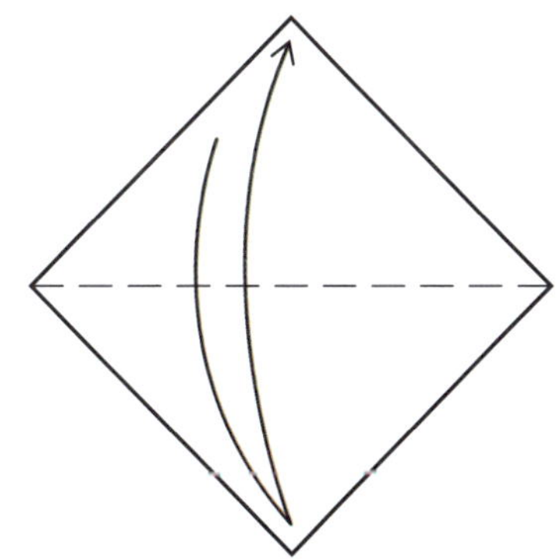

Start with white side up. Fold and unfold diagonal.

2

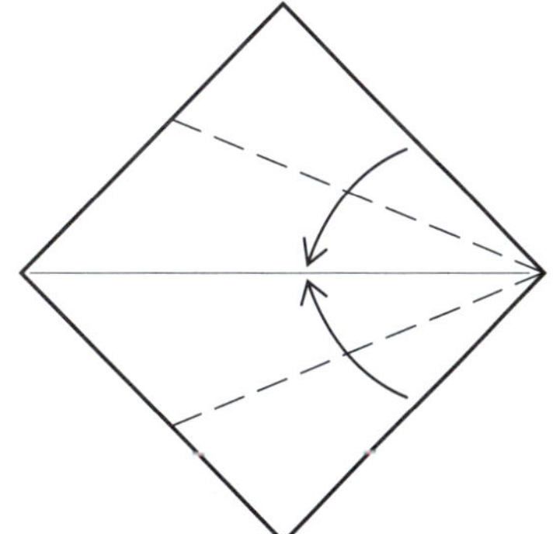

Fold both sides to the middle.

3

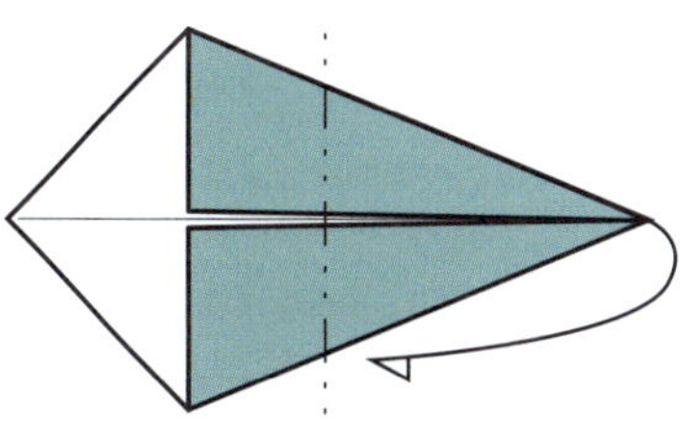

Mountain fold in half behind.

4

Squash fold both sides.

5

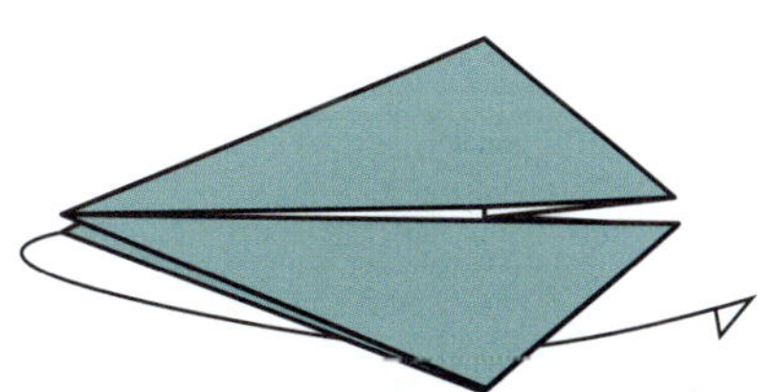

Mountain fold the back layer behind.

6

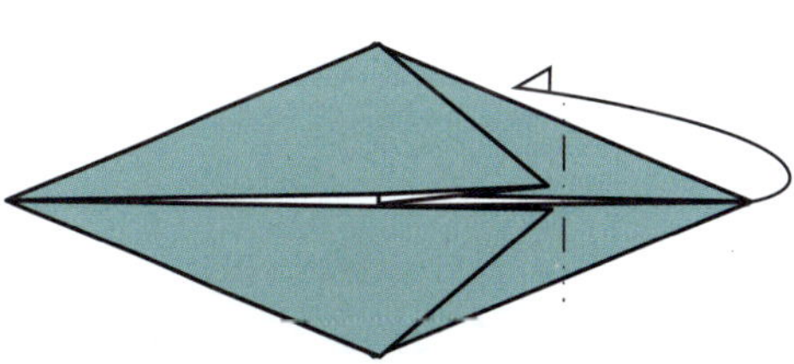

This is known as the fish base.
Mountain fold the point.

7

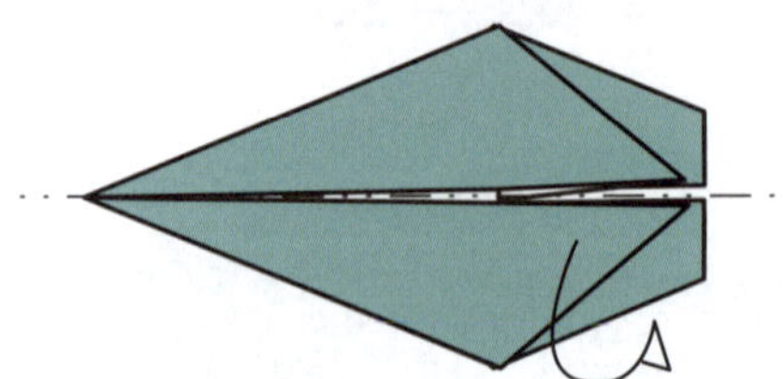

Mountain fold in half behind.

8

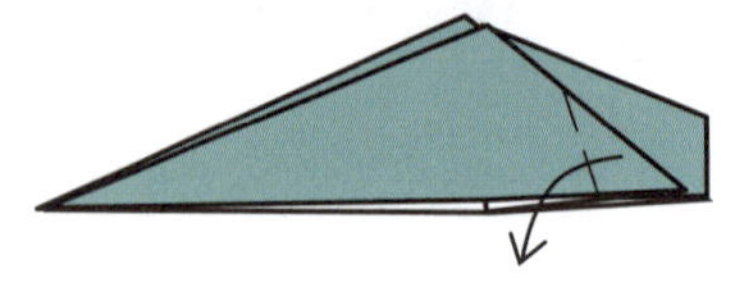

Fold the fins down on both sides.

9

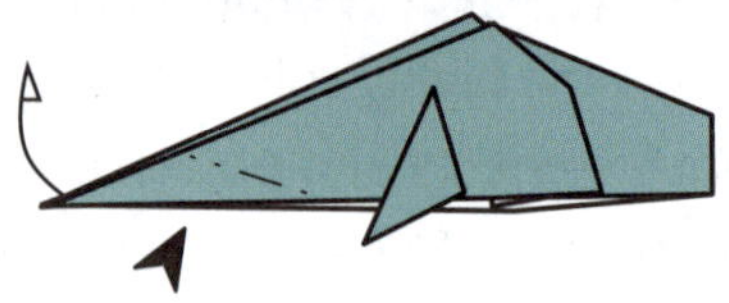

Inside reverse fold the tail.

10

Completed fish.

IRIS

MODEL: TRADITIONAL, JAPAN
DIAGRAM: MATTHEW GARDINER

The iris takes its name from the Greek word for rainbow. Its name reflects the wide range of colors of the iris. This model looks best when folded from a blended or two-toned paper.

The iris is a popular symbol, appearing on the flag of Brussels, and in the fleur-de-lis, the symbol of Florence, Italy.

1

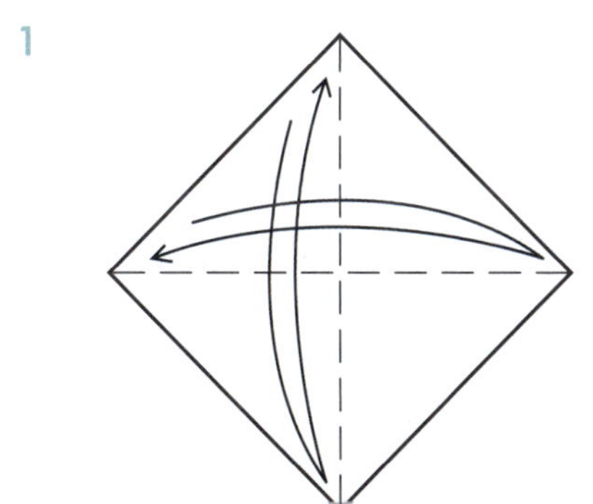

Fold and unfold diagonals. Turn over.

2

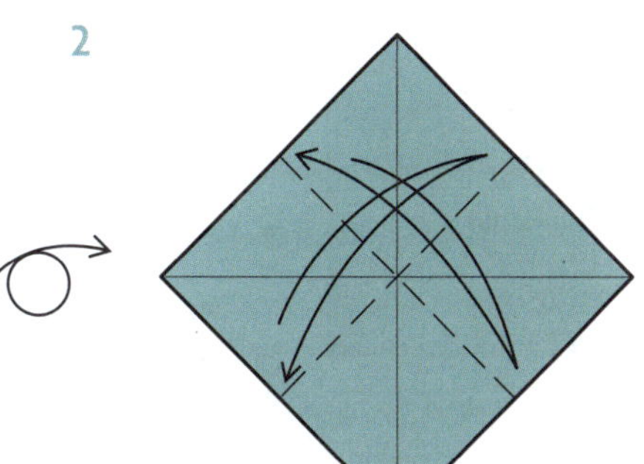

Book fold and unfold.

3

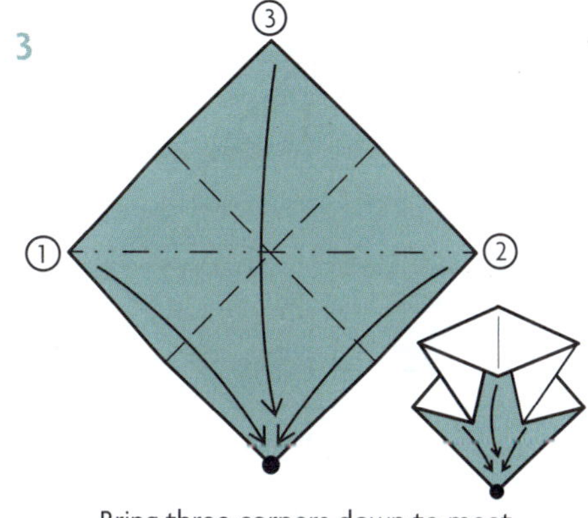

Bring three corners down to meet bottom corner. Start with corners 1 and 2 together followed by corner 3.

4

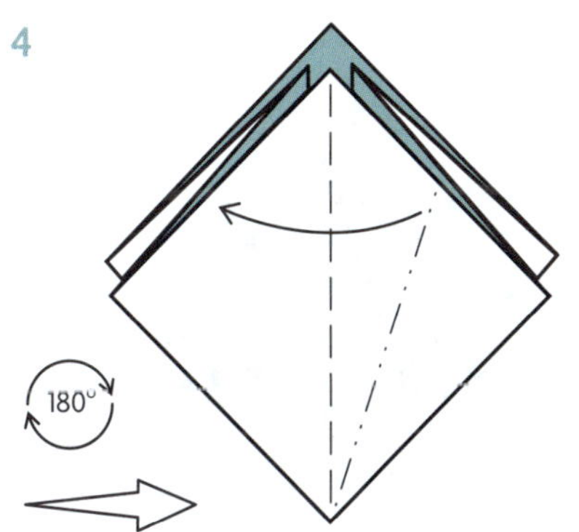

Pre-crease then squash fold.

5

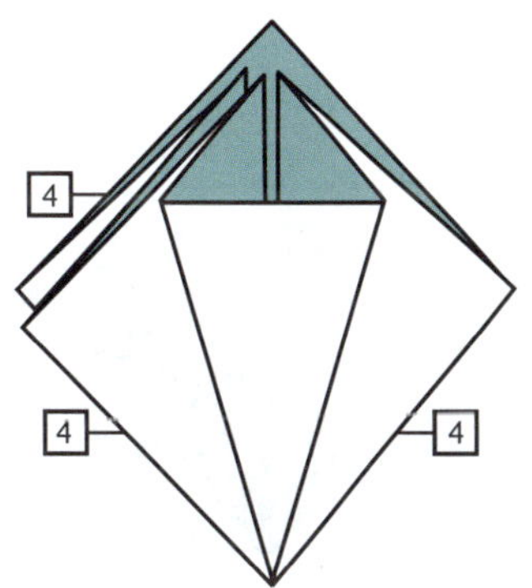

Repeat step 4 on the other three sides.

6

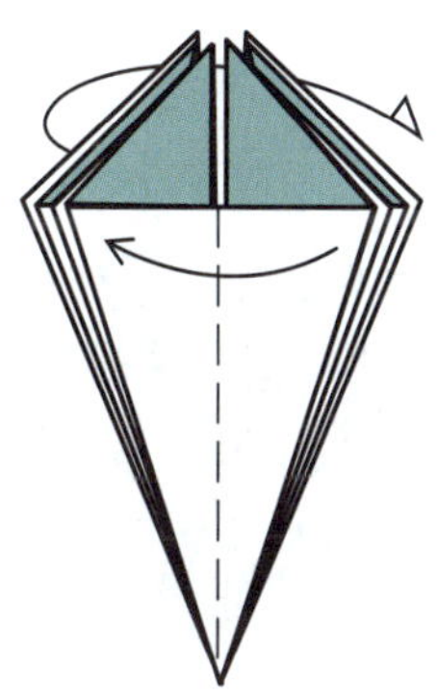

Turn top and back layer over.

WATER LILY

MODEL: TRADITIONAL, JAPAN
DIAGRAM: MATTHEW GARDINER

The water lily is a beautiful form, invoking the charm of the lily floating on the water.

1

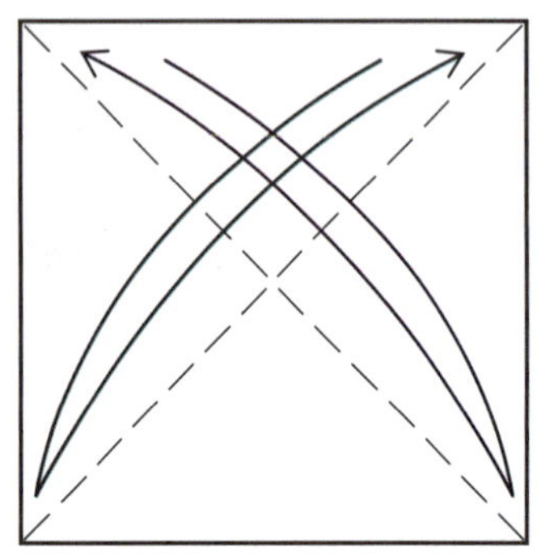

Fold and unfold diagonals.

2

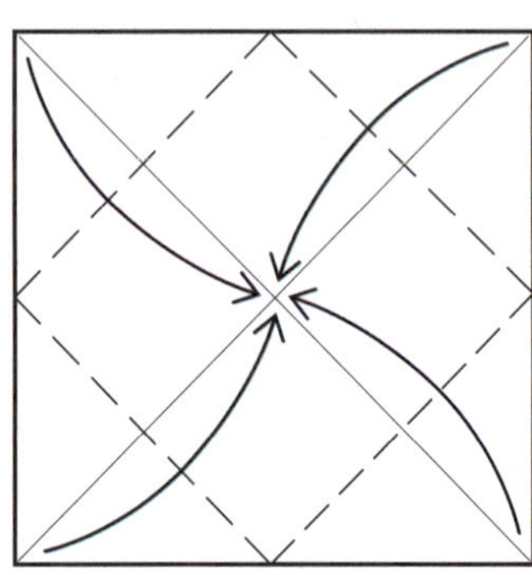

Fold corners to the center.

3 4 5

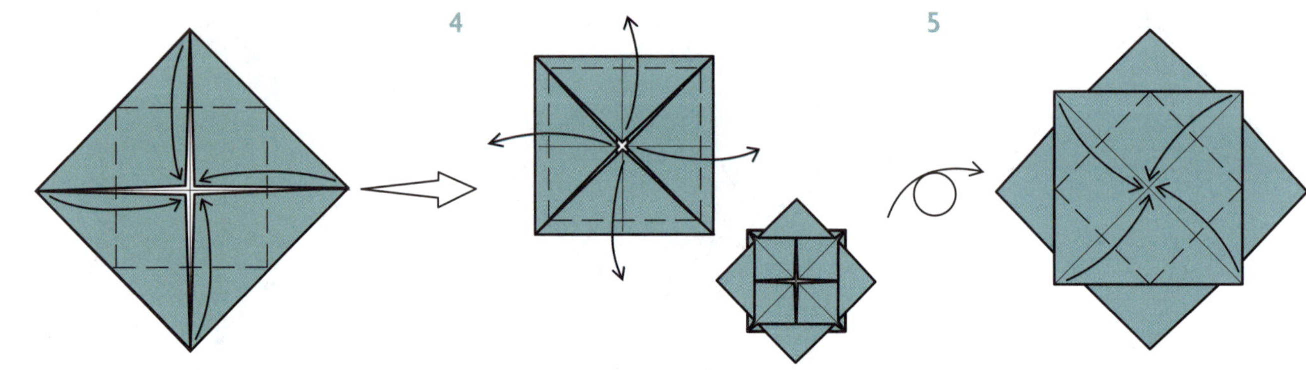

3. Fold corners to the center again.

4. Fold indicated corners outwardv leaving a small gap at the edges. Turn over.

5. While folding the indicated corners to the center, the model will change into 3D.

6 7 8

6. Completed step 5. Turn over.

7. Fold indicated corners outside leaving a little gap at the edges. Turn over.

8. Completed water lily.

LILY

MODEL: TRADITIONAL, JAPAN
DIAGRAM: MATTHEW GARDINER

Follow the instructions for the iris on the previous page up to step 7, but start with the colored side up.

1

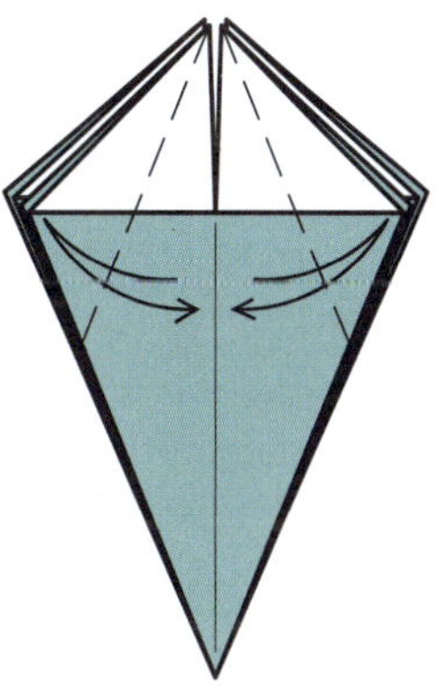

Start from step 7 of the iris. Fold the top layer only to the center crease.

2

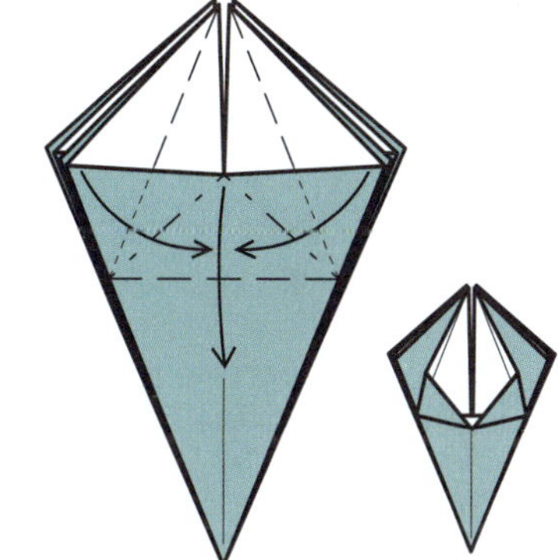

Petal fold; pull down the top layer, and fold the sides to the middle. Lastly, make the mountain folds.

3

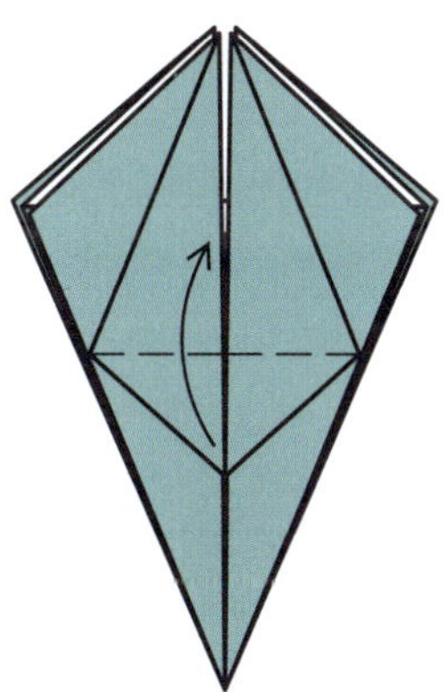

Completed petal fold. Fold the triangle flap upward.

4

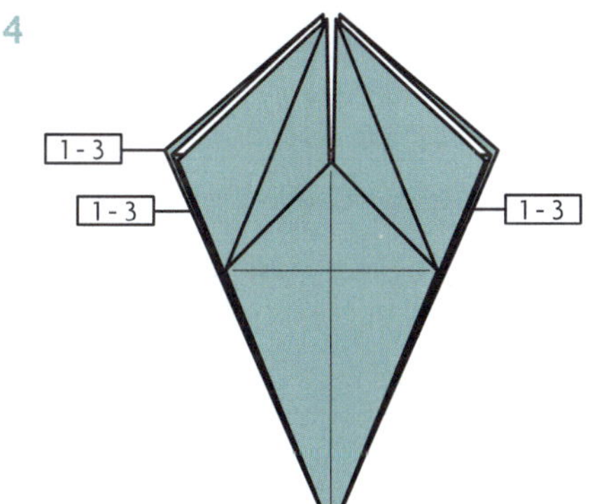

Repeat steps 1-3 on the three remaining sides.

5

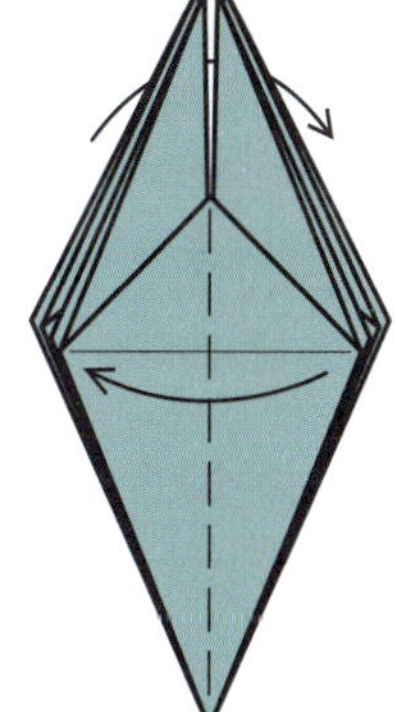

Fold one layer in front and behind.

6

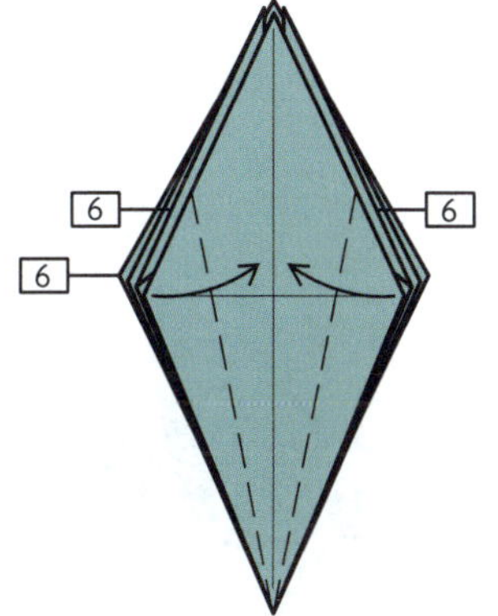

Fold edges to the middle, thinning the lily. Repeat on the other three sides.

7

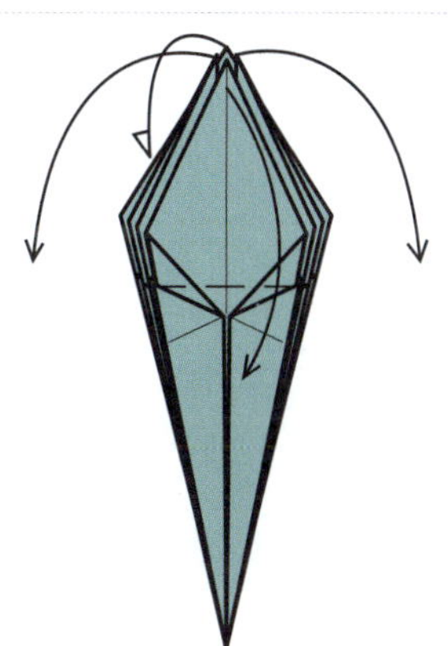

Make a soft, curved valley fold on all four sides to open out the lily.

8

Completed lily.

7

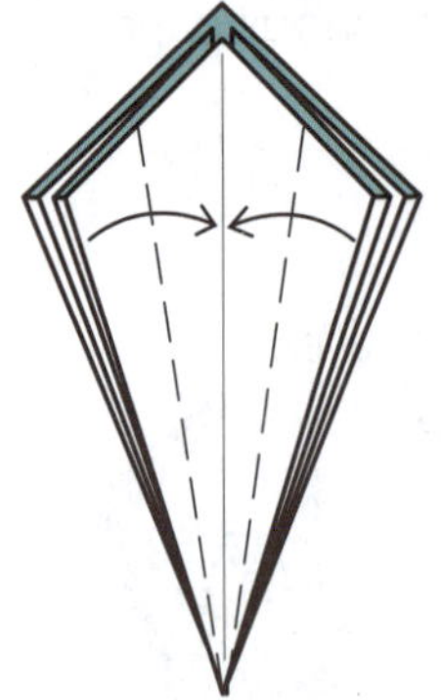

Fold top layer edges to meet the middle.

8

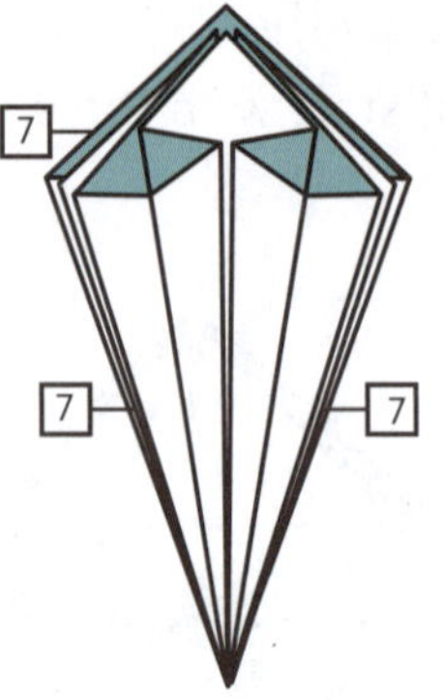

Repeat step 7 to both sides and behind.

9

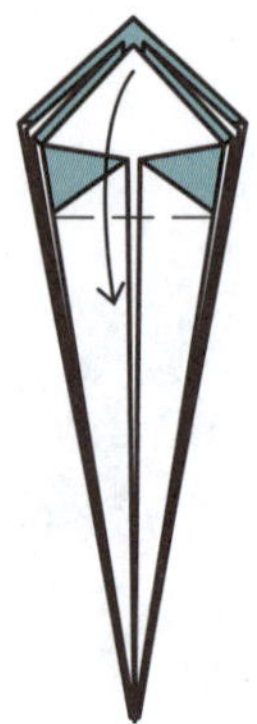

Fold front petal down.

10

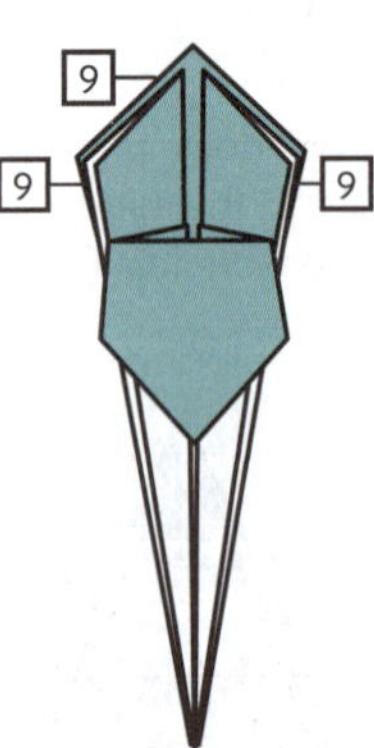

Repeat step 9 on all three sides making the model 3D. Start with both side petals followed by the back petal.

11

Completed iris.

YAKKO-SAN

MODEL: TRADITIONAL, JAPAN
DIAGRAM: MATTHEW GARDINER

Yakko-san is a very old, very well-known traditional origami form. It originates from the era of the samurai. Yakko-san comes from the word Yatsuko meaning servant. Yakko-san was the man carrying the baggage for his master. In contemporary Japanese society, Yakko-san has come to mean "young man."

Yakko-san is a popular design in Japanese kimono prints.

1 Fold and unfold both diagonals.

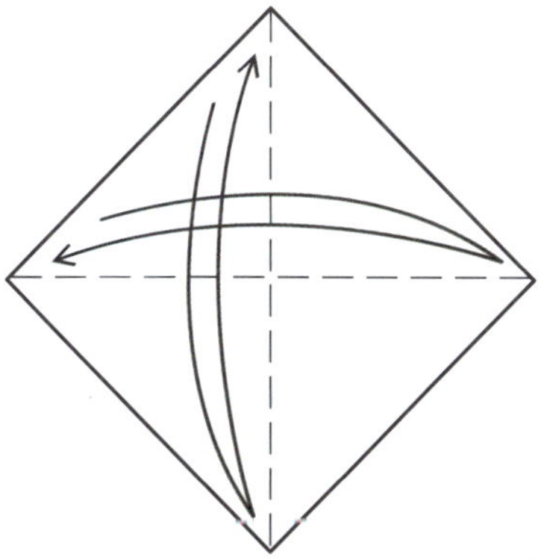

2 Blintz fold and turn over.

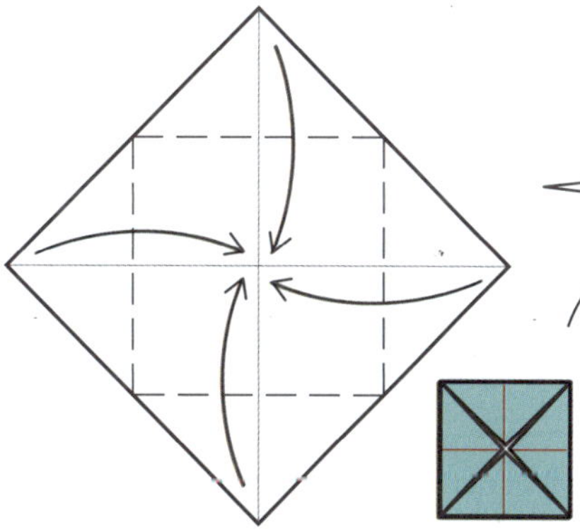

3 Blintz fold for the 2nd time, and turn over.

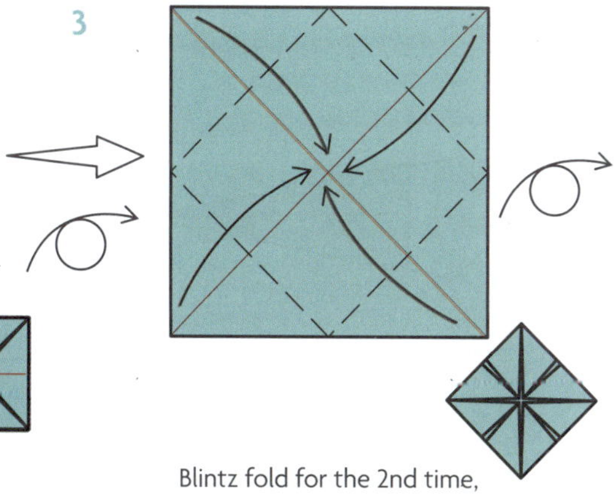

4 Blintz fold and turn over for the 3rd time.

5 Squash fold the three corners as shown. The corners will open outward and form the square arms and feet.

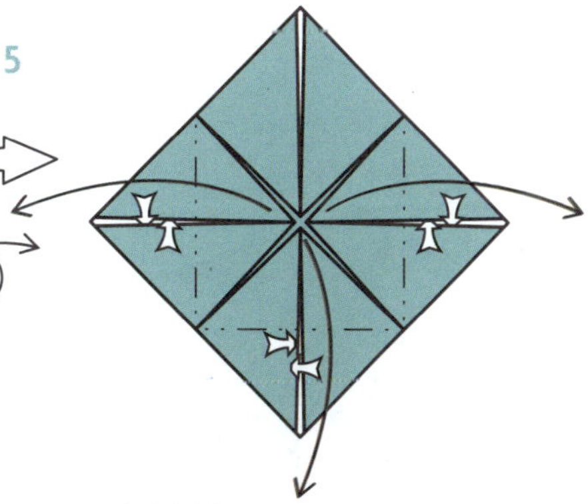

6 Completed Yakko-san, konnichi-wa.

SWAN

MODEL: TRADITIONAL, JAPAN
DIAGRAM: MATTHEW GARDINER

This simple origami swan expresses the form of this elegant bird swimming on the water of a lake.

1

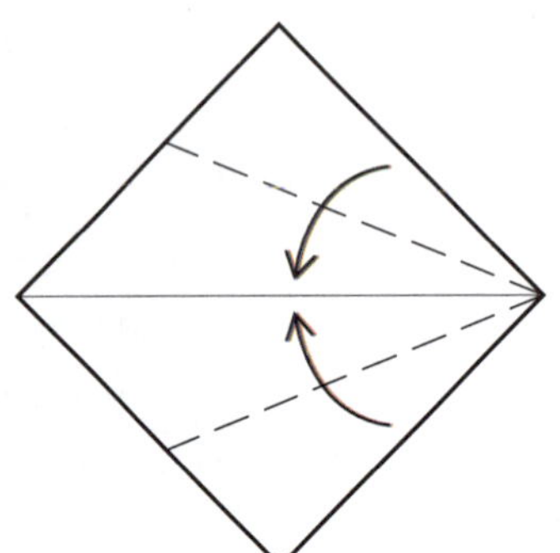

Pre-crease diagonal. Fold sides to the middle.

2

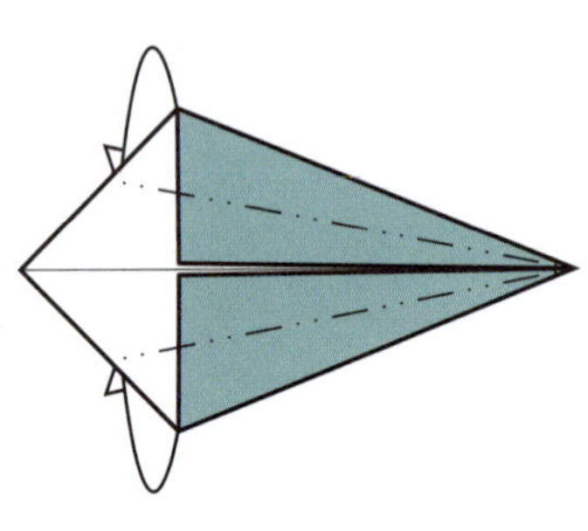

Mountain fold both sides to the middle.

3

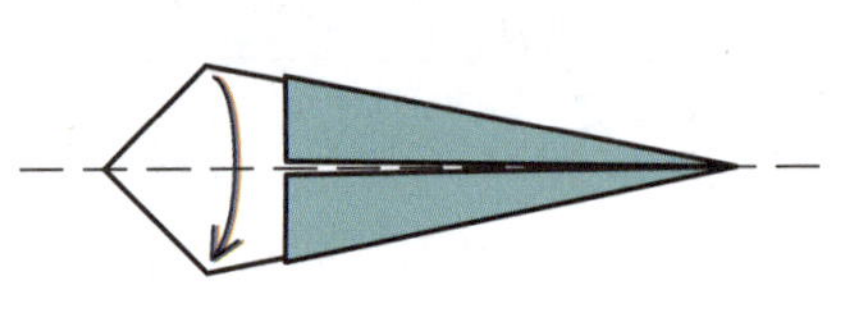

Fold in half.

4

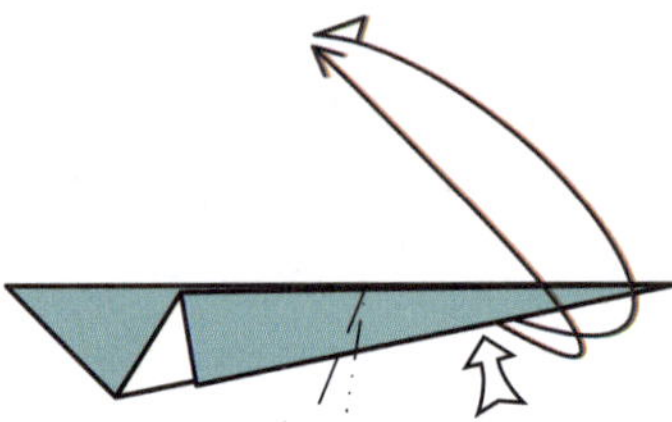

Outside reverse fold the neck.

5

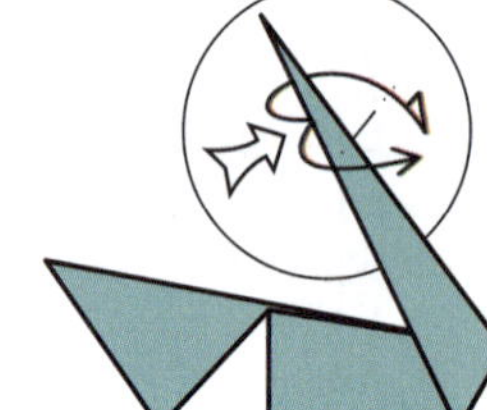

Outside reverse fold the head.

6

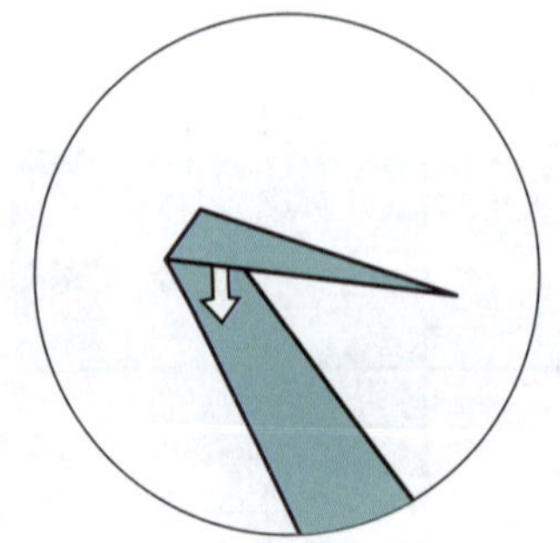

Pull out hidden paper on both sides of the head.

7

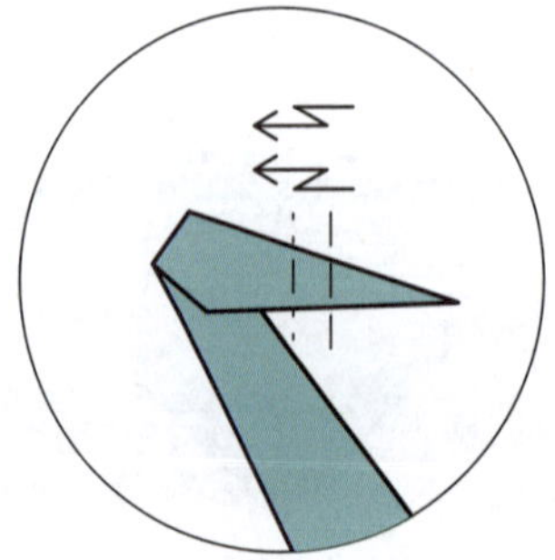

Pleat, then double reverse fold the head to form the beak.

8

Completed swan.

PAJARITO

MODEL: TRADITIONAL, JAPAN
DIAGRAM: MATTHEW GARDINER

Pajarito, or "Little Bird" is the most famous traditional design from Spain. Historically, Spanish origami was born from the geometric fascination of the Moors. The model requires a 3D transformation move at the end. Be careful when folding to make sure the mountain and valley folds are placed correctly. Then the final move will be almost "natural" for the paper.

The pajarito is the icon of Spanish origami. Papiroflexia is the Spanish way of saying paper folding.

1

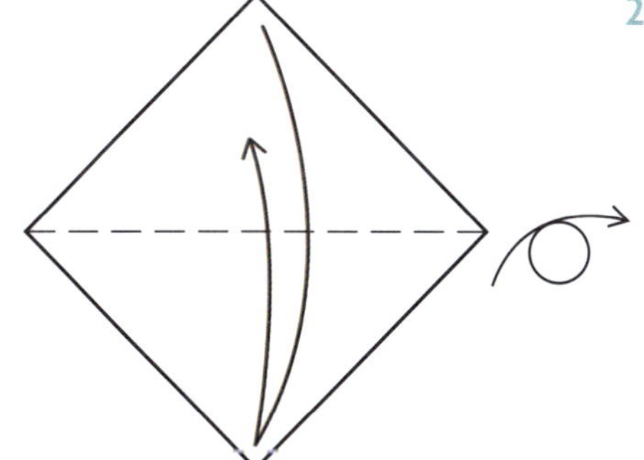

Begin white side up.
Fold and unfold diagonal. Turn over.

2

Fold and unfold diagonal.

3

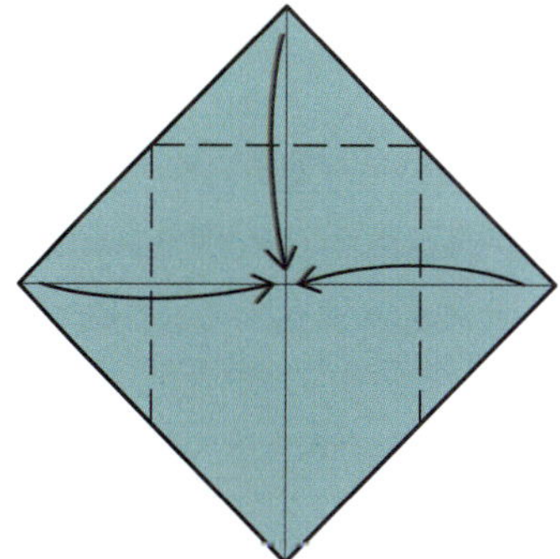

Fold three corners to the center.

4

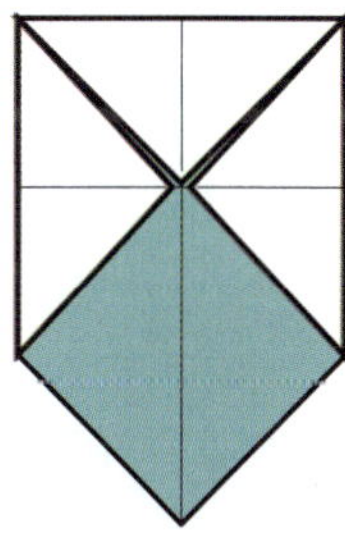

Completed step 3.
Turn over.

5

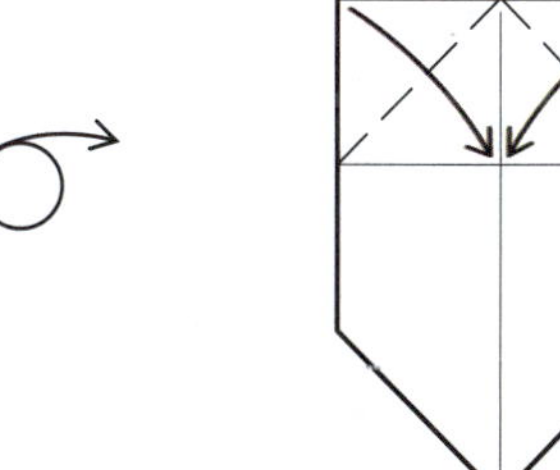

Fold top corners down to center point.

6

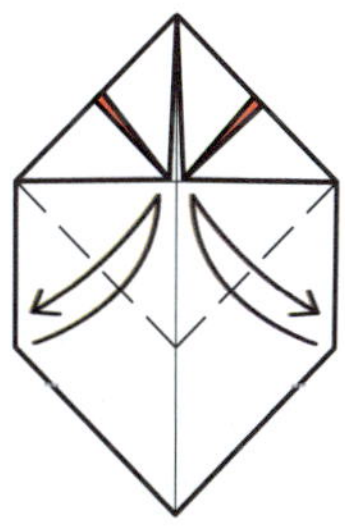

Fold and unfold, be careful to only crease as shown.

7

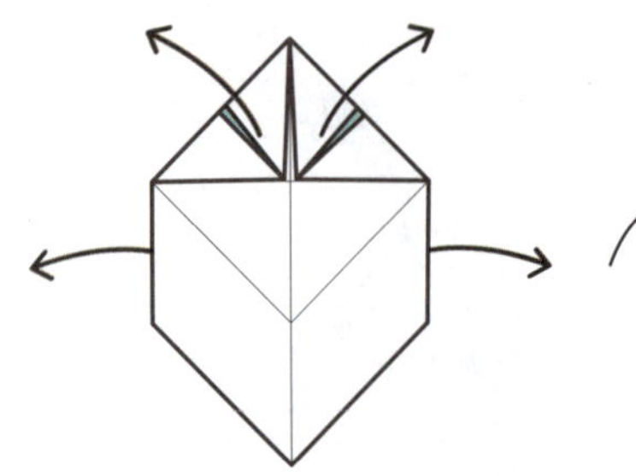

Unfold corners and side flaps.
Turn over.

8

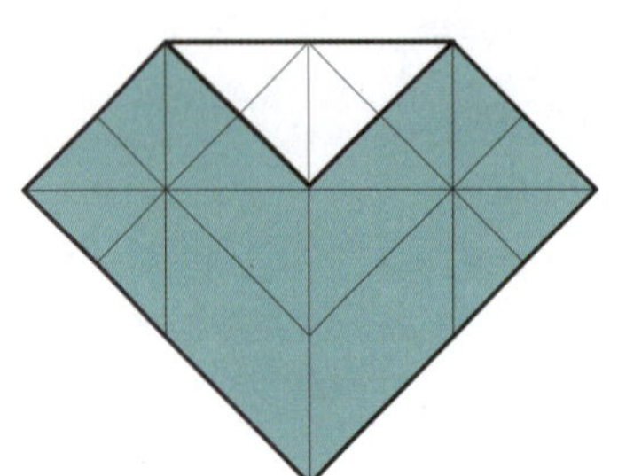

Your model should look like this.
Turn over.

9

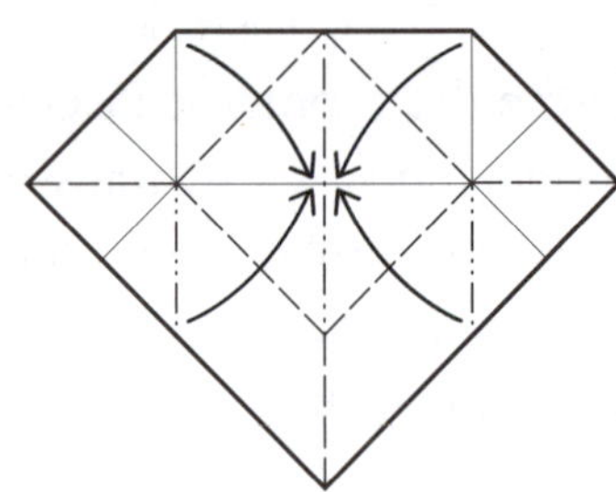

Fold on existing creases. Pay attention to the mountain and valley folds.

10

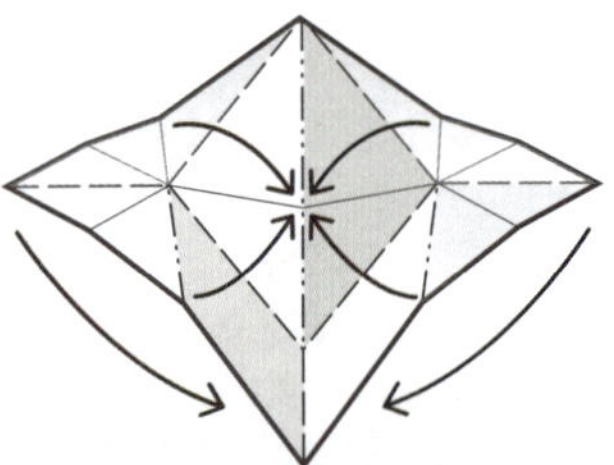

The 3D move in progress.

11

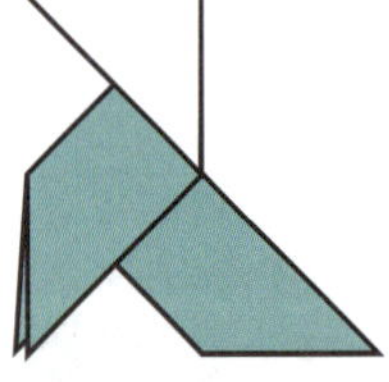

Completed pajarito.

PAPER CRANE

MODEL: TRADITIONAL, JAPAN
DIAGRAM: MATTHEW GARDINER

The traditional Japanese paper crane or orizuru is famous throughout the world. It is a symbol of origami and a symbol of peace. An ancient Japanese legend says that whoever folds 1000 cranes will be granted a wish.

Today, in Hiroshima, stands the peace memorial of Sadako Sasaki built by her classmates in her memory to inspire peace around the world. Sadako was a victim of atom-bomb disease and she folded cranes until she died. She never gave up on her wish to be well.

1

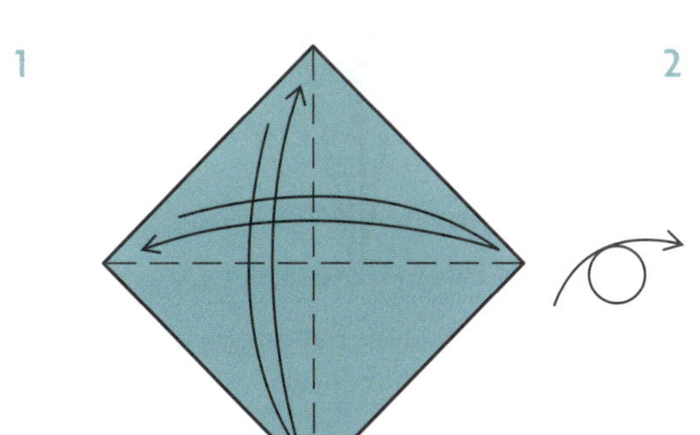

Start colored side up.
Fold and unfold diagonals. Turn over.

2

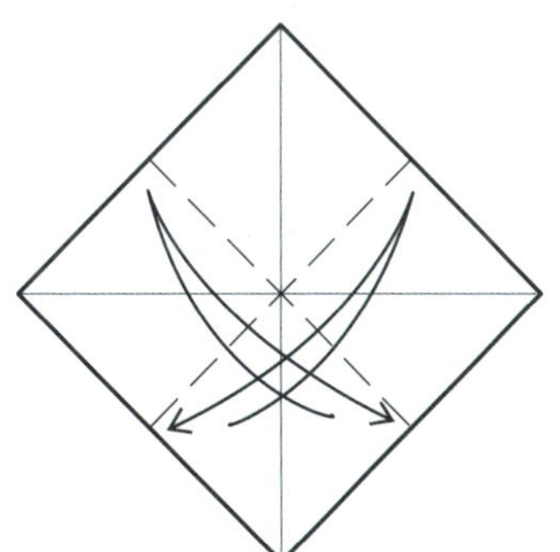

Book fold and unfold.

3

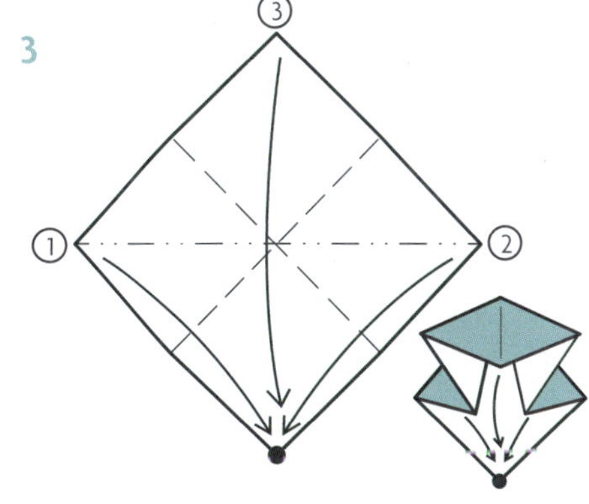

Bring three corners down to meet bottom corner. Start with corners 1 and 2 together followed by corner 3.

4

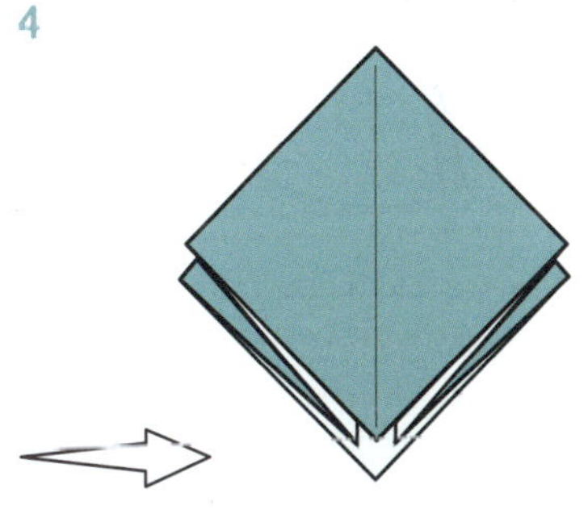

Completed preliminary base.

5

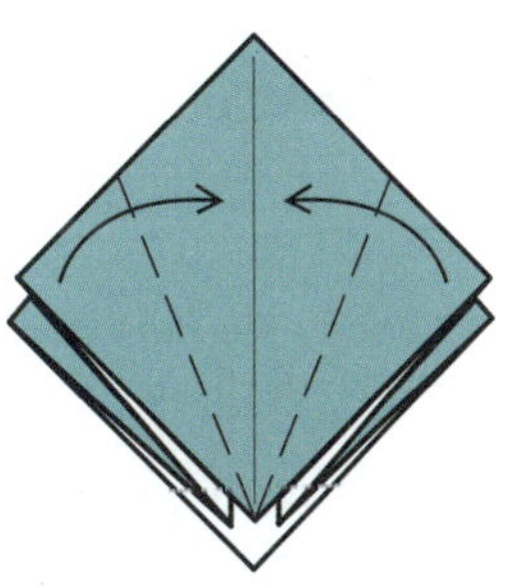

Fold top layer to the center crease.

6

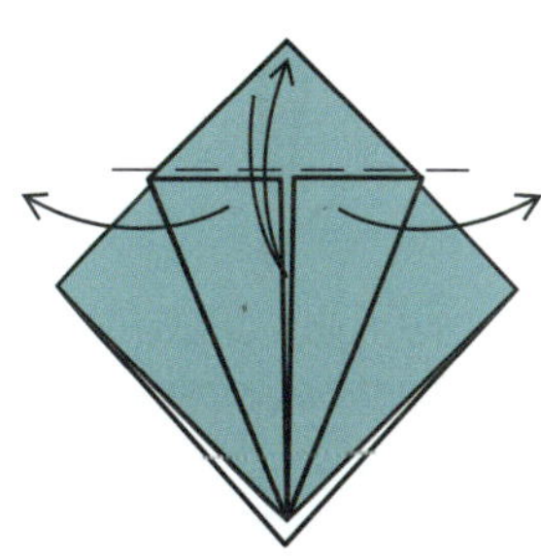

Fold and unfold the top triangle down.
Unfold flaps.

7

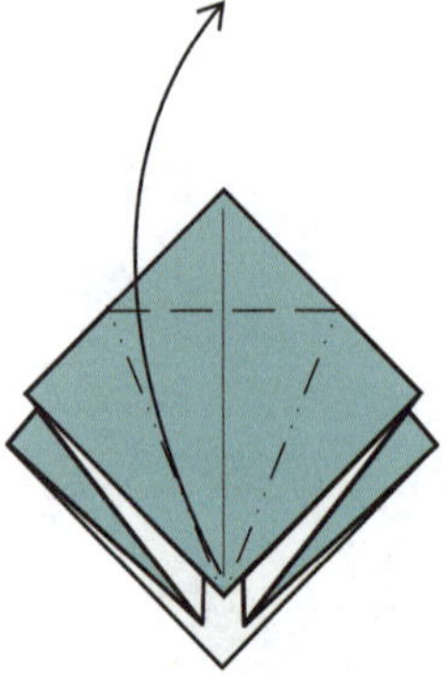

Lift the top layer upward.

8

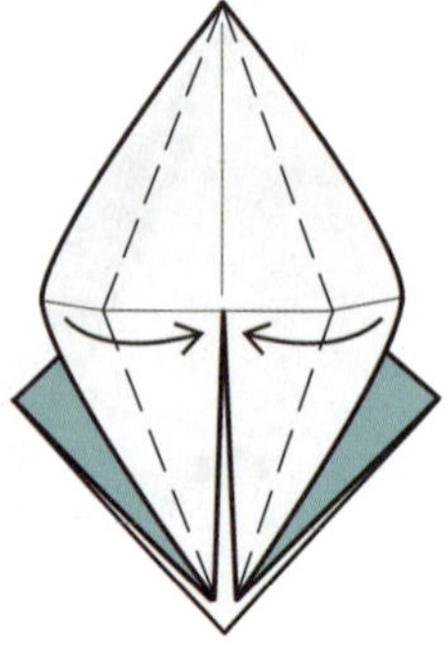

Step 7 in progress, the model is 3D. Fold the top layer inward on existing creases.

9

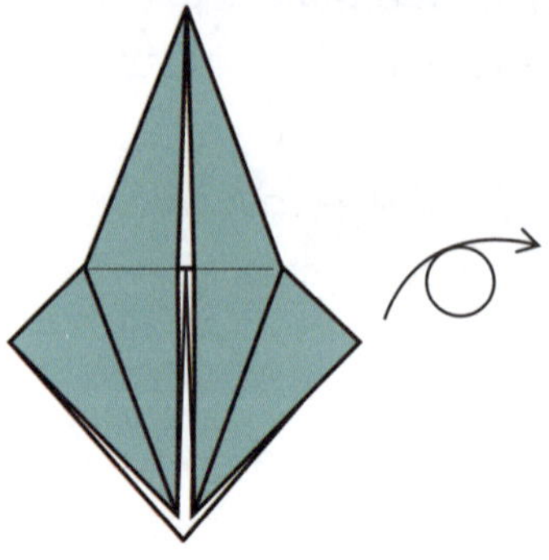

Step 7 completed, the model will be flat. Turn over.

10

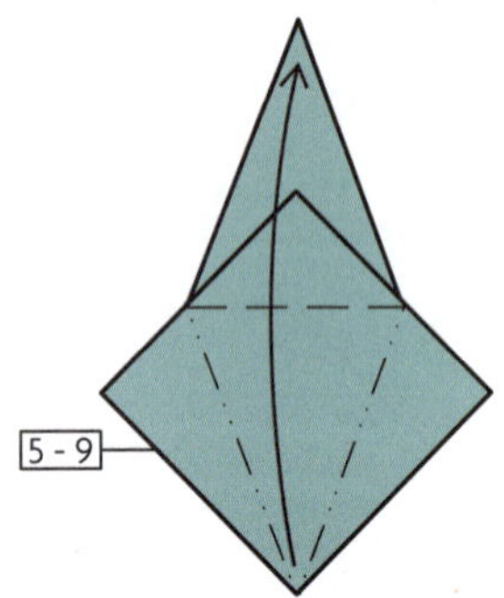

Repeat steps 5-9 on this side.

11

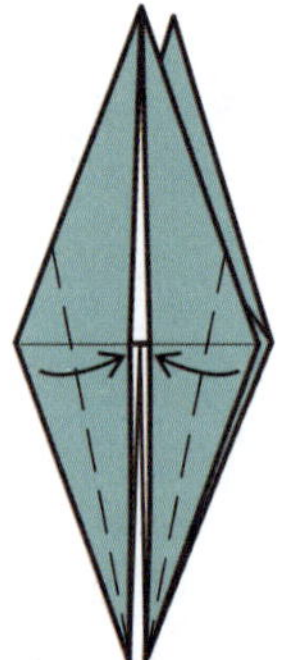

Narrow the bottom points on the top layer only. Repeat behind.

12

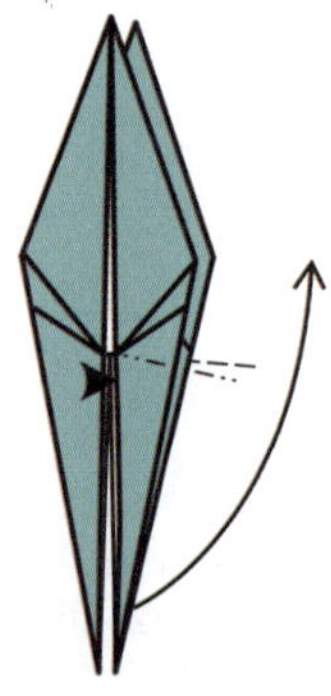

Reverse fold the bottom point upward.

13

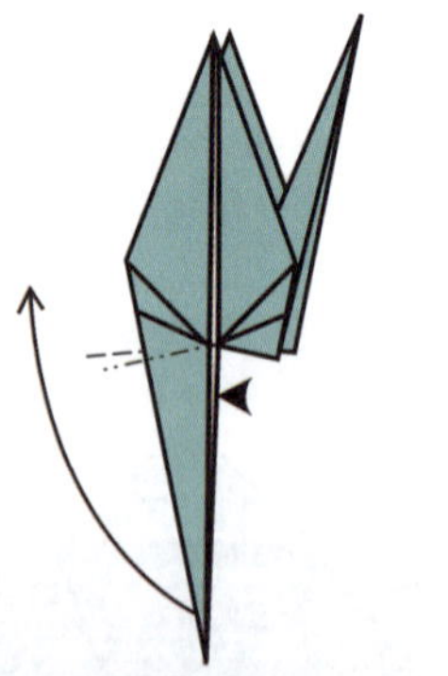

Your model should look like this. Repeat on the other side.

14

Completed body. The next steps focus on the head.

15

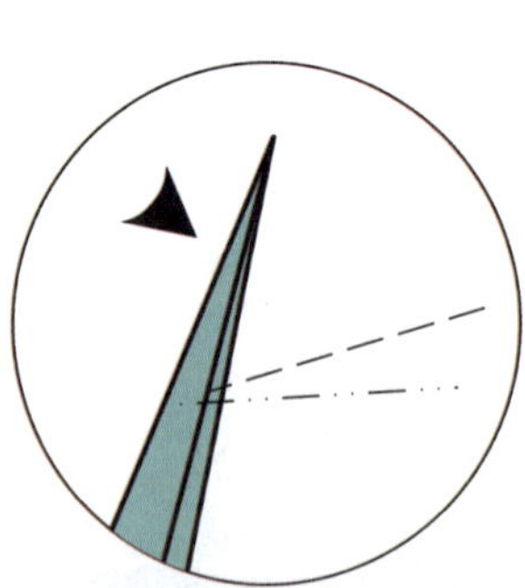

Reverse fold the point to create the head.

16

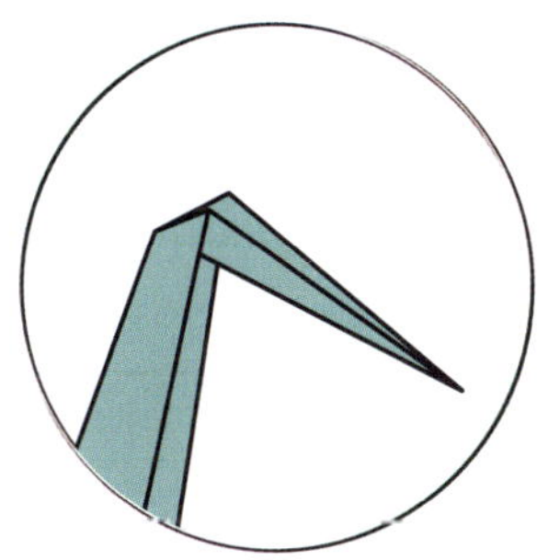

Head completed.

17

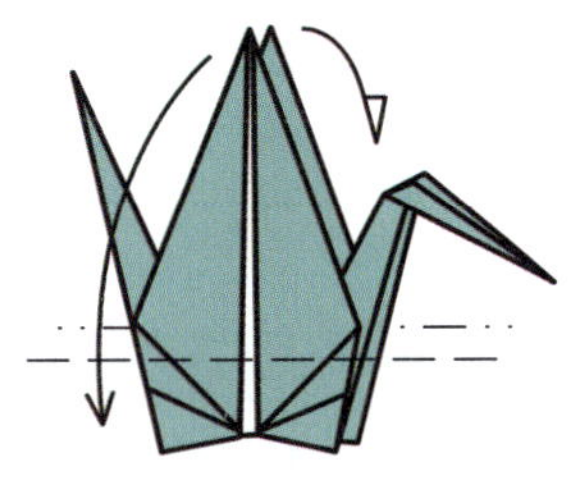

Fold wings down.

18

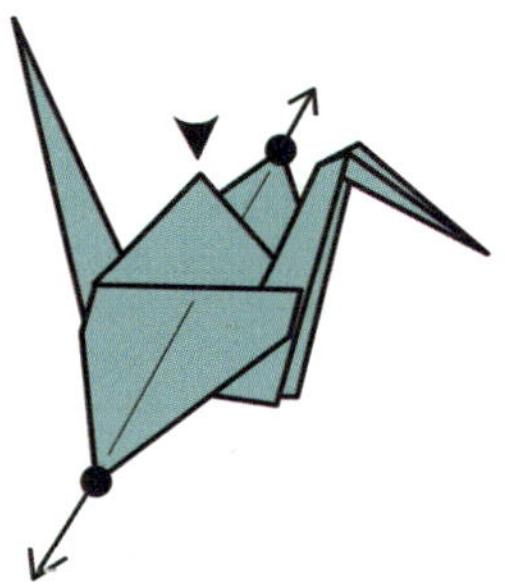

Pull the wings gently to shape the body.

19

Completed paper crane—repeat 1000 times for a wish.

HEART

MODEL: MATTHEW GARDINER
DIAGRAM: MATTHEW GARDINER

This heart can be a folded love letter, or used as a decoration on the front of a card. Use letter (8.5 x 11in) paper.

1 2

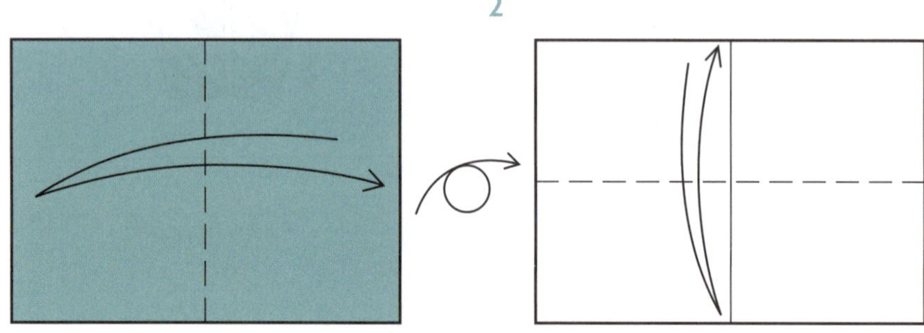

1. Book fold and unfold. Turn over.

2. Fold in half lengthways and unfold.

3

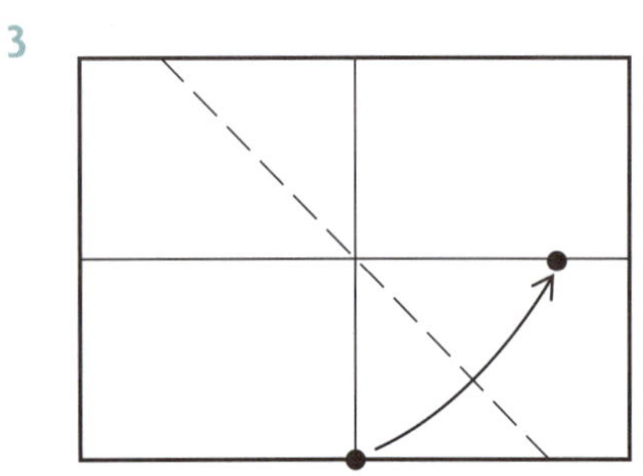

Valley fold a diagonal so that the vertical crease touches the horizontal crease.

4 5

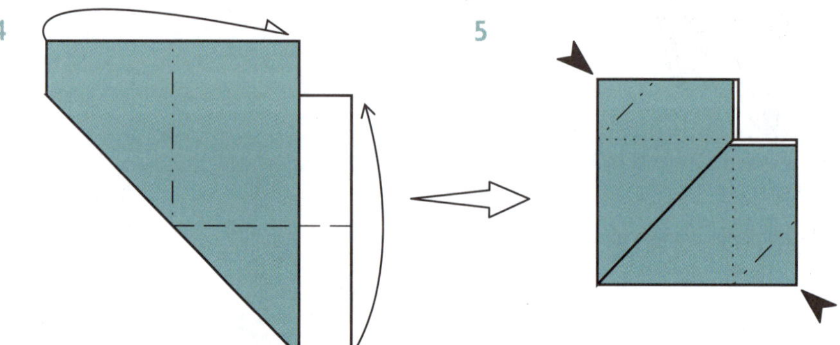

4. Fold the corners together, noting the mountain fold on the upper part and the valley fold on the lower part.

5. Inside reverse fold the points. The edge of the crease should match with the inner layer of the paper.

6

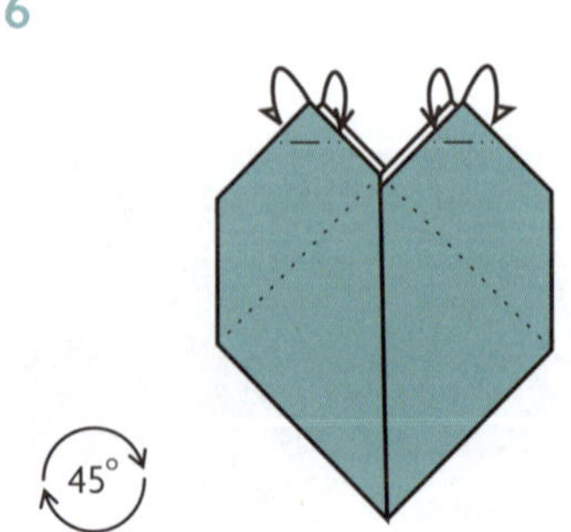

Fold the tips inside the heart.

7

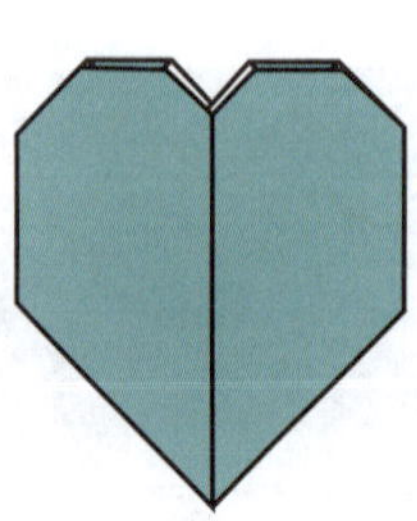

Completed heart.

ADVANCED PROJECTS

SPANISH BOX

MODEL: TRADITIONAL, SPAIN
DIAGRAM: MATTHEW GARDINER

The traditional Spanish box was brought to the world origami stage by the British magician and origami expert Robert Harbin during his famous BBC television series. It's a practical decorative model, and if you use a 12in (30cm) sheet, or larger, of stiff card you can create a strong vessel for sweets and foods at parties.

The Spanish box is so named because of the decorative pleating on the rim of the box.

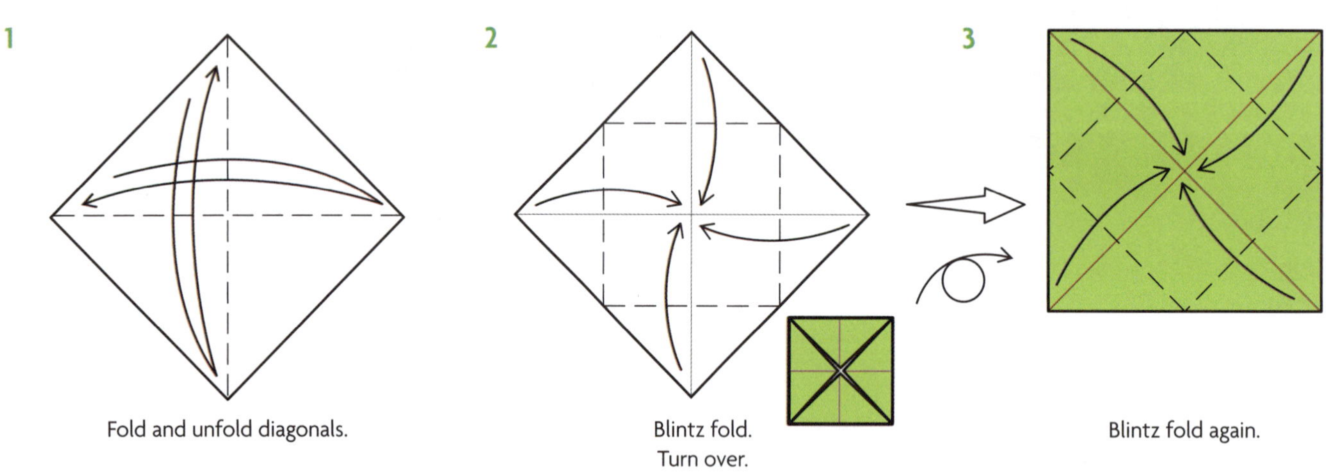

1 Fold and unfold diagonals.

2 Blintz fold. Turn over.

3 Blintz fold again.

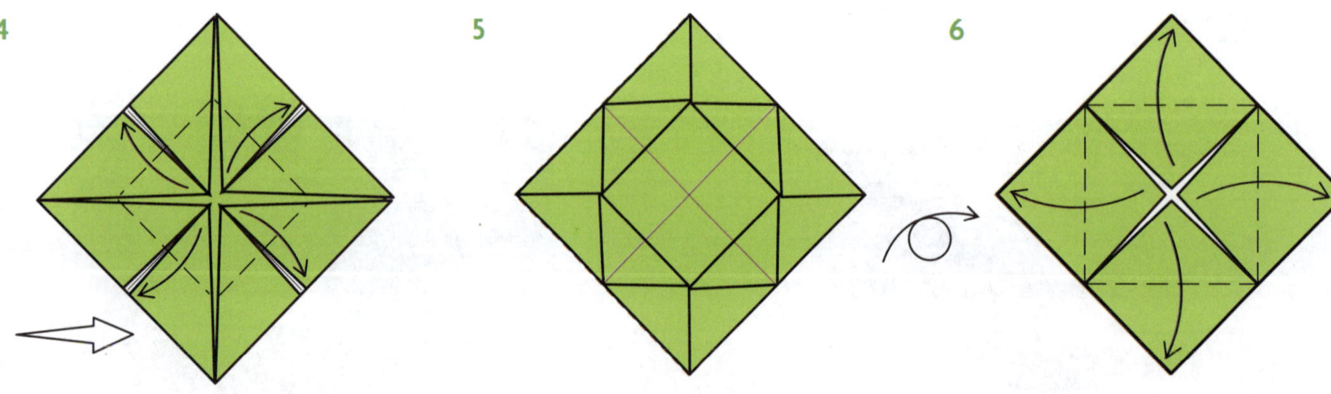

4 Fold top layers from the center to corners.

5 Completed step 4. Turn over.

6 Fold top layers from the center to corners.

7

Detail of corner.

8

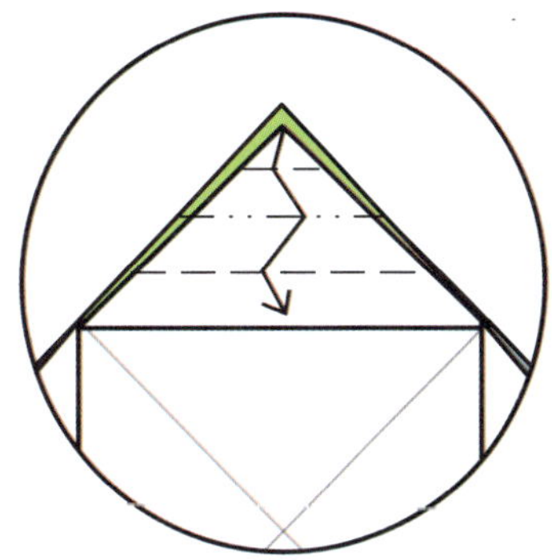

Fold over as shown.

9

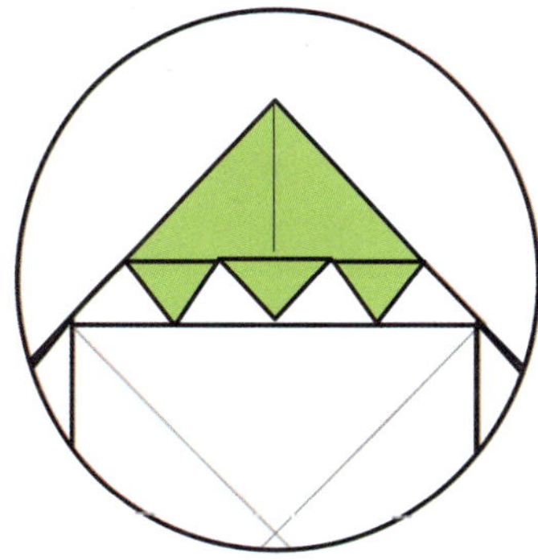

Completed step 8.

10

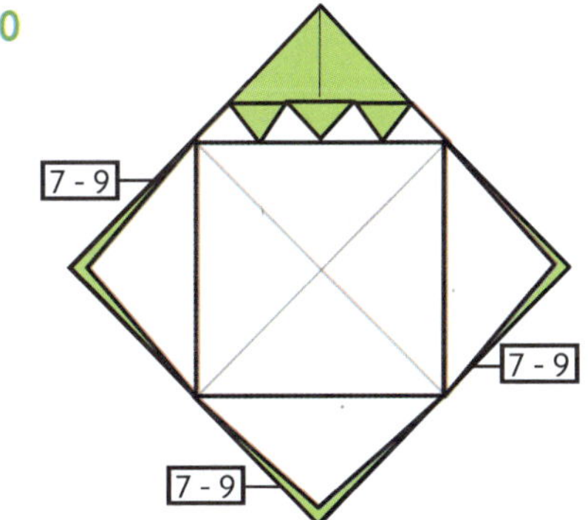

Repeat steps 7-9 on other three corners.

11

Pinch each corner as shown by the white arrows making the box 3D.

12

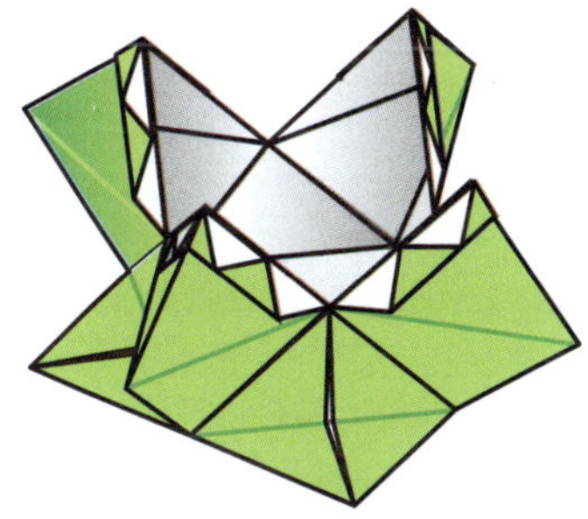

Completed Spanish box.

MASU BOX

MODEL: TRADITIONAL, JAPAN
DIAGRAM: MATTHEW GARDINER

The masu box is a very practical origami model. Traditionally it was used as a measure for rice, as certain sheet sizes produced set volumes of rice. The masu, as you will see later in this section, has many new variations, and perhaps the best variation is that by making a slightly bigger or smaller box, you can make a lid or a base.

The masu box is handy for holding almost anything.

1

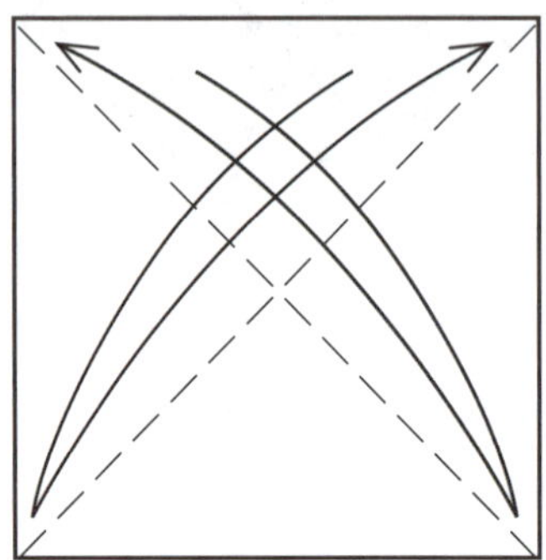

Begin white side up. Fold and unfold diagonals.

2

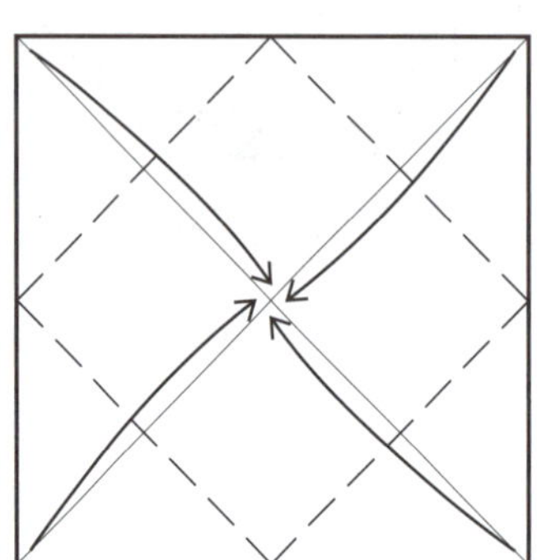

Blintz fold.

3

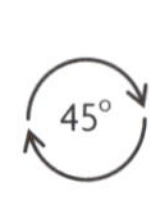

Cupboard fold and unfold.

4

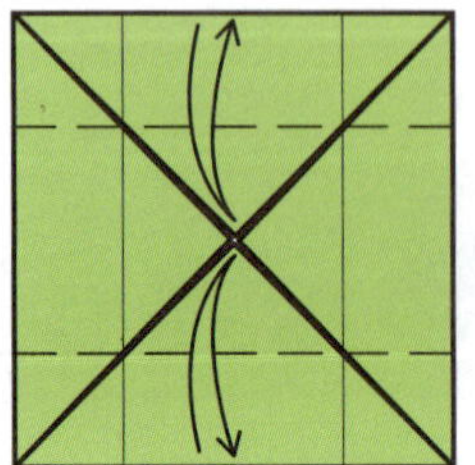

Cupboard fold and unfold the other edges.

5

Unfold two side points.

6

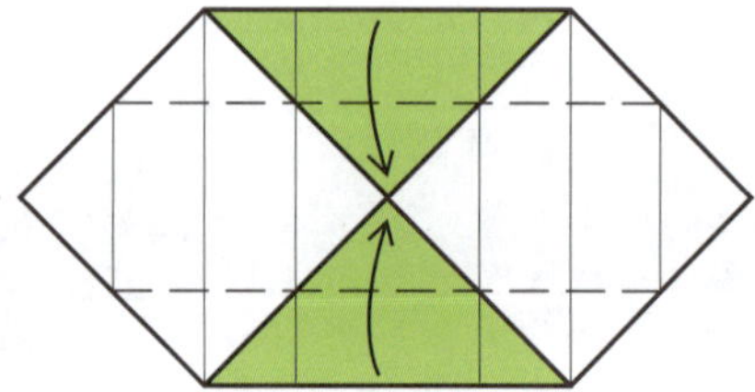

Fold on existing creases.

7

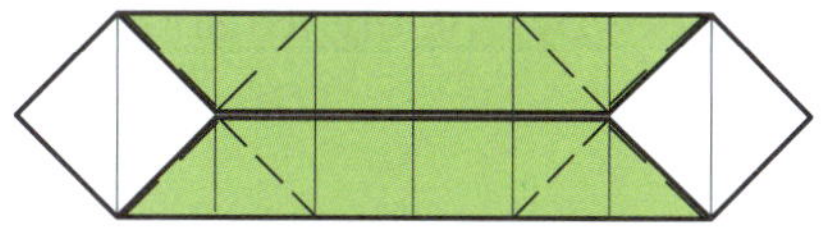

Fold and unfold on diagonals.

8

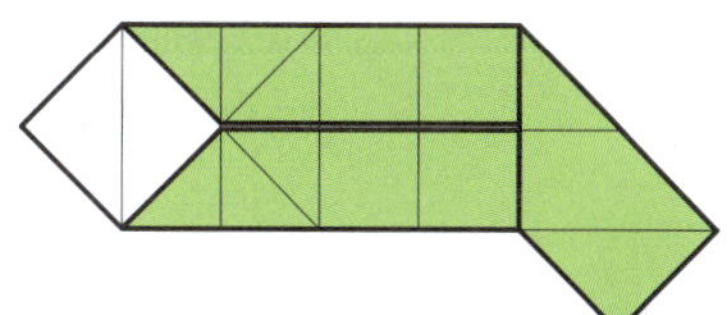

Step 7 in progress.

9

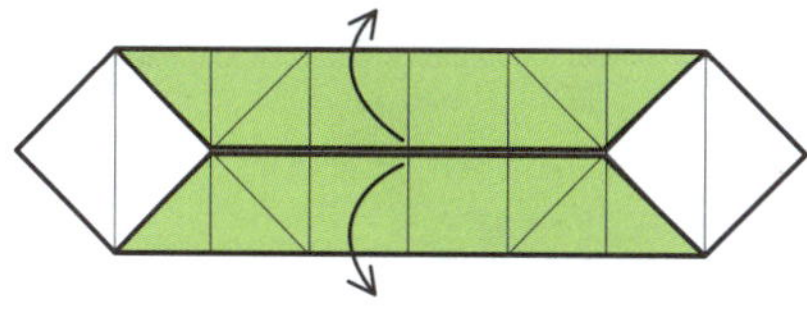

Lift sides to 90º.

10

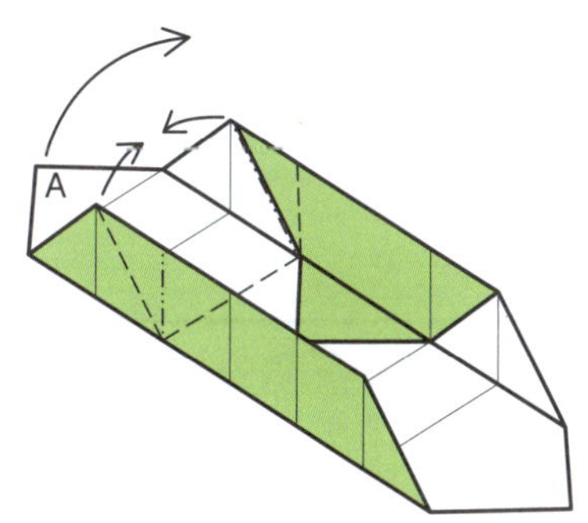

To make the side of the box, lift point A upward—the existing sides will naturally collapse to points.

11

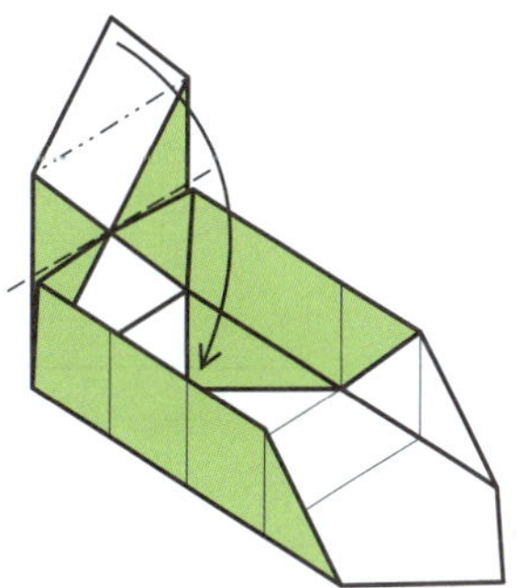

Fold the point down into the box, and press the point to the center.

12

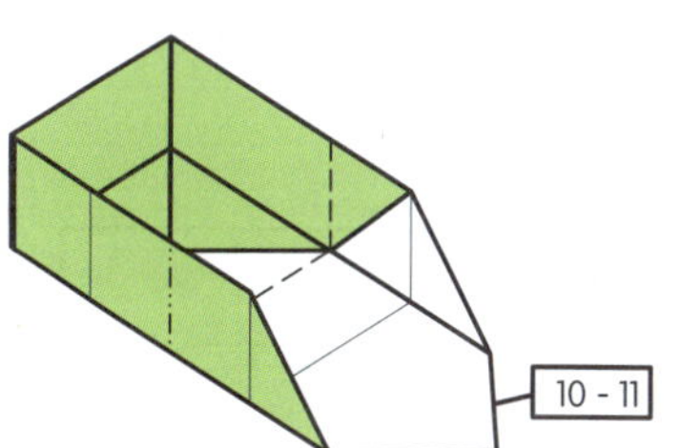

Repeat steps 10-11 on this side.

13

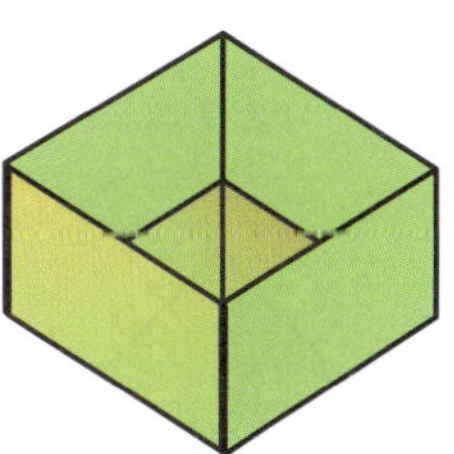

Completed masu box.

STAR BOX MASU

MODEL: DARREN SCOTT
DIAGRAM: DARREN SCOTT

This box lid fits the traditional masu box. There are lots of possible variations—see what you can create yourself. To get a perfect fit, make this lid first, and then trim the same size sheet by one eighth and make the masu box.

1

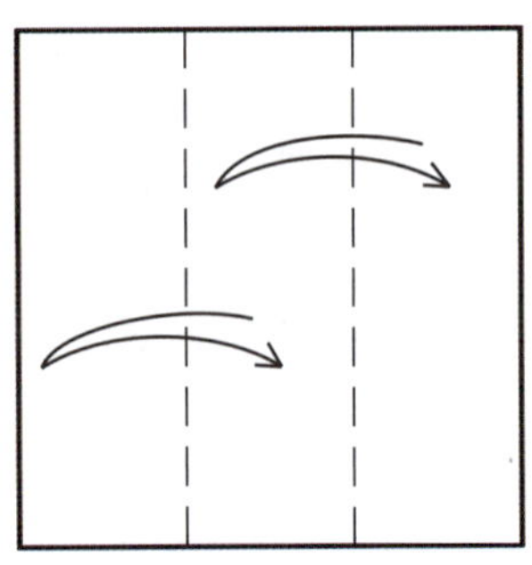

Start with the square white side up and divide into thirds and unfold.

2

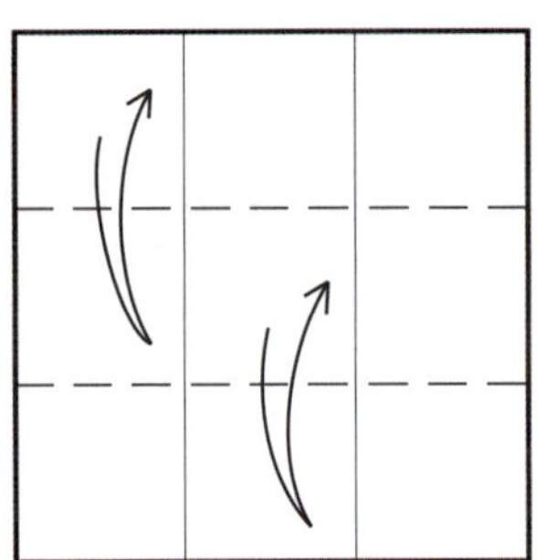

Divide into thirds in the horizontal direction and unfold.

3

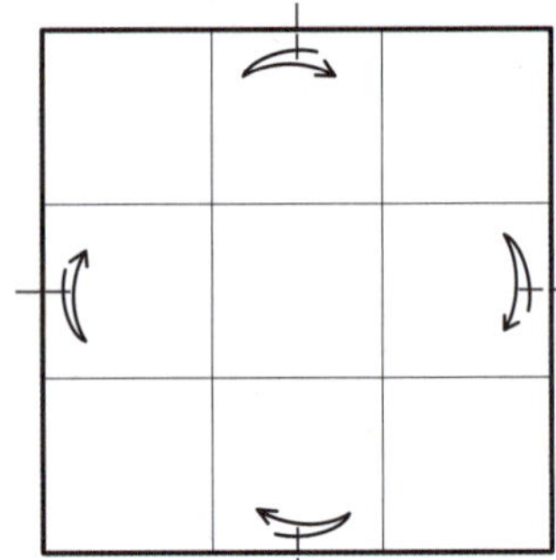

Make small pinches at the midpoint on all four sides.

4

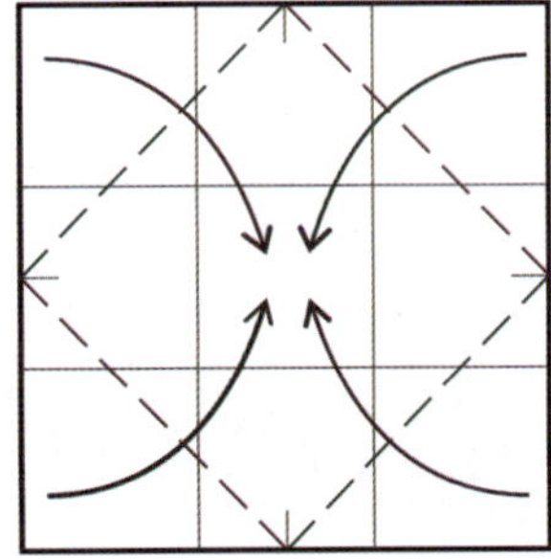

Using the creases in step 3 blintz fold.

5

This should be the result. Now turn over.

6

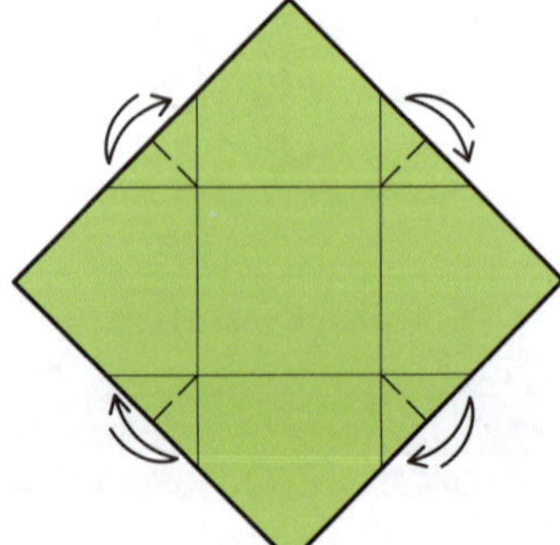

Make four more small creases.

7

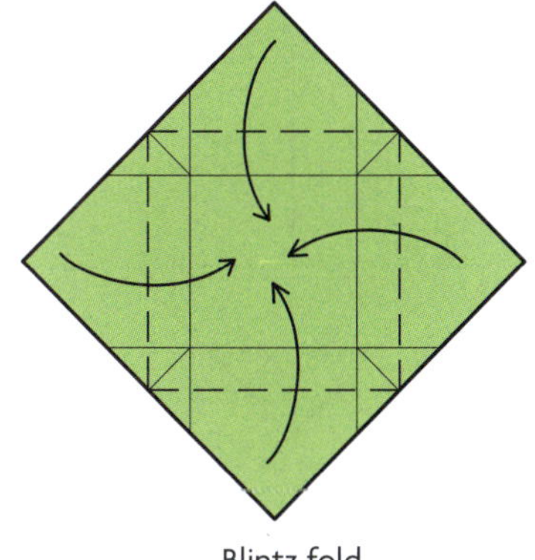

Blintz fold.

8

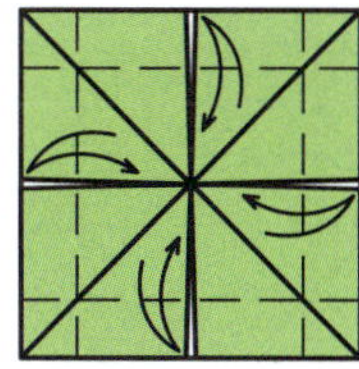

Fold and unfold over existing creases. These will form the edges of the box. Turn over.

9

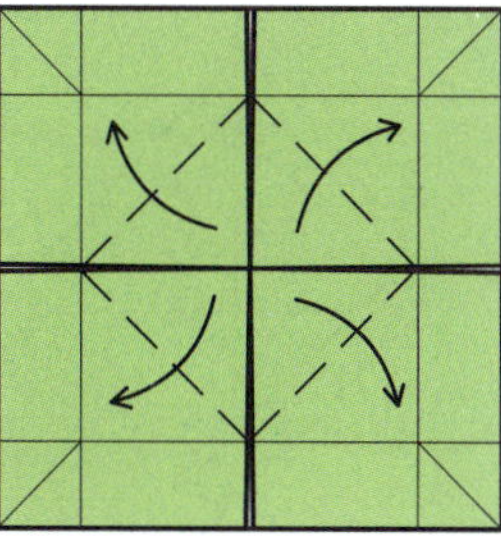

Fold the corners from the middle to the corners made by the creases.

10

Fold the corner of each flap to meet the edge of the crease.

11

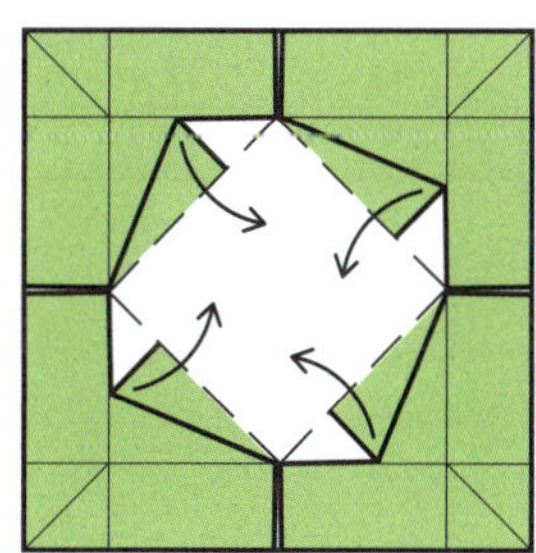

Fold each flap along the existing crease.

12

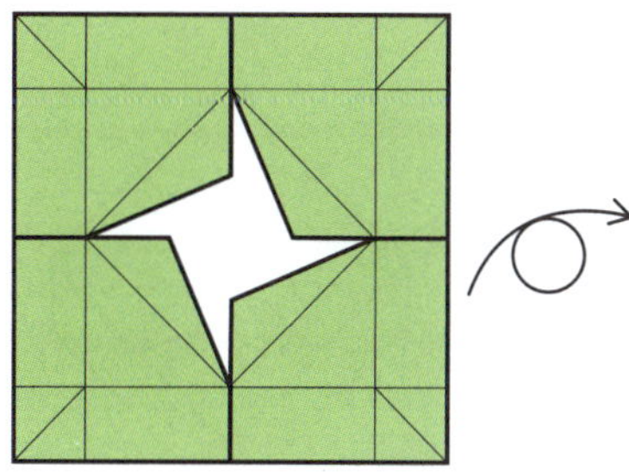

This should be the result. Turn over.

13

Open out the two side points.

14

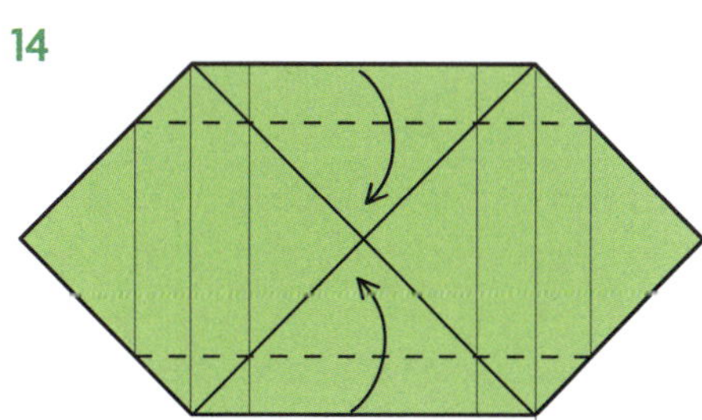

Fold the edges upward to 90º.

15

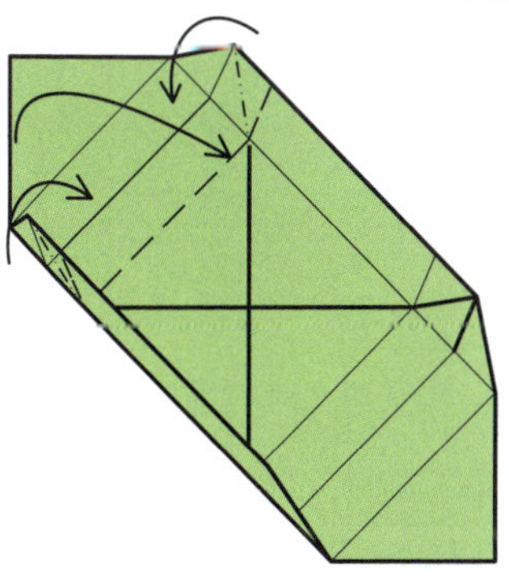

Using the existing creases lift the flap upward and then bring the edges towards the center.

16

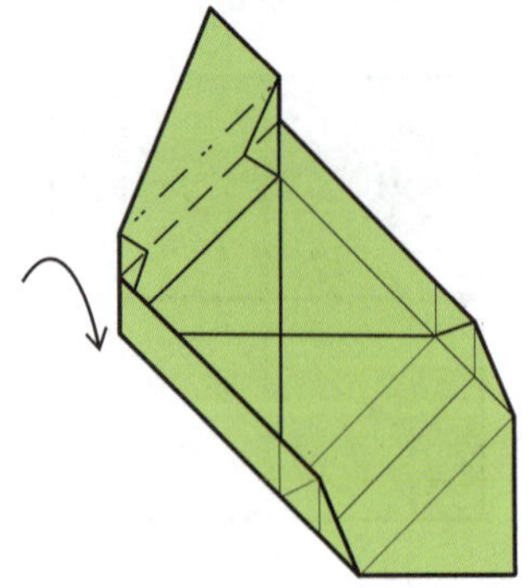

Now that you have formed the edge you need to lock the corners in place. This is done by making two folds along existing creases.

17

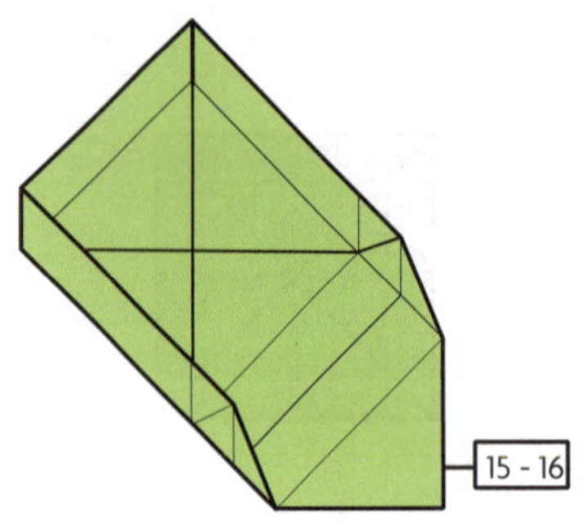

Repeat steps 15-16 on the other end.

18

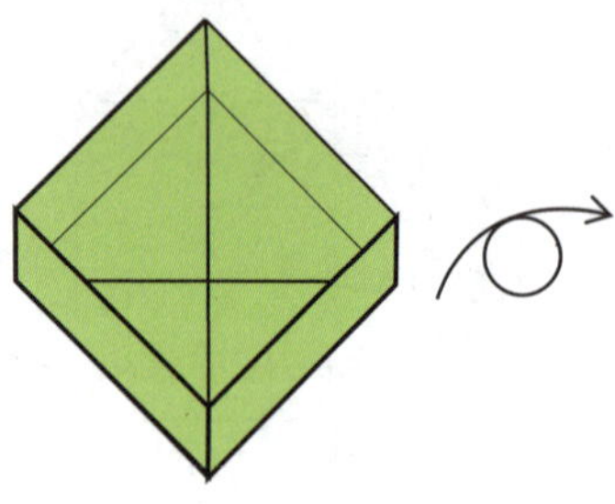

Turn over.

19

Complete star masu box.

20

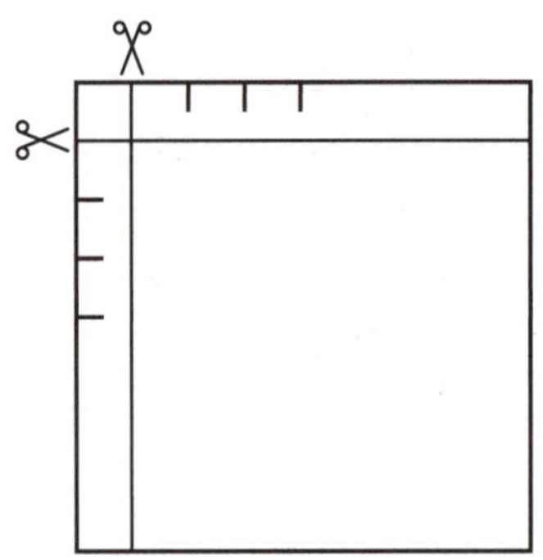

Trim 1/8 (one eighth) off the same size sheet to make the base.

21

Use the trimmed sheet to fold the masu. The base will fit in the star box masu.

BOOKMARK

MODEL: GARETH LOUIS
DIAGRAM: GARETH LOUIS

The checkered bookmark is a useful and decorative bookmark that slips over and locks onto a page. This unique and practical kind of bookmark is a favorite subject for origami designer Gareth Louis.

The checkered bookmark will keep your page marked for you in paper folding style.

1

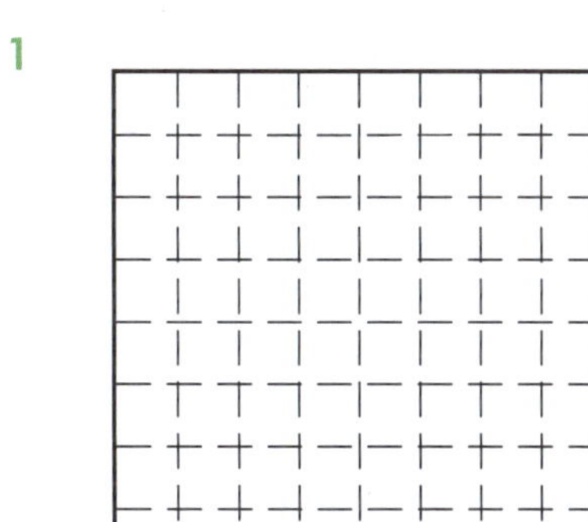

Begin white side up. Pre-crease into a grid of eighths.

2

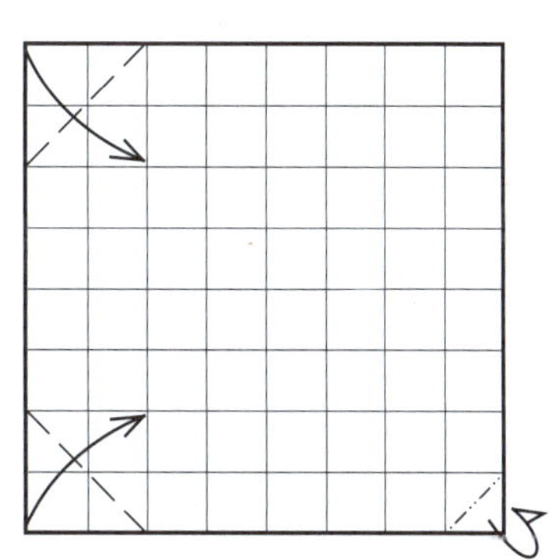

Valley fold the two left corners, and mountain fold the bottom right corner.

3

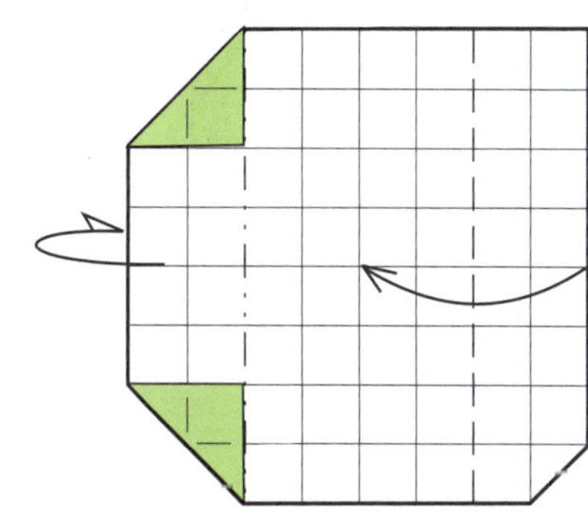

Mountain fold on the left side, and valley fold on the right.

4

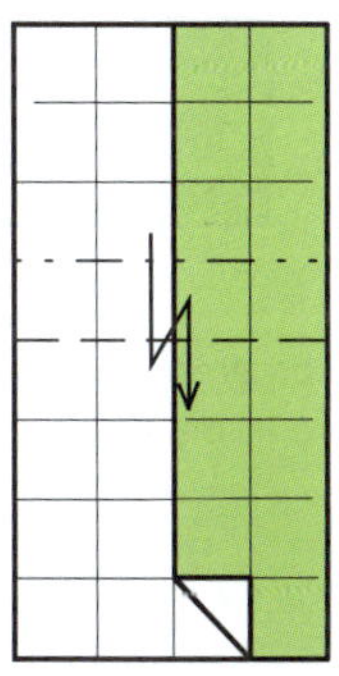

Pleat downward.

5

Completed step 4. Turn over.

6

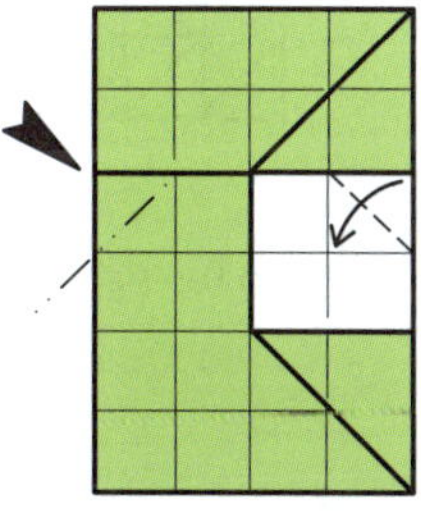

Reverse fold on the left point and valley fold on the right-hand side.

7

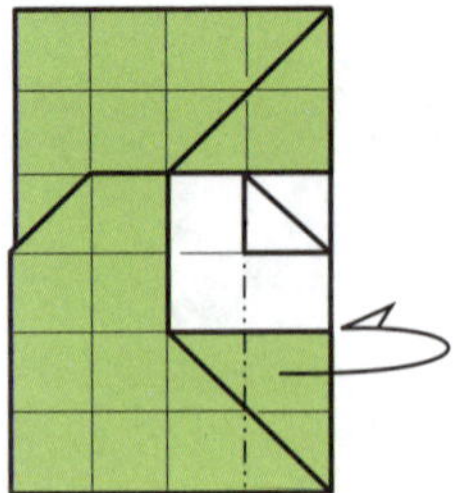

Mountain fold behind.

8

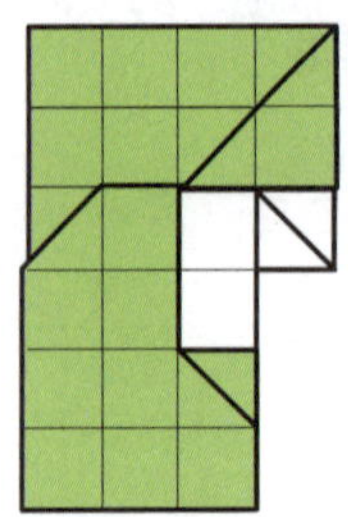

Completed step 7. Turn over.

9

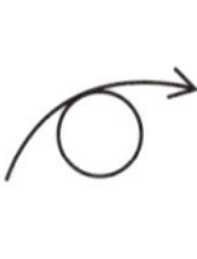

Pull out hidden layers from beneath.

10

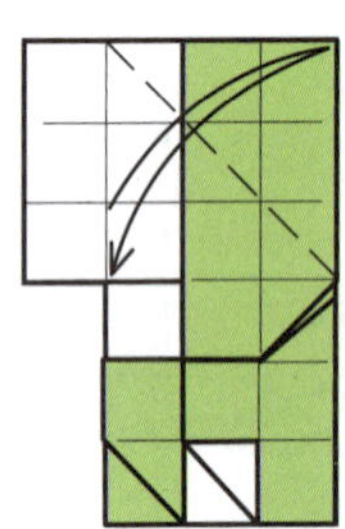

Pre-crease top right corner.

11

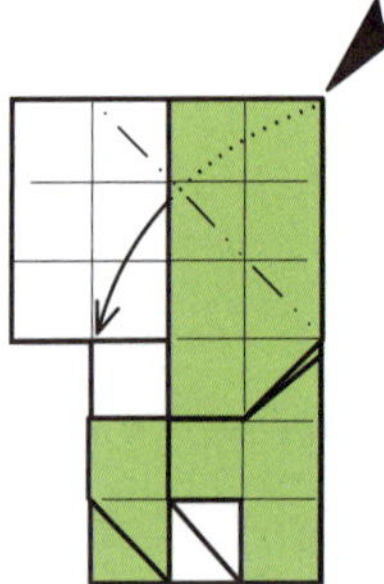

Reverse fold on creases from step 10.

12

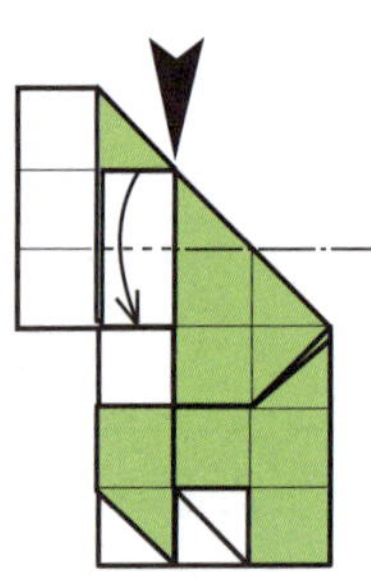

Reverse fold inside.

13

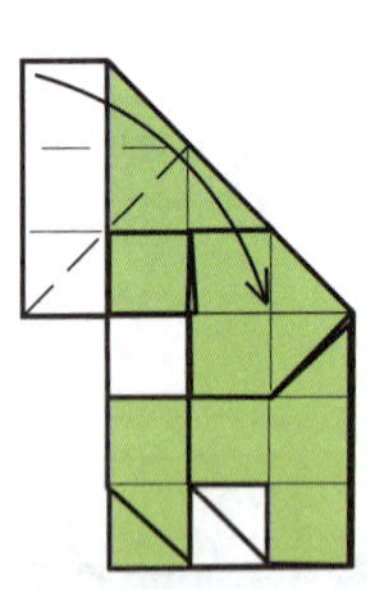

Valley fold top right flap.

14

Collapse upward by valley folding and making a reverse fold at the end.

15

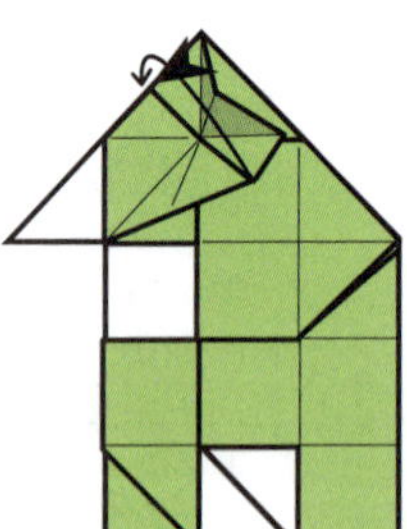

Step 14 in progress. The black arrow shows where to make the reverse fold.

16

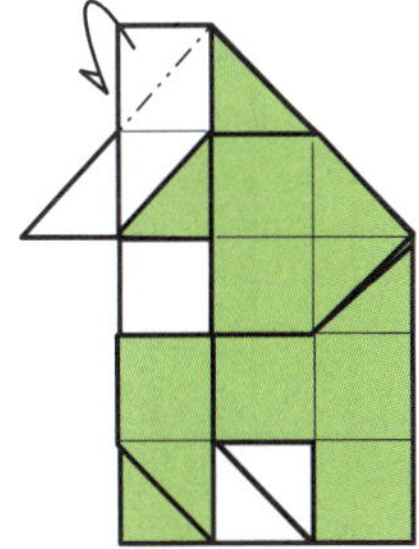

Mountain fold corner into the pocket behind.

17

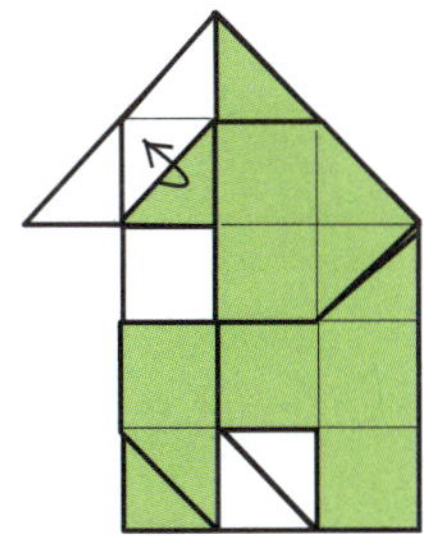

Pull out the colored layer from behind.

18

Valley fold up while incorporating a reverse fold.

19

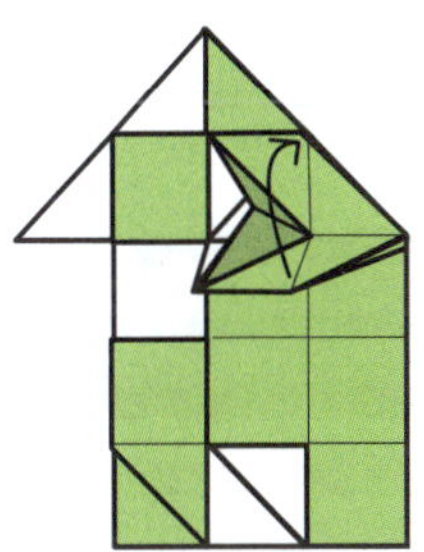

Collapsing in progress.

20

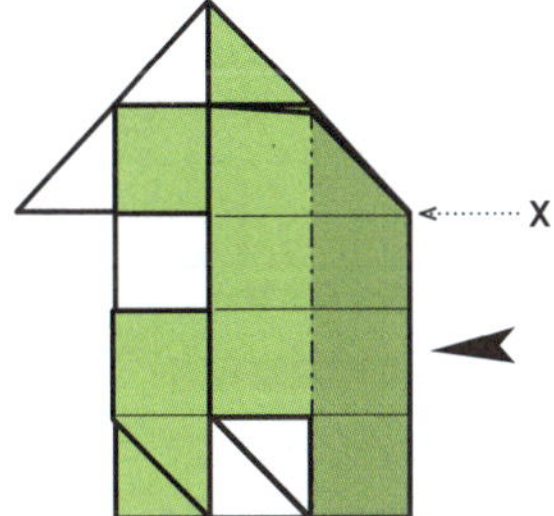

Open sink the darkened portion, but leave point X as it is, sticking out.

21

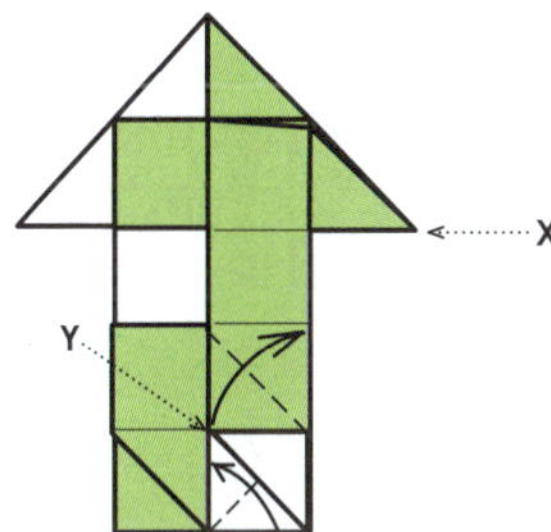

After the sink, you can still see point X. Valley fold point Y, at the same time swiveling the bottom white triangle.

22

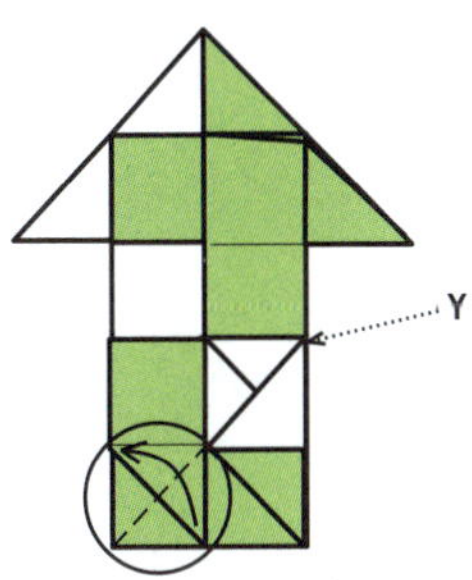

Note the new location of corner Y. Valley fold the lower corner to effect a color change.

23

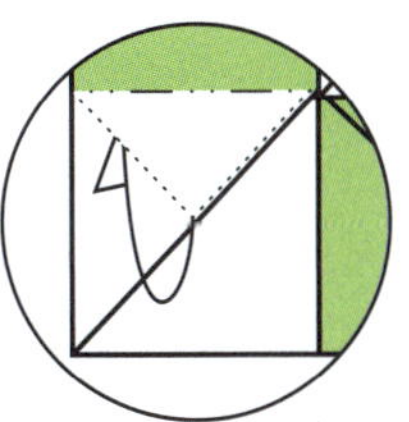

Close-up X-ray view: Mountain fold a tiny tip beneath the white layer. (It will help if you loosen the side flaps.)

24

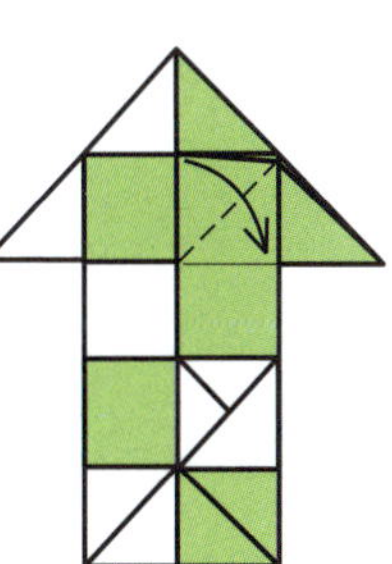

Valley fold for one last color change.

25

Completed checkered arrow.

26

To transform the pattern into a plain simple two colored arrow, just flip the flaps as shown.

27

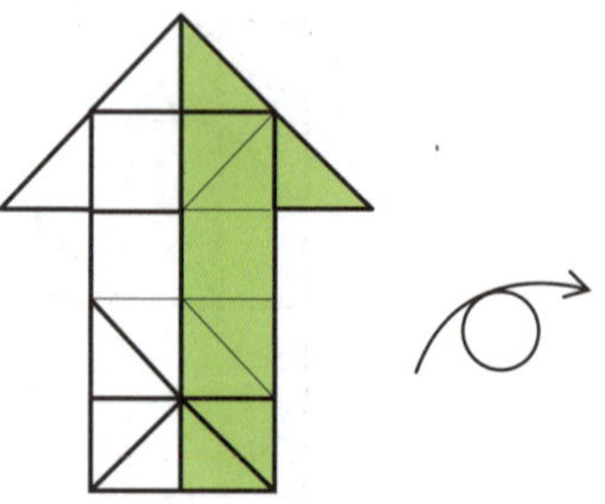

And no fancy patterns, just a normal two colored arrow. Either way, turn over...

28

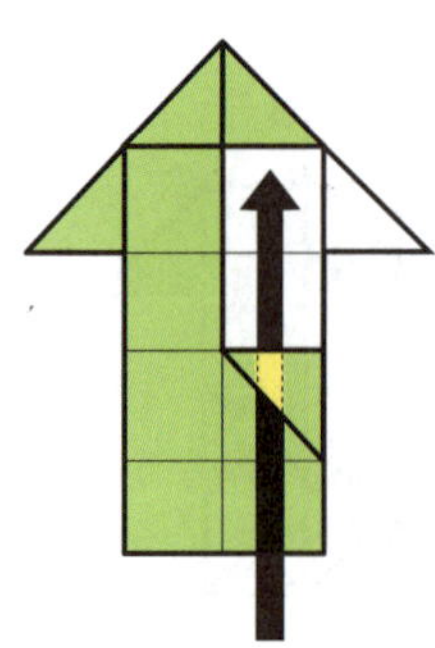

...and you will note the pocket to slip into a page.

29

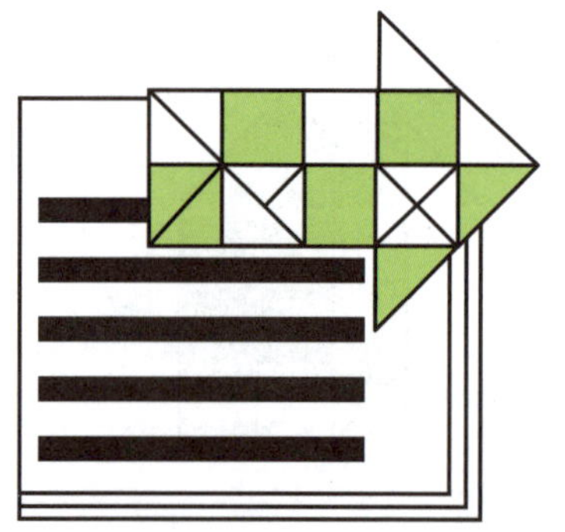

Slotted into a book, this model makes a very nice bookmark.

30

FANS OF ASIA EARRINGS

MODEL: TRADITIONAL, CHINA
DIAGRAM: DR MATTHEW GARDINER

Hand fans from Asia are usually made from intricately painted silk or paper. The fans are both decorative and practical. This earring design is inspired by their simple folds. The large folding bone is useful for making the many pleats very strong.

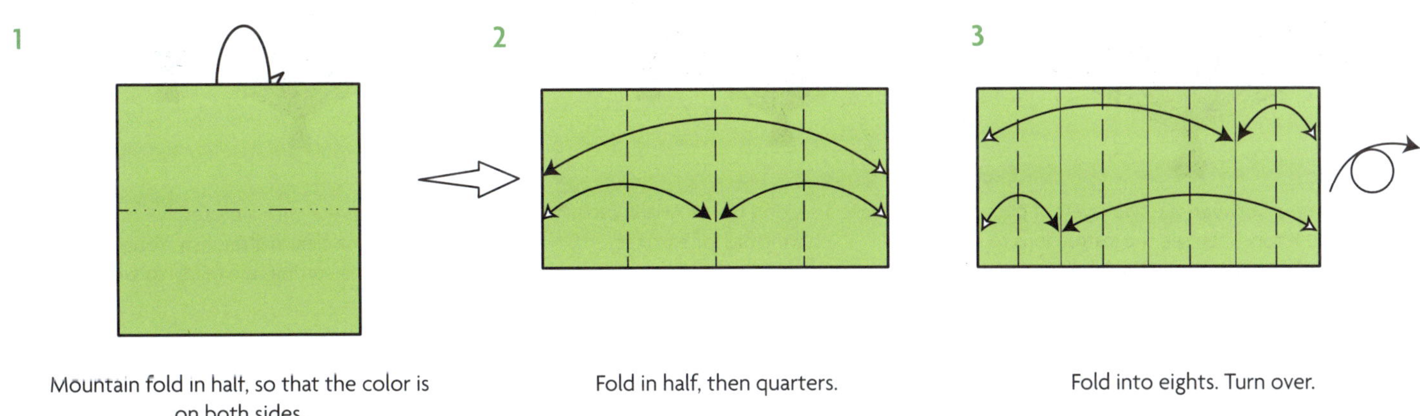

1 Mountain fold in half, so that the color is on both sides.

2 Fold in half, then quarters.

3 Fold into eights. Turn over.

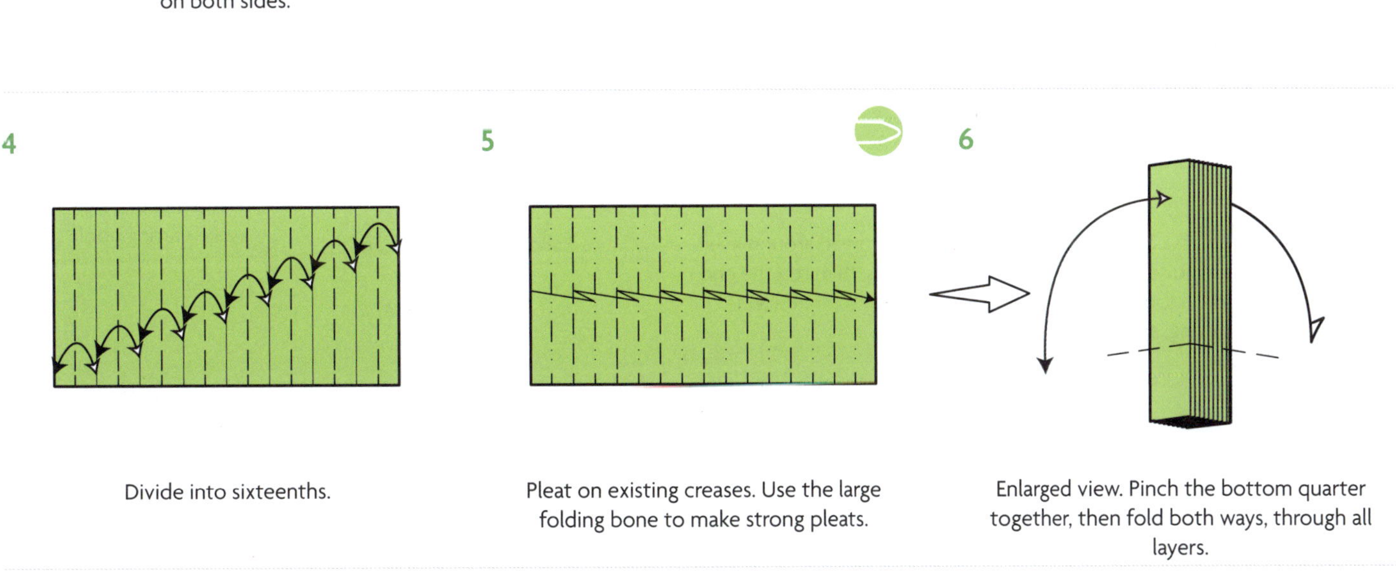

4 Divide into sixteenths.

5 Pleat on existing creases. Use the large folding bone to make strong pleats.

6 Enlarged view. Pinch the bottom quarter together, then fold both ways, through all layers.

7

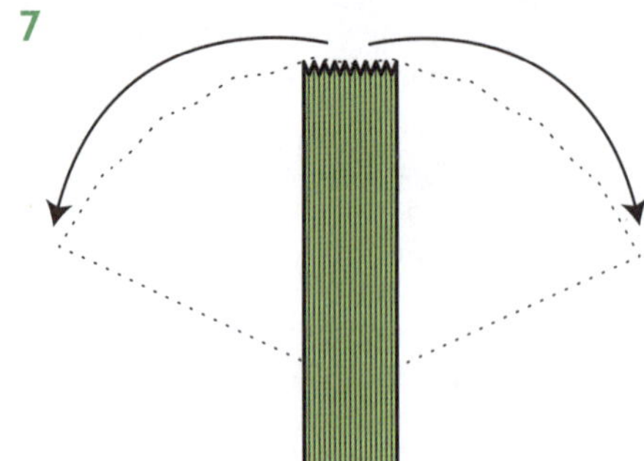

Pinch the bottom, and spread out the upper layers of the fan.

8

Your fan should look like this.

9

Pierce the bottom of the fan with a needle, then bind it tightly with thread and trim.

10

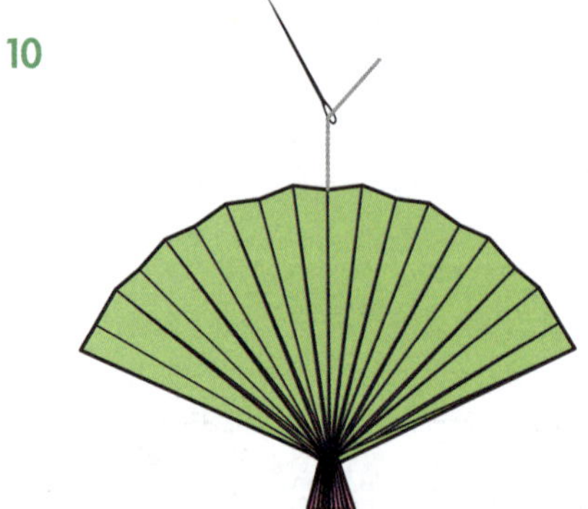

Run the thread between the two layers of paper and out the top. Then see the instructions to attach it to an earring hook below.

11

Make a second fan of Asia in order to have a pair of earrings.

12

Complete with a protective coating, such as clear nail varnish. Your fan of Asia earrings are ready to wear.

HOW TO ATTACH EARRING HOOKS

1

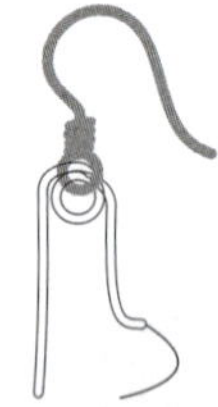

Take the thread that's coming out the top of the fan model (see step 10 above), and make a loop through the earring hook ring, as shown.

2

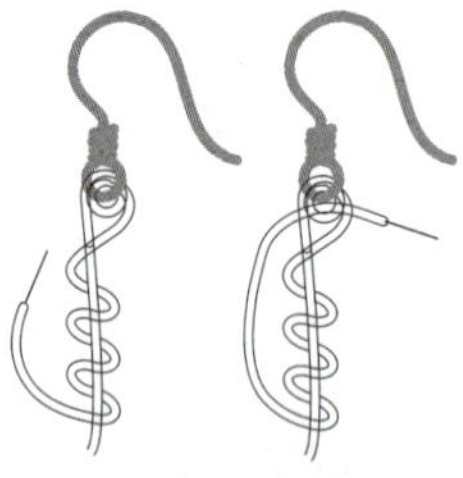

Wrap the thread around itself 3—4 times, then run the end through the first loop.

3

Pull the thread tight and trim the excess.

Optional:
If you like, you can add an extra decorative element to your earrings by stringing small beads onto the thread before you attach your earring hooks.

ANGELINA'S PURSE

MODEL: DR MATTHEW GARDINER
DIAGRAM: DR MATTHEW GARDINER

Angelina's Purse has a diamond as its key motif in the overall shape and also in the details such as the clasp that holds the purse together.

Use the folding bone to get extra sharp creases in steps 1–5 and 7.

1

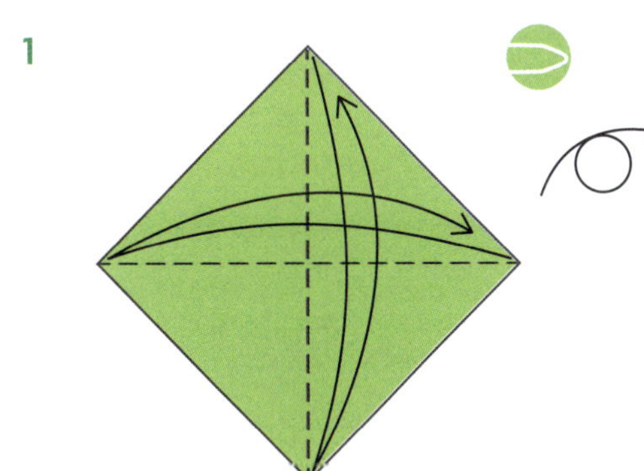

Fold and unfold diagonals. Turn over.

2

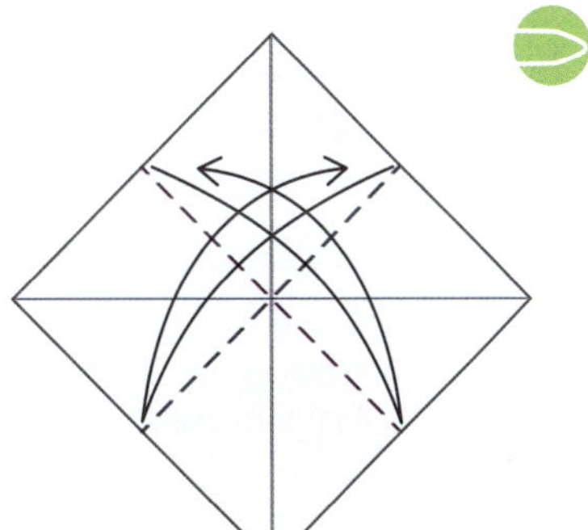

Book fold and unfold.

3

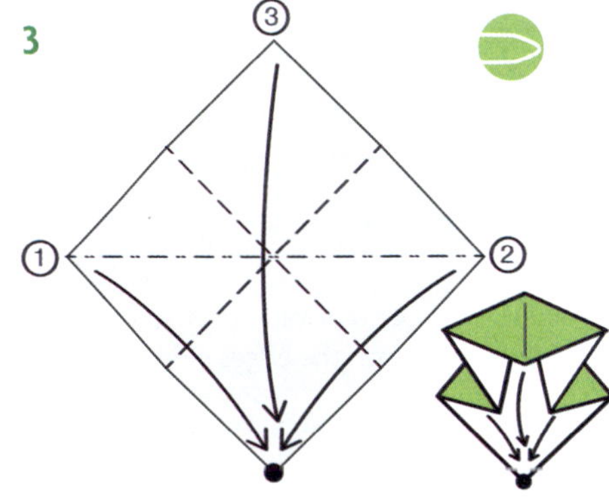

Bring three corners down to meet the bottom corner. Start with corners 1 and 2 together followed by corner 3.

4

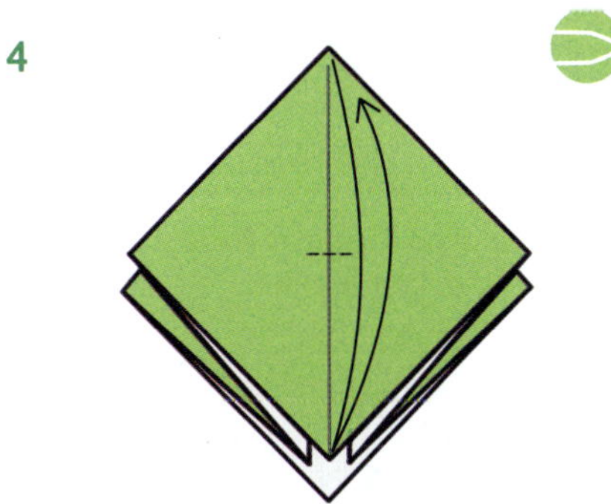

You've completed the preliminary base. Make a small pinch to mark the center on the top layer.

5

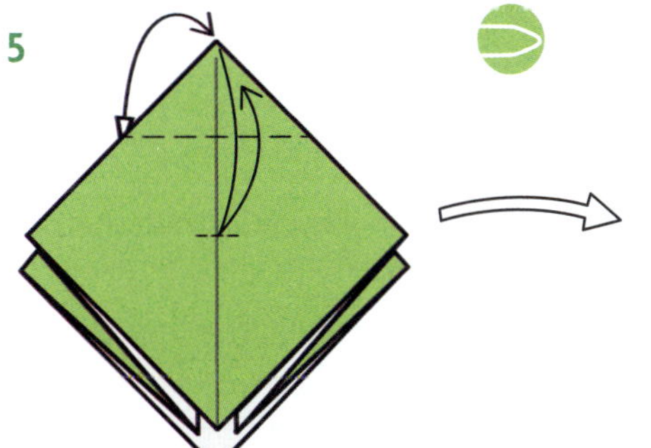

Use a folding bone to double crease, mountain and valley fold firmly. Unfold the paper flat.

6

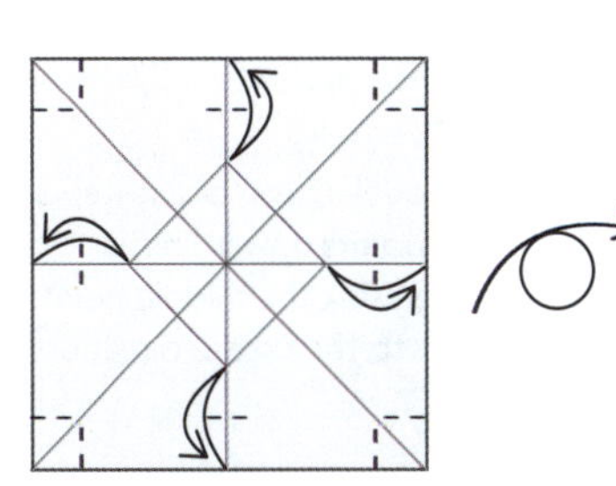

Make four small pinch creases, then turn the paper over.

7

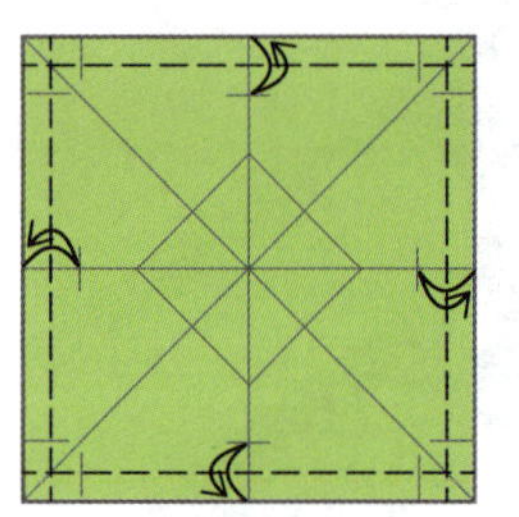

Fold each edge to the pinch crease and unfold, then turn over.

8

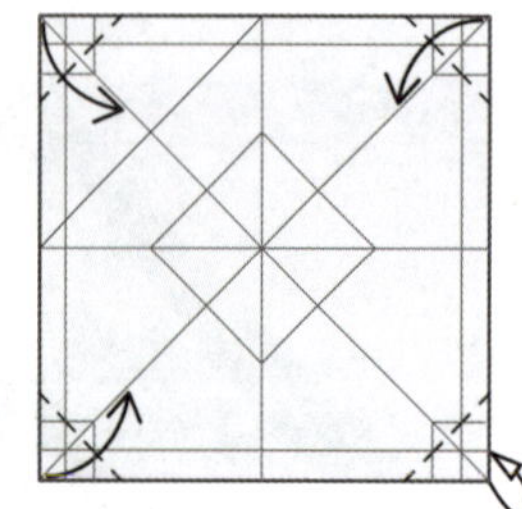

45°

Valley fold three of the corners inward, mountain fold the last one.

9

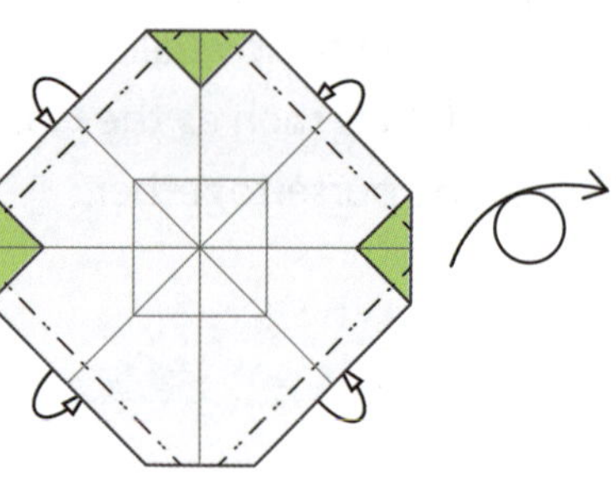

Mountain fold the edges behind.

10

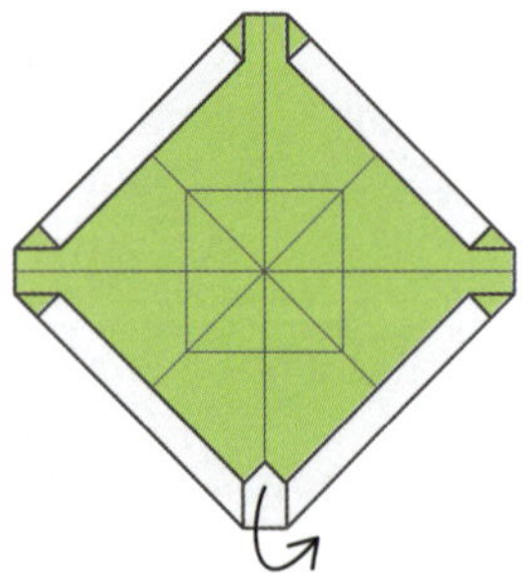

Pull the mountain folded corner out from underneath the edges either side.

11

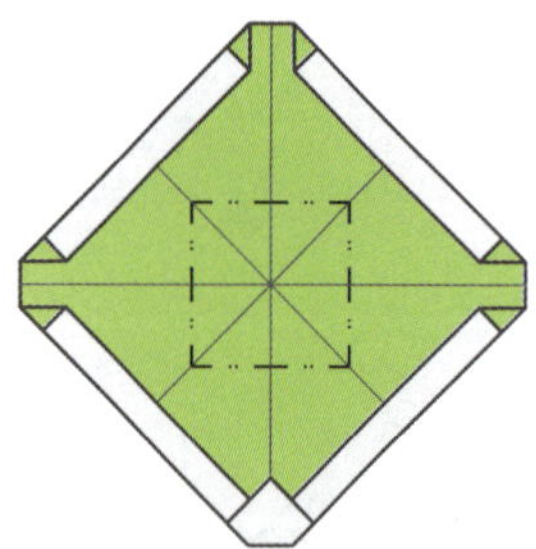

Fold the corner over again on top, like this, then turn over.

12

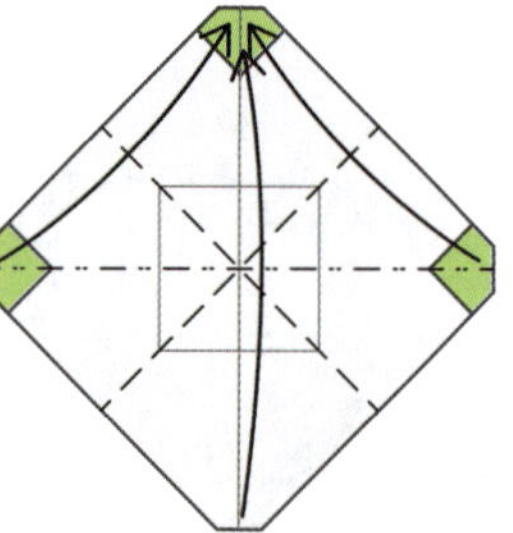

Re-fold the inner square, making sure all of the folds are valleys.

13

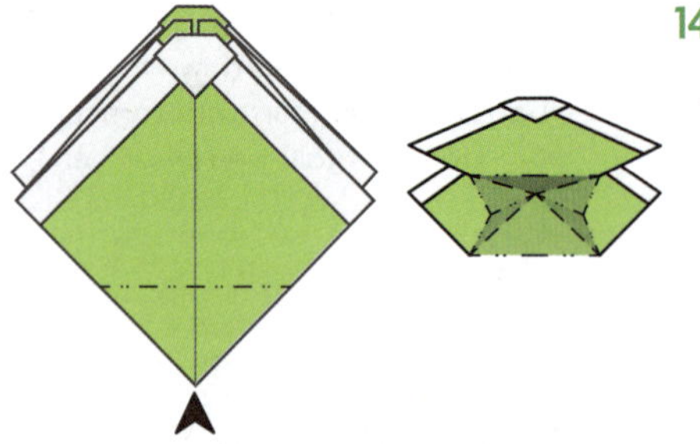

Collapse the model as you did in step 3, but drawing the points upward rather than downward. Then sink the middle point, paying attention to the crease directions.

14

Tuck the two front layers under the back diamond shaped flap to close the purse.

15

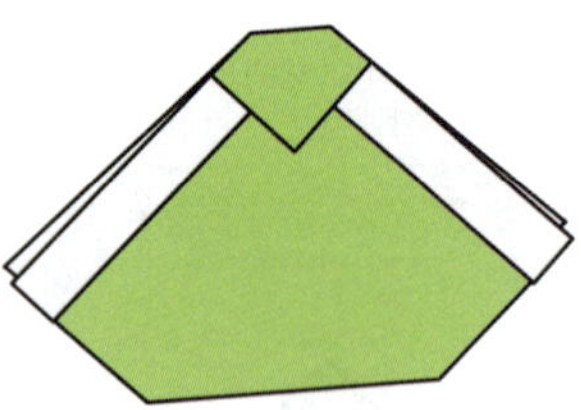

Your finished Angelina's Purse should look like this.

TATO

MODEL: TRADITIONAL, JAPAN
DIAGRAM: MATTHEW GARDINER

The tato is a form of paper purse or puzzle in Japan. Tatogami is a folded paper that is used to store expensive kimonos, however this tato design is for smaller objects. Origami masters Shuzo Fujimoto and Michio Uchiyama are renowned for their innovation in expanding tato designs. The primary method involves dividing the square radially, in this case into eight segments, that fold inward over each other.

Tato can be folded from fabric, or two laminated sheets of paper for maximum durability and effect.

1

Start colored side up.
Fold and unfold diagonals. Turn over.

2

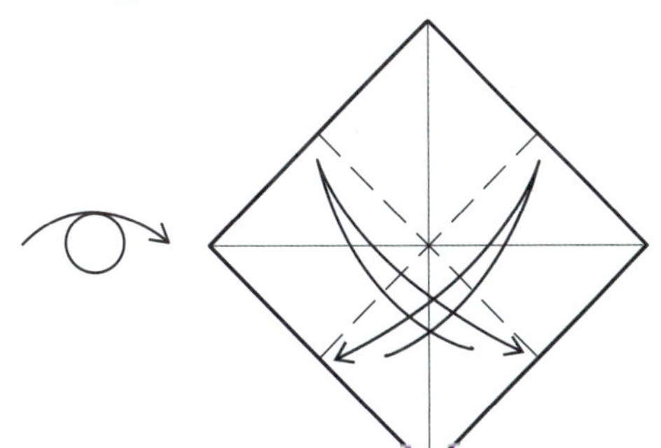

Book fold and unfold.

3

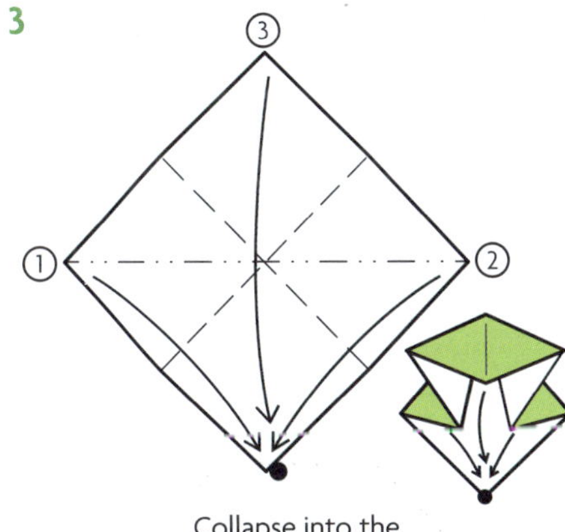

Collapse into the preliminary base.

4

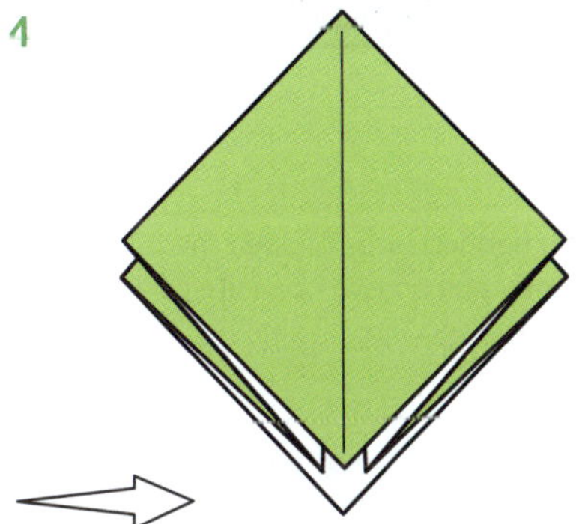

The preliminary base.

5

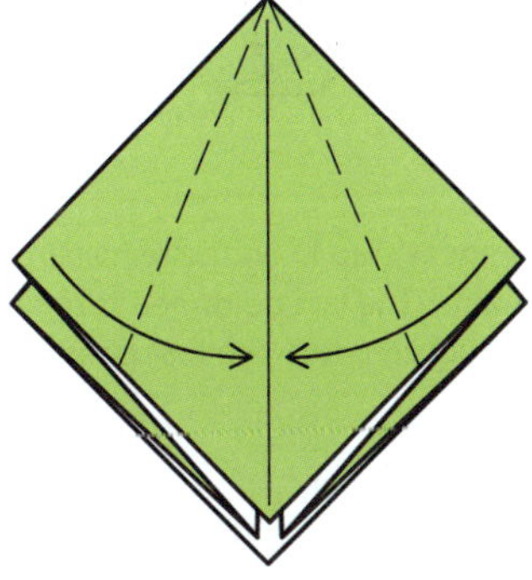

Fold edges of top layer to the center.

6

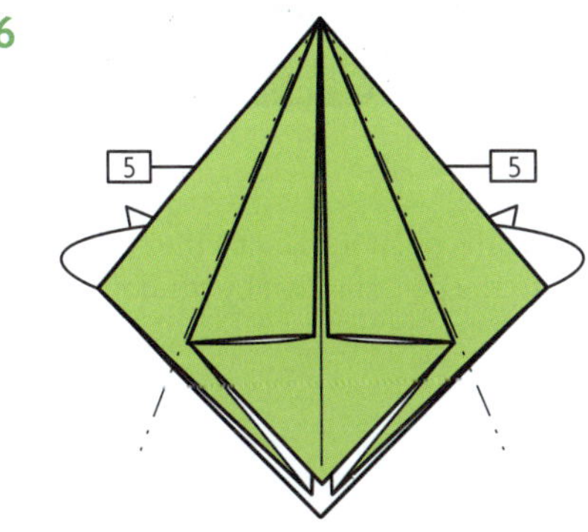

Repeat step 5 on the other side.

7

Unfold to a flat sheet.

8

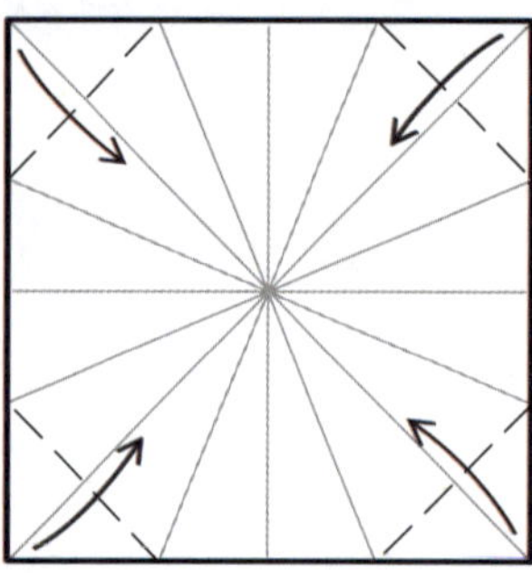

Fold corners in at the intersection of existing creases. This makes a perfect octagon.

9

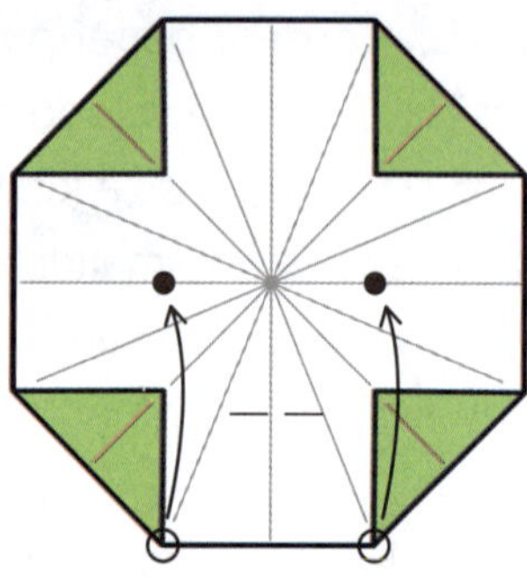

Fold the edge to the middle. Be careful to only crease as shown.

10

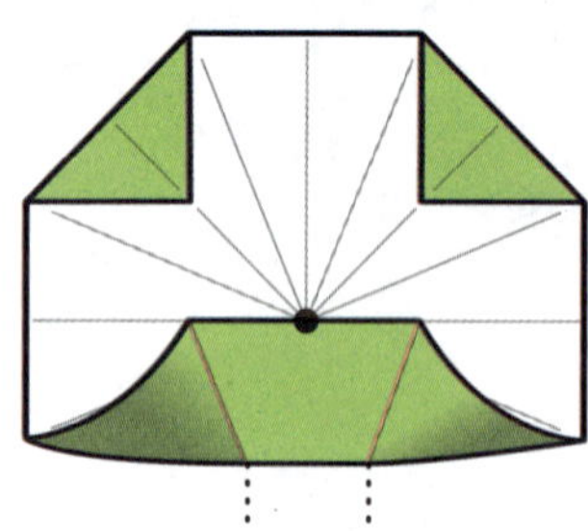

Step 9 in process. Only crease between the dotted lines.

11

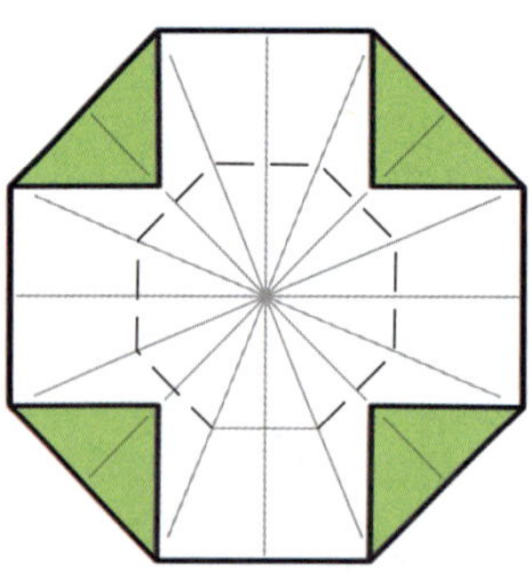

Repeat step 9 all around the octagon.

12

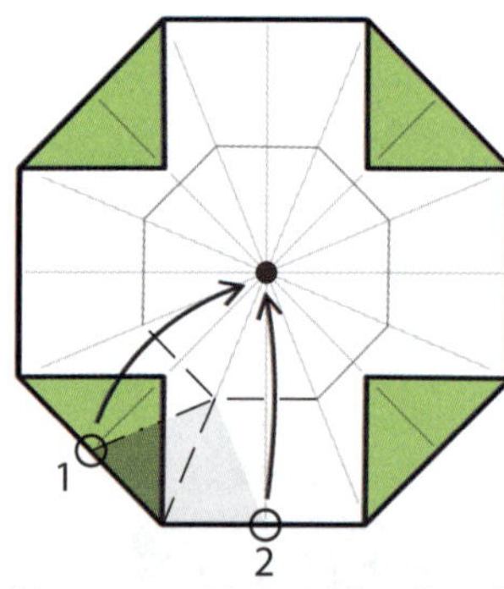

Fold point 1 to the middle. Then fold point 2. This will create a point with the grayed-out paper. Fold this point to the left. Look ahead to step 13, to see the result.

13

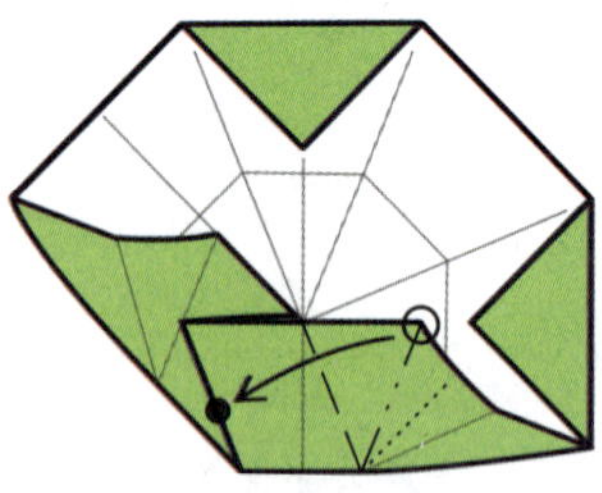

Fold the point marked by the circle to the point marked by the dot.

14

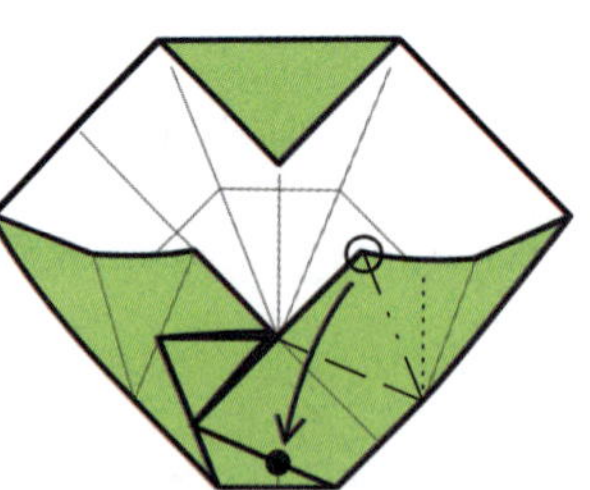

Repeat step 13 on the remaining points. The last point needs to be tucked under the first point.

15

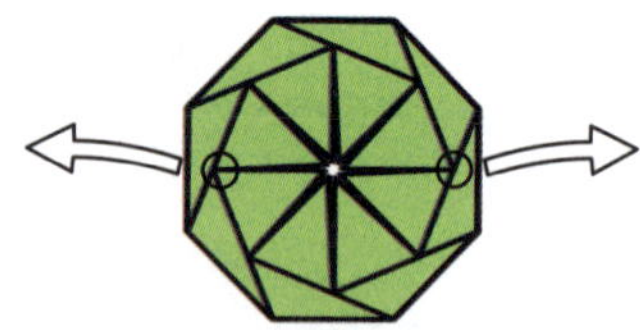

The finished tato. To open the purse gently pull on two opposite points.

JADE'S BOWL

MODEL: DR MATTHEW GARDINER
DIAGRAM: DR MATTHEW GARDINER

Jade's bowl is a rotund geometric bowl with interlocking corners that looks as good on top as it does on the bottom. A simple design, it's useful as a small vessel to keep tiny precious objects, or when folded from heavier card, it can be used a decorative item by itself. Experiment with the fold angle in step 10 to alter the profile of the bowl.

Use the folding bone to make sharp creases throughout, especially on diagonal creases.

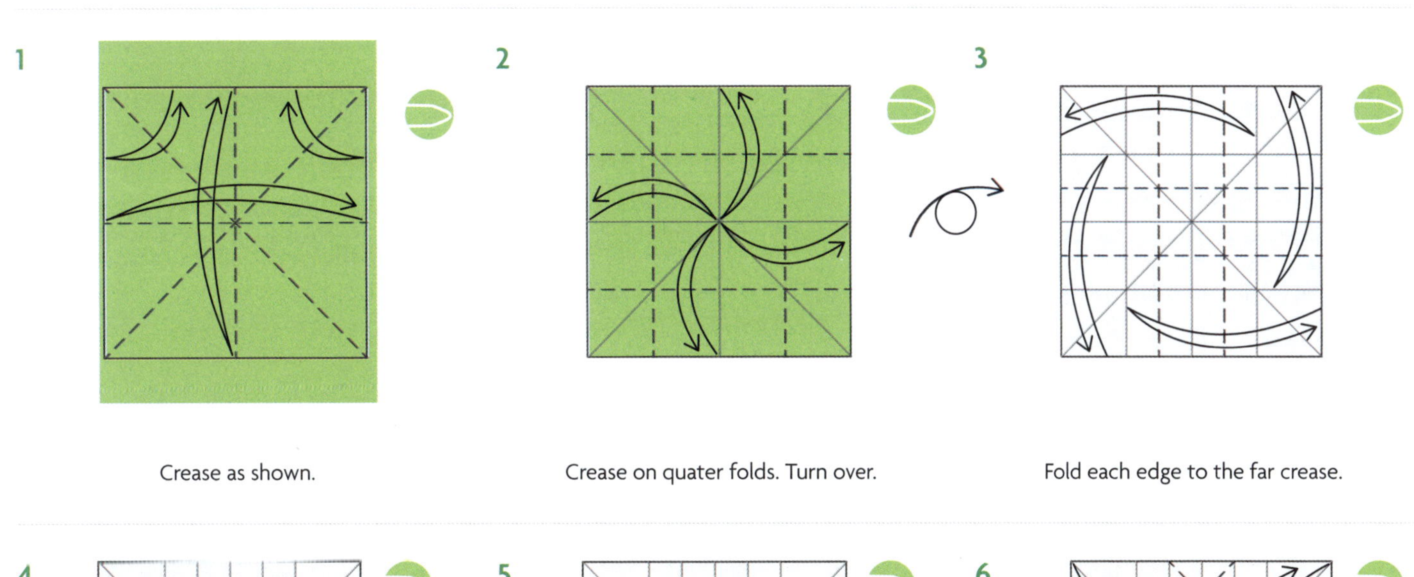

1 Crease as shown.

2 Crease on quater folds. Turn over.

3 Fold each edge to the far crease.

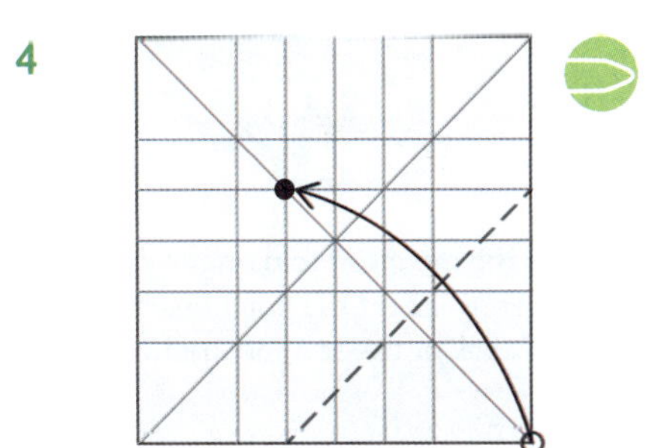

4 Now, begin to crease the diagonals. The reference point for the first fold is marked here.

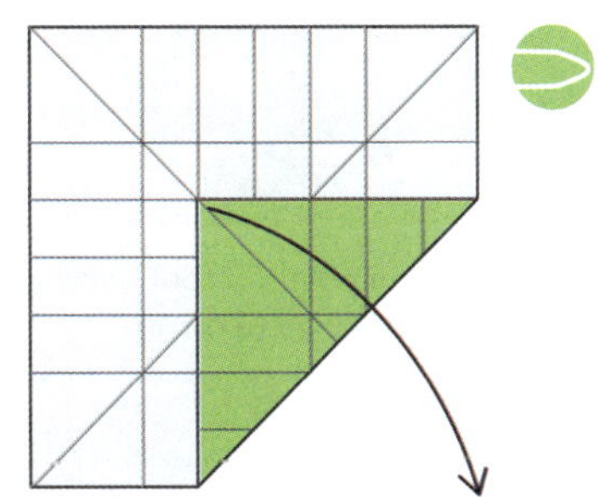

5 This is the first fold. Unfold it afterwards.

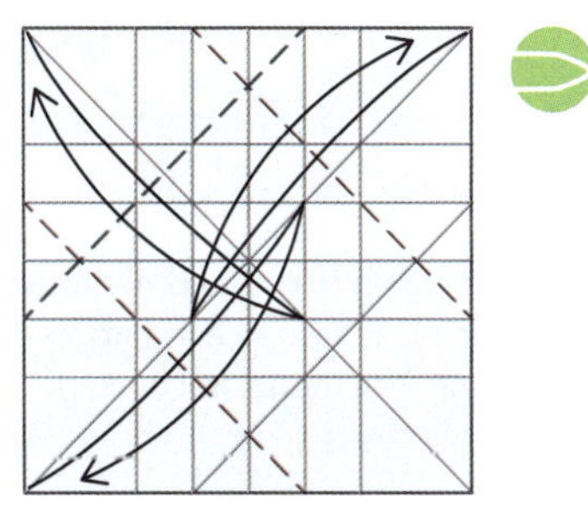

6 Crease the remaining three diagonals as per steps 4–5.

7

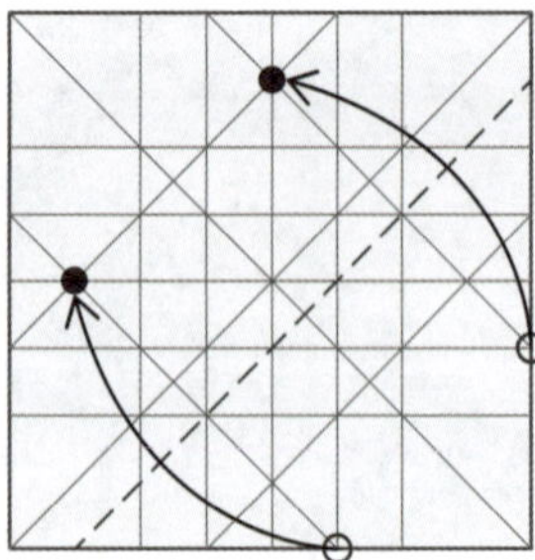

Fold the diagonal using the marked points to position the fold correctly.

8

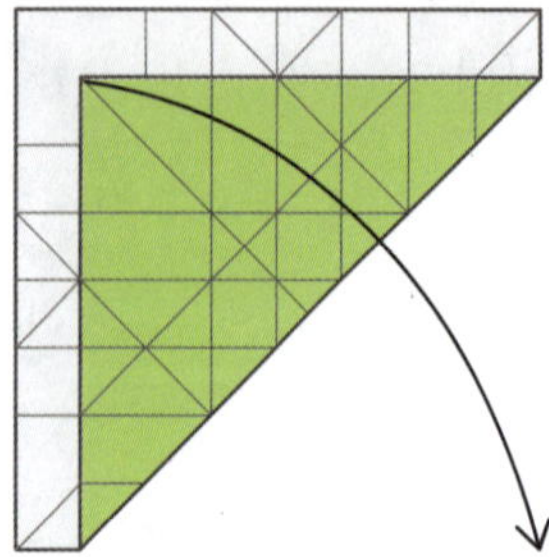

The fold should look like this. Unfold.

9

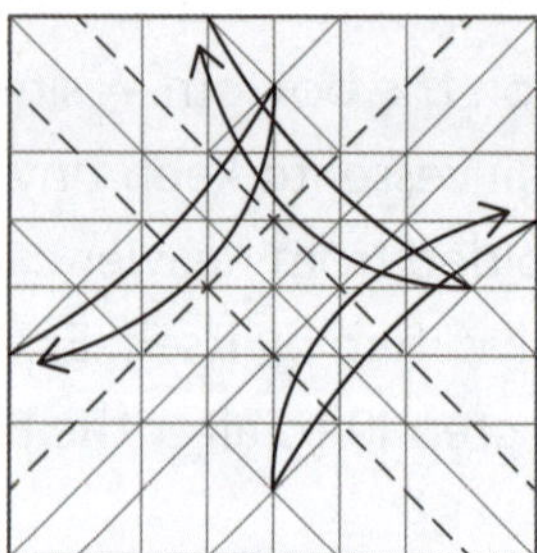

Crease the remaining diagonals as per steps 7–8.

10

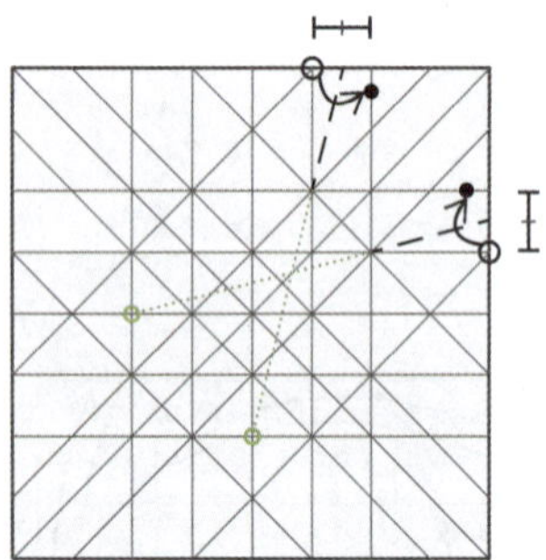

Fold the intersection to meet the crease. The fold can be pre-scored using the scoring tool. Use the green dotted lines as a guide.

11

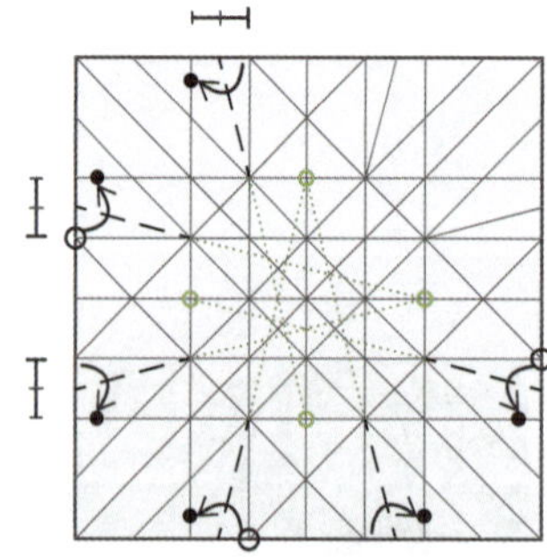

Repeat step 10 on the remaining corners. Turn over.

12

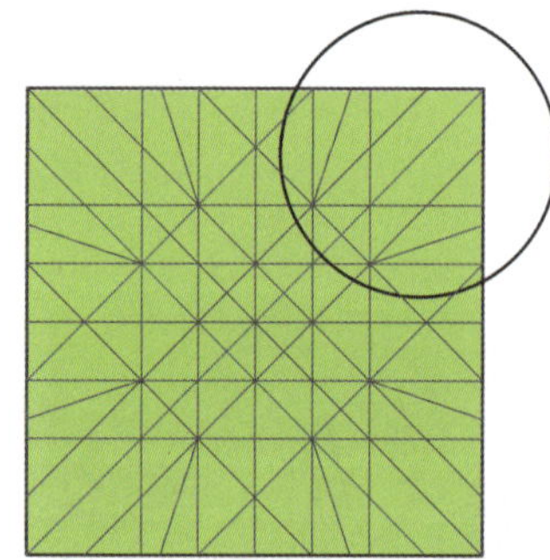

This is completed crease pattern. See detail in the next few steps.

13

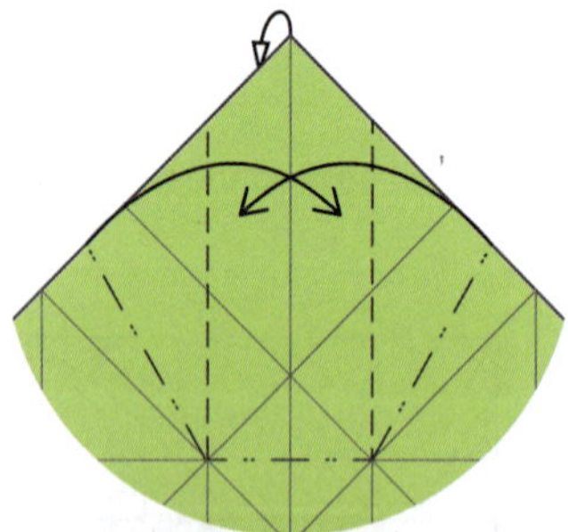

Mountain fold the corner forward, then pleat each side inward, one at a time. The model will become 3-D.

14

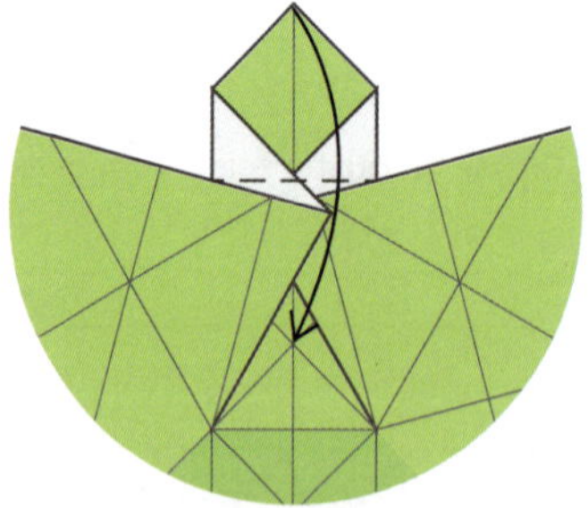

Fold the top point in front, locking the layers underneath.

15

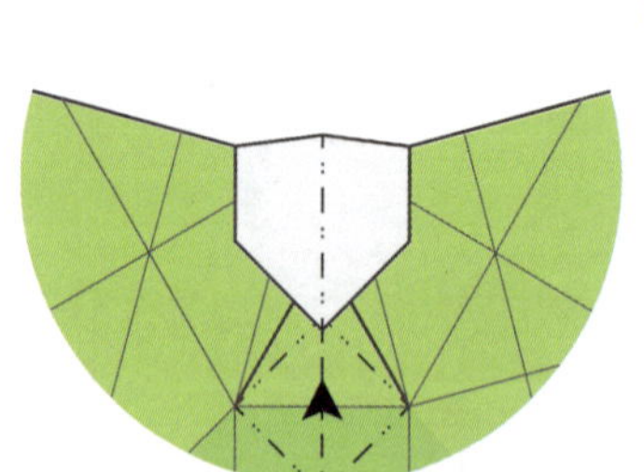

Firm up the mountain fold on the corner and gently indent the point below. A pointed stick or tweezers are useful here.

16

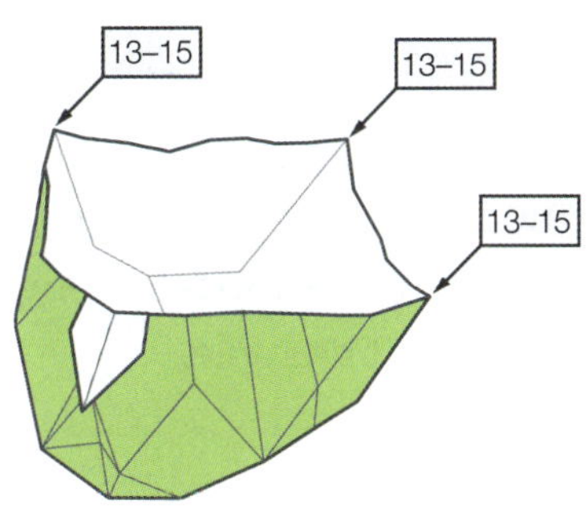

Repeat steps 11–13 on the other three corners. The shape of the bowl will become clearer with each corner.

17

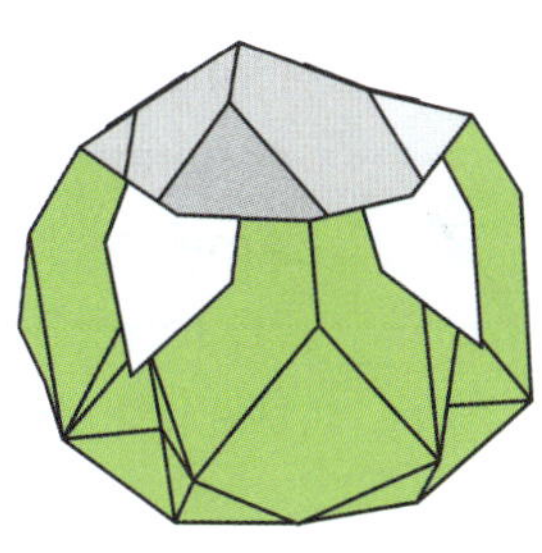

The basic bowl shape after folding all the corners. Turn model over.

18

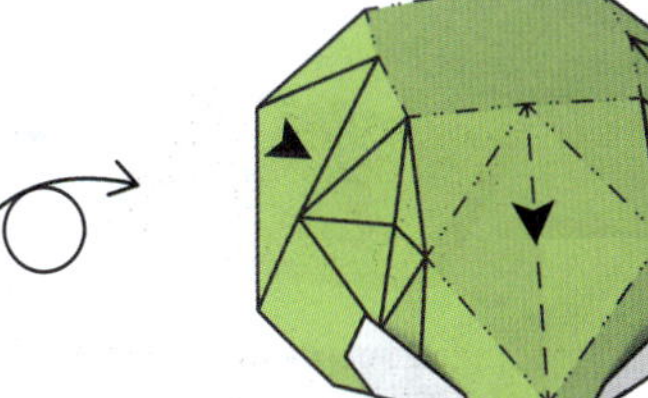

Shape the bottom and sides of the bowl by gently pushing the creases from outside or inside with a pointed stick or tweezers.

19

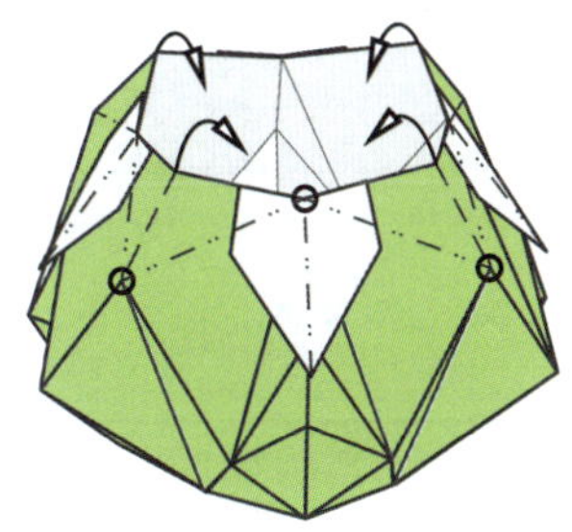

Make the mountain folds around each point by creasing between the marked circles, then fold the four points inward.

20

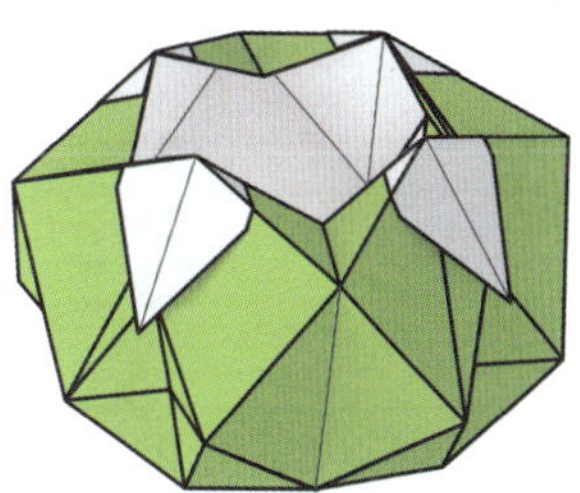

This is what Jade's bowl looks like completed.

VERDI'S VASE

MODEL: TRADITIONAL, CHINA
DIAGRAM: MARK KENNEDY

This traditional Chinese vase was popularized in the United States by Verdi Adams, who taught it to a generation of paperfolders at The Origami Center of America. It is a fantastic model that produces a solid 3D form. Be careful when opening the model during the last steps so the paper doesn't crumple.

These diagrams were originally published in the OUSA Newsletter # 34, Fall 1989. They are reproduced here with permisson from Mark Kennedy.

1

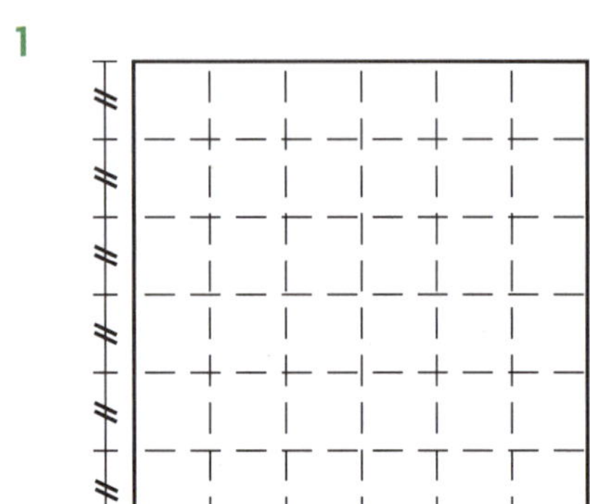

White side up. Crease into sixths in both directions.

2

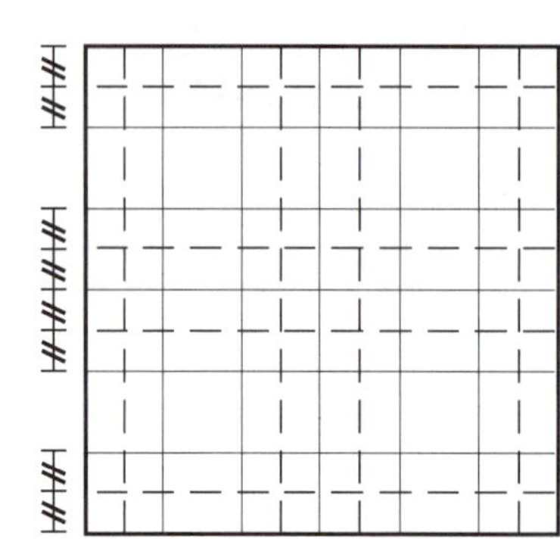

Crease in half the first, third, fourth and sixth sixths in both directions.

3

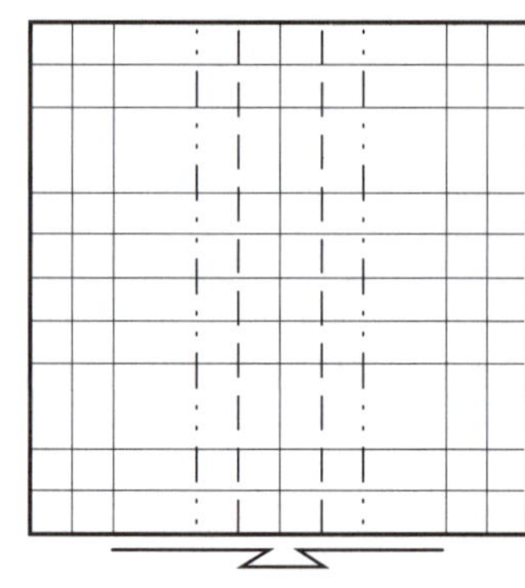

On existing creases, pleat to the center line.

4

5

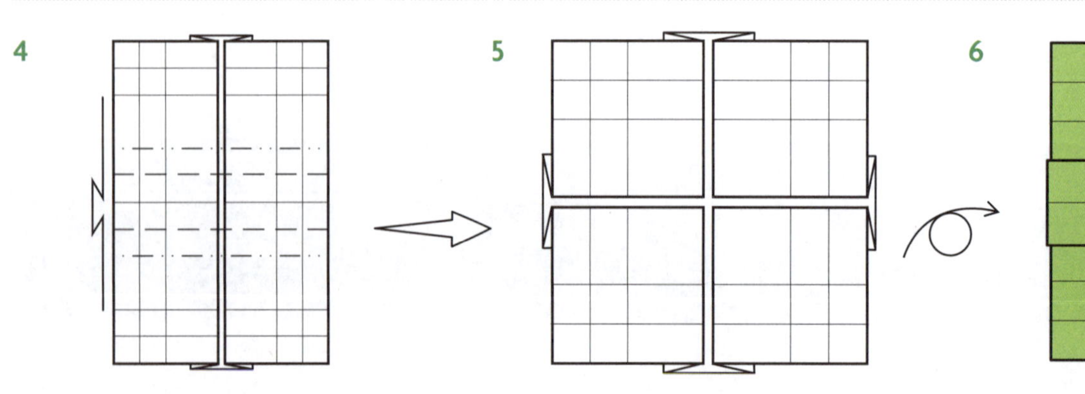

On existing creases, pleat to the center line.

The model should look like this. Turn over.

6

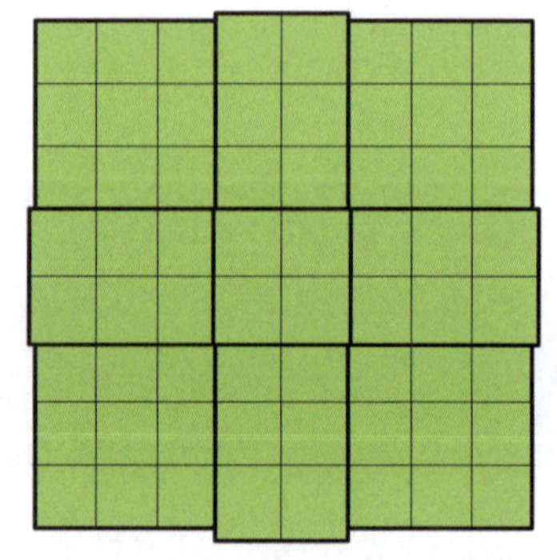

Completed step 5.

6A

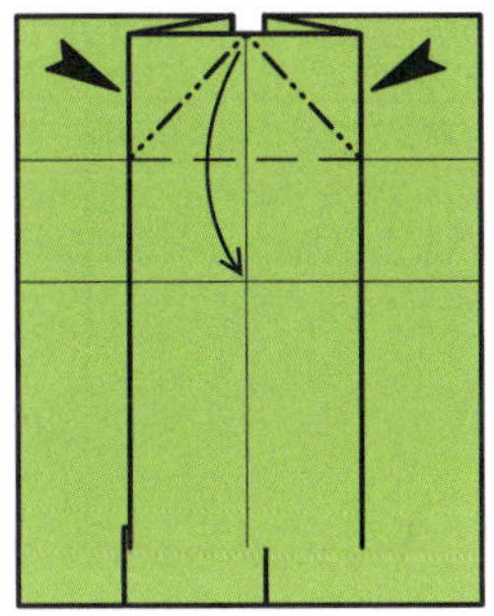

Pull down top layer while squashing in the sides.

6B

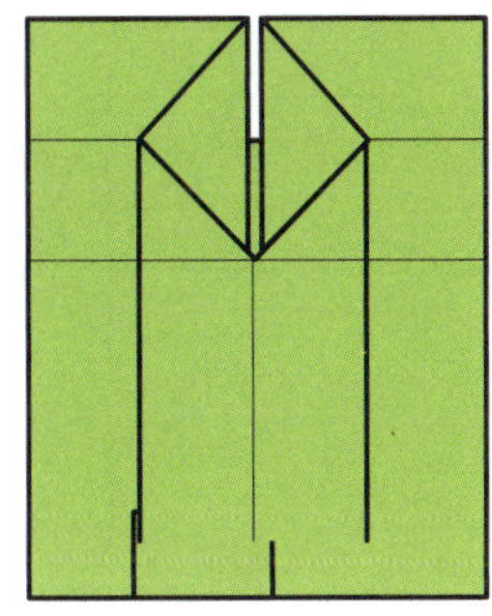

Squashes complete.

7

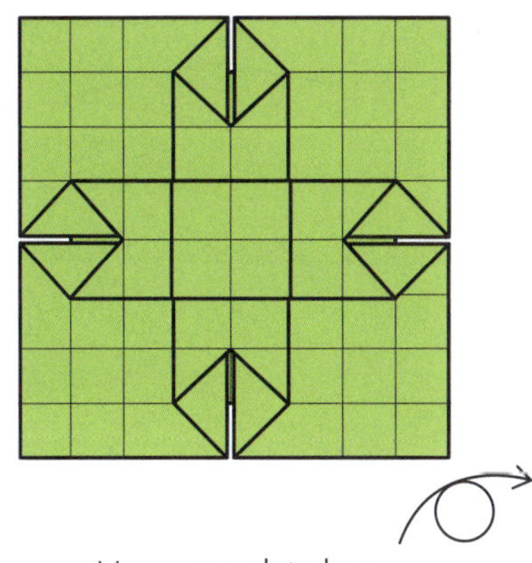

Moves completed on all four sides. Turn over.

8

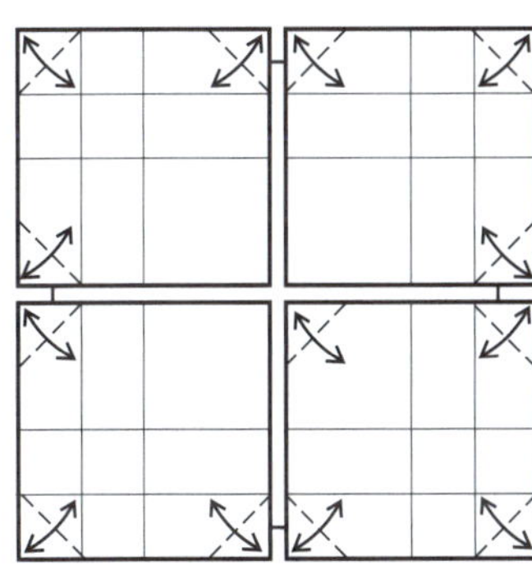

Pre-crease corners as shown to make step 11 easier.

9

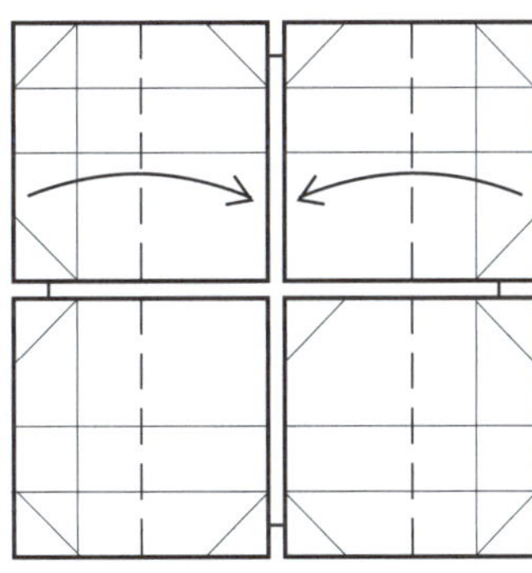

Cupboard fold sides to the center.

10

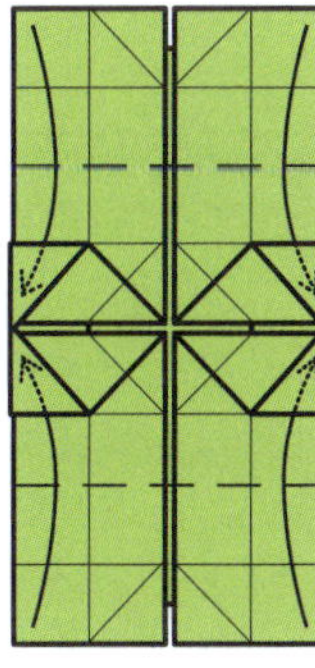

Cupboard fold top and bottom to center and tuck the corners into the pockets.

11

Cupboard fold top and bottom to center and tuck the corners into the pockets.

12

All folding is done. Turn over.

13

Start to open out vase by pulling out the extra layers along the sides. Be careful and work slowly.

14

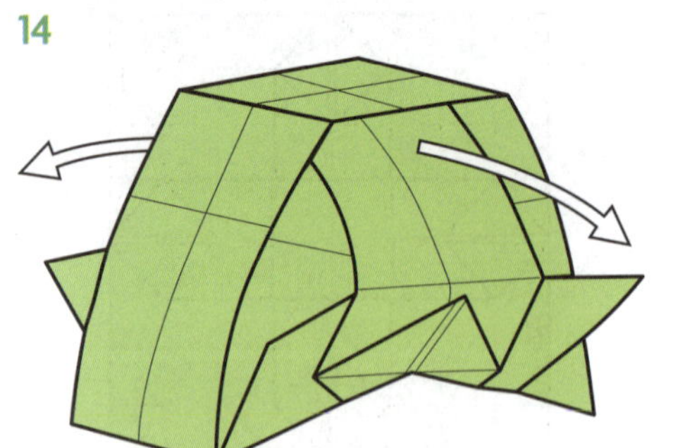

One pair of sides already pulled out. Pull out the other side.

15

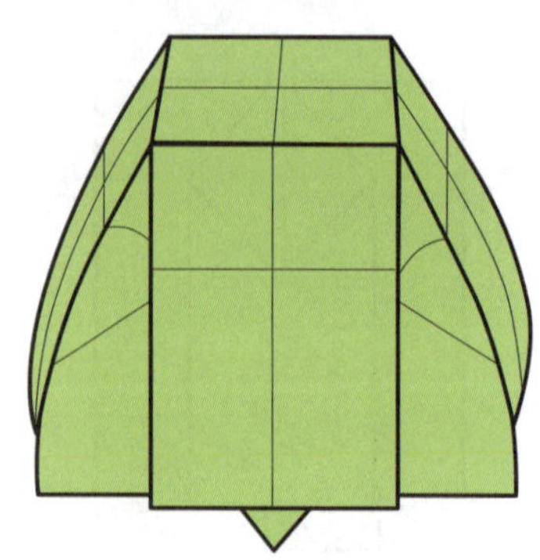

All sides are pulled out.

16

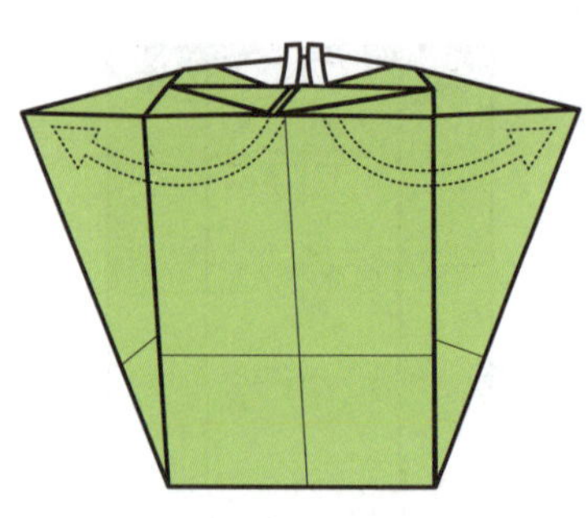

Turn over. Reach inside the top of the vase, poke out and round the corners.

17

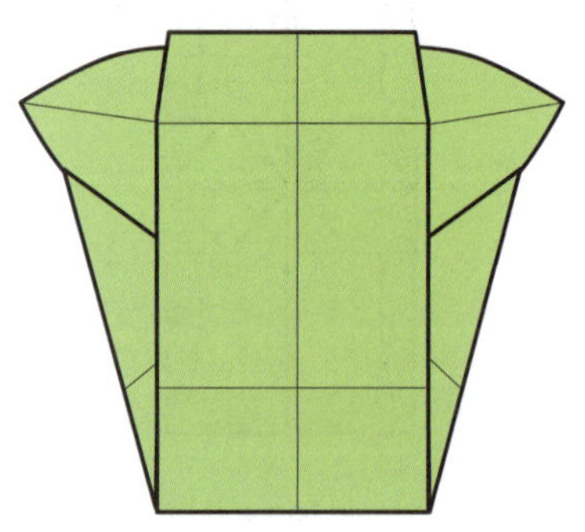

Completed vase—side view.

18

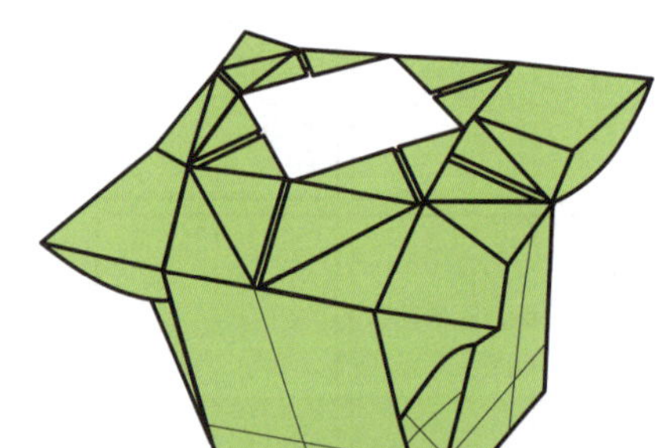

Completed vase—top view.

WINGED SONOBE

MODEL: TRADITIONAL, JAPAN
DIAGRAM: MATTHEW GARDINER

This unit pays homage to a unit origami classic, the Sonobe unit by Mitsunobu Sonobe. The variation on this unit is that it has a "wing" with pockets. It can be assembled into the same range of configurations as the Sonobe unit. It's a great unit for experimenting and folding platonic solids.

1

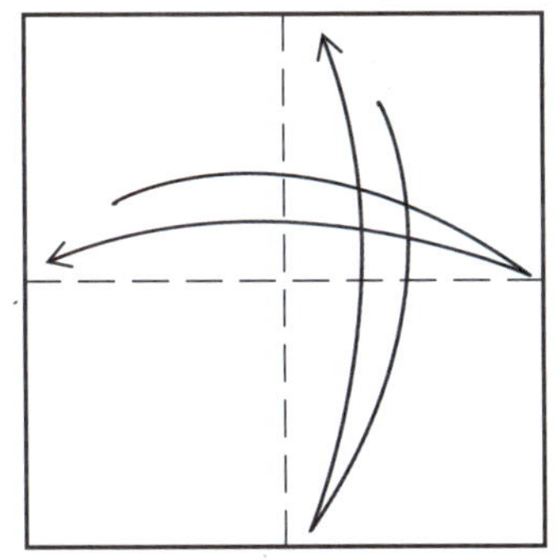

Begin white side up. Book fold and unfold.

2

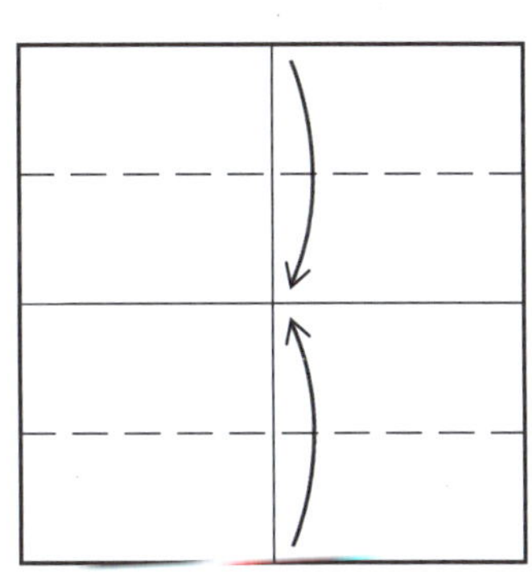

Cupboard fold.

3

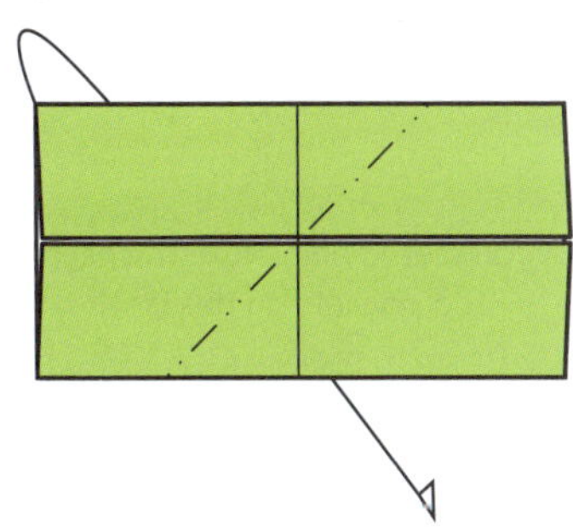

Mountain fold behind.

4

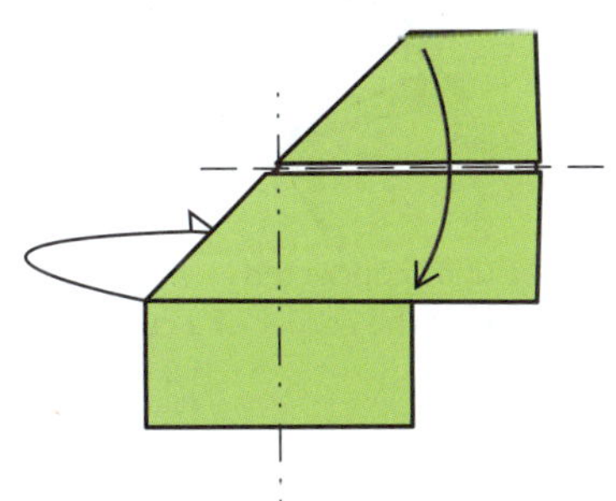

Fold flaps in half, valley fold on top, and mountain fold on the side.

5

Valley fold through all layers except bottom layer.

6

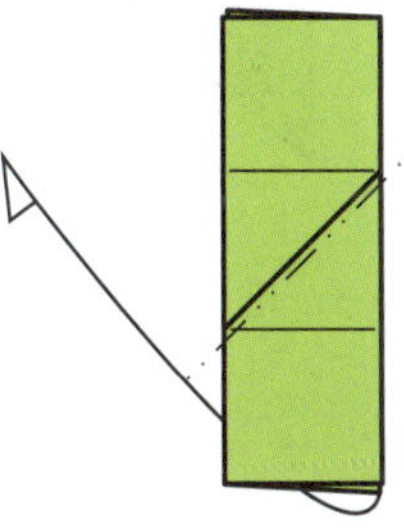

Mountain fold underneath the center diagonal.

7

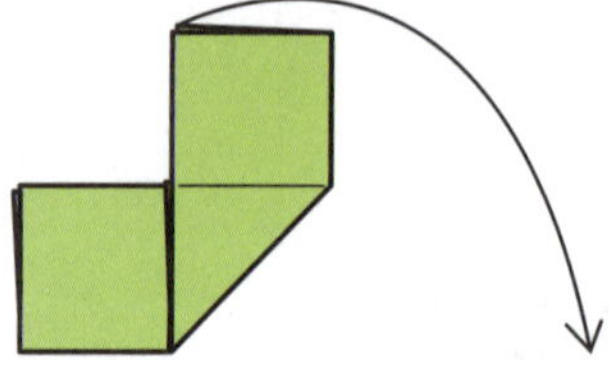

Fold the front flap down to turn it back into a strip.

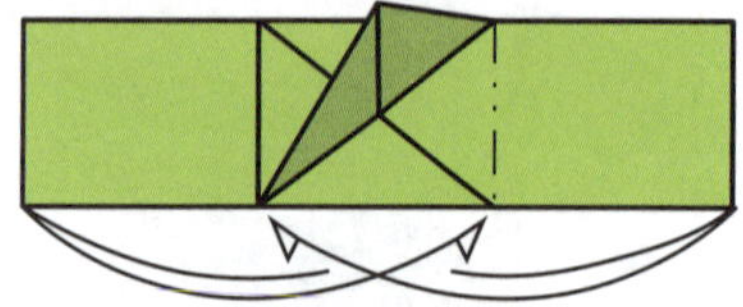

Mountain fold and unfold along the paper ridge on either side.

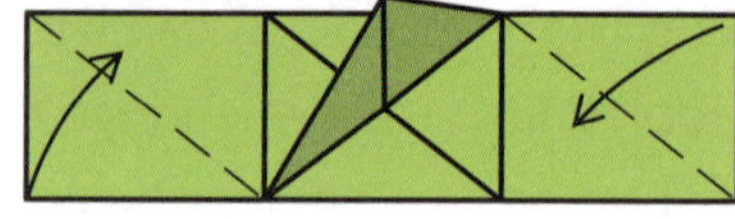

Fold the corners up to 90º.

10

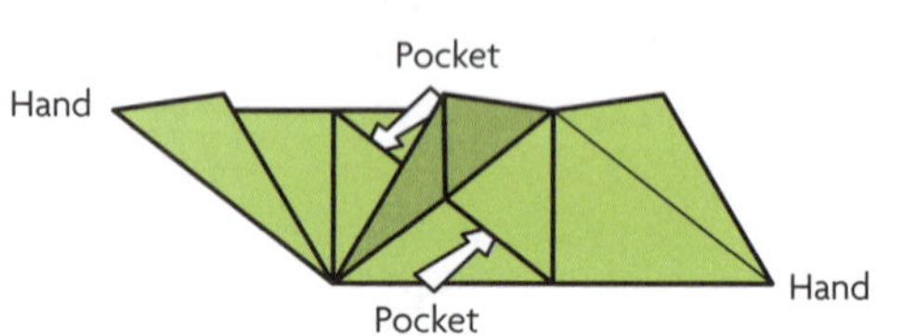

A completed unit. Note the hands and pockets on this unit.

11

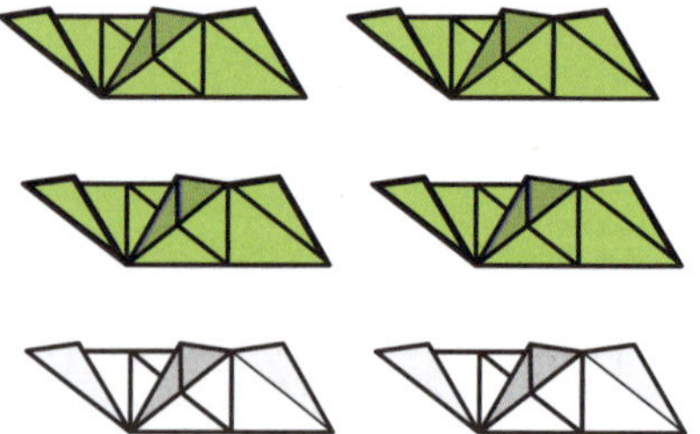

To make a cube, you need six units. Three colors look best—use two sheets of each color.

12

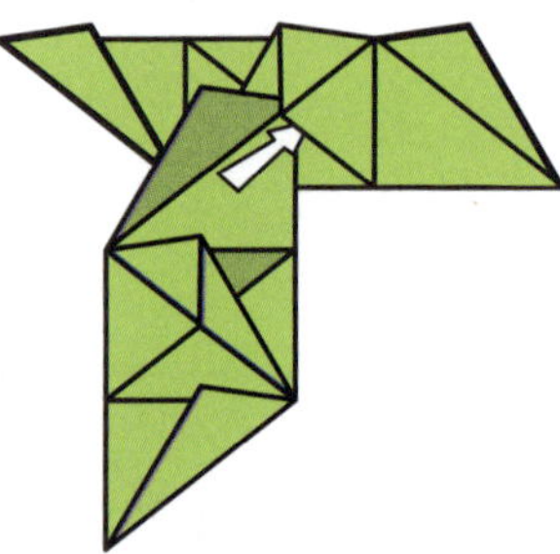

To assemble two units, insert the hand from one unit into the pocket of another.

13

Two units assembled.

14

Insert the 3rd unit into the 2nd and the 1st into the 3rd to connect three units.

15

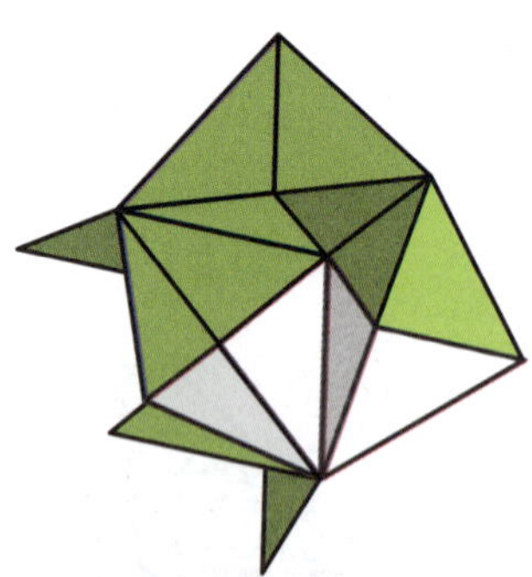

Three units connected—the joined point is the corner of a cube.

16

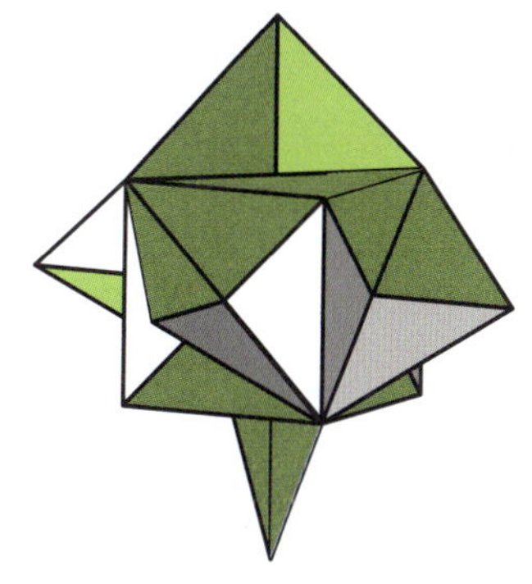

Add three more units in the same way to make a complete cube.

17

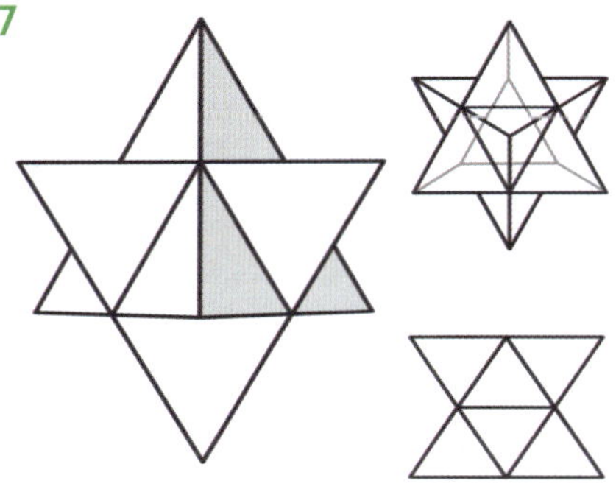

This shape is called a star tetrahedron. It's made from two tetrahedrons, one pointing up and one pointing down.

x 4

x 4

x 4

Use twelve units—three colors, four of each color.

Twelve units!

18

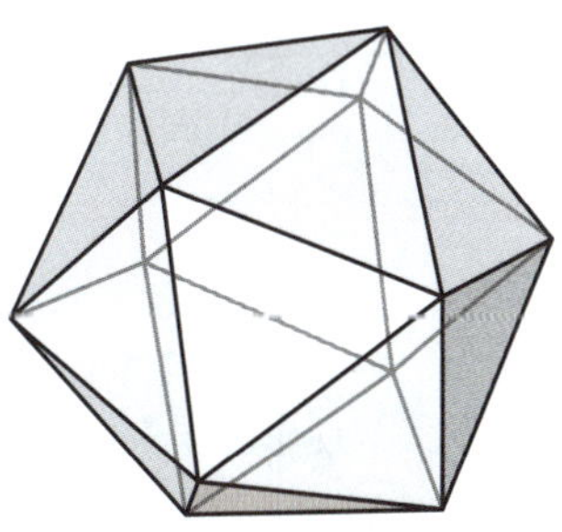

Using this icosahedron as a reference, start by assembling units around one of the pentagonal points.

x 10

x 10

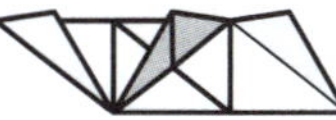

x 10

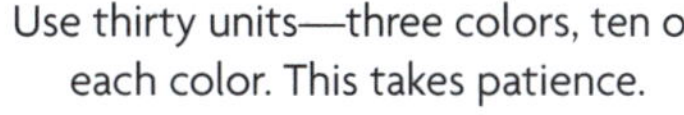

Use thirty units—three colors, ten of each color. This takes patience.

Thirty units!

KUSUDAMA

MODEL: TRADITIONAL, JAPAN
DIAGRAM: MATTHEW GARDINER

The kusudama is a traditional origami decoration with a very geometric feel. The kusudama is often thought to be the precursor to unit origami. This model requires glue to complete the assembly.

Kusudama literally means medicine ball, from kusuri (medicine) and tama (ball). They are now used as gifts.

1

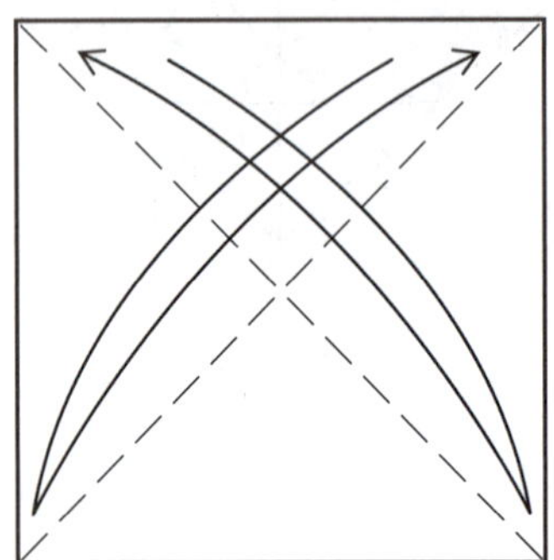

Begin white side up.
Fold and unfold diagonals.

2

Blintz fold and unfold.

3

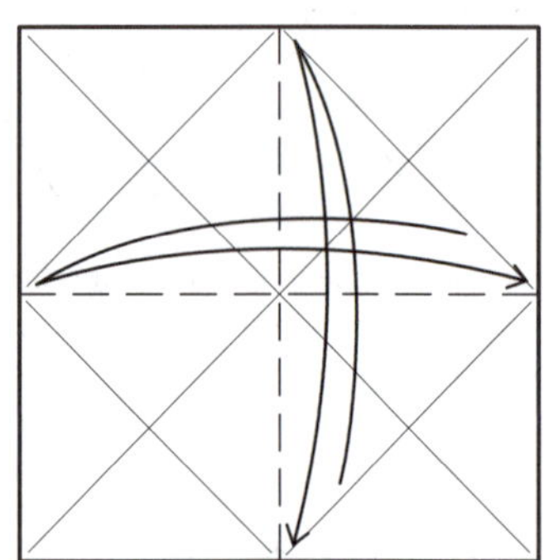

Book fold and unfold.

4

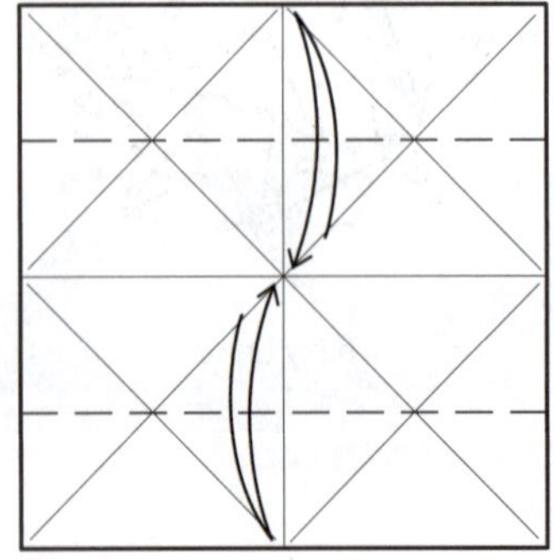

Cupboard fold and unfold.

5

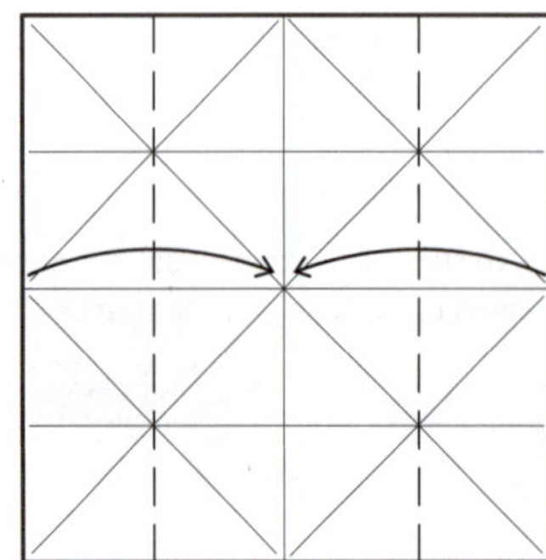

Cupboard fold.

6

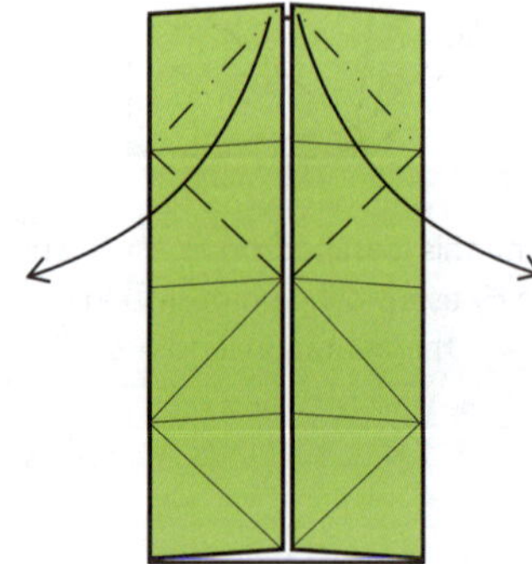

Squash fold using existing creases.

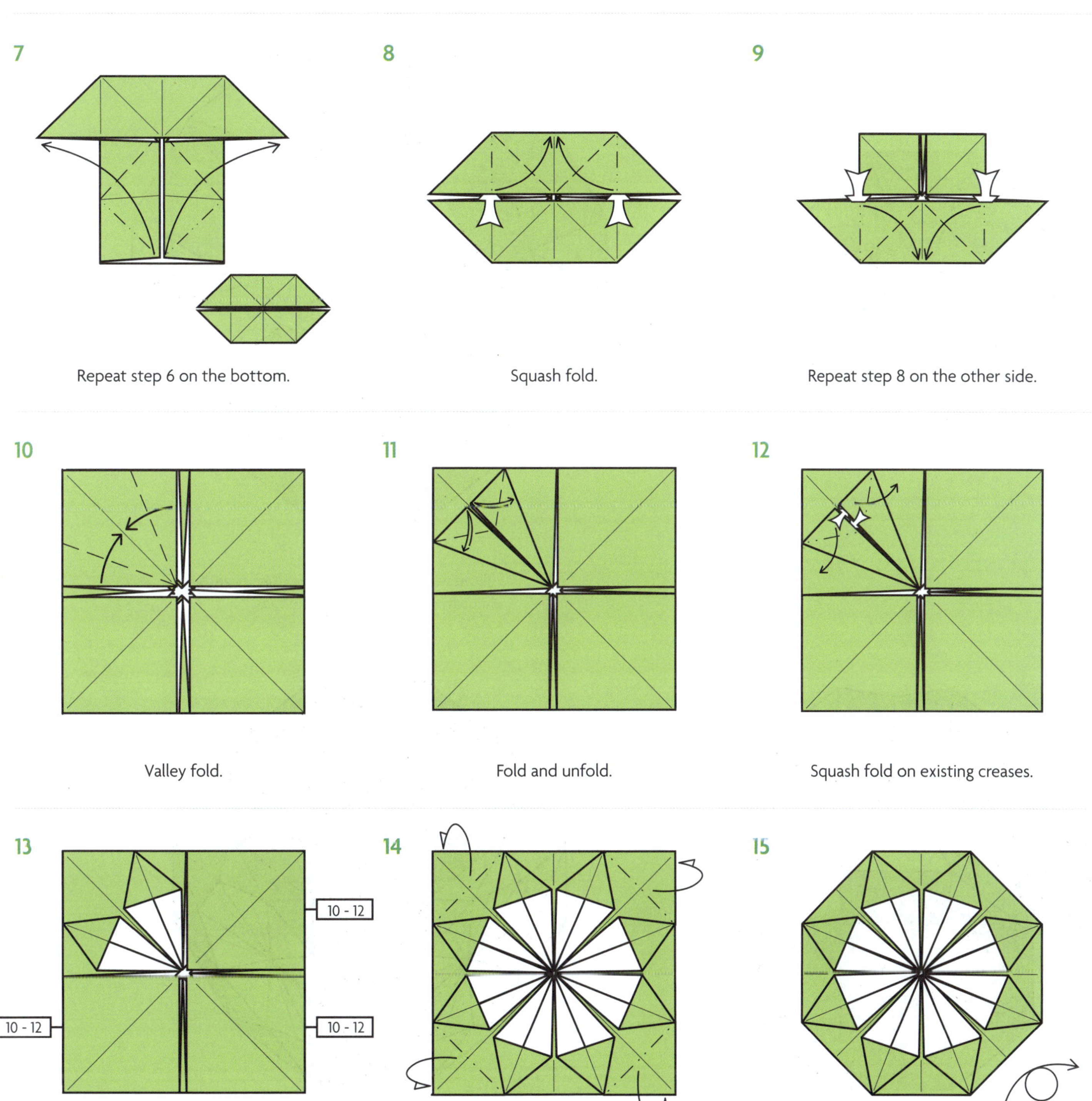

Repeat steps 10-12 on the other three sides.

Fold four corners behind.

Completed unit. Turn over.

16

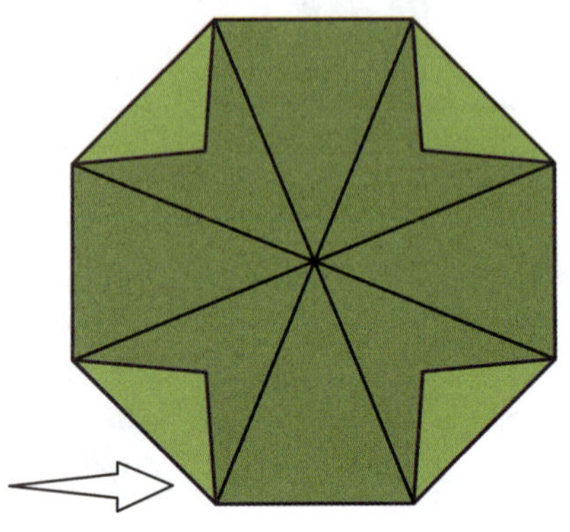

Like this.

17

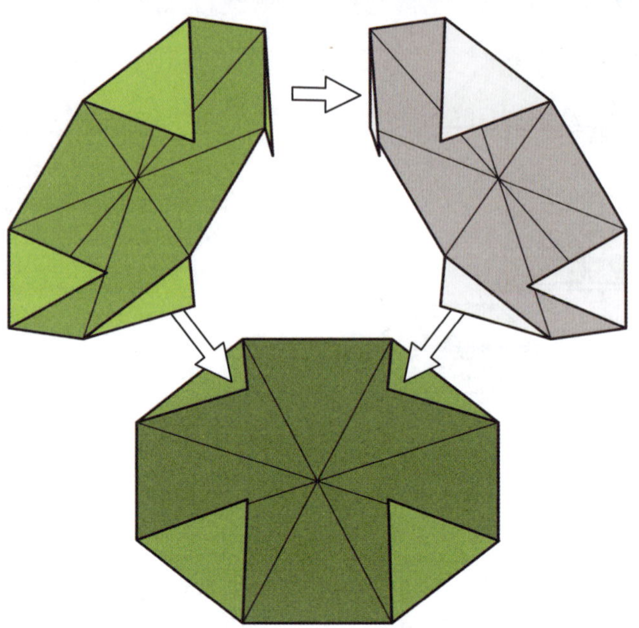

This is a 3D view. Use glue to join the units together.
Put the glue on the triangle tabs.

18

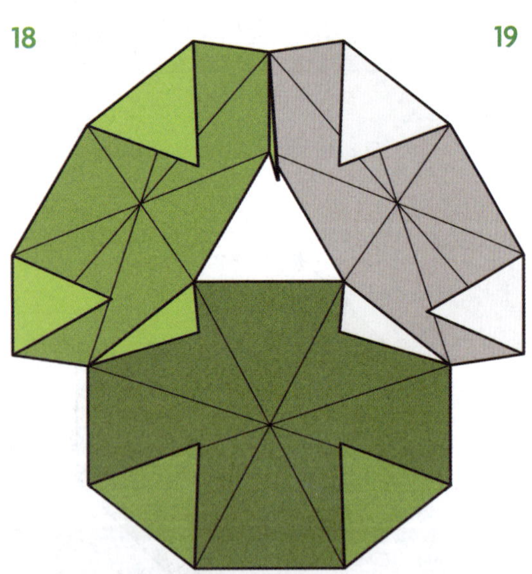

Three units joined together. Glue the last three units in the same way.

19

Completed kusudama.

WINDMILL RODS

MODEL: DARREN SCOTT
DIAGRAM: MATTHEW GARDINER

This unit is made from a windmill base, and is very versatile. With conveniently located hands and pockets, it is easy to assemble and can be made into many different geometric forms.

1

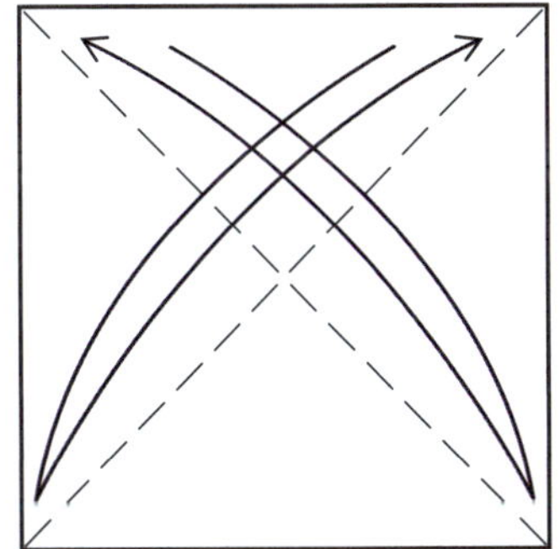

Fold and unfold diagonals.

2

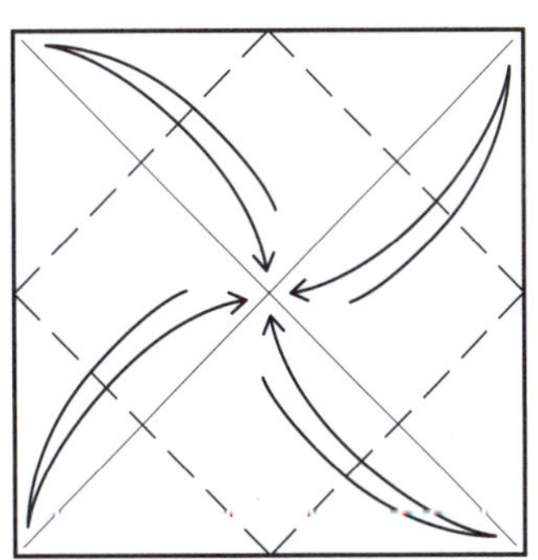

Blintz fold and unfold.

3

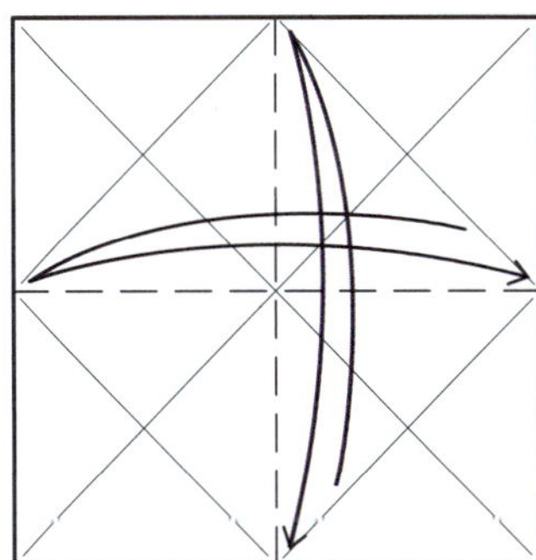

Book fold and unfold.

4

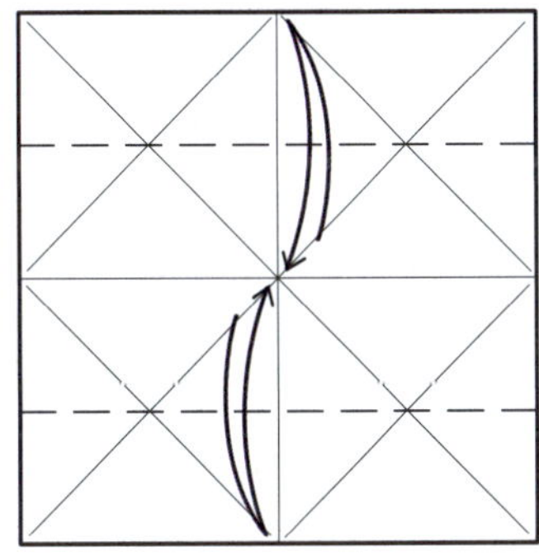

Cupboard fold and unfold.

5

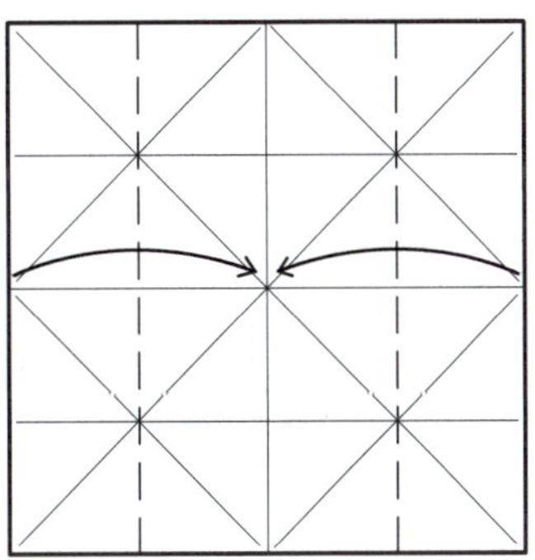

Cupboard fold.

6

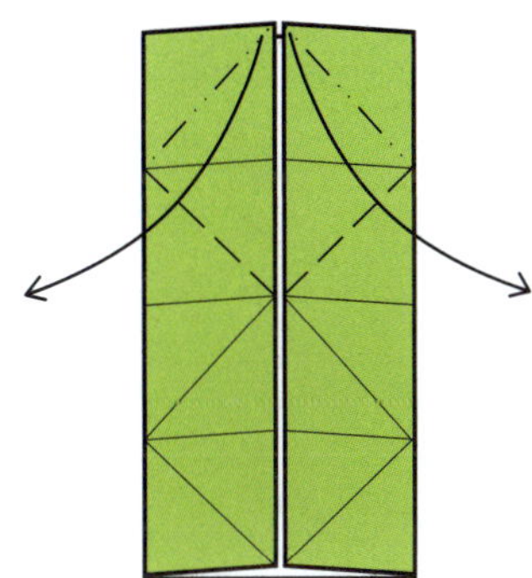

Squash fold using existing creases.

7

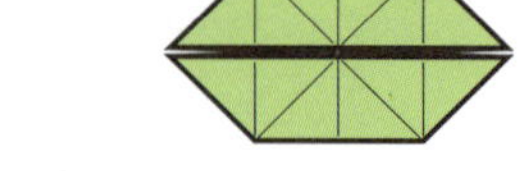

Repeat step 6 on the bottom.

8

Fold two corners to the middle.

9

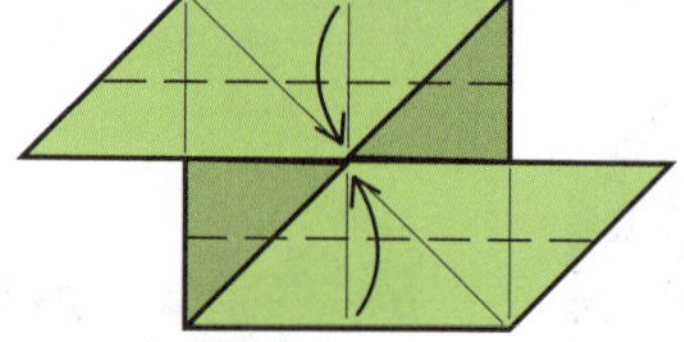

Fold edges to meet the middle.

10

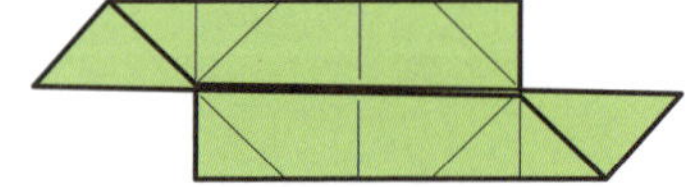

This is the bottom of the unit. Turn over.

11

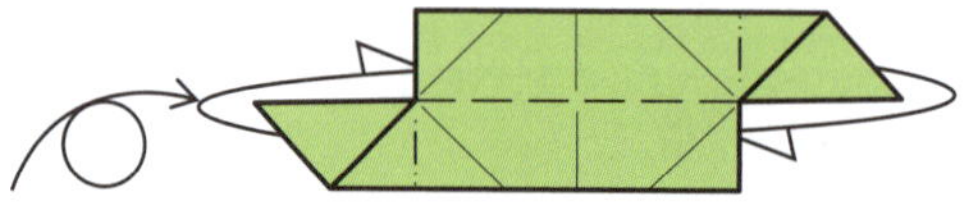

Mountain fold the tips, and valley fold lengthways to 90º.

12

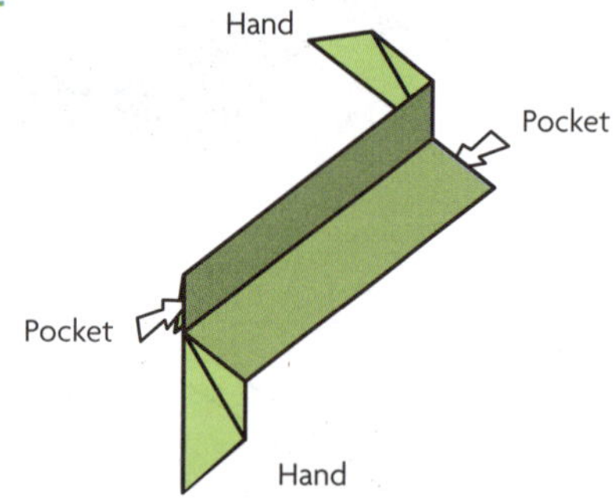

The completed unit.

13

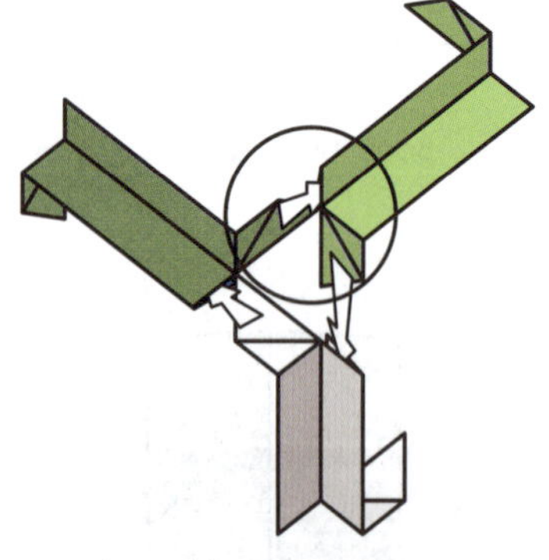

Assemble units as shown.

14

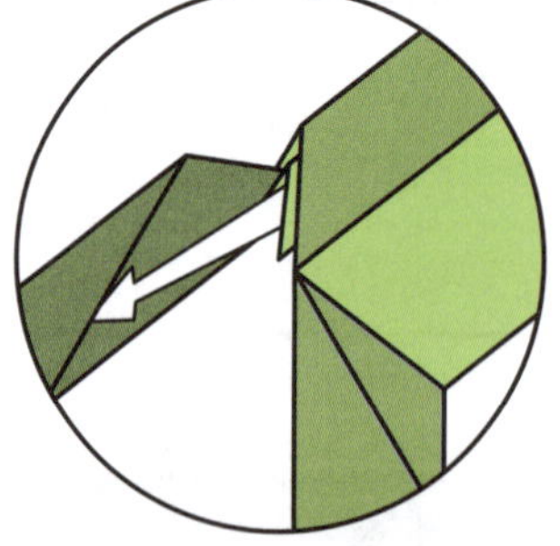

Note the way in which the units slot together. The lock is quite strong.

15

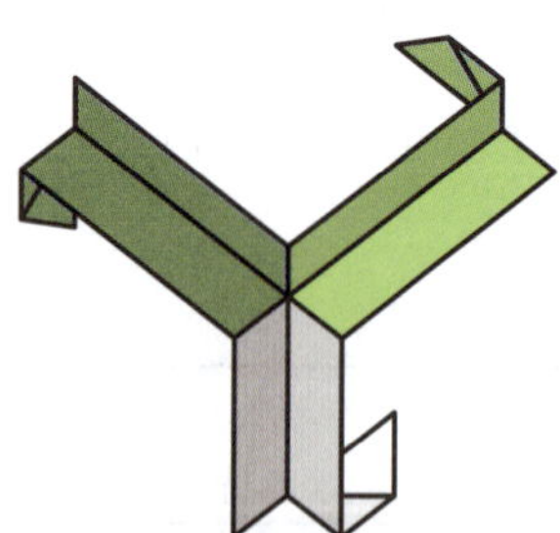

Three units assembled.

16

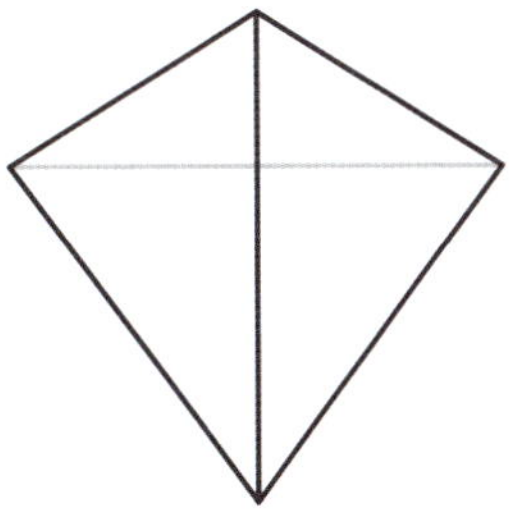

Tetrahedron

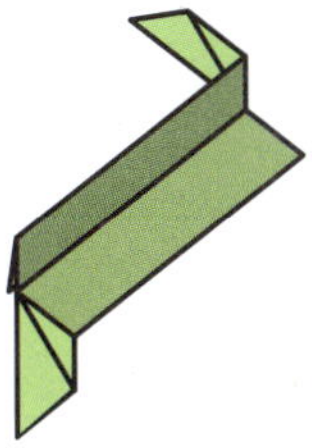

x 6

Use six units.

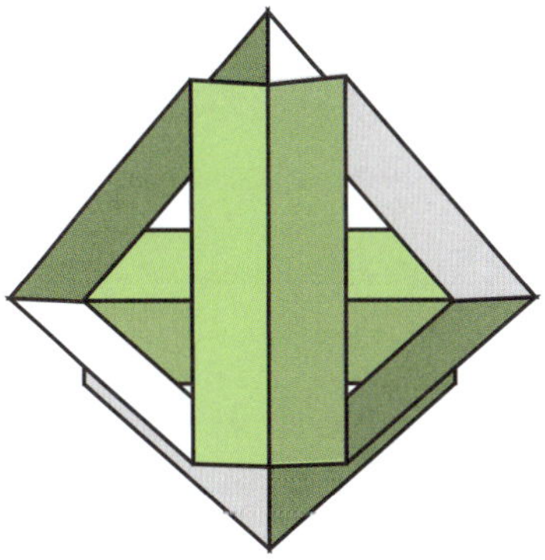

Completed tetrahedron.

17

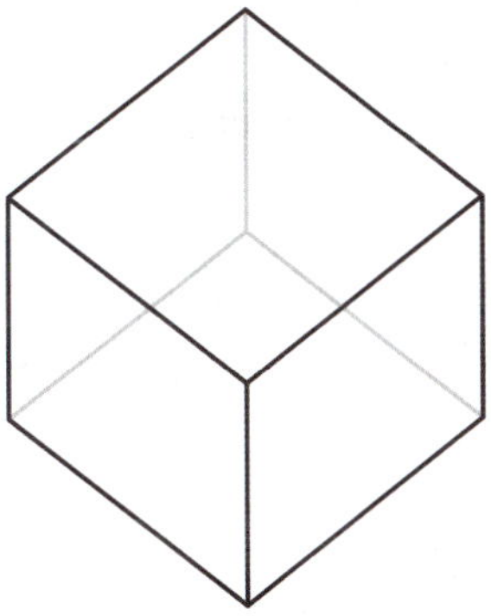

Hexahedron

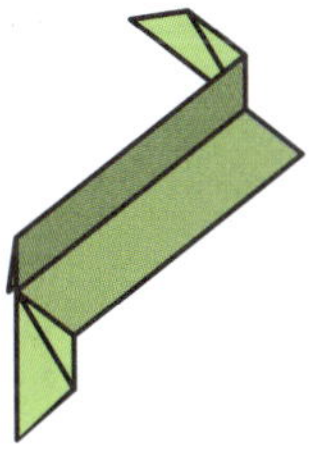

x 12

Use twelve units.

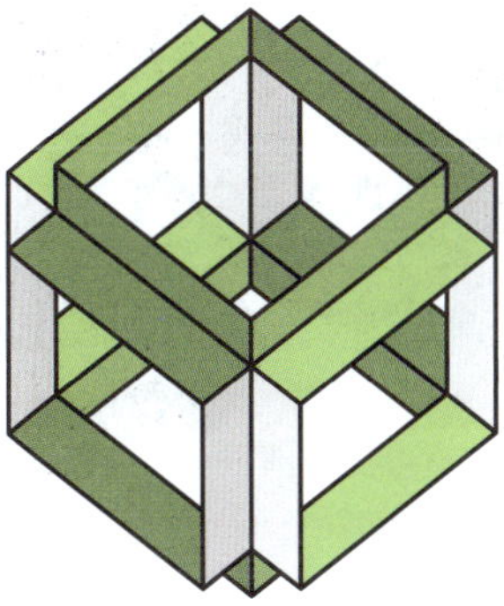

Completed hexahedron.

18

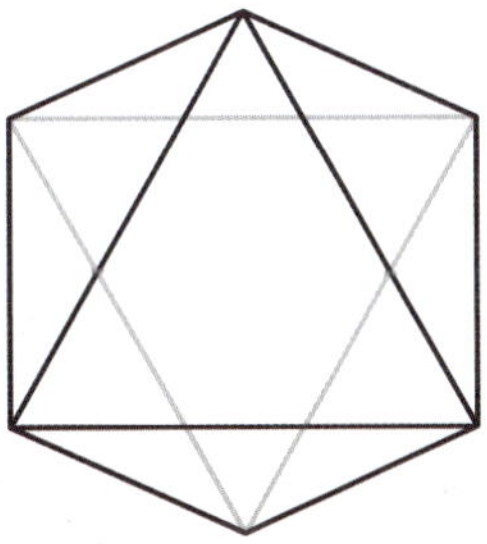

Octahedron.

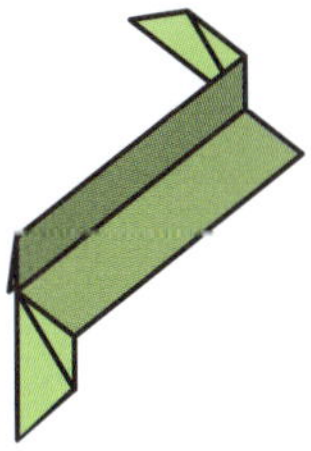

x 12

Use twelve units.

Completed octahedron.

EXPERT PROJECTS

FOUR-LEAF CLOVER BOWL

MODEL: EVI BINZINGER
DIAGRAM: EVI BINZINGER

Count your lucky folds! This delightful bowl is perfect as a vessel for little knick-knacks around the house. Try folding the bowl from a larger sheet of heavier paper stock to make your luck last longer.

1

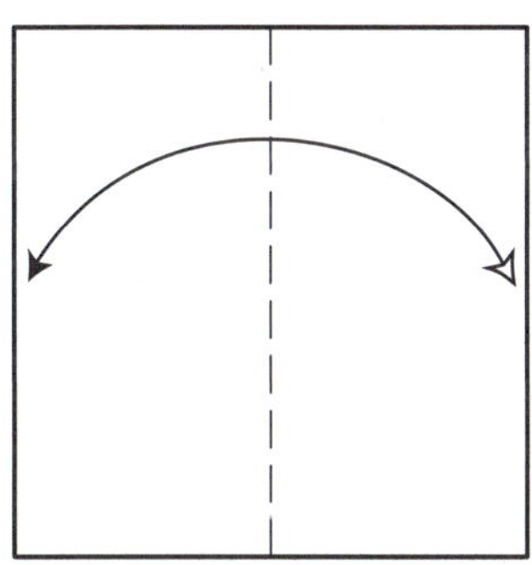

Book fold in half and unfold.

2

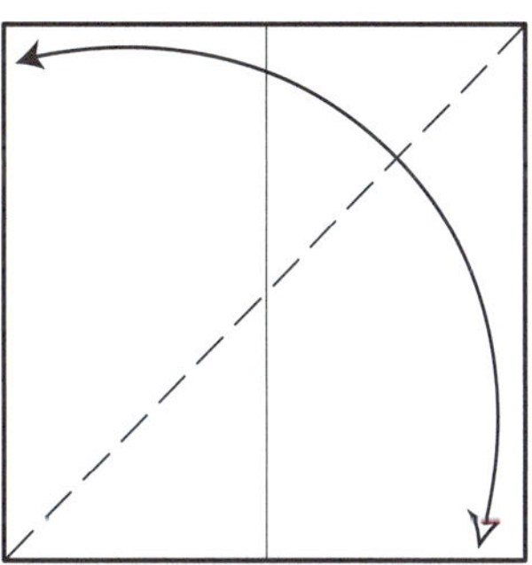

Crease across the diagonal.

3

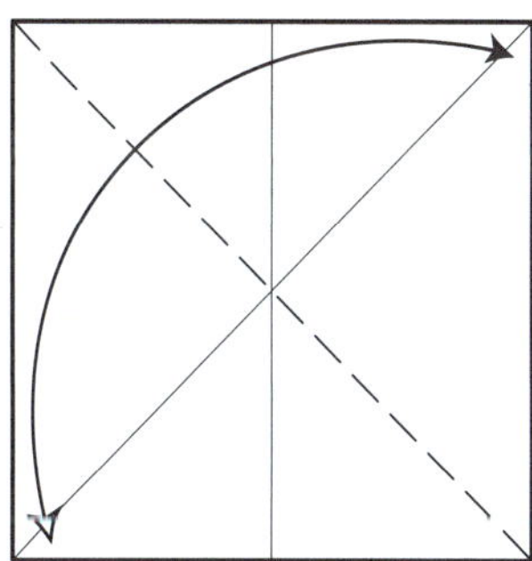

Crease across the other diagonal.

4

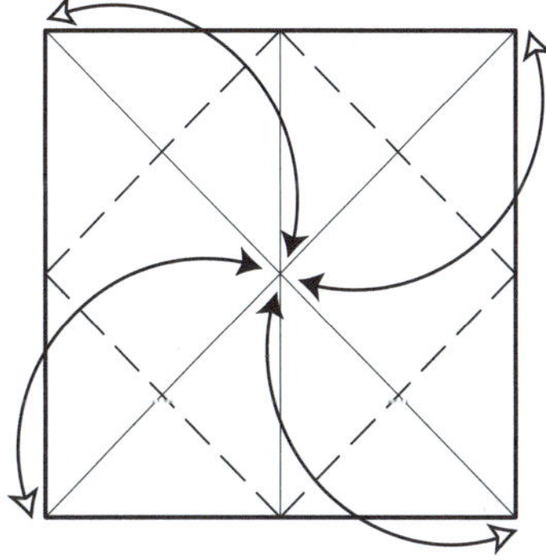

Blintz fold all corners to the centre and unfold.

5

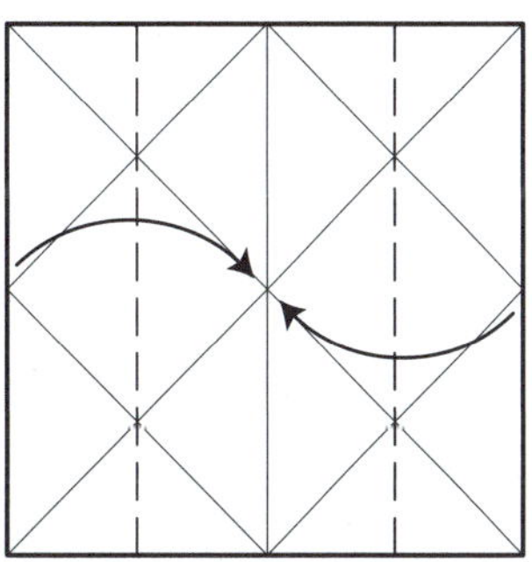

Valley fold the side edges to the center crease.

6

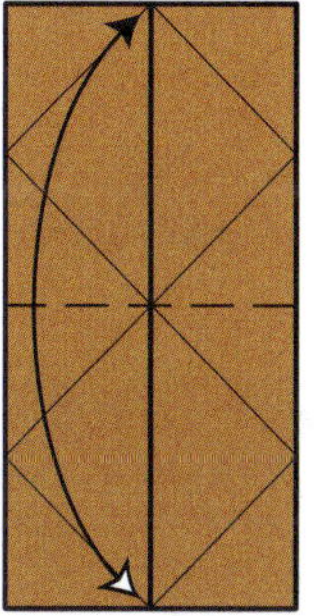

Book fold in half vertically and unfold.

7

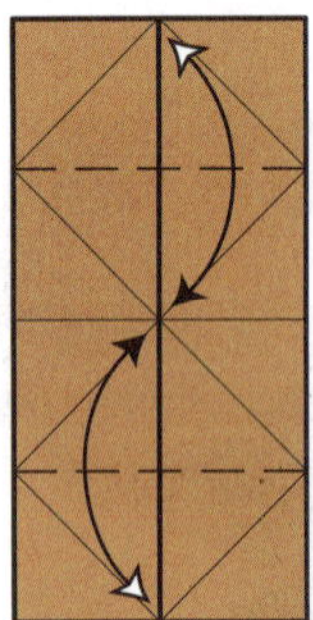

Valley fold the top edges to the center crease and unfold.

8

Crease diagonally through the center.

9

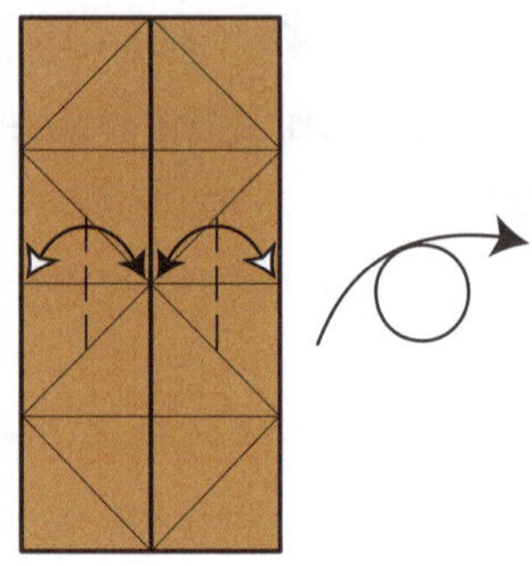

Make creases as shown, folding both sides to the center.

10

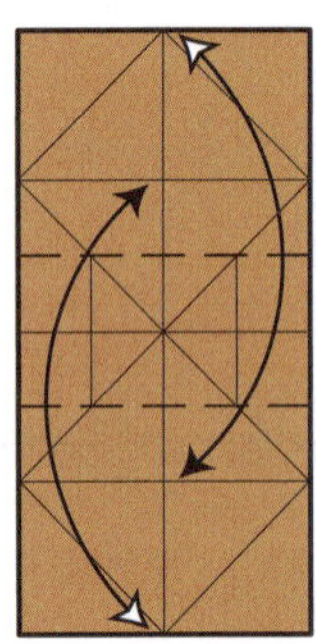

Valley fold and unfold as shown.

11

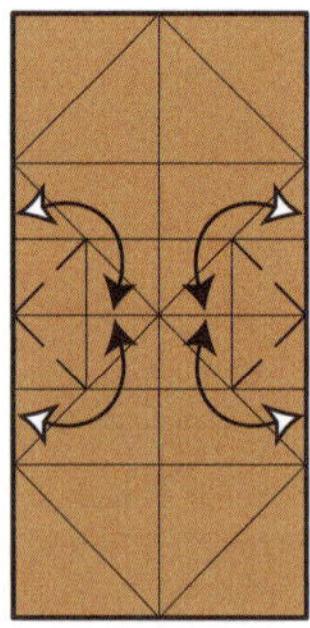

Valley fold and unfold through all layers, creasing as indicated.

12

Valley fold and unfold through all layers, creasing as indicated.

13

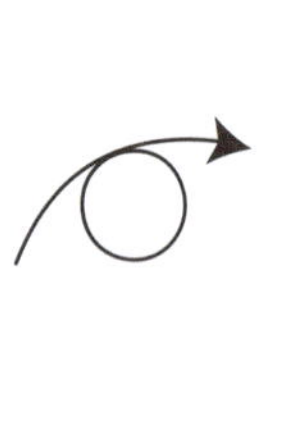

Valley fold and unfold through all layers, creasing as indicated.

14

Make squash folds at each corner.

15

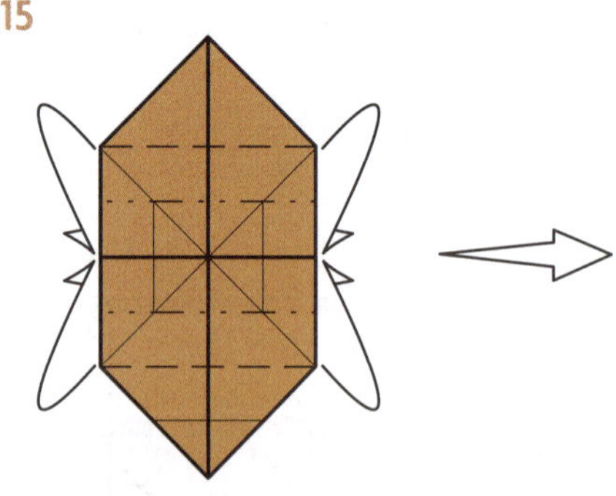

Pleat, forming mountains and valleys as shown.

16

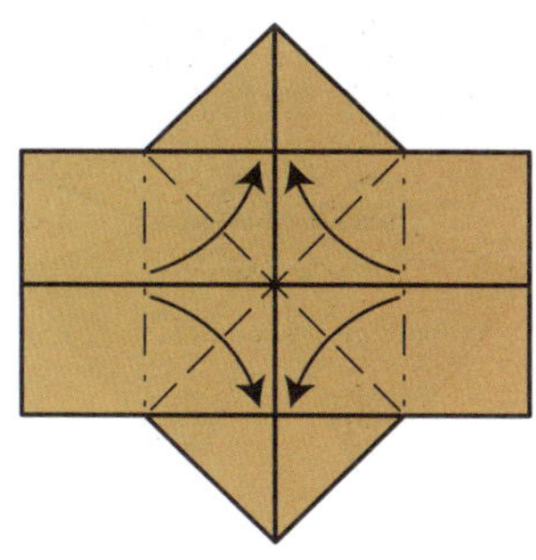

Lift the inner edges outward, forming a box shape.

17

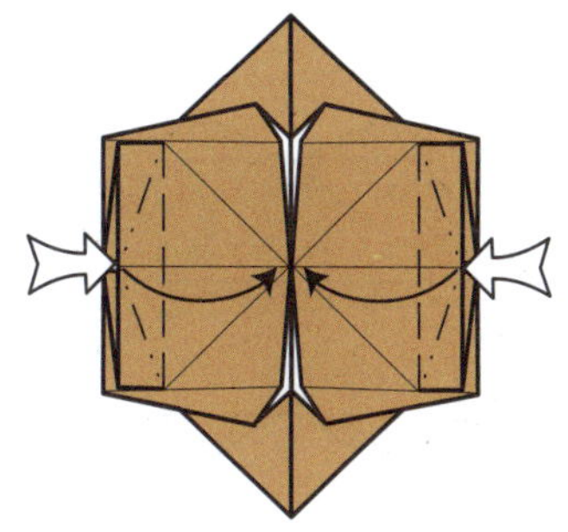

3D view. Squash fold the inner layer to the center of the model.

18

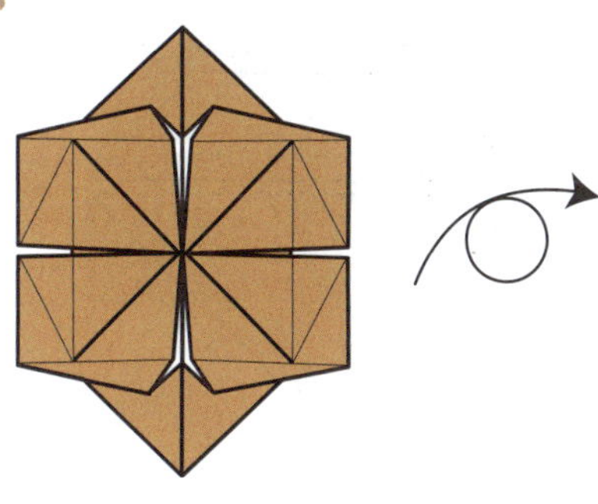

Like so. Turn over.

19

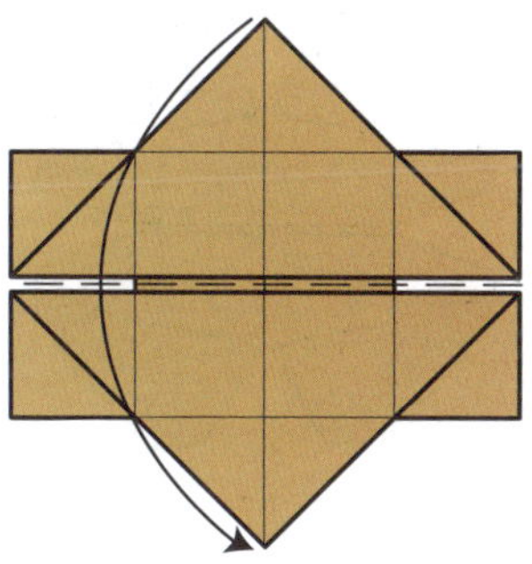

Valley fold top to bottom.

20

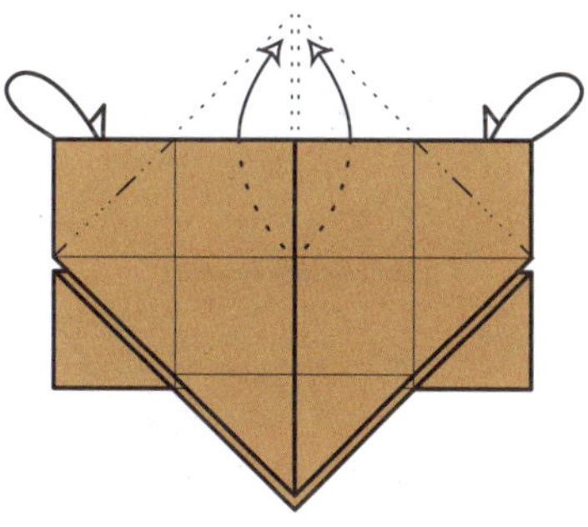

Pull up layer of paper from behind and mountain fold the corners.

21

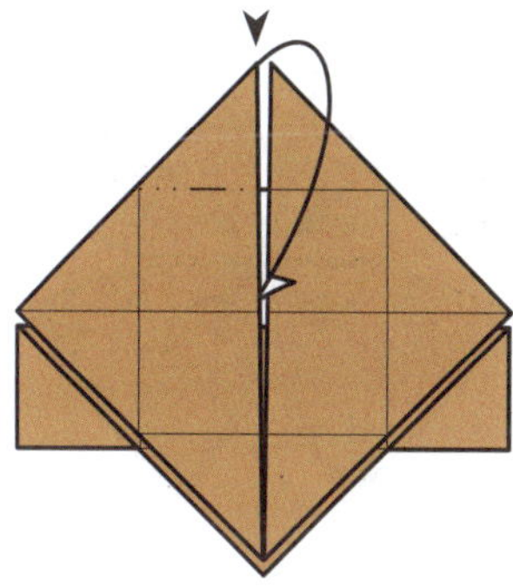

Reverse fold the point inside the model.

22

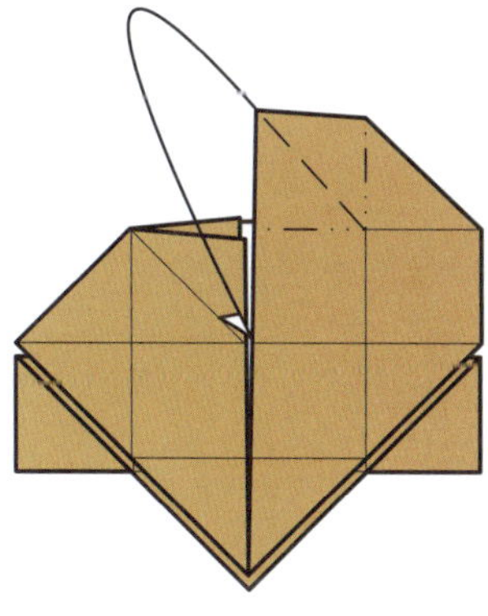

Repeat on the other side.

23

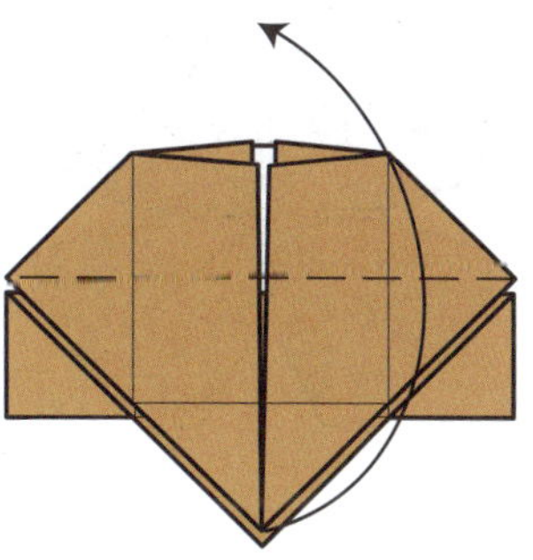

Valley fold upward.

24

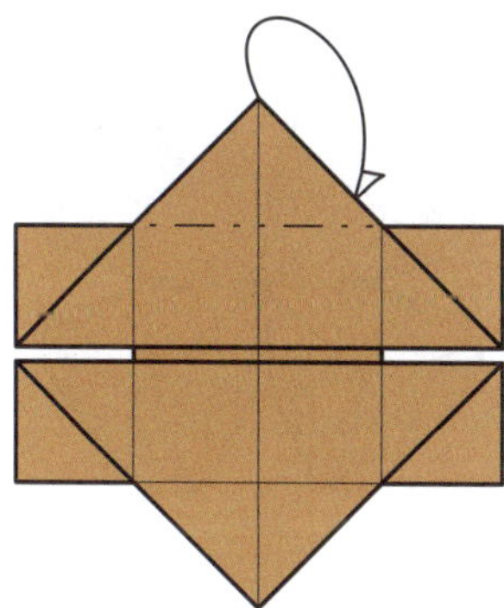

Mountain fold behind and insert into the pocket.

25

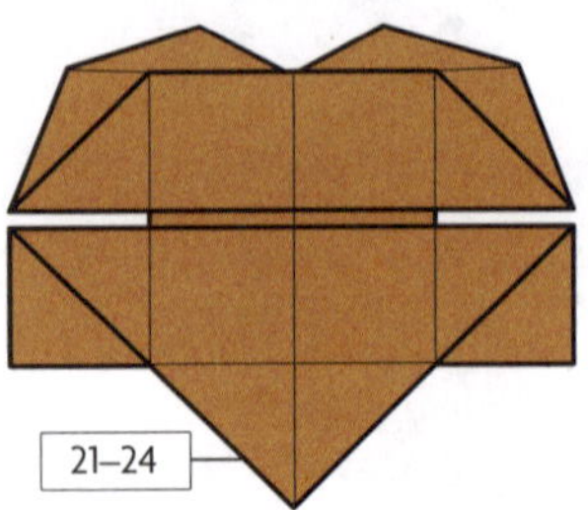

Repeat steps 21–24 on the bottom side.

26

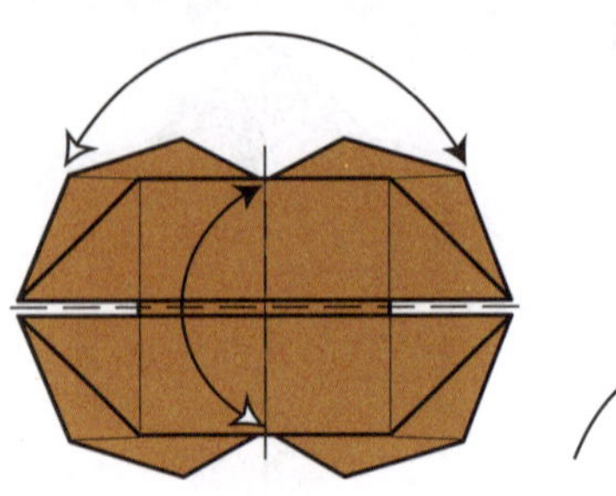

Fold and unfold horizontally and vertically. Push the center point upward to balance the petals' shape.

27

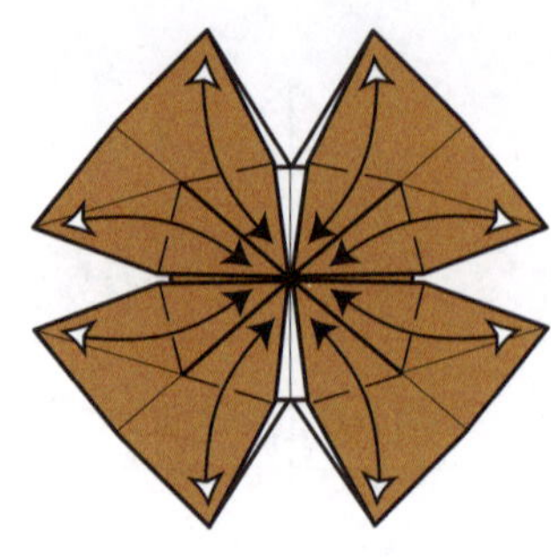

Fold all points to the center and unfold.

28

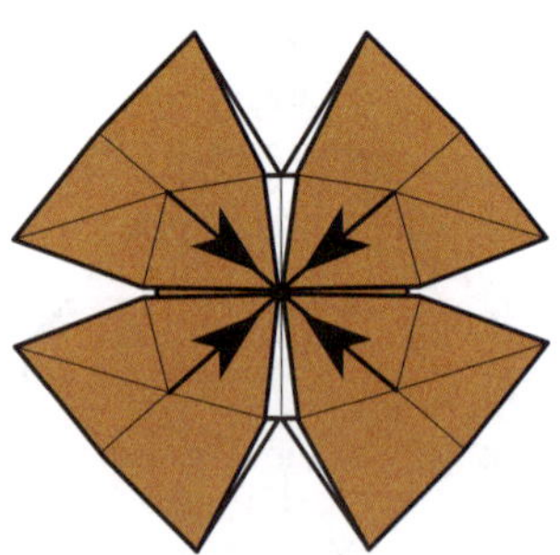

Curve all points towards the middle to round the bottom of the bowl.

29

Fold the points behind to shape the leaves.

30

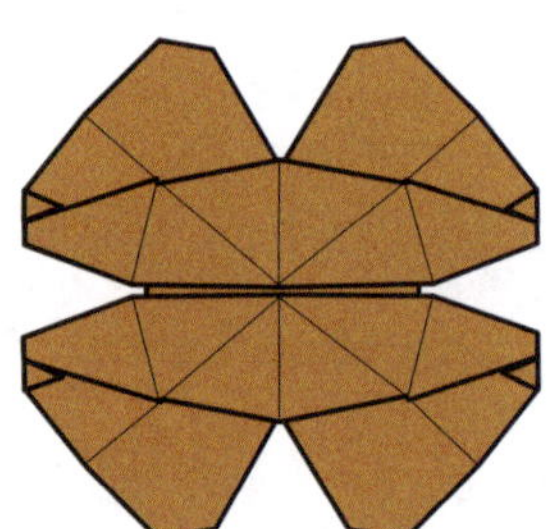

Sink fold the points to hide them. The result will look like this.

31

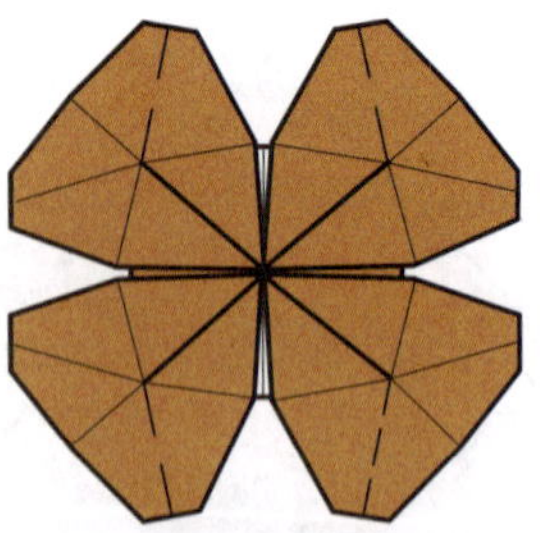

If you like, add extra creases to make the model look symmetrical.

32

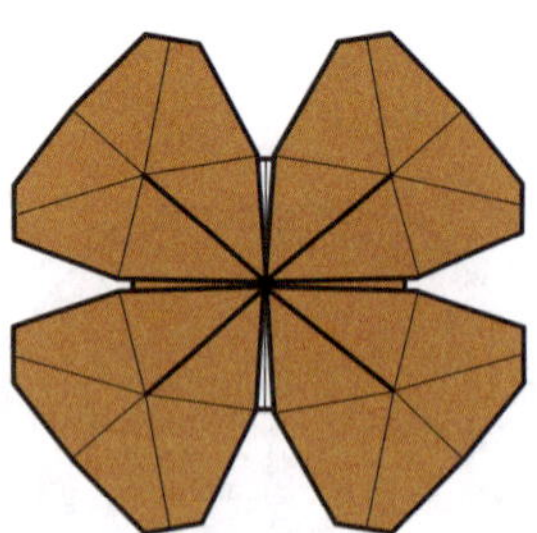

The finished four-leaf clover bowl.

SOPHIA'S TILE

MODEL: TRADITIONAL, JAPAN
DIAGRAM: MATTHEW GARDINER

This tile is directly inspired by a walk through San Marco Basilica in Venice where the floors are adorned with ingenious tiling patterns. These patterns contain geometric wisdom from centuries ago. The six-sided geometric face can also be found in work by origami legend Shuzo Fujimoto, whose pioneering origami work inspired the field of origami tessellations. This work pays homage to both sources.

Use the folding bone to mark sharp creases throughout and the scoring tool to score the short creases, if you prefer, rather than folding them.

1

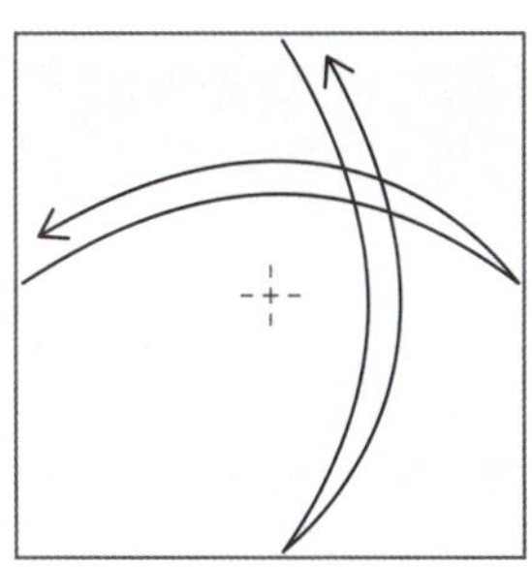

Pinch at the midpoint of each fold to mark the center of the paper.

2

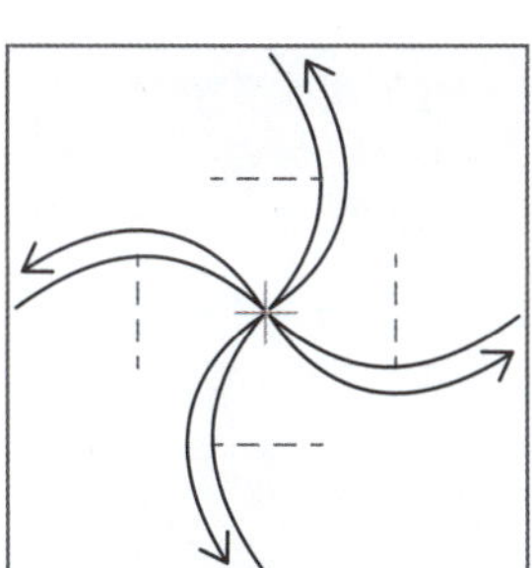

Fold each of the edges to the center and crease just the middle quarter of the sheet on all four sides.

3

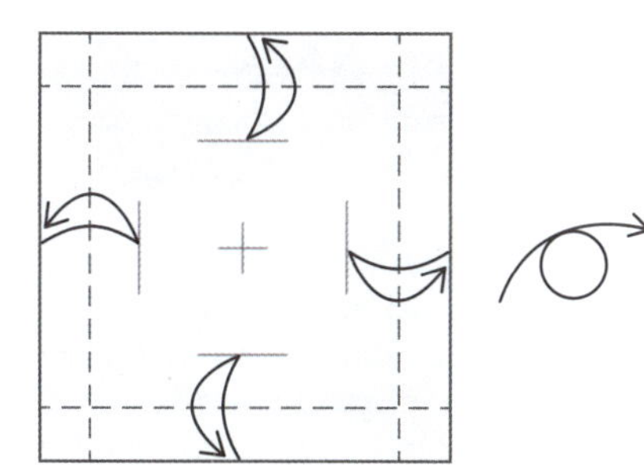

Fold the edges to the creases you made in step 2 and crease the full width of the sheet. Turn over.

4

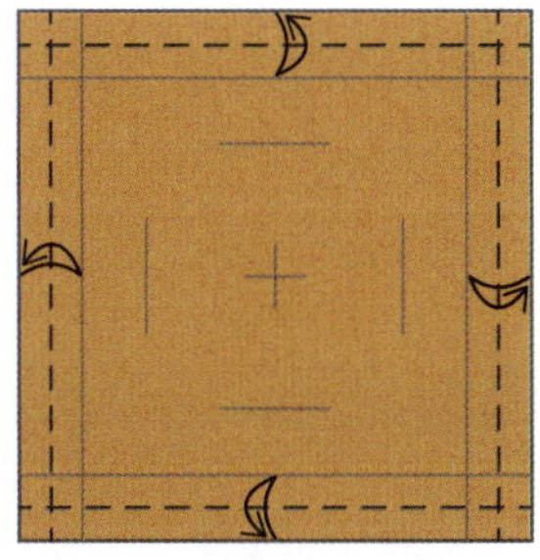

Crease one-sixteenth width creases on all sides.

5

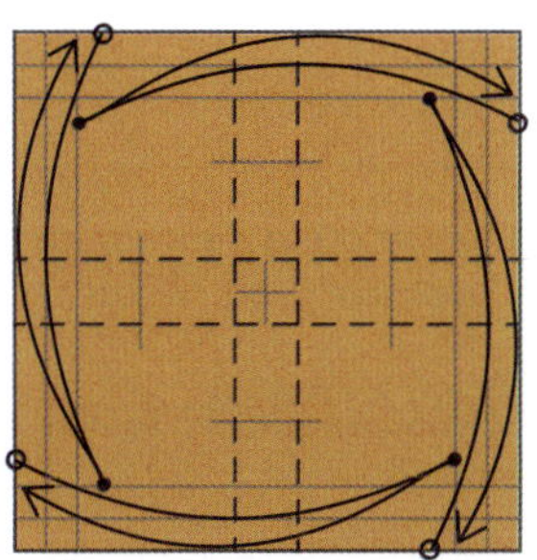

Fold each edge to the far one-eighth crease line made in step 3. Turn over.

6

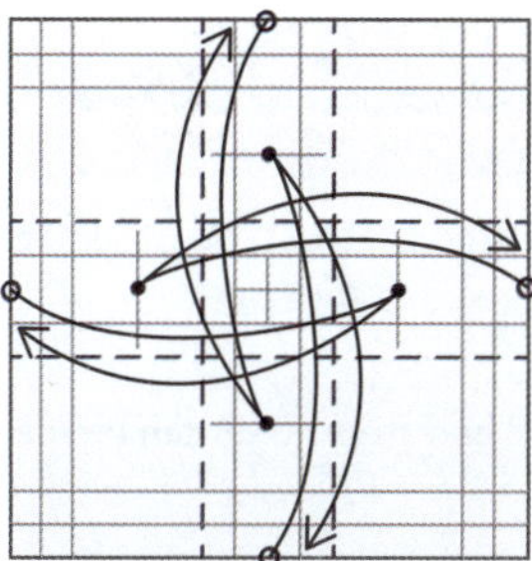

Fold each edge to the far quarter crease made in step 2.

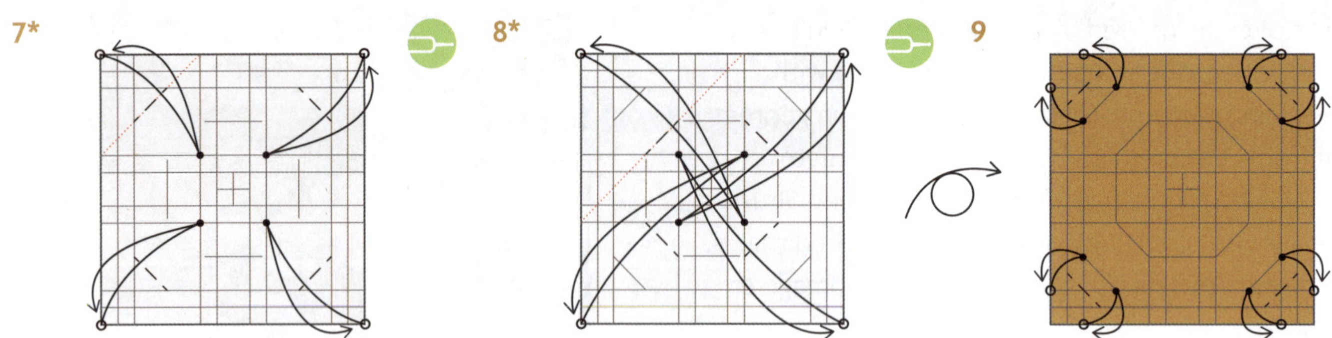

Fold each corner to the dotted intersection and make a short diagonal crease.

Fold circled corners to the dotted intersections and make a short diagonal crease. Turn over.

Fold so that the circled intersections touch the fold from step 7, and make a short diagonal crease.

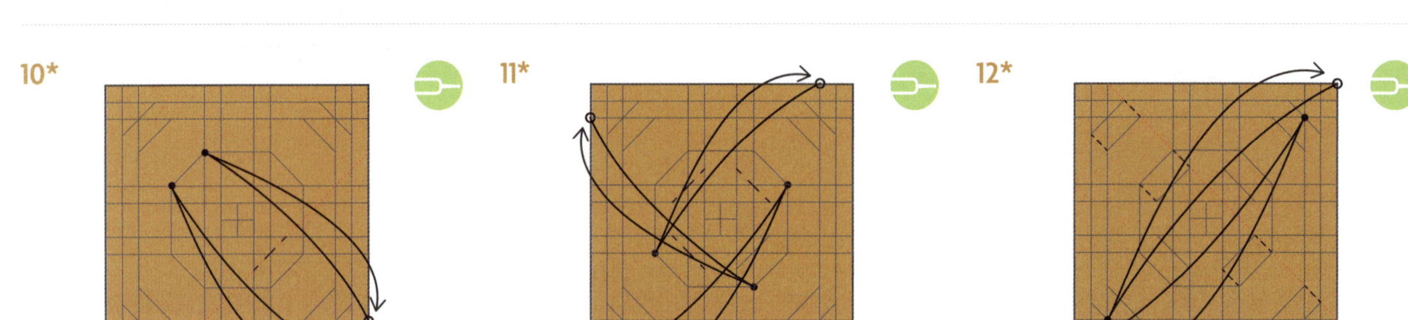

Fold the circled intersections to touch the fold line form step 8, and make a short diagonal crease.

Repeat step 10 with the remaining 3 corners.

Fold the circled intersection to touch the dotted intersection and make eight short diagonal creases between existing fold lines.

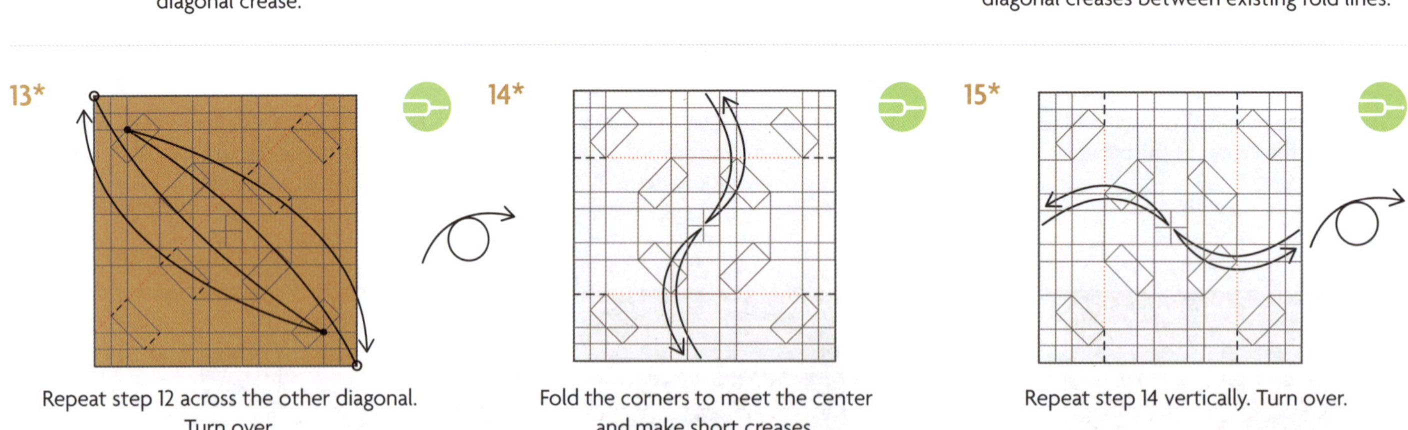

Repeat step 12 across the other diagonal. Turn over.

Fold the corners to meet the center and make short creases.

Repeat step 14 vertically. Turn over.

* Steps 7–8 and steps 10–16 can be marked with the scoring tool and ruler prior to folding. Use the red dotted lines as a guide to line up your ruler.

16*

Fold the corners to meet the dotted intersections and make short creases.

17

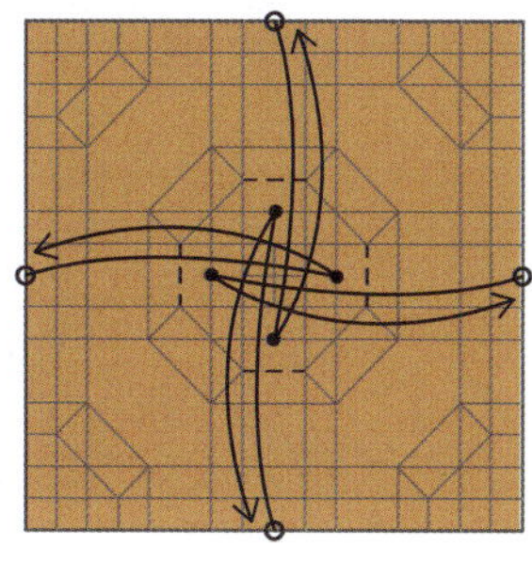

Fold the edge to meet the one-eighth crease past the center and make a short crease.

18

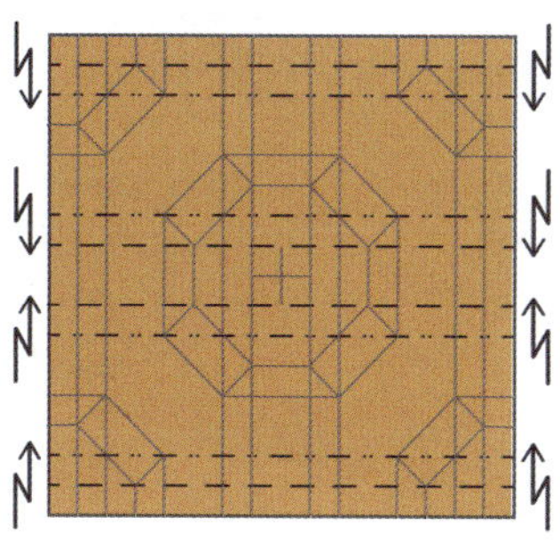

Make four pleats as shown. Pay attention to the mountains and valleys.

19

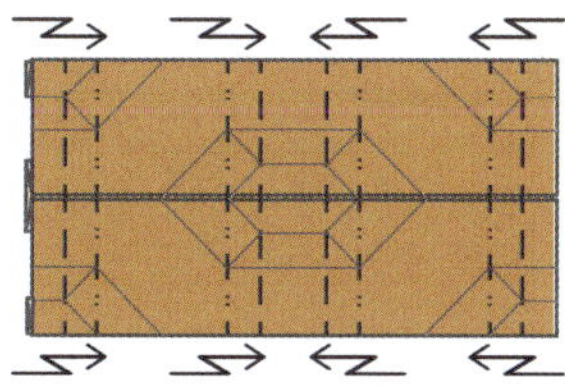

Repeat and pleat across the other direction. Take care folding through many layers.

20

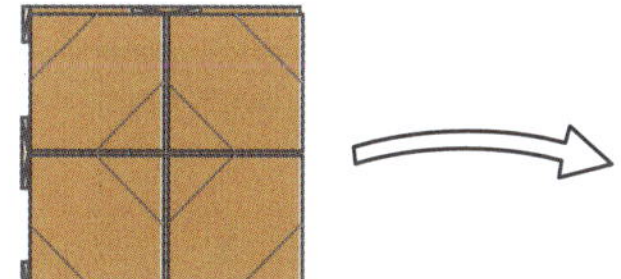

This is what it will look like completely pleated. Unfold completely flat.

21

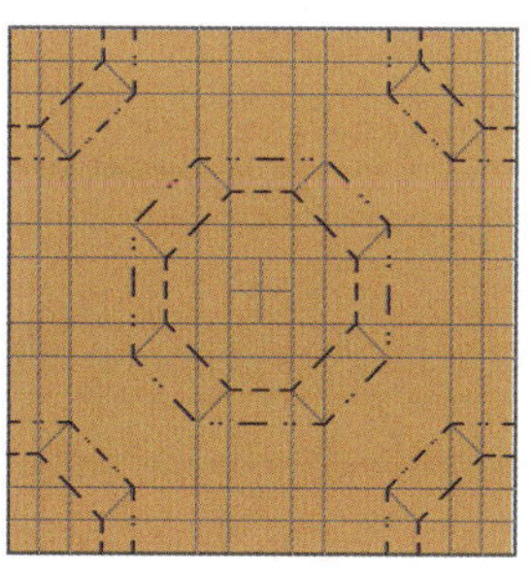

Re-fold along the crease loops, making sure that the folds are mountain and valley as shown. The model will not lie flat in steps 22–24.

22

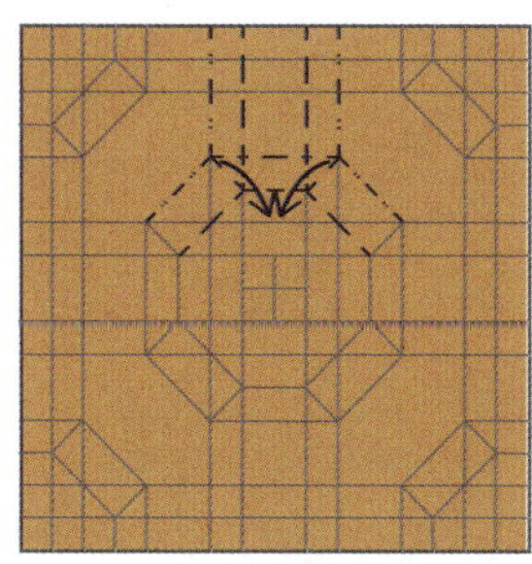

Steps 22–25 show the collapse of the central section of the pattern. Firstly, shape the fold directions carefully.

23

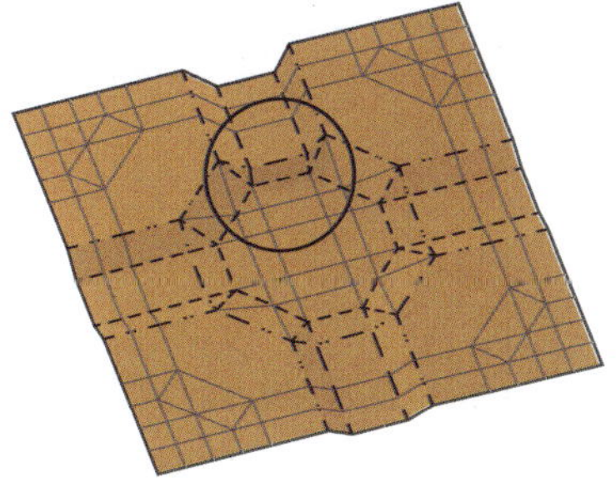

As the collapse progresses, shape the folds on the remaining sides. See detail in the next step.

24

Close-up of the collapse in process.

25

Creases in step 23 are now completely collapsed and the model should lay flat.

26

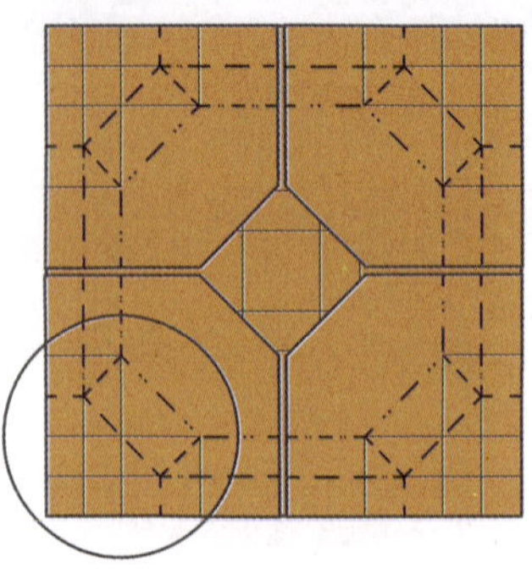

Each corner is creased similarly to steps 22–25. Shape the crease directions. See detail in the next step.

27

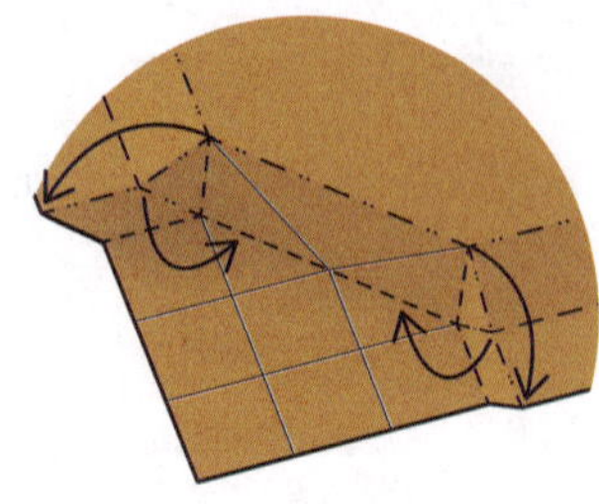

Collapse one corner at a time, pleating the edges in between them at the same time. The model will not lie flat until all of the corners are collapsed.

28

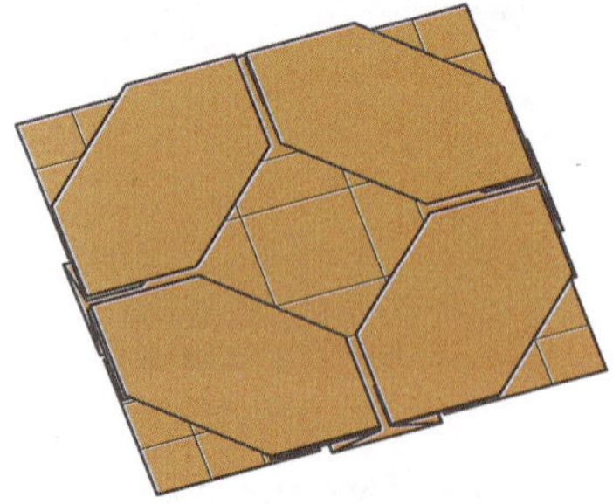

The tile is completely collapsed.

29

It looks like this from above.

30

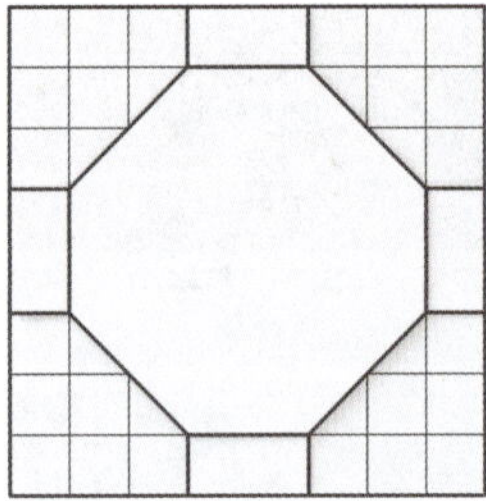

It looks like this from below.

31

It is possible to make a larger pattern from different sheets, by repeating steps 1–30 with three more sheets of paper. Use tape on the back to join the sheets together.

32

Or for a more complex origami challenge, you can fold the full crease pattern (shown over the next page) from a single, larger sheet.

Remember, solid lines are mountain folds and dashed lines are valley folds.

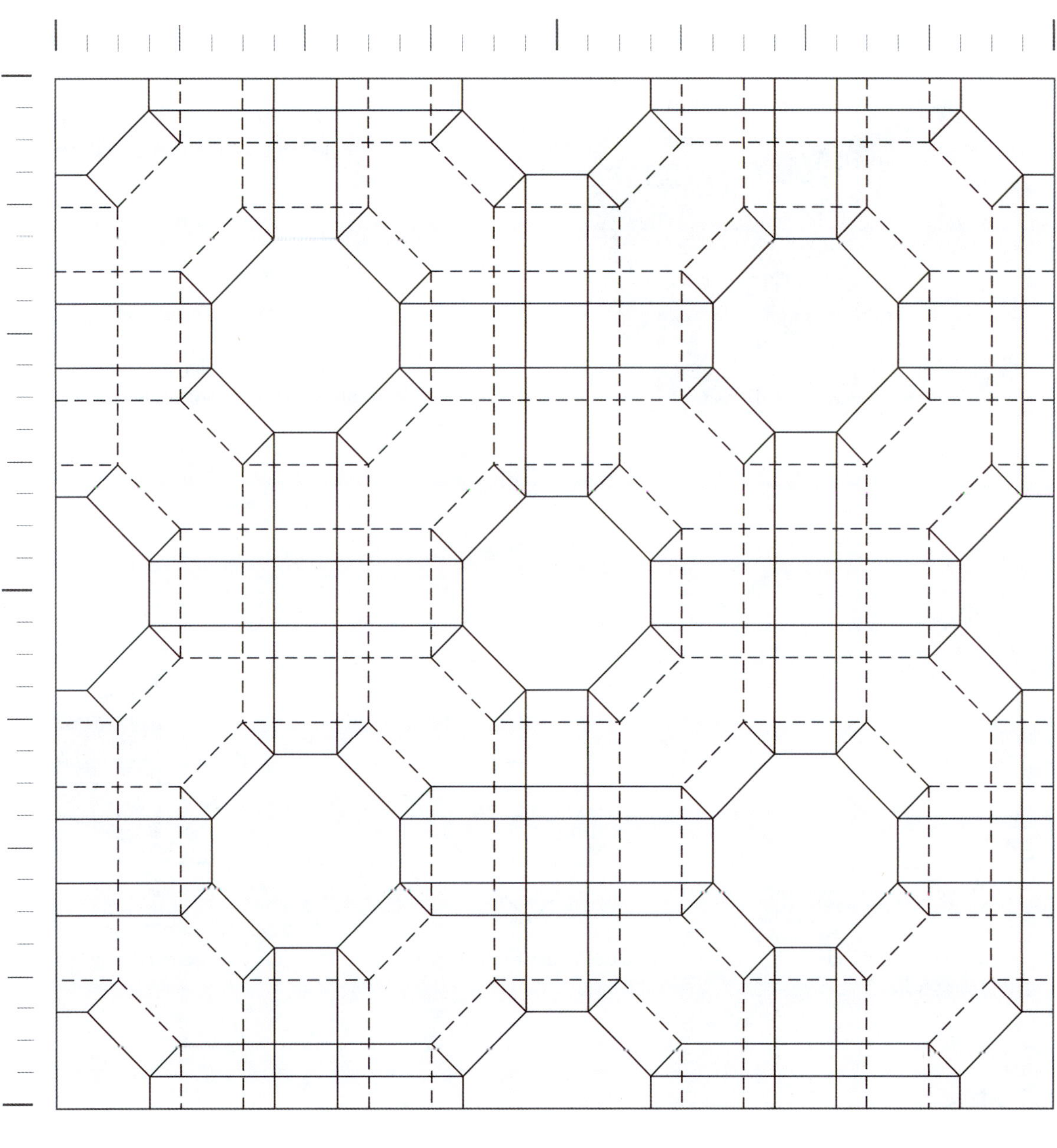

1

Crease all the vertical and horizontal folds and then pleat. Unfold.

2

Score and then crease all of the small folds.

3

Collapse the pattern, focusing on one center section at a time, as per steps 22–25. Finally, complete the edges as per steps 26–27.

MANDARIN DUCK

MODEL: STEVEN CASEY
DIAGRAM: STEVEN CASEY

The mandarin duck is inspired by a traditional model. The mandarin duck is a migratory bird, and flies to southern China and Japan during the winter months. The male mandarin duck has very distinctive patterning on its head, so use a decorative sheet of paper.

A Chinese proverb relates loving couples to "two mandarin ducks playing in water."

1

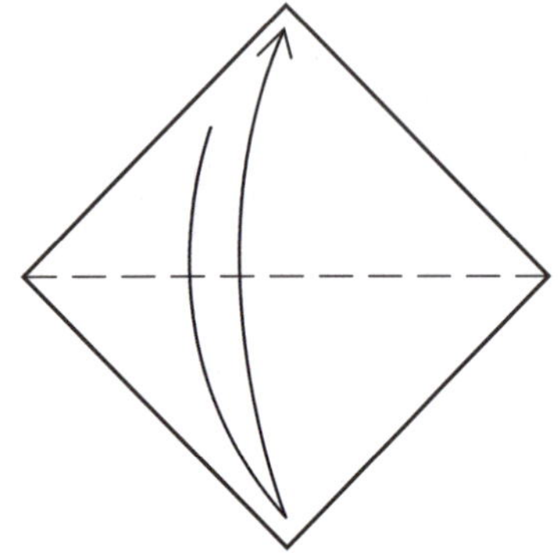

Start with white side up. Fold and unfold diagonal.

2

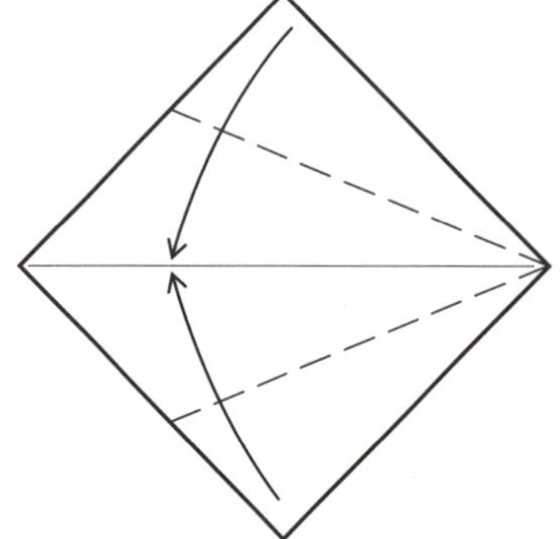

Fold both sides to the middle.

3

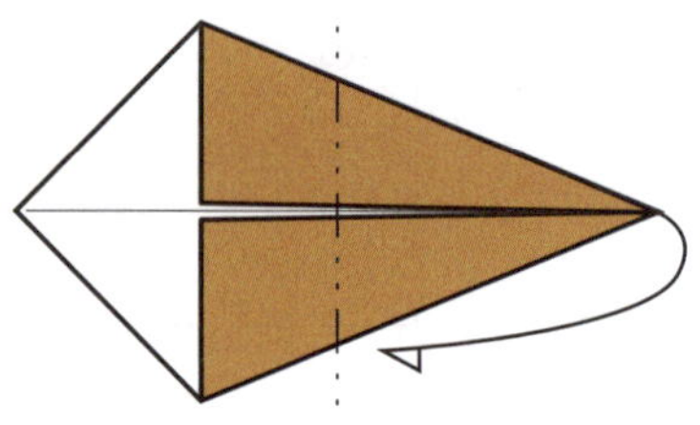

Mountain fold in half behind.

4

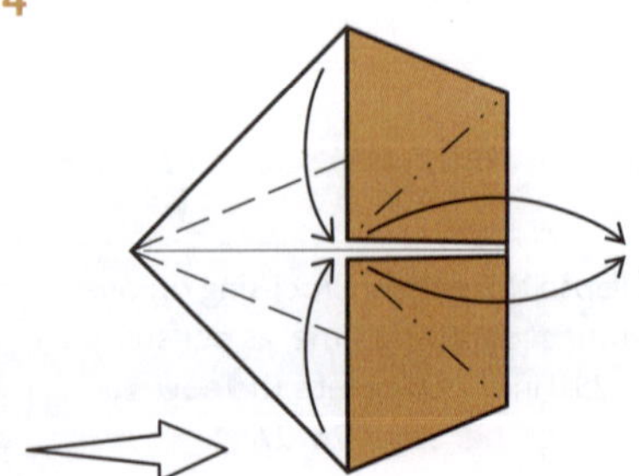

Squash fold both sides.

5

Mountain fold the back layer behind.

6

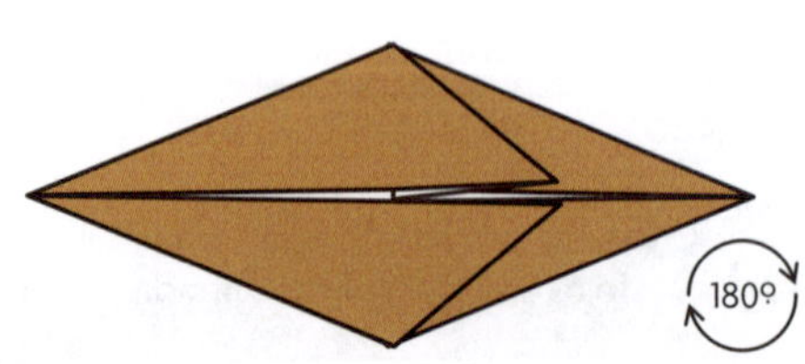

This is known as the fish base. Rotate 180º.

7

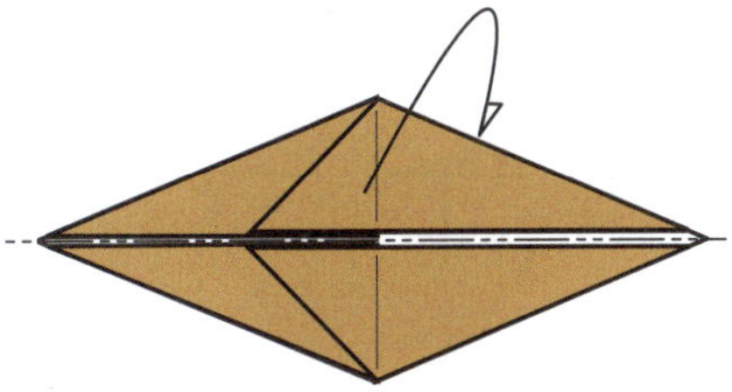

Fold top half behind.

8

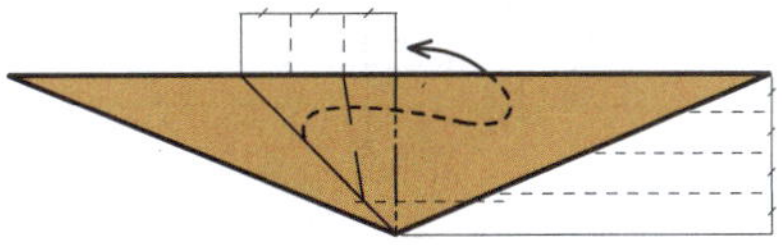

Double reverse fold small flaps. Repeat behind.

9

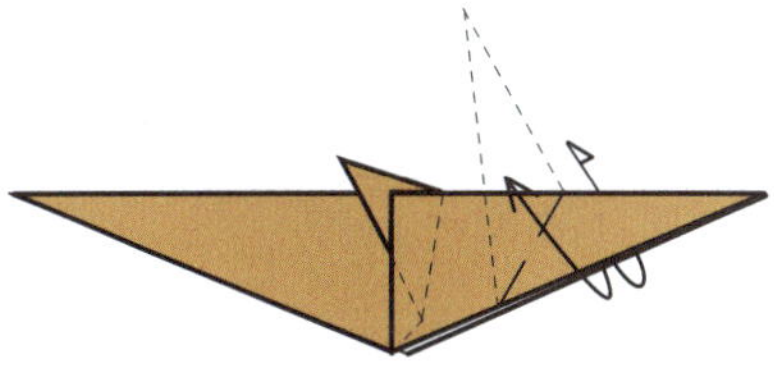

Outside reverse right point.

10

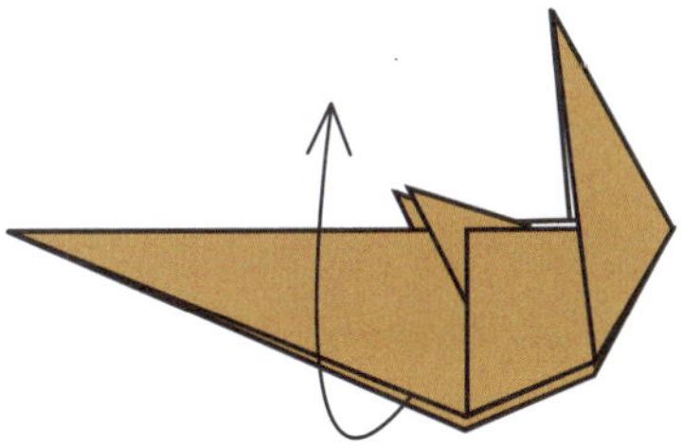

Lift layer upward.

11

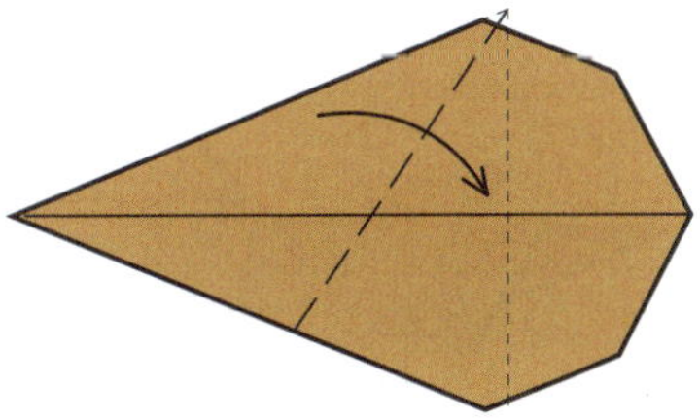

Fold top edge in line with dotted vertical line.

12

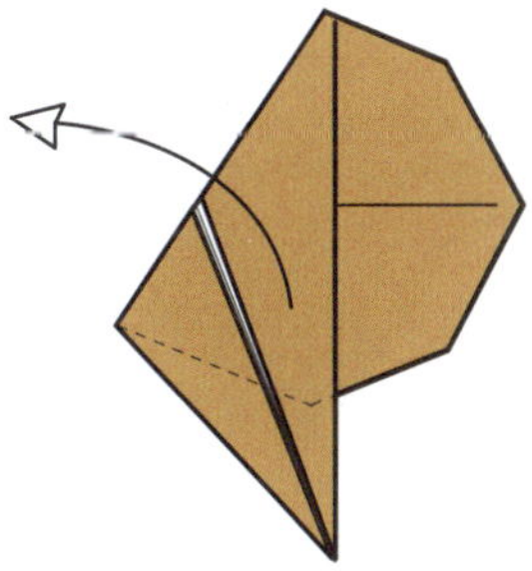

Unfold.

13

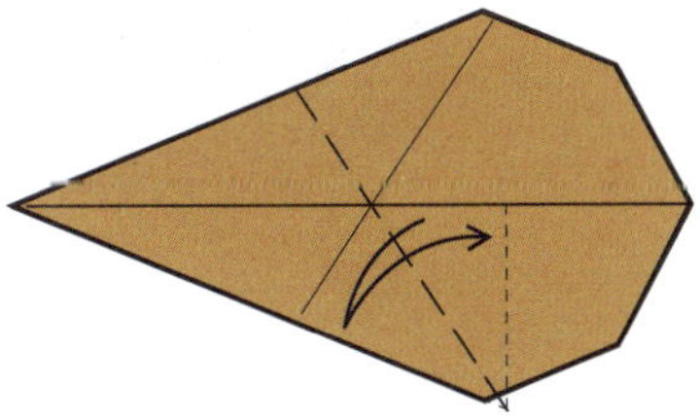

Repeat in other direction.

14

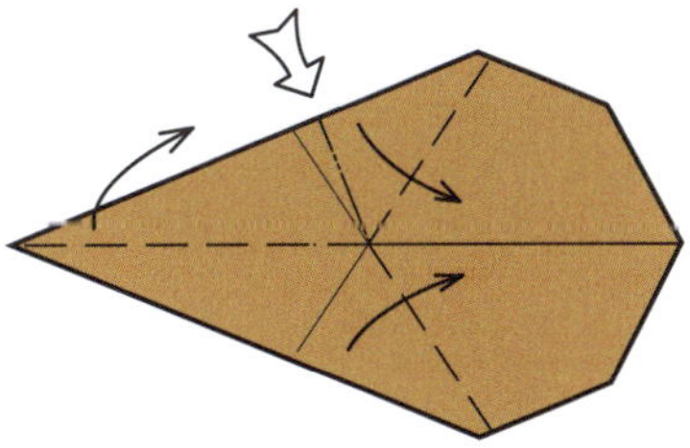

Rabbit ear on existing creases.

15

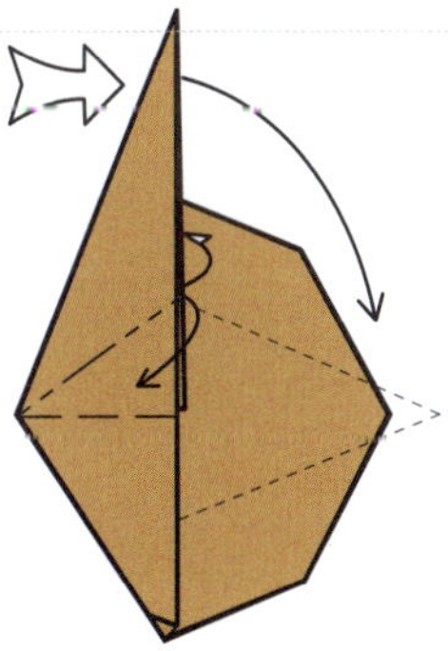

Lift the point upward and squash fold.

16

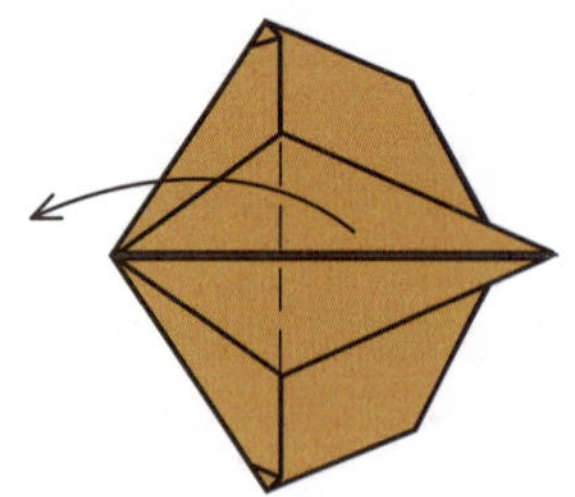

Valley fold the top point to the left.

17

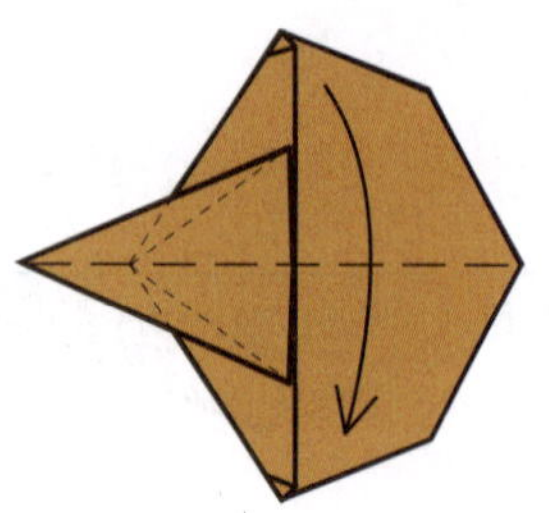

Fold top half down in front.

18

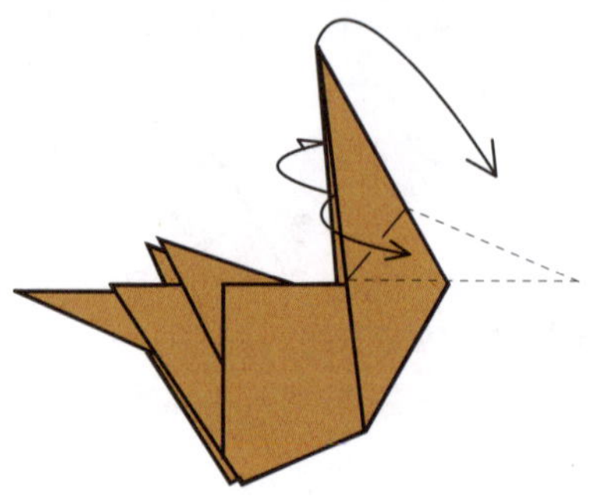

Outside reverse.

19

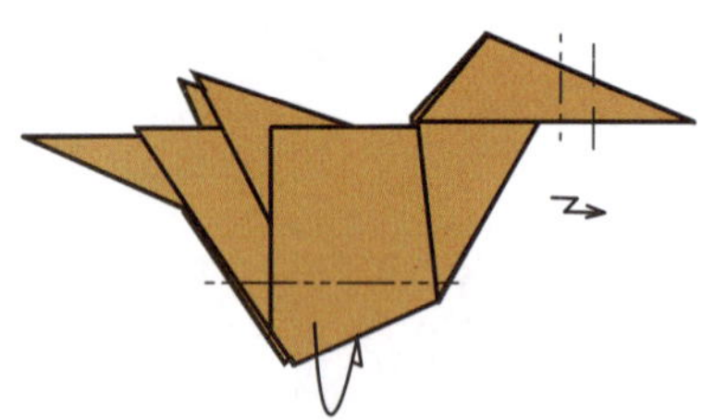

Fold bottom edge under and into body.
Double reverse point to form bill.

20

Completed mandarin duck.

MOUSE

MODEL: STEVEN CASEY
DIAGRAM: STEVEN CASEY

The mouse is a member of the rodent family. This mouse resembles the well-known common house mouse, with alert ears and a long tail. Attempt this model first with a 12in (30cm) sheet before progressing onto a smaller sheet size for a life-size mouse.

The mouse is regarded as the third most successful mammal on the planet, due to its ability to adapt to almost any environment.

1

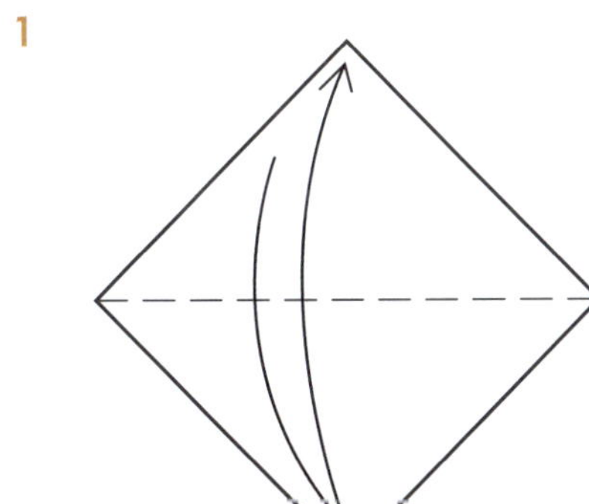

Begin white side up.
Fold and unfold diagonal.

2

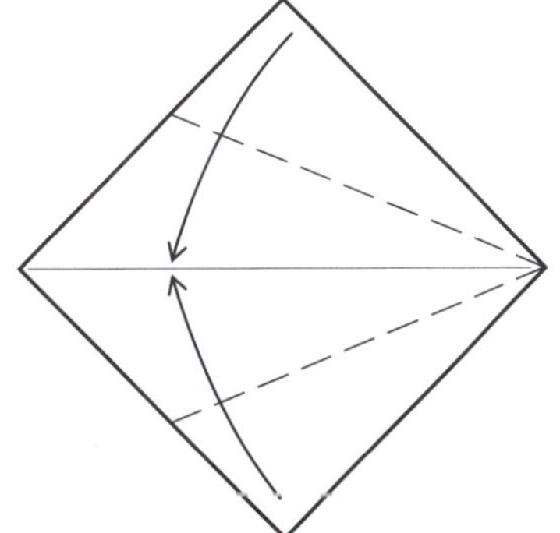

Fold both sides to the middle.

3

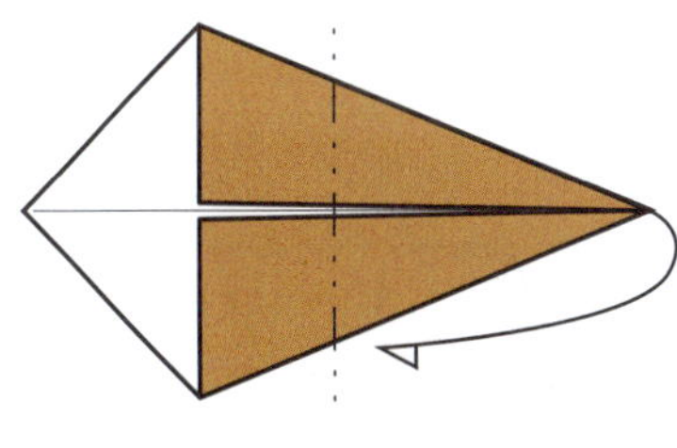

This is known as the kite base.
Mountain fold in half.

4

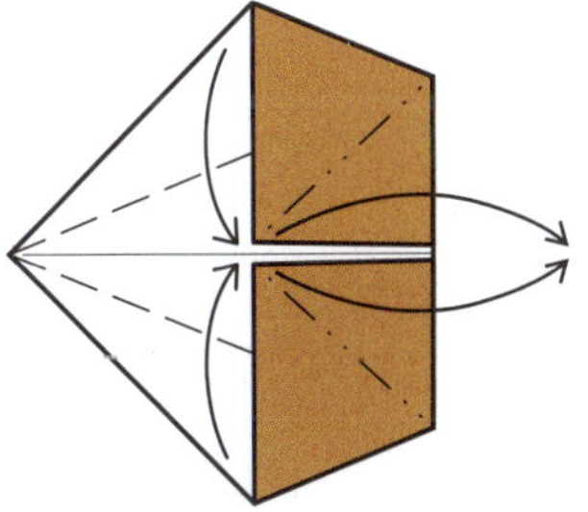

Squash fold both sides.

5

Mountain fold the point behind.

6

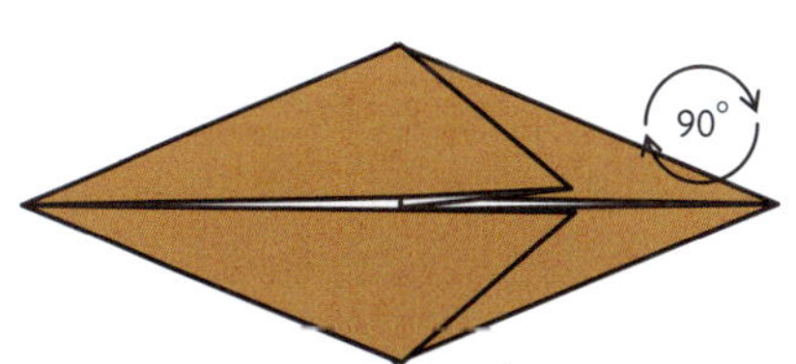

This is known as the fish base.
Rotate 90º.

7

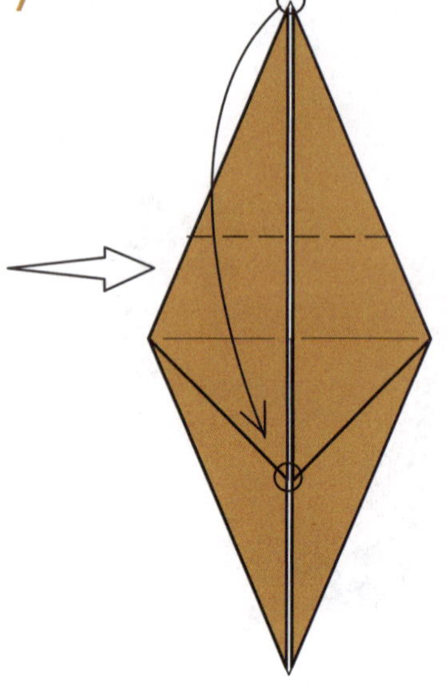

Fold the top down to the tip of the small triangles.

8

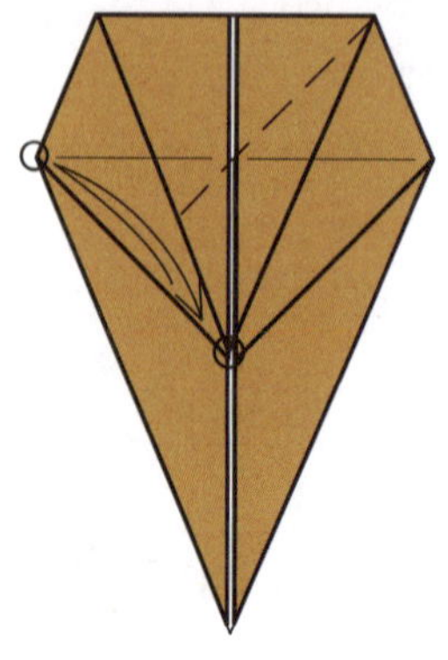

Bring the middle point to the outside corner then unfold.

9

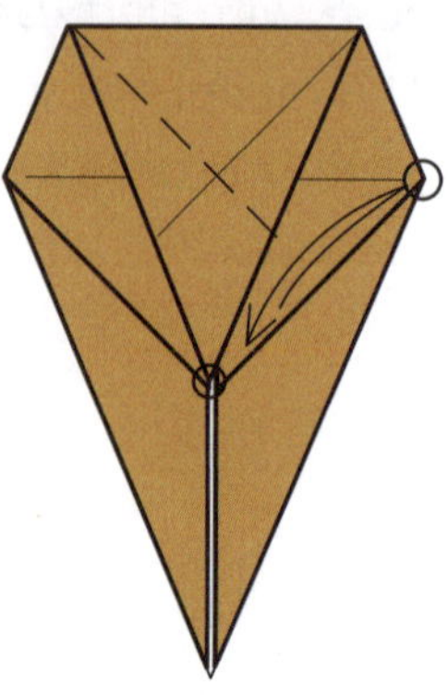

Repeat step 8 in the other direction.

10

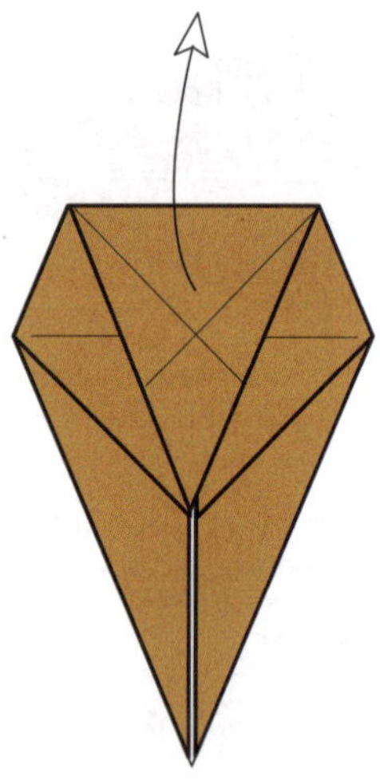

Unfold point to original position.

11

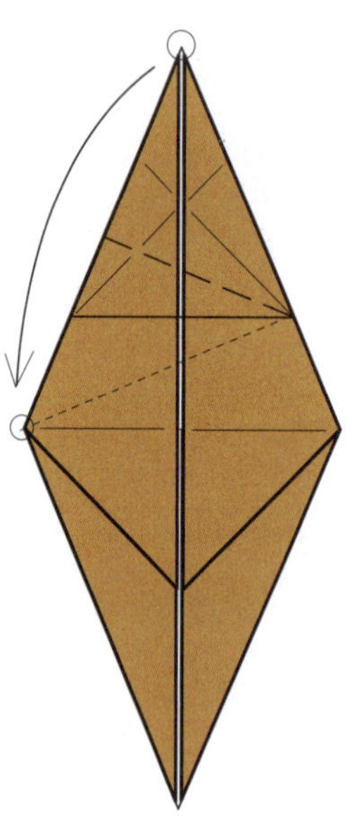

Fold tip down to corner.

12

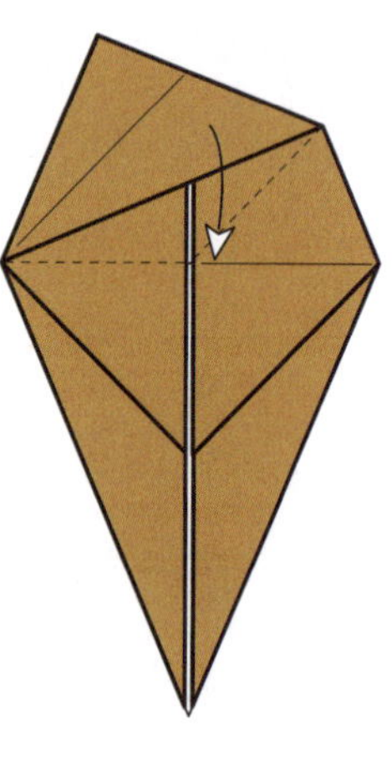

Ease out extra paper.

13

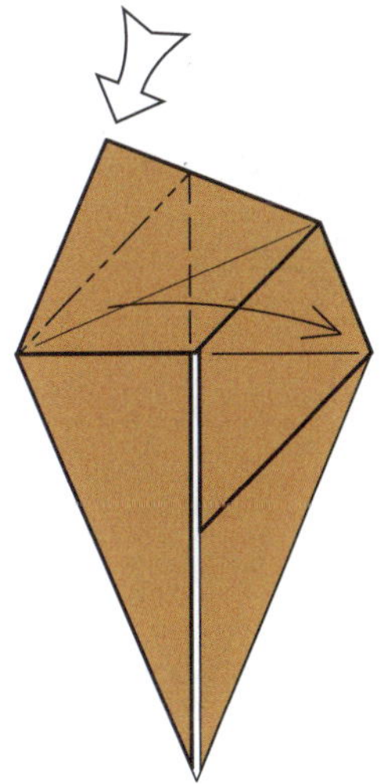

Fold the top layer across, to make a squash fold on the top point.

14

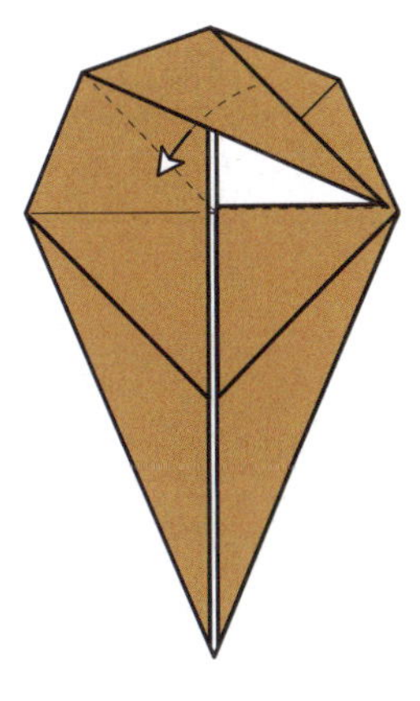

Pull out extra paper.

15

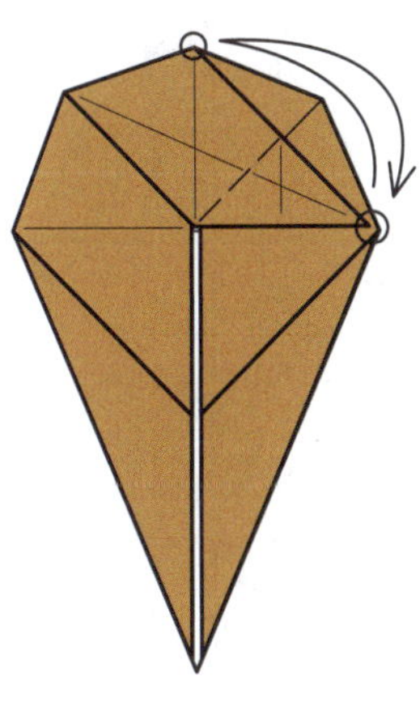

Pre-crease.

16

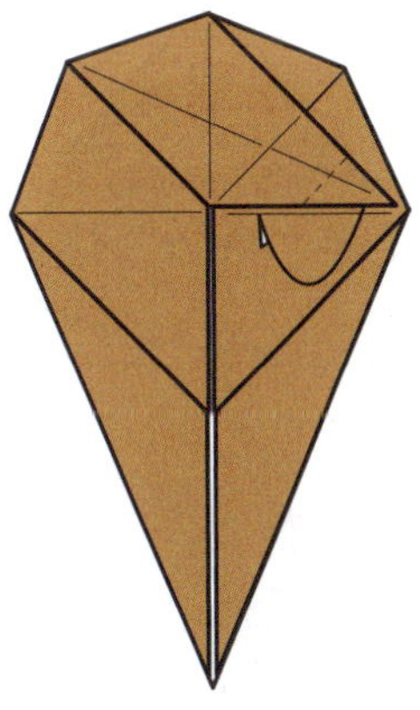

Inside reverse.

17

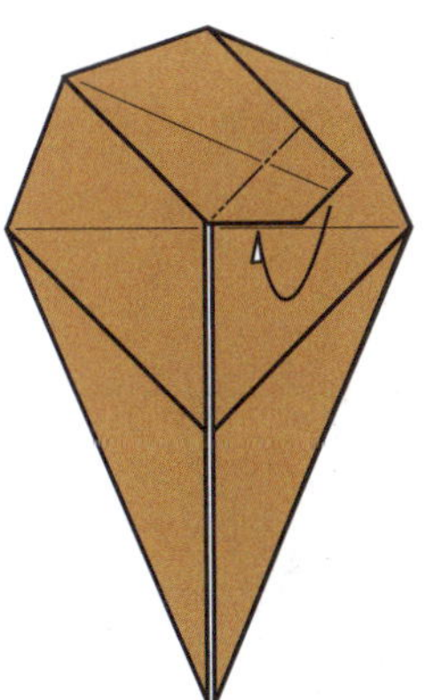

Do another inside reverse fold.

18

Flip back.

19

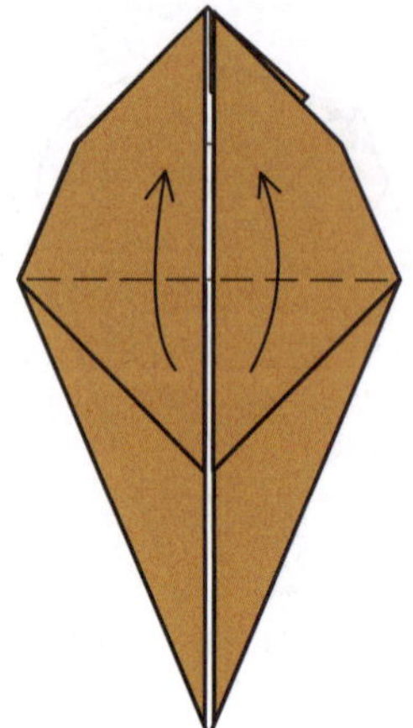

Valley fold small flaps up.

20

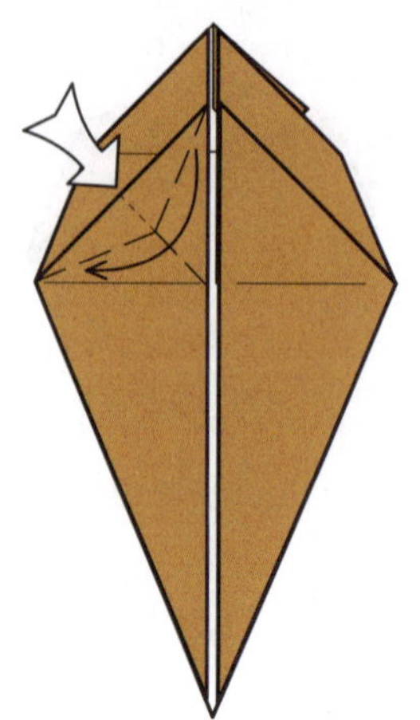

Rabbit ear the top layer.

21

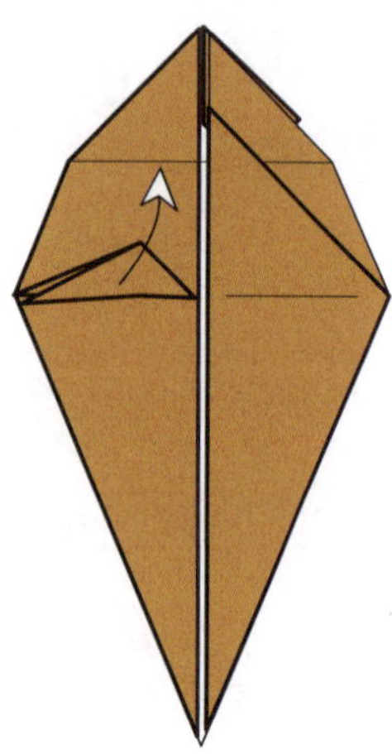

Unfold the rabbit ear.

22

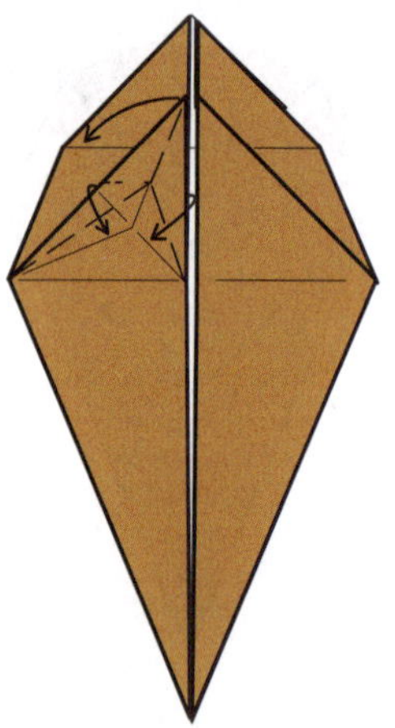

Add a new rabbit ear around the creases of the original. Place the tip near the side corner.

23

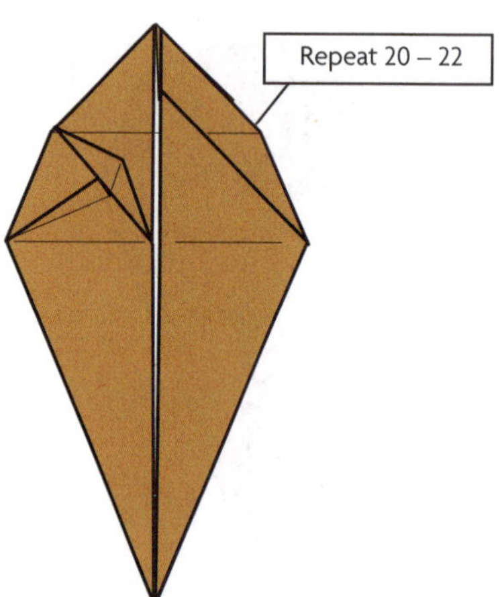

Repeat the folds on the right-hand flap.

24

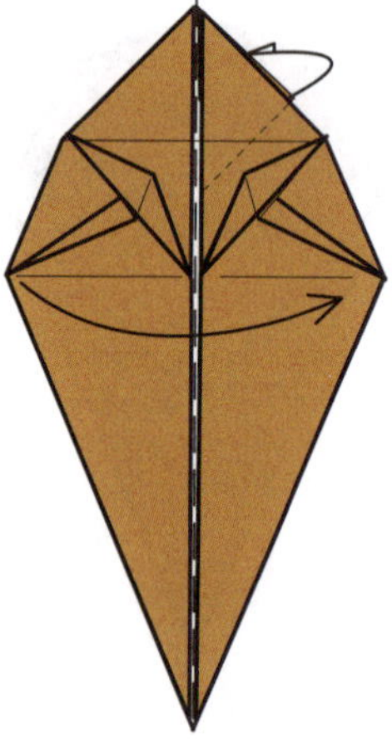

Fold in half. Allow hidden flap on the right to flip behind to the left.

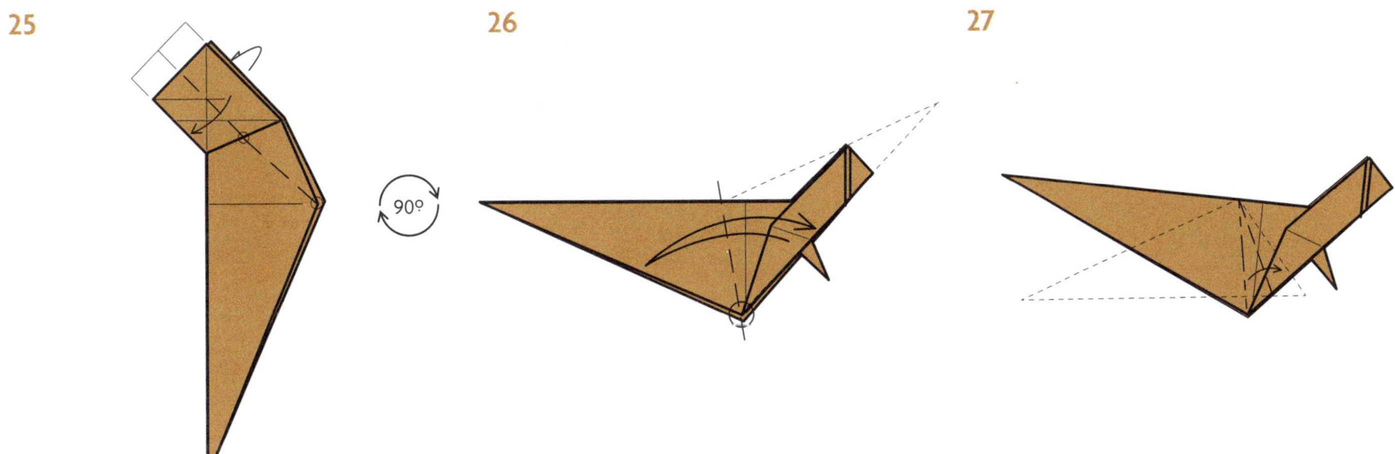

Valley fold in front, mountain fold behind. Rotate to position in next step.

Fold the lower left edge in line with the right. The crease runs through the lower corner.

Crimp back legs and tail section.

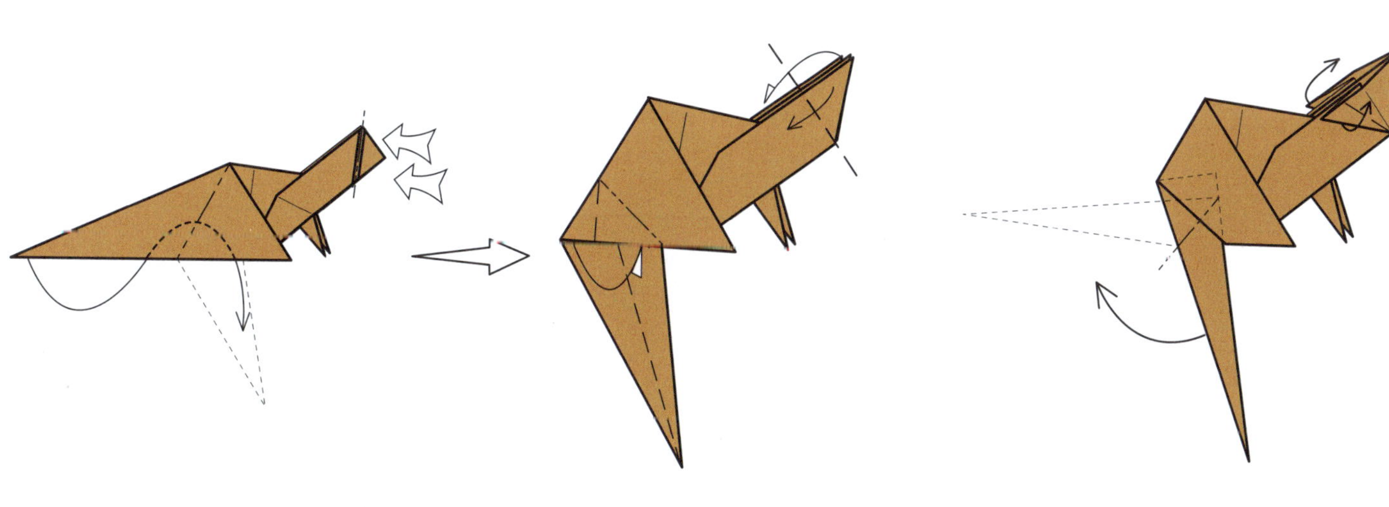

Reverse fold tail. Push in two corners.

Swivel fold tail on both sides. Fold ears back.

Reverse fold tail. Fold ear flaps forward.

31

Crimp head down. Swivel fold tail. Repeat behind.

32

Tuck the back points into the body and close sink the top point. Curl the tail.

33

Completed mouse.

TURTLE

The turtle is a member of the reptile family. Its bony shell gives it shelter from predators, and its webbed feet allow it to swim quickly in water, but still walk on land for nesting. Use a 30cm (12in) or larger sheet for this model, as there are a few layers in the head and tail, and the details require more paper.

The turtle cannot breathe in water, but it can hold its breath for a long time.

1

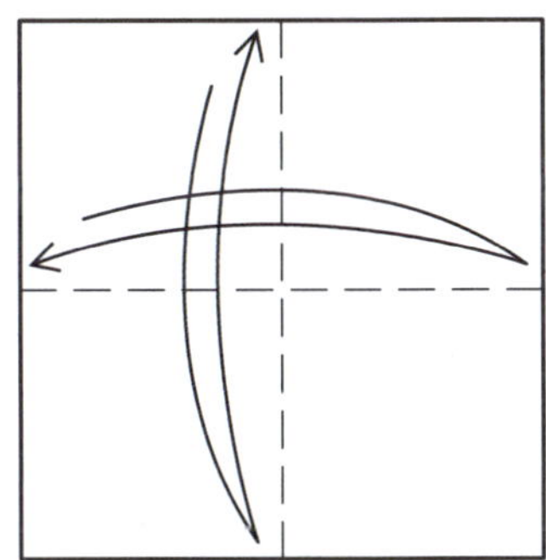

Begin white side up.
Book fold and unfold.

2

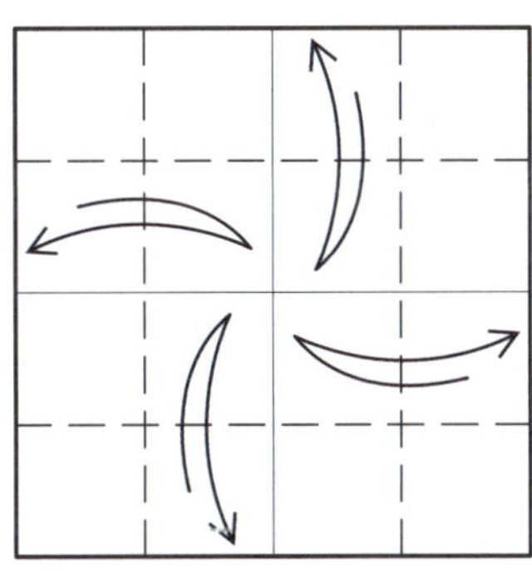

Fold each edge into the centre then unfold.

3

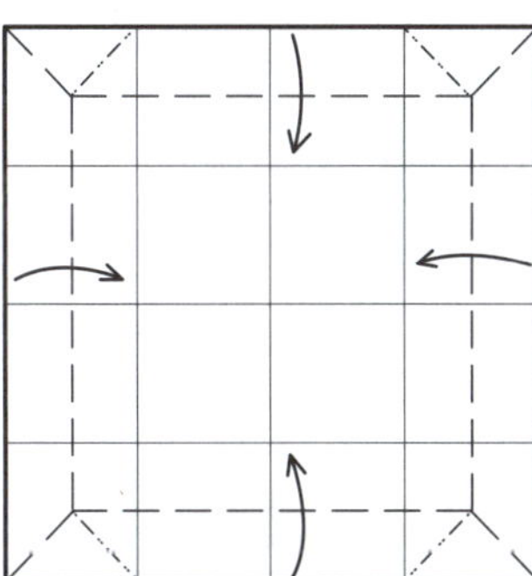

Fold edges in, and rabbit ear corners.

4

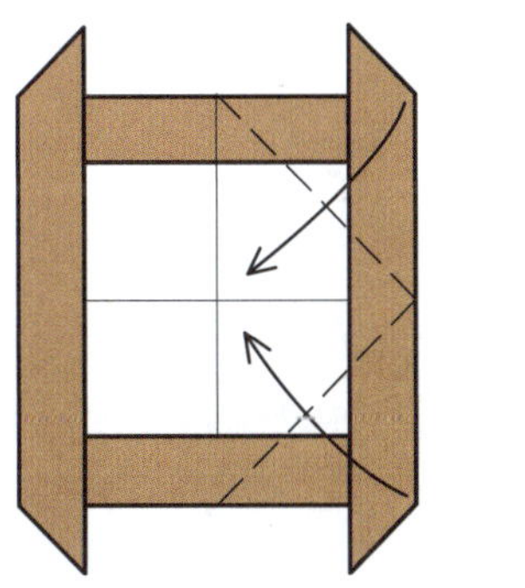

Fold right corners into centre.

5

Completed step 4. Turn over.

6

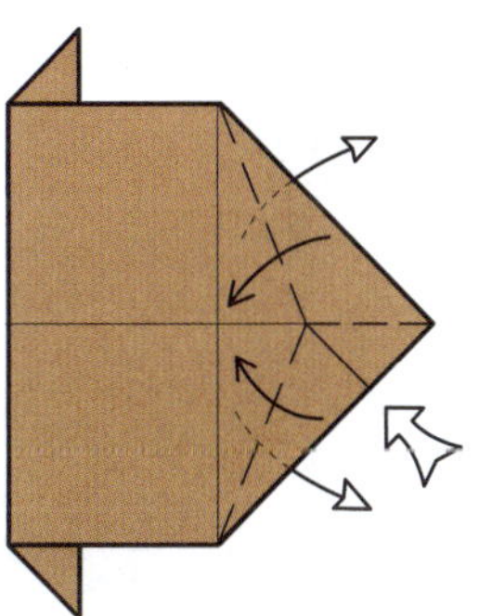

Rabbit ear on right side. Allow layers from behind to flip out.

7

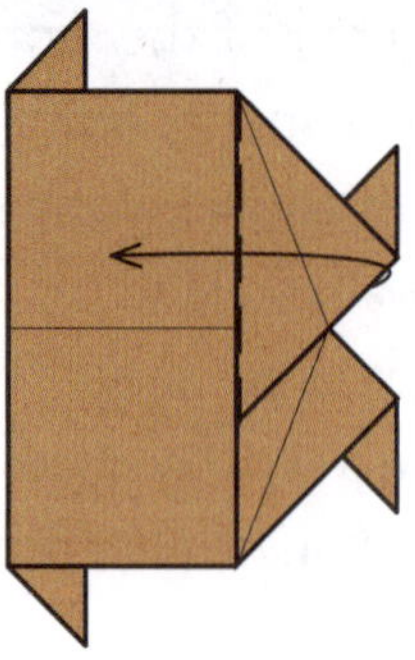

Fold single flap over to the left.

8

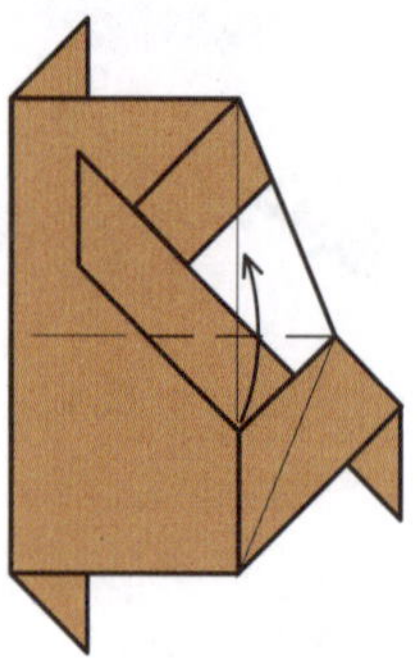

Fold small flap upwards.

9

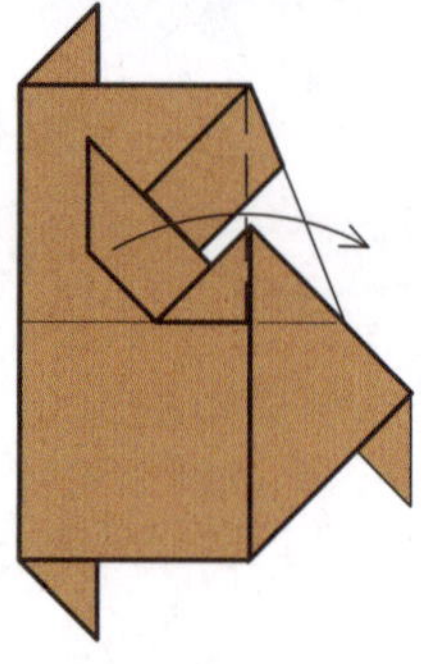

Fold flap over to the right.

10

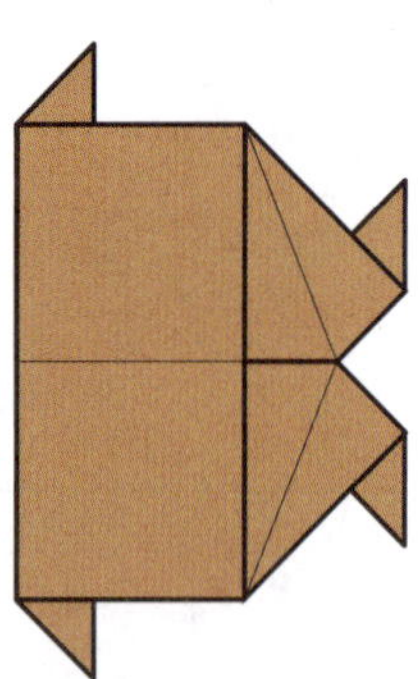

Turn over top to bottom.

11

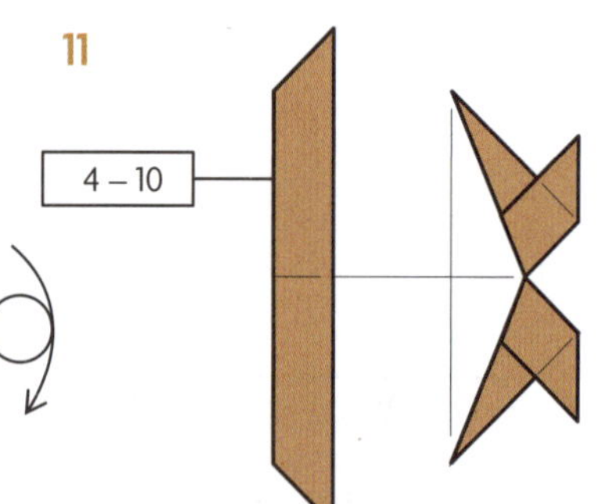

Repeat steps 4–10 on the left half of the model.

12

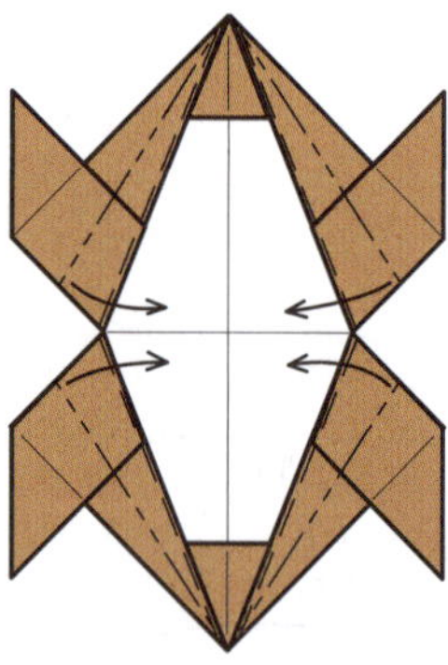

Crimp all four flaps.

13

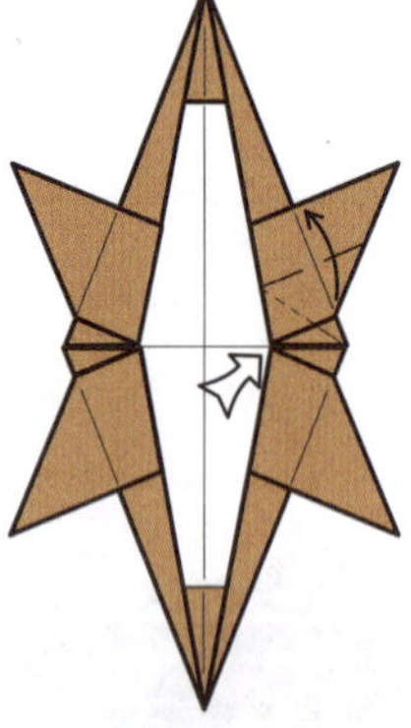

Squash fold.

14

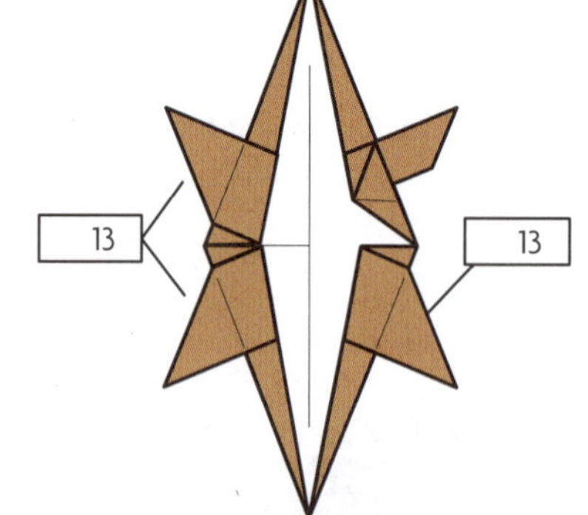

Repeat step 13 on remaining flaps.

15

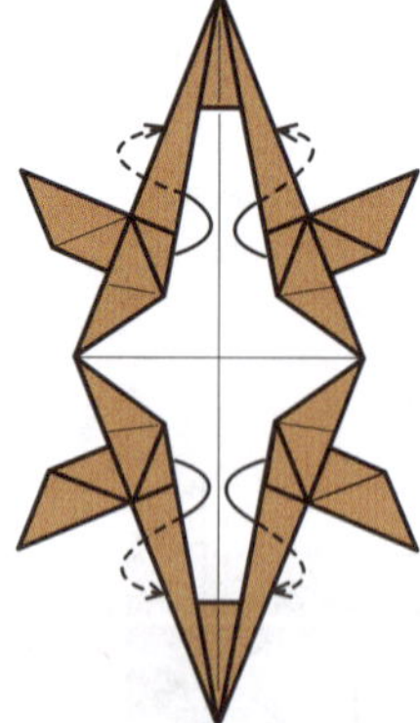

Tuck flaps under the white layer. The top flaps go between the small hidden flap and the white layer.

16

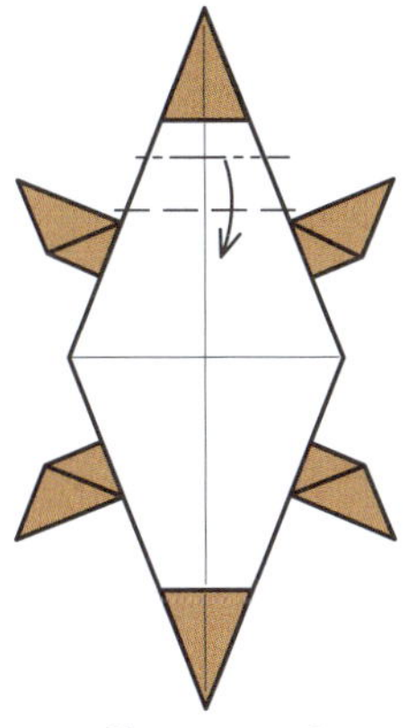

Pleat top point.

17

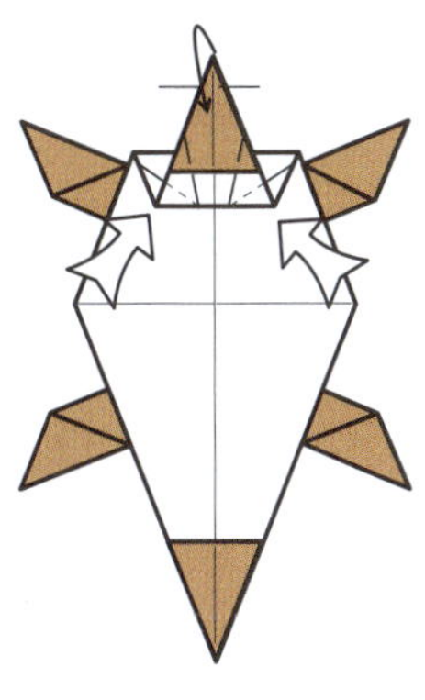

Squash fold corners. Valley fold the top point down.

18

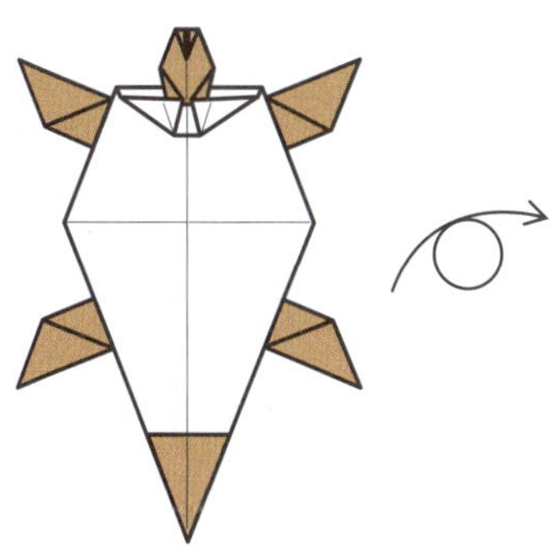

Turn over.

19

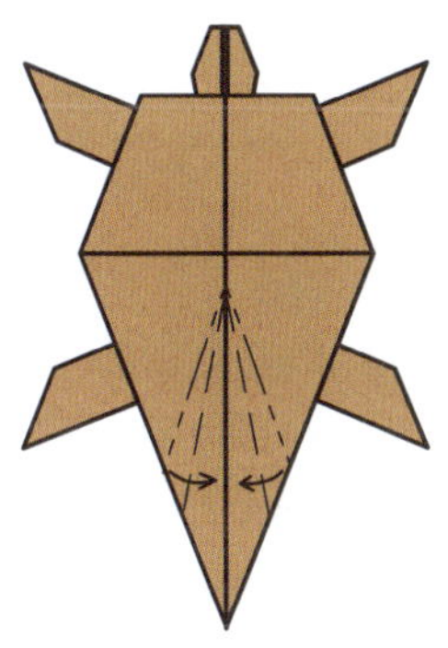

Crimp tail section. Model become 3D.

20

21

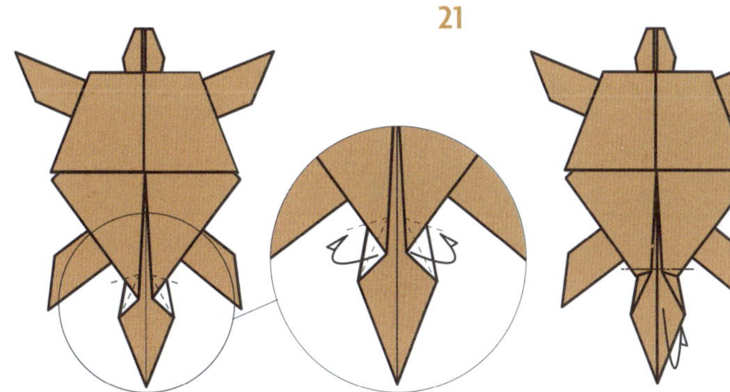

Swivel edges under.

Fold tail under.

22

Completed step 21. Turn over.

23

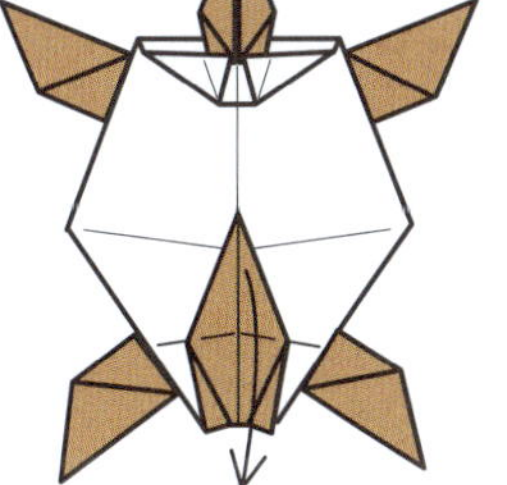

Valley fold tail. Turn over.

24

Completed turtle.

MOVEABLE ORIGAMI PROJECTS

FORTUNE TELLER

MODEL: TRADITIONAL, JAPAN
DIAGRAM: MATTHEW GARDINER

The fortune teller, also known as the "cootie catcher" or "salt cellar," is perhaps the best known origami game in the west. The game, played by children, uses colors and numbers to magically reveal the player's fortune.

The fortune teller is best made from a 12in (30cm) square of white paper.

1

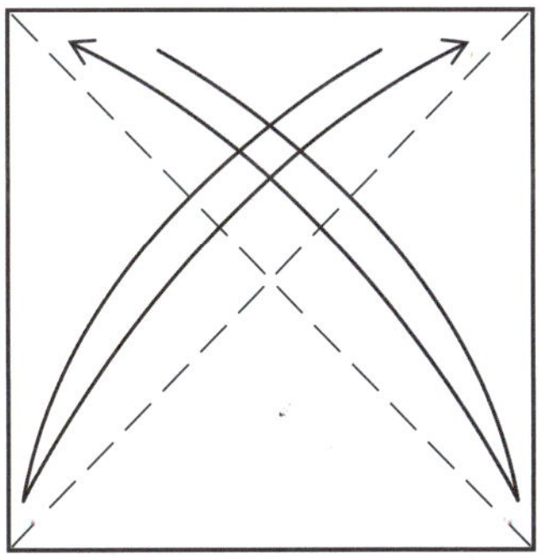

Fold and unfold diagonally.

2

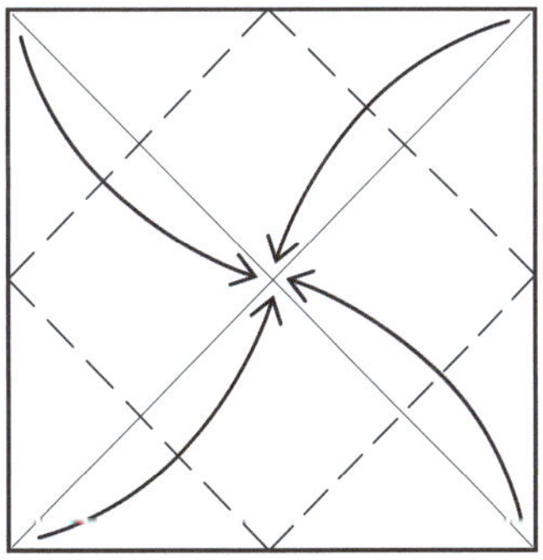

Blintz fold. Turn over.

3

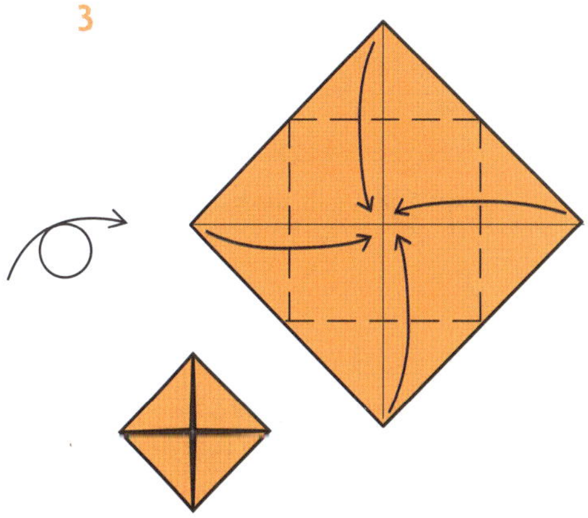

Blintz fold again.

4

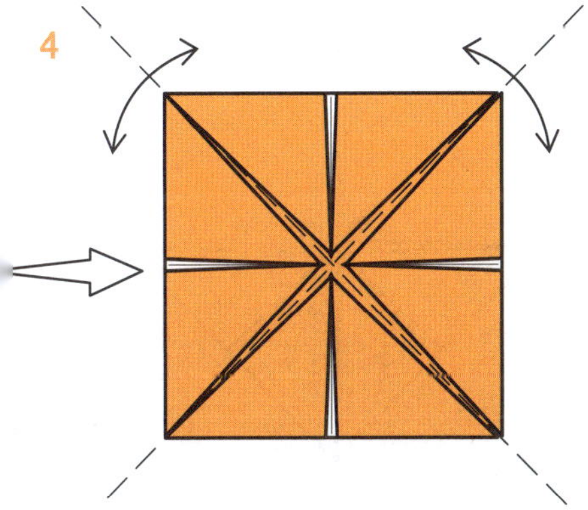

Fold and unfold through all layers to make the 3D opening process easier. Turn over.

5

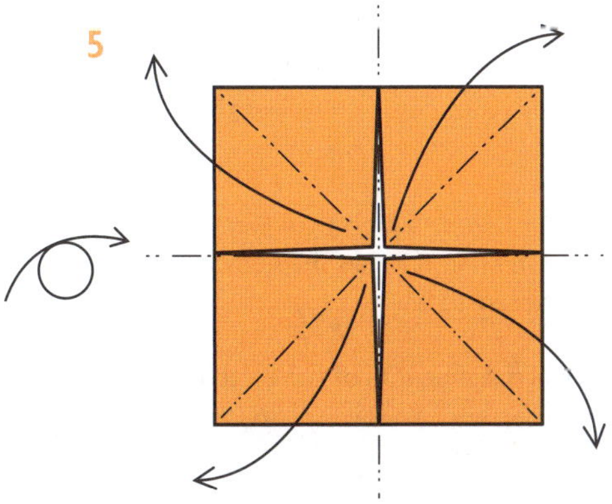

Lift the flaps outward: the fortune teller will become 3D. Turn over.

6

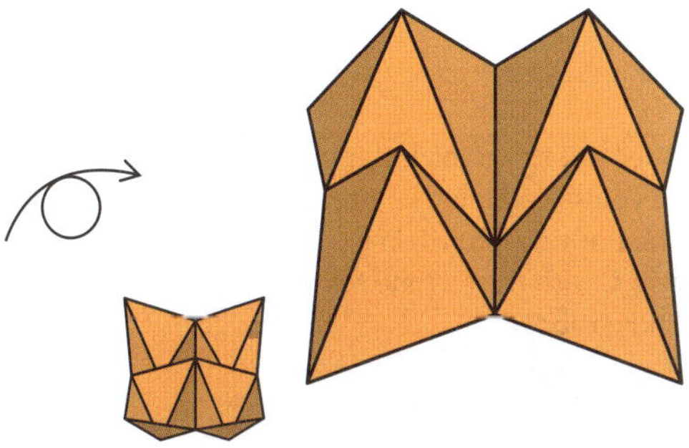

Completed fortune teller.

HOW TO PLAY:

DRAW

Flatten the model to step 5. Decorate your fortune teller with four colors.

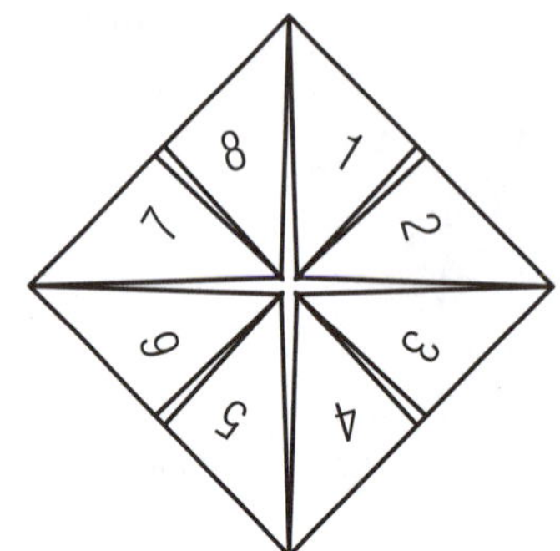

Turn over, and write the numbers from 1 to 8 on each of the triangles.

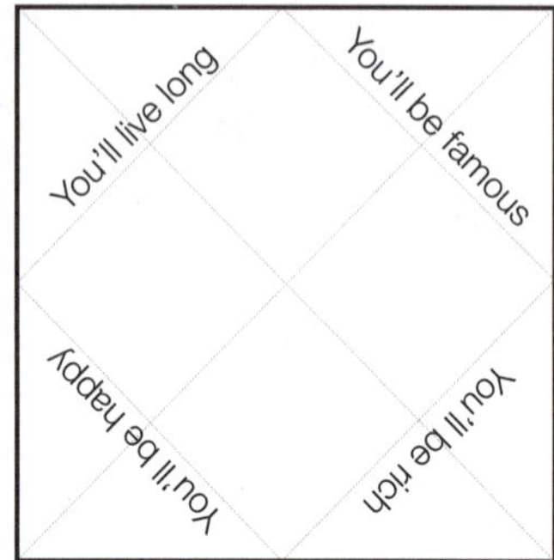

Open up all the points and write in your fortunes. Write one for each number.

MOVE

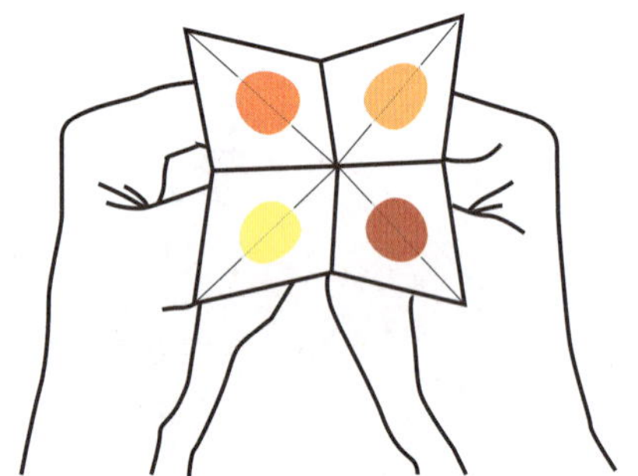

The "start" position. Thumbs and forefingers of both hands are together.

A

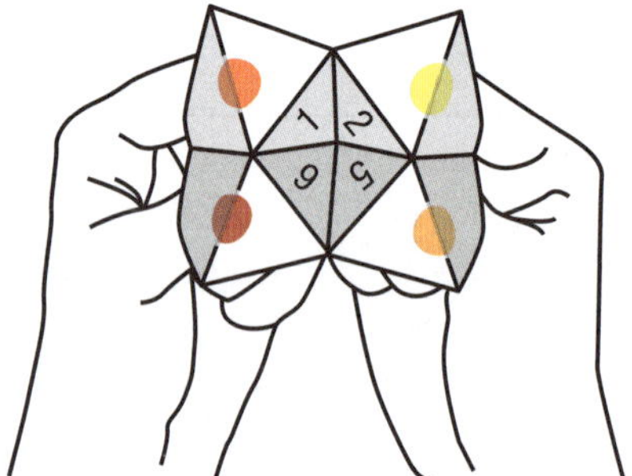

One count/letter. Thumbs and forefingers of each hand are together.

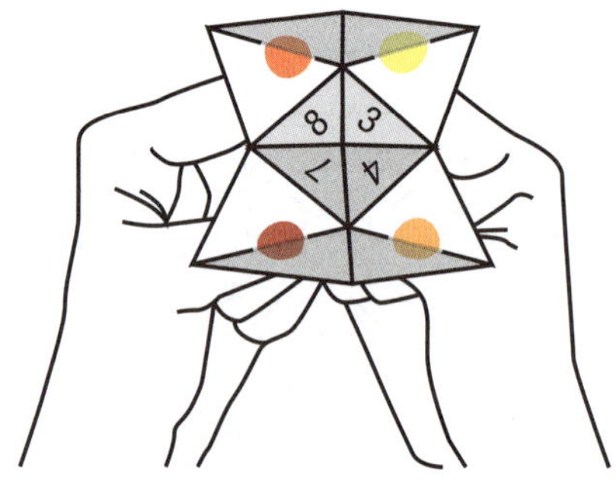

Next count. Both thumbs are together, and both forefingers are together.

PLAY

Begin in the "start" position.

Ask your friend to pick a color.

Spell out the color, letter by letter, and as you say each letter, alternate between the positions shown in B and C with the fortune teller, as shown above.

Ask your friend how many boyfriends/ girlfriends they have, and count the number they say.

Ask your friend to pick a number. Unfold the flap that has the number, and read their fortune.

You can make up lots of fun fortunes.

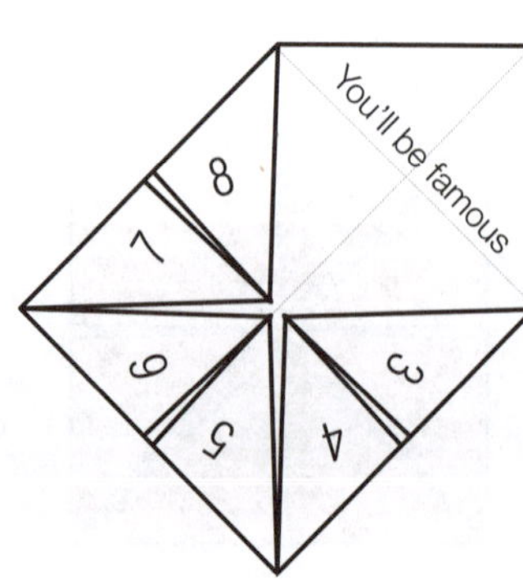

FOX

MODEL: TRADITIONAL, JAPAN
DIAGRAM: MATTHEW GARDINER

The fox is a cunning creature. In Japanese mythology, foxes possess magical abilities and wisdom, and some have the ability to change into human form. This fox is a fun little hand puppet that gives the wearer special fox abilities. Use this puppet with care, and respect the animals of the world.

The Japanese say that a sunshower (rain falling from a clear sky) is the sign of a fox wedding.

1

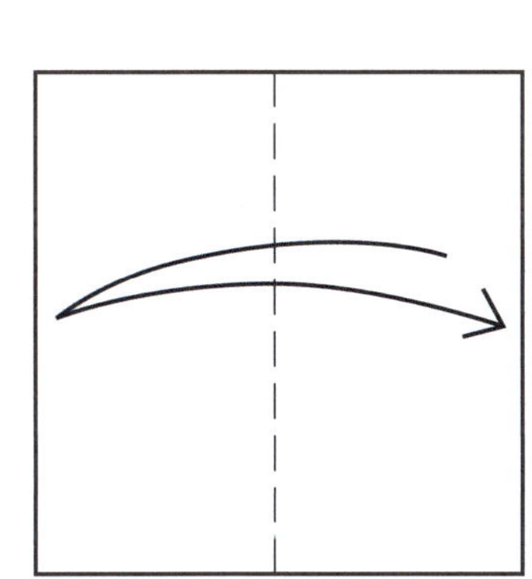

Book fold and unfold.

2

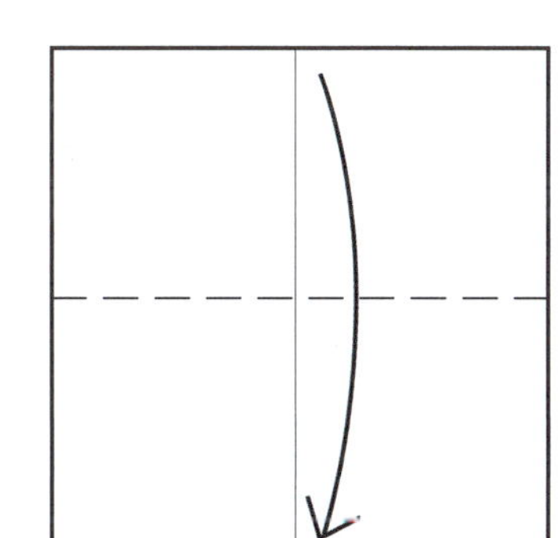

Book fold.

3

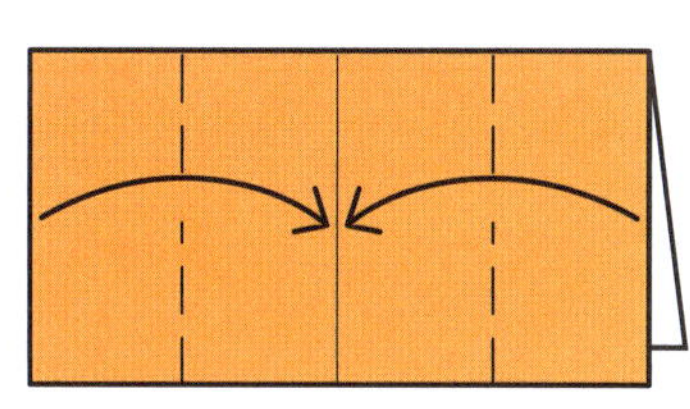

Cupboard fold.

4

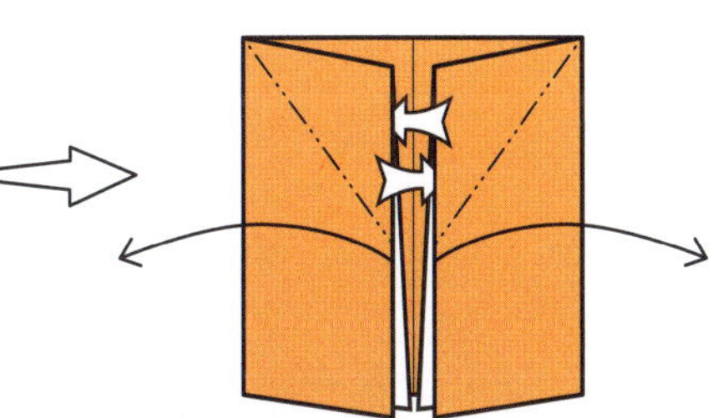

Open up the pocket and squash fold.

5

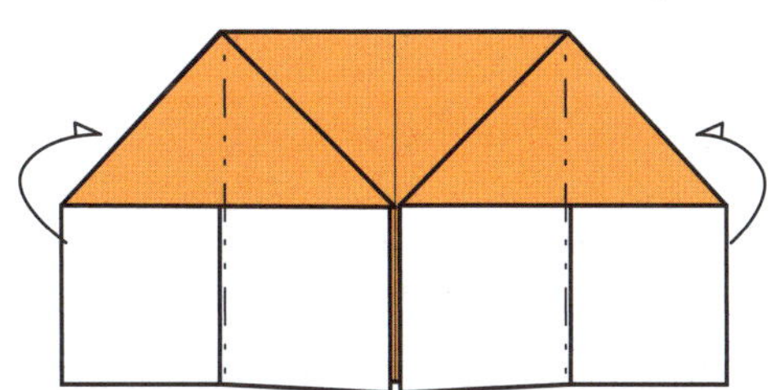

Mountain fold sides.

6

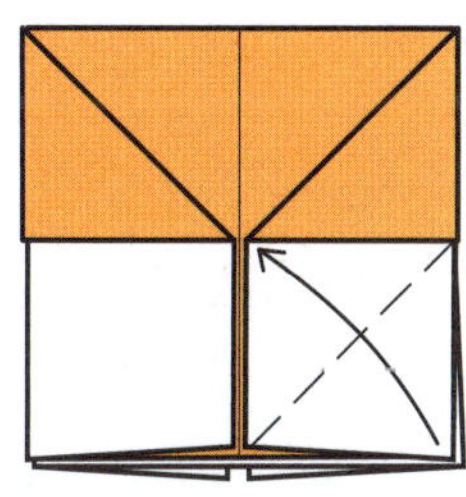

Fold up corner of top layer.

7

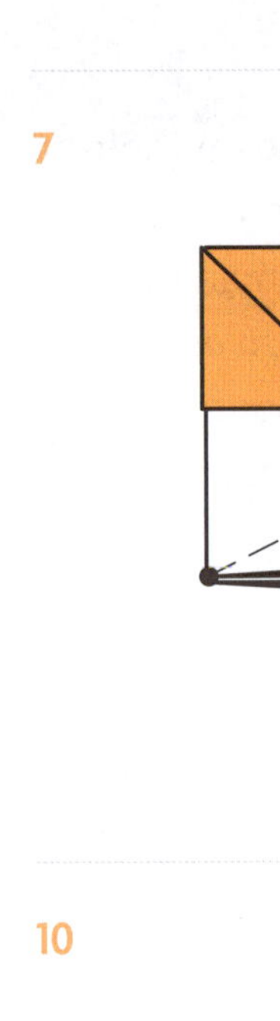

Fold up.

8

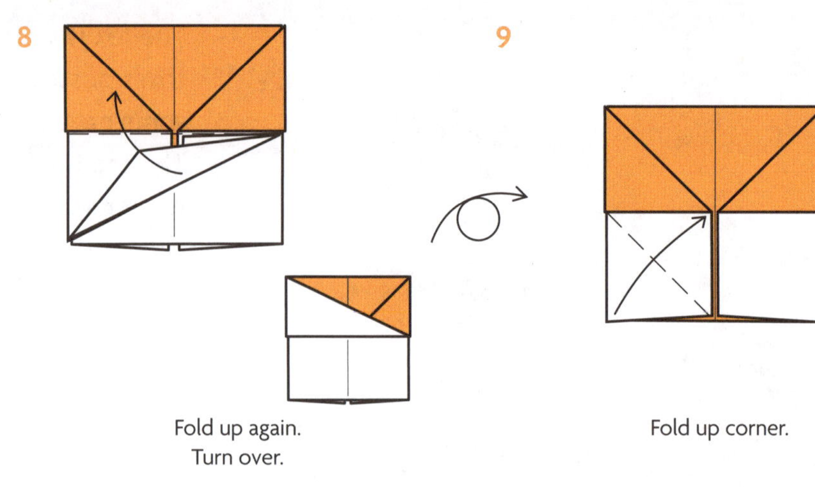

Fold up again.
Turn over.

9

Fold up corner.

10

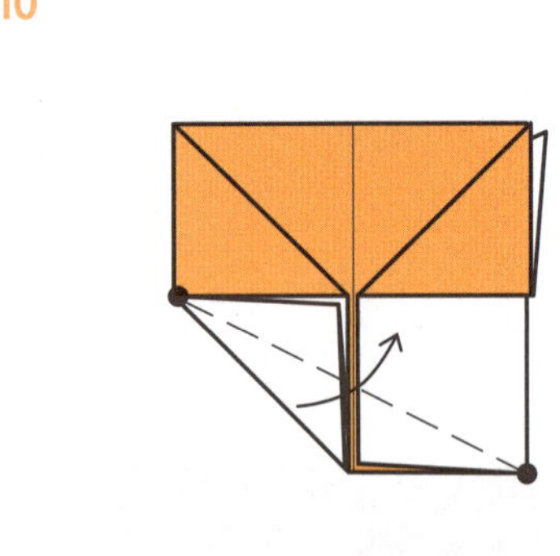

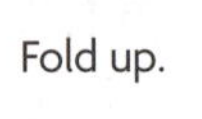

Fold up.

11

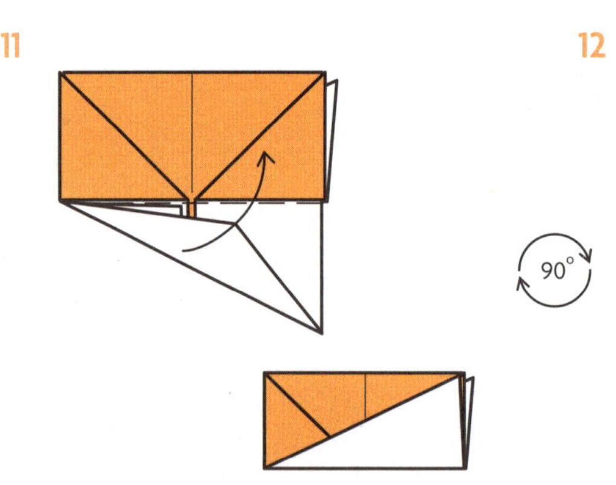

Fold up again.

12

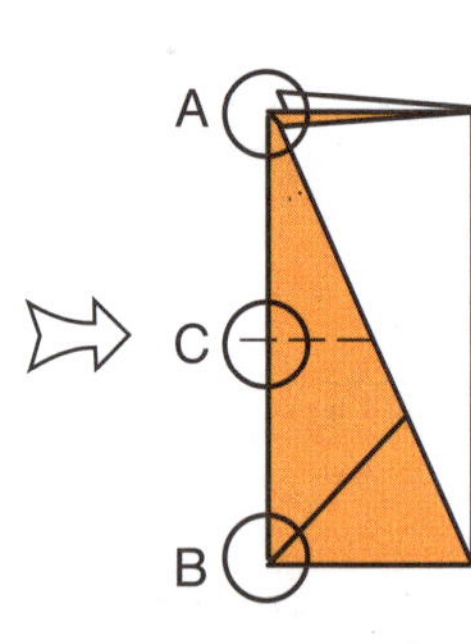

Push point C further in so point A and B touch.

13

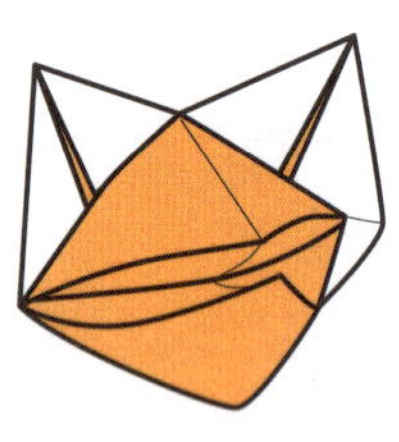

Completed fox.

14

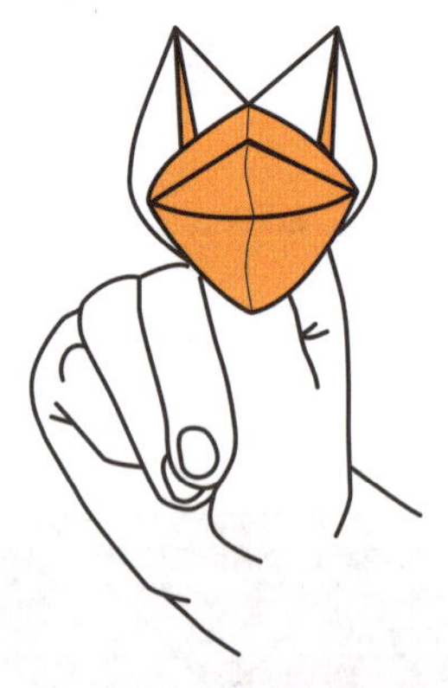

Insert your hand in the back and use as a puppet.

JUMPING FROG

MODEL: TRADITIONAL, JAPAN
DIAGRAM: MATTHEW GARDINER

The jumping frog is a paper racing game waiting to happen. All you need are a few friends, some jumping frogs and the game is on! High performance frogs can be made from card. Business cards make small dynamic frogs, but index cards are a more foldable size.

At the 2007 Australian Origami Convention, special guest Michael LaFosse used a secret racing frog design to win the Melbourne Paper Cup.

1

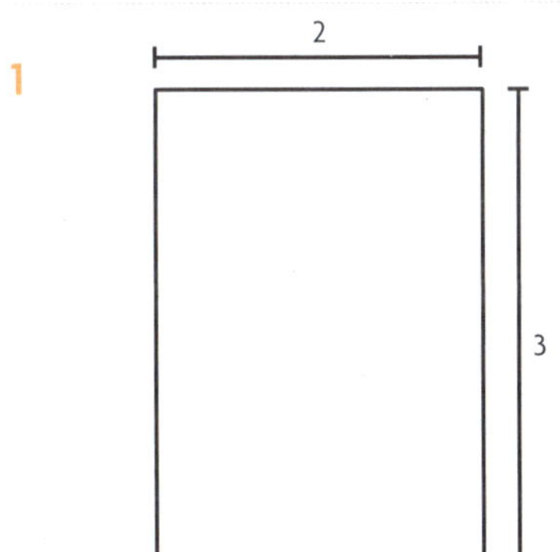

Choose a rectangle piece of paper with a ratio of 2:3. Index cards are a good size.

2

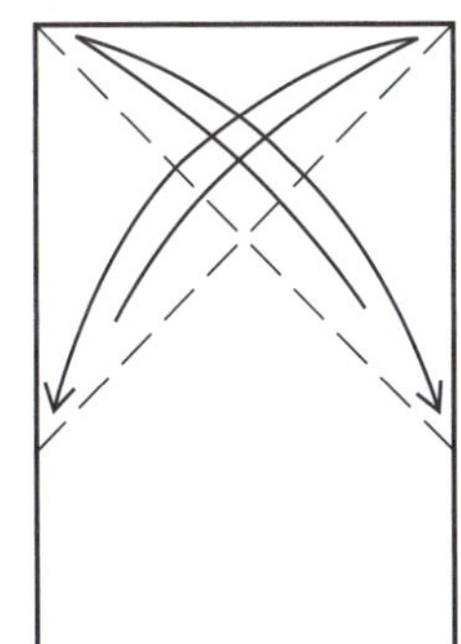

Begin white side up. Fold and unfold diagonally so that the top edge lines up with the side edge. Turn over.

3

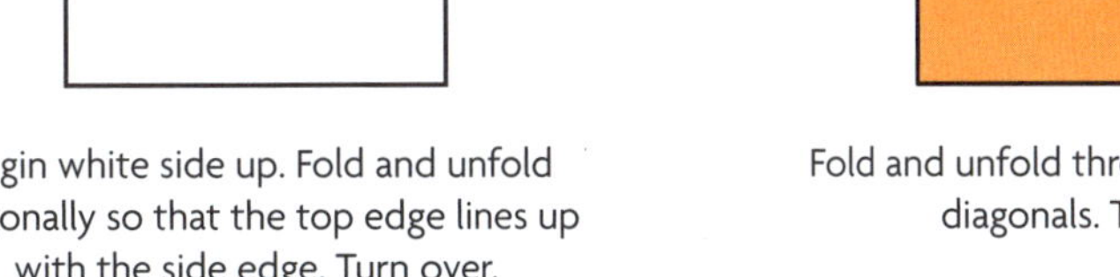

Fold and unfold through the crossing diagonals. Turn over.

4

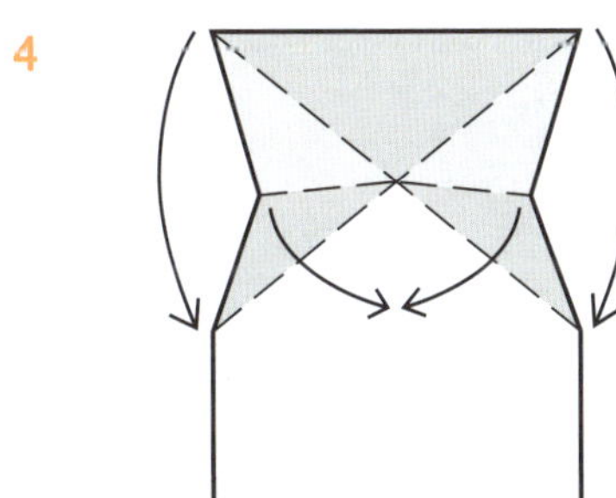

Fold top corners down. Fold midpoints inward.

5

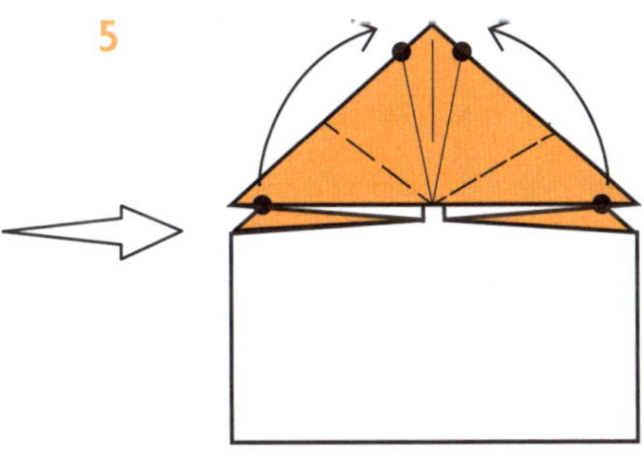

The top triangular shape is called a water bomb base. Fold up the top two corners just short of the center line, so they point out a little.

6

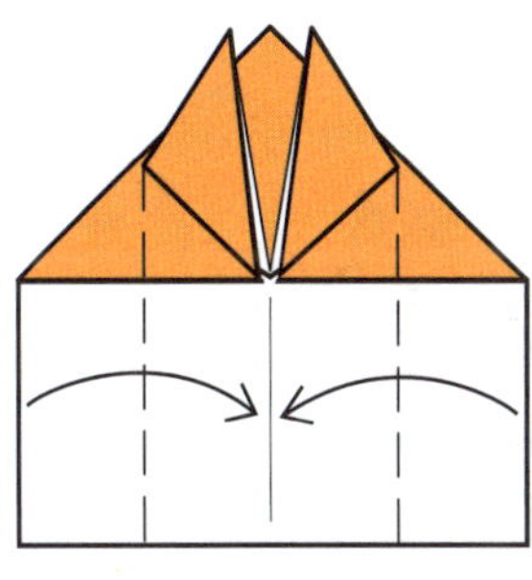

Cupboard fold.

7

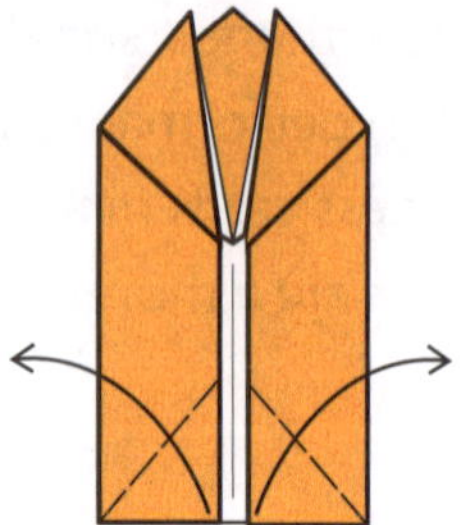

Fold out rear legs.

8

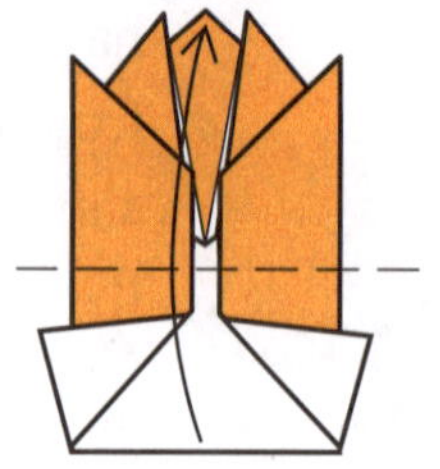

Fold in half, bringing the bottom to the top.

9

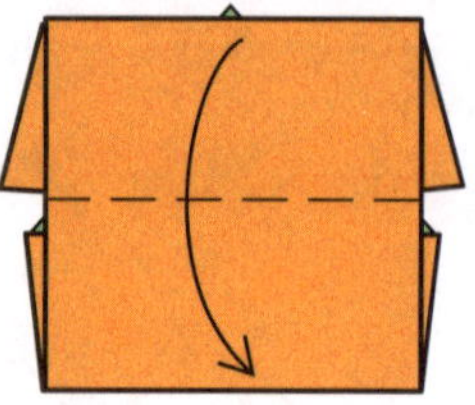

Fold the top layer in half, bringing the top to the bottom.

10

Turn the model over.
Completed jumping frog.

11

To make the frog jump gently press and release at the point marked.

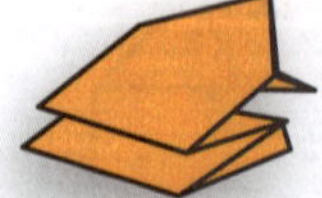

WALKING CRAB

MODEL: SHOKO AOYAGI
DIAGRAM: SHOKO AOYAGI

The walking crab is a fun design that walks sideways when you tap it. Shoko is well known for her fun origami style—she likes to use stick-on eyes to add character to her origami creations. You cut out circles of white and black paper and glue them together, or use pre-cut circles that are available at office suppliers.

The walking crab is a contemporary Japanese design.

1

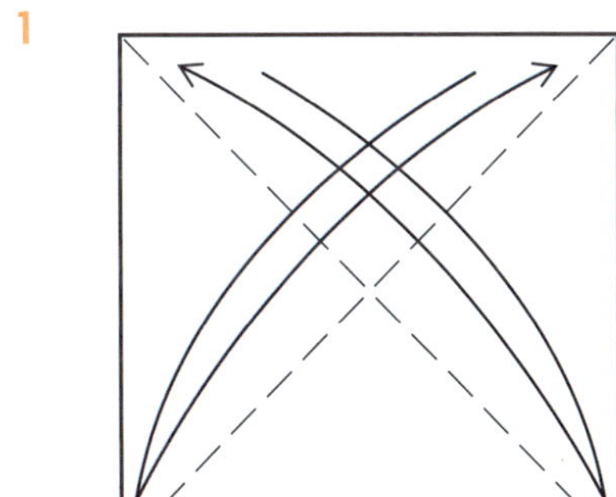

Fold and unfold diagonals.
Turn over.

2

Blintz fold.

3

Completed step 2. Turn over.

4

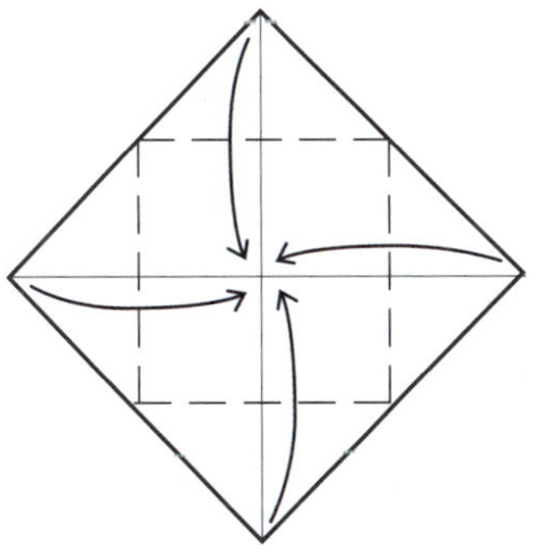

Blintz fold again.

5

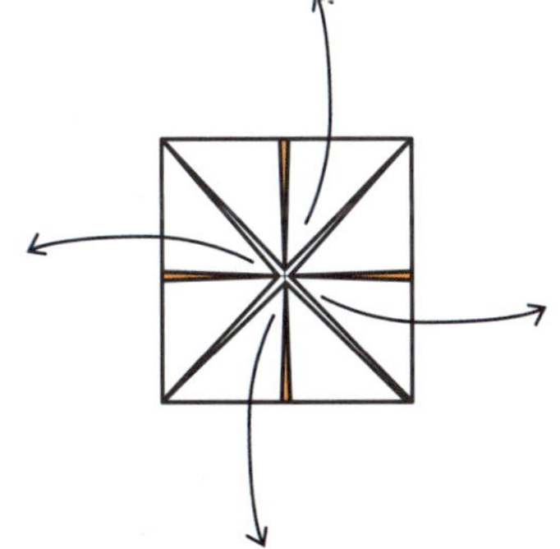

Completely unfold the paper.

6

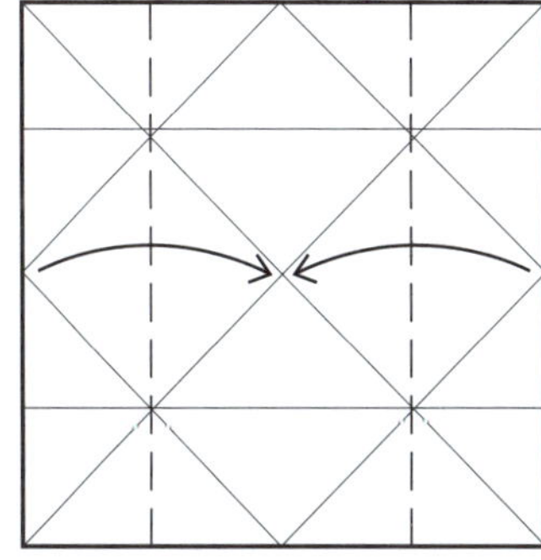

Then fold sides to center.

7

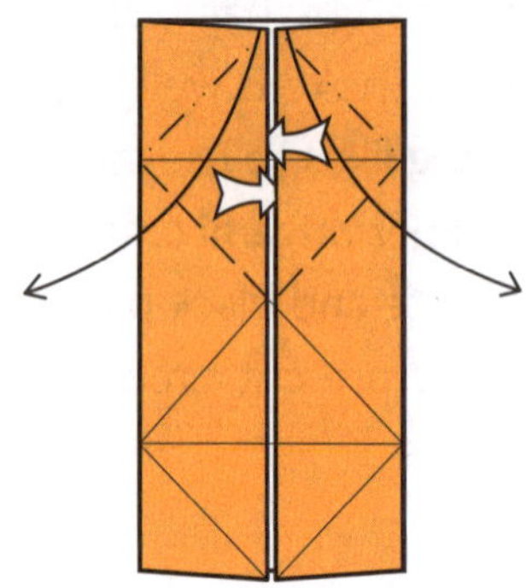

Bring both corners forward and squash fold.

8

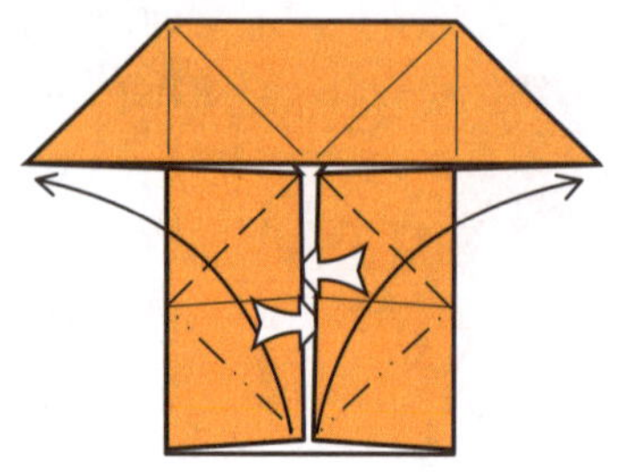

Repeat step 7 on other end.

9

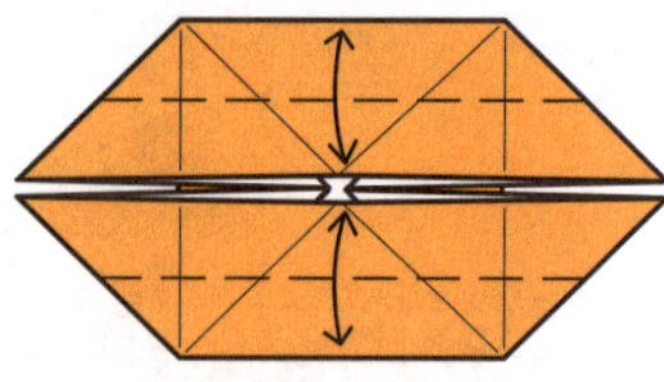

Fold and unfold top and bottom edge to the center.

10

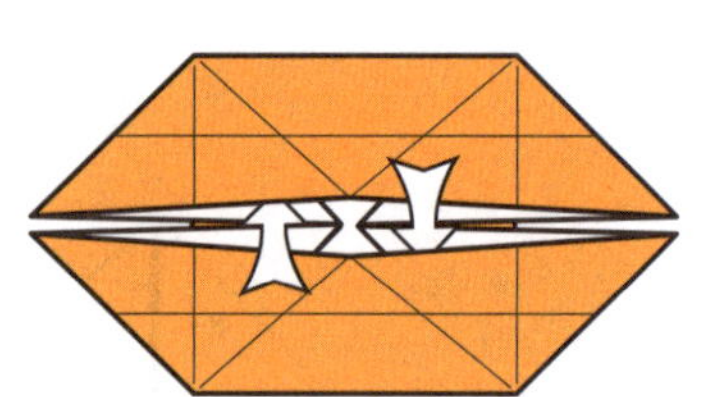

Open up pockets.

11

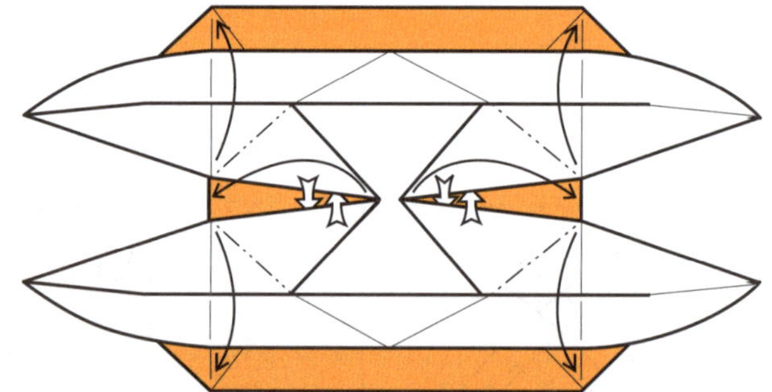

This shows the pockets open. Lift up inside corners, and fold the edges outward.

12

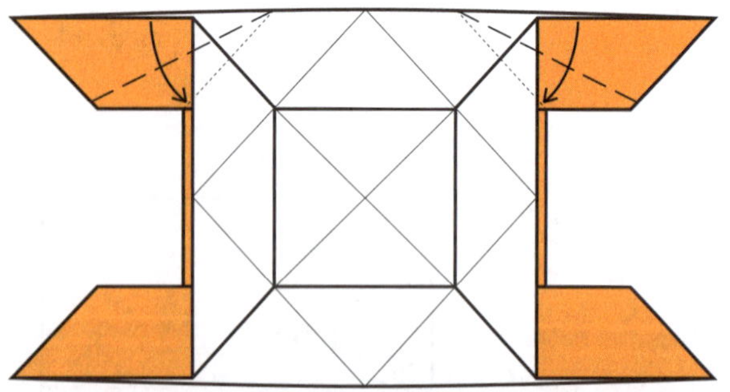

Fold edge to corner.

13

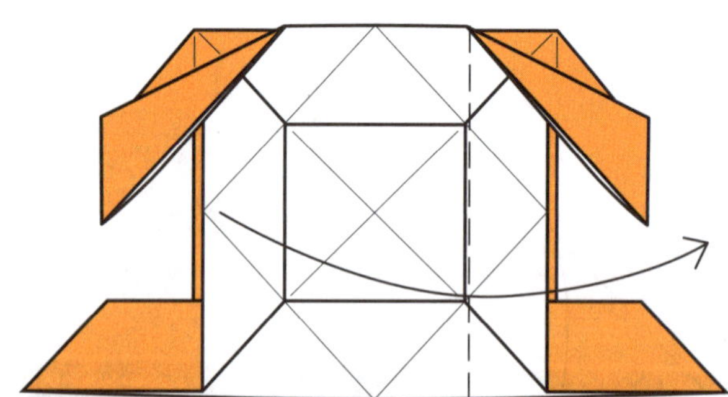

Fold over.

14

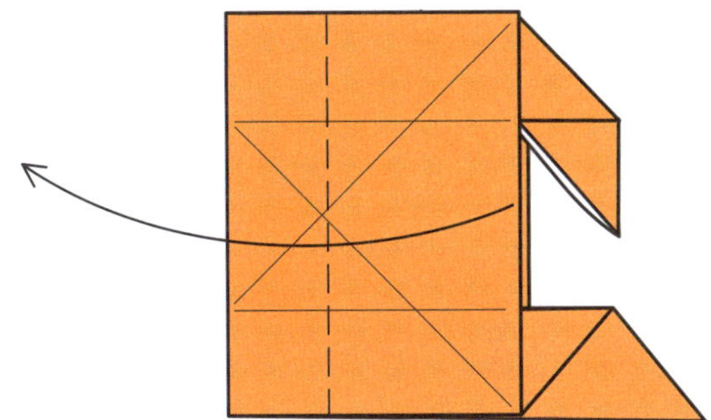

Fold over.

15

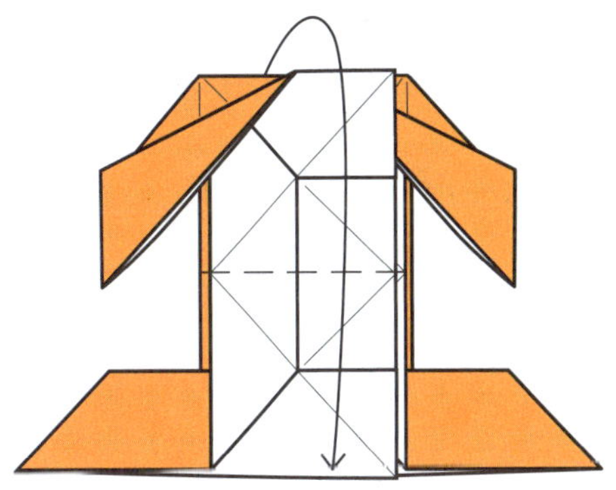

Fold in half through all layers.

16

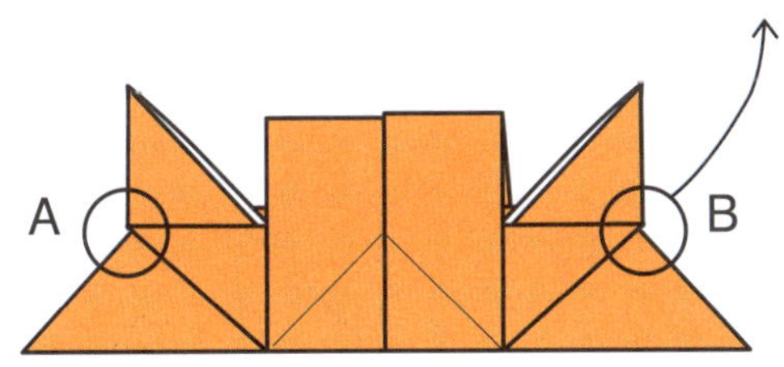

Hold "A" with one hand. Pull "B" upward.

17

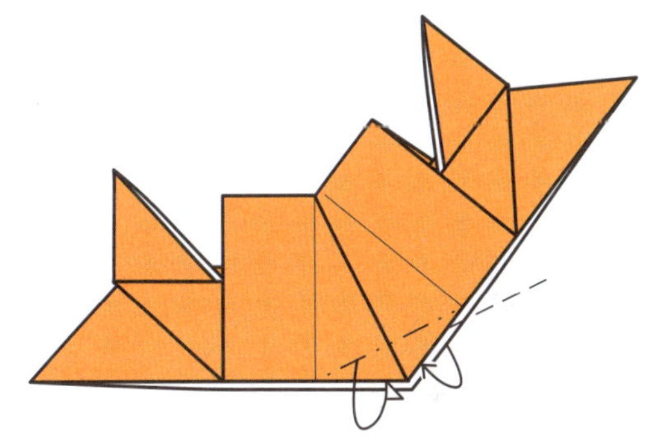

Fold inside the base of the front flap as shown. Repeat on the other side.

18

Completed walking crab.

19

When you tap the C, the crab will walk sideways. Attach the round stickers for eyes and draw eyeballs.

FLAPPING BIRD

MODEL: TRADITIONAL, JAPAN
DIAGRAM: MATTHEW GARDINER

The flapping bird is a variation of the paper crane. This variation has a beautiful mechanism that pulls the paper of the wings, causing them to flap. There are a few varieties of flapping birds—this one is the original and a classic.

The smallest flapping bird in the world was folded by Akira Naito in Japan. His smallest ever model so far is a paper crane folded from a 0.0039in (0.1mm) square, using plastic film instead of paper, a microscope and special handmade micro origami tools.

1

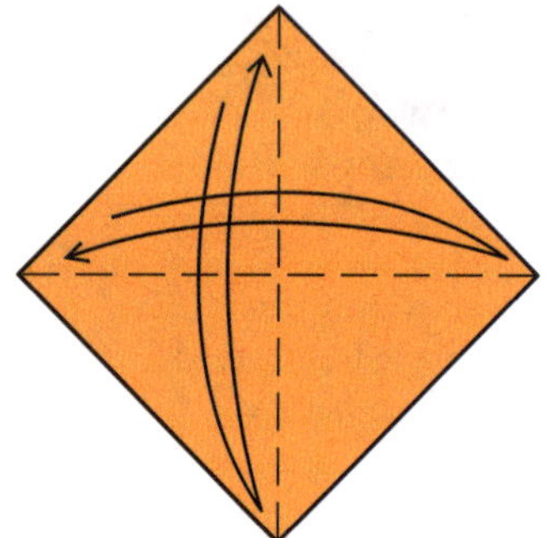

Start colored side up.
Fold and unfold diagonals. Turn over.

2

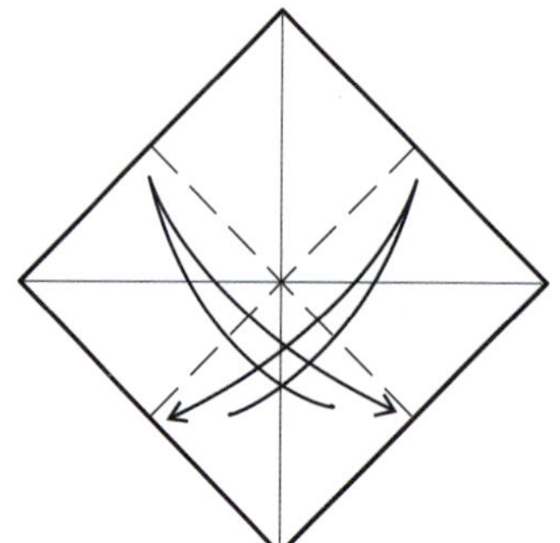

Book fold and unfold.

3

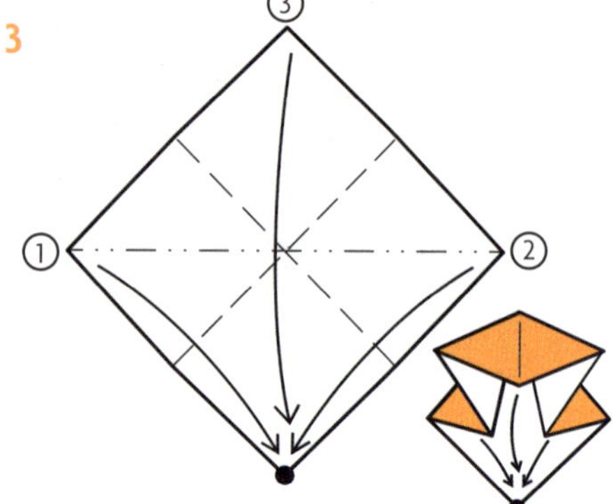

Bring three corners down to meet bottom corner. Start with corners 1 and 2 together followed by corner 3.

4

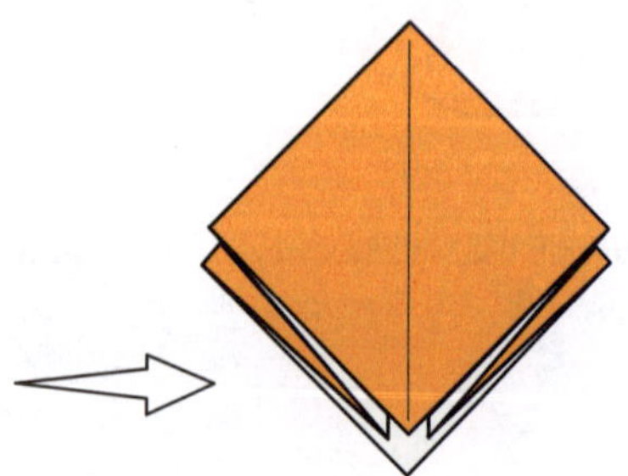

Completed preliminary base.

5

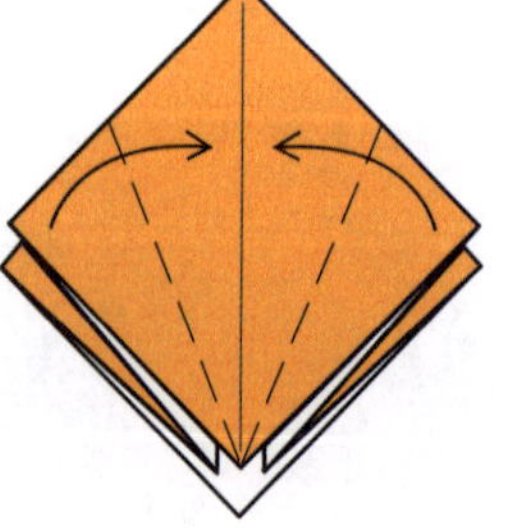

Fold top layer to the center crease.

6

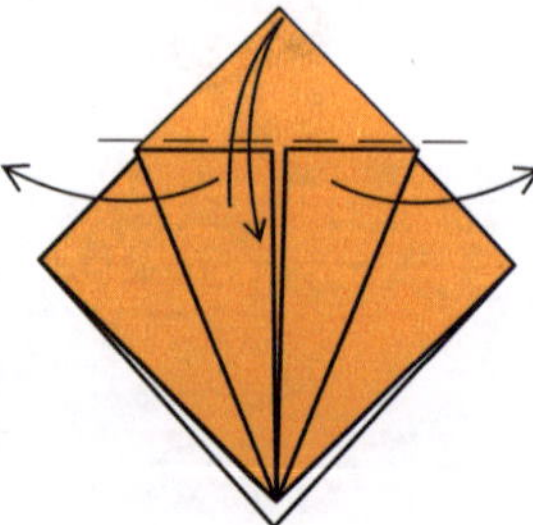

Fold the top triangle down and unfold.
Unfold flaps.

7

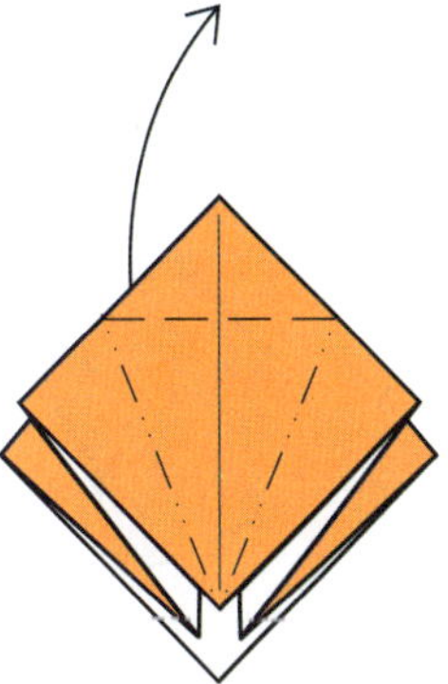

Lift the top layer upward.

8

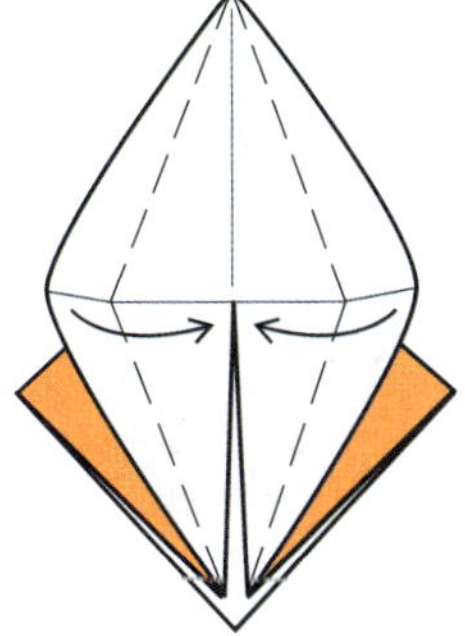

Step 7 in progress, the model is 3D. Fold the top layer inward on existing creases.

9

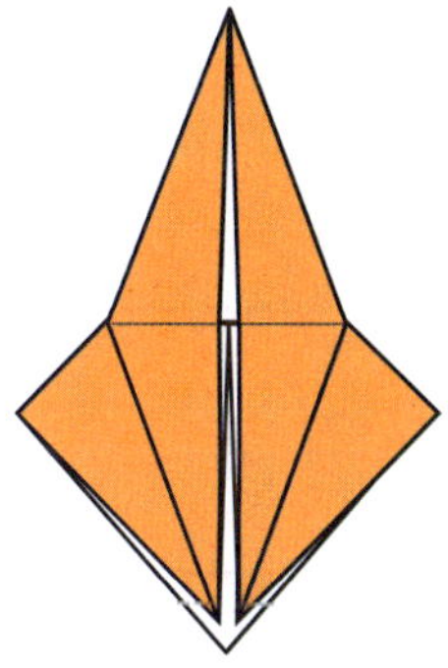

Step 7 completed, the model will be flat. Turn over.

10

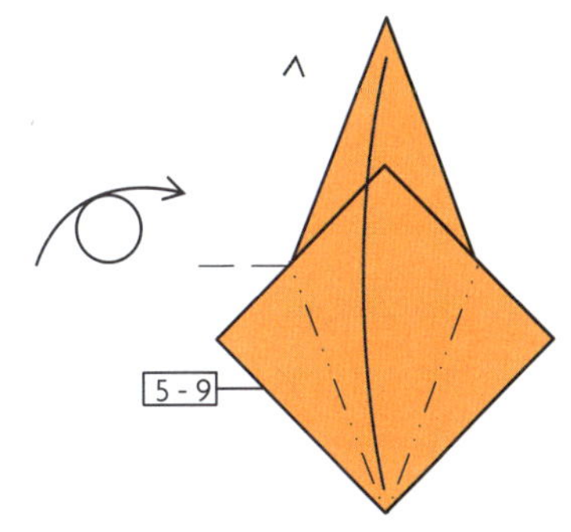

Repeat steps 5-9 on this side.

11

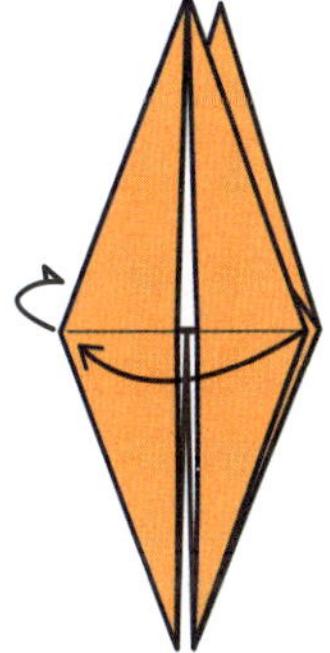

Turn front and back flap over.

12

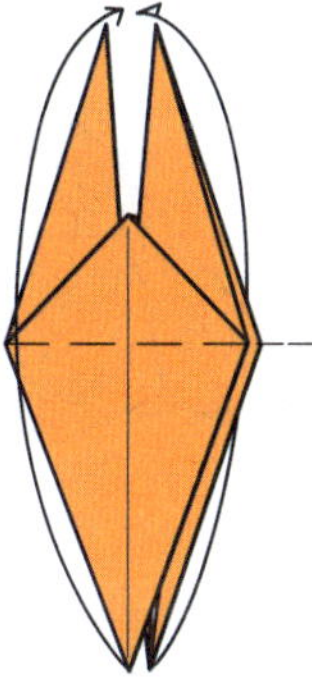

Fold flaps up.

13

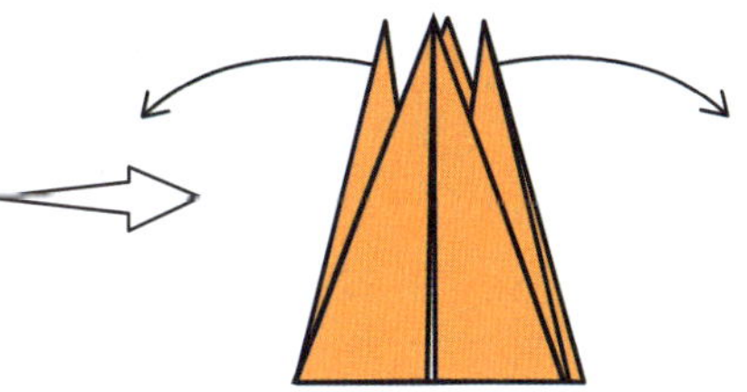

Swivel the two points outward. These form the head and tail.

14

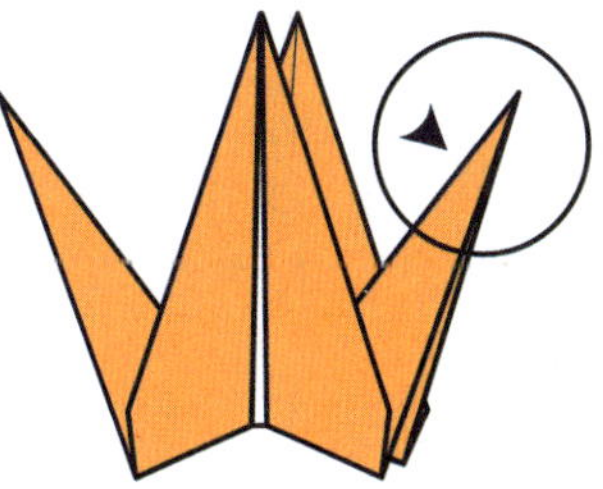

The next steps show details of forming the head.

15

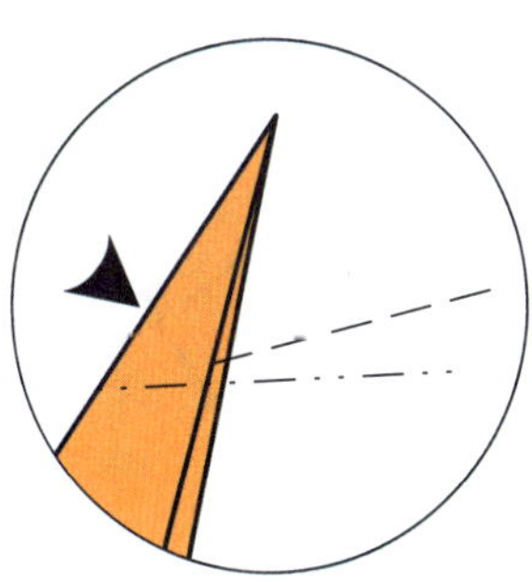

Reverse fold.

16

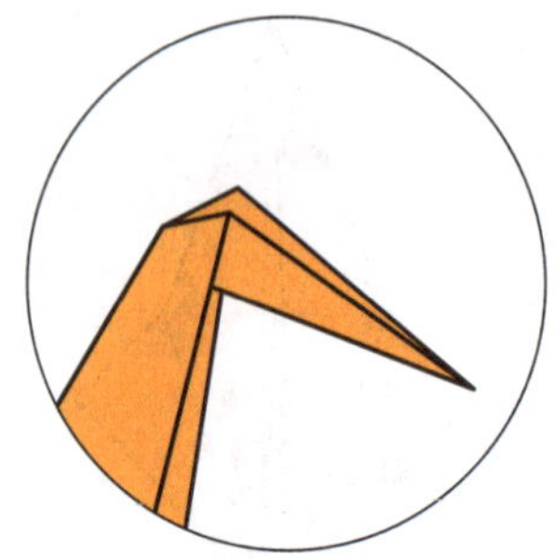

Step 15 completed.

17

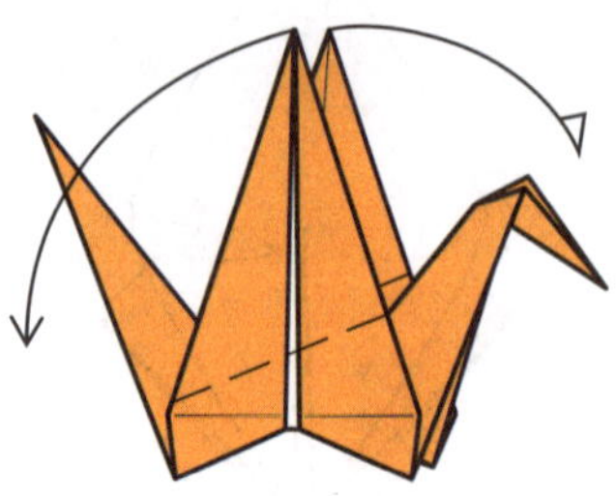

Fold down wings. Make soft folds.

18

Completed flapping bird.

19

To make the bird flap hold the model at the black dots. Gently pull on the tail and the wings will flap down. Gently release and the wings will go back up. Repeat.

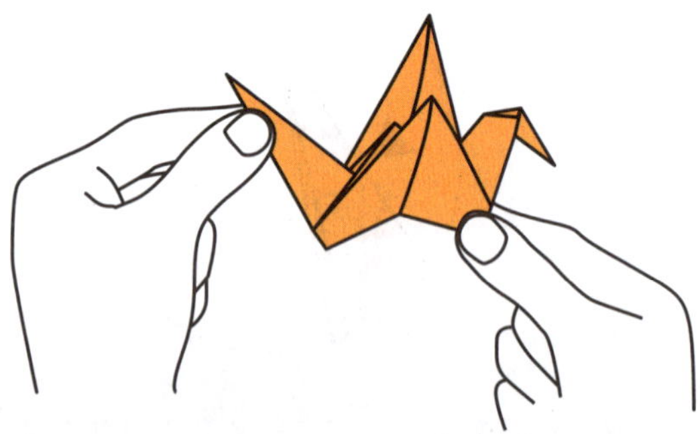

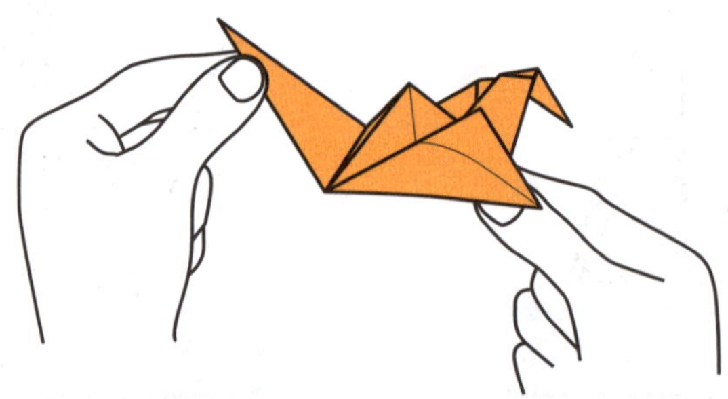

NINJA STAR

1

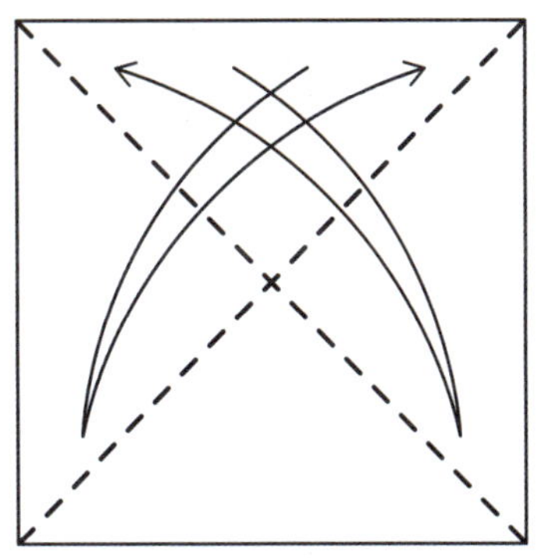

Begin colored side up. Fold and unfold diagonals.

2

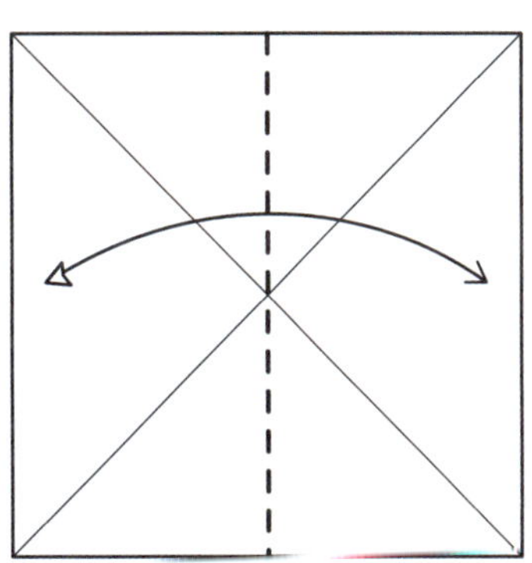

Book fold and unfold.

3

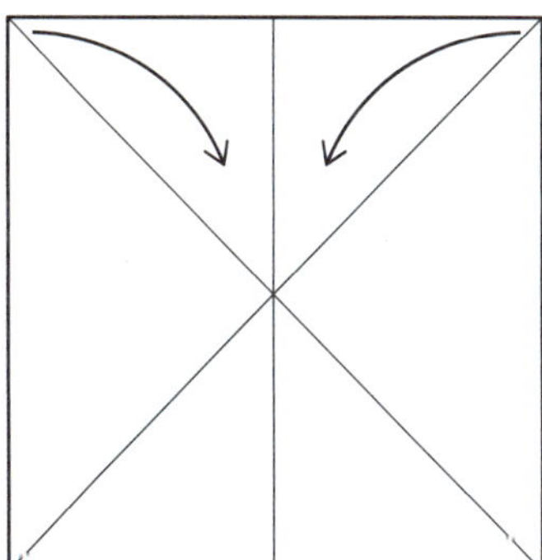

Fold top corners to the middle.

4

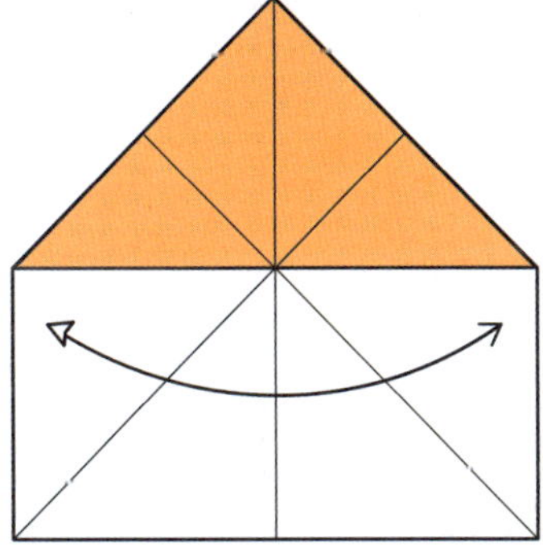

Rotate 90° and fold in half on existing crease.

5

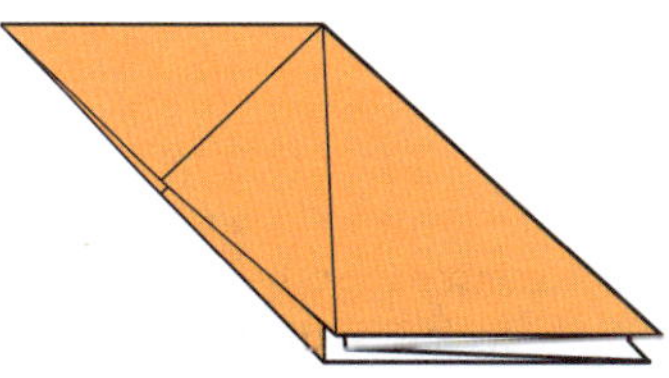

Push the square end into itself, using existing crease lines. This will make a completed unit.

6

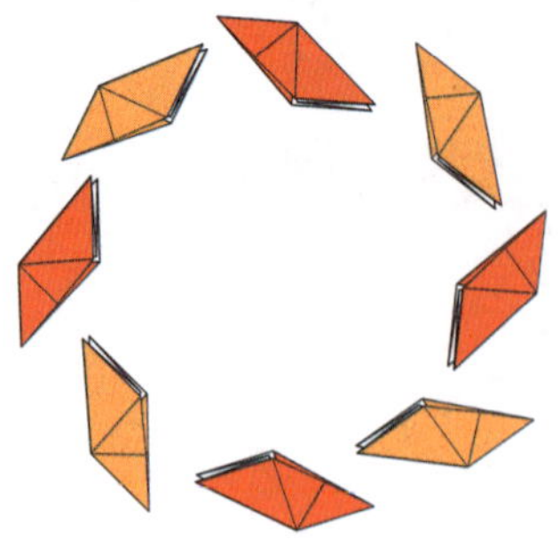

To make a ninja star, you need eight units. Two colors look best—use four sheets of each color.

7

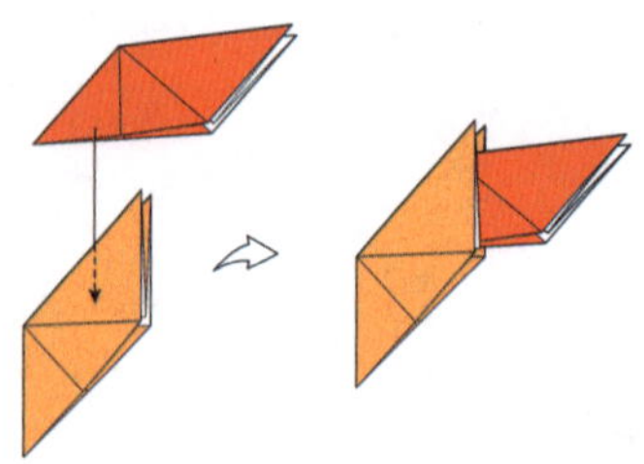

Join two units together. Insert closed front of one unit in between back flaps of next.

8

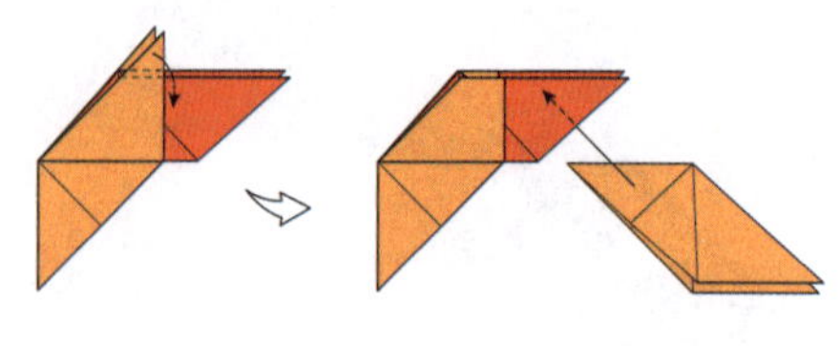

Fold the back flap tips inward to lock the units in place. A sliding motion should be possible between pieces.

9

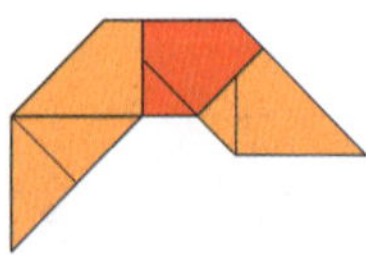

Lock the remaining units together. Ensure that the flaps are always tucked to either side of the closed front.

10

When locking in the final unit, tuck the flaps on either side of the closed front already in the crevice.

11

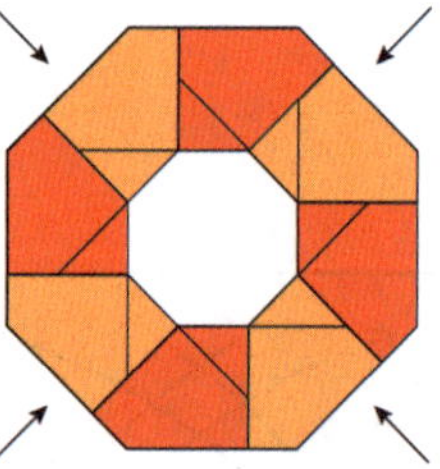

This is the untransformed version of the ninja star.

12

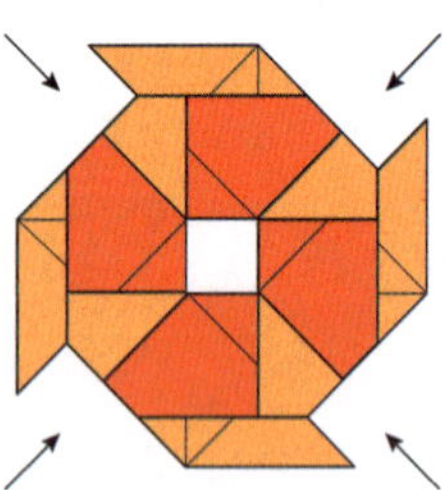

Push opposite sides of the octagon inward toward the center, allowing the pieces to slide against each other and reveal the "blades" of the ninja star.

13

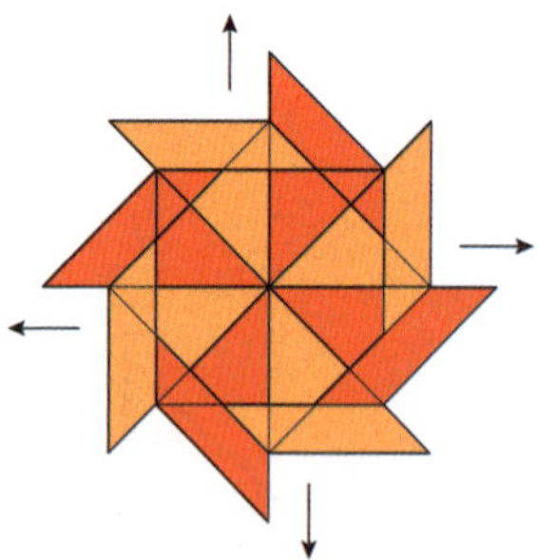

The ninja star is fully transformed when the hole in the center is closed and all 8 edges of the ninja star are revealed.

14

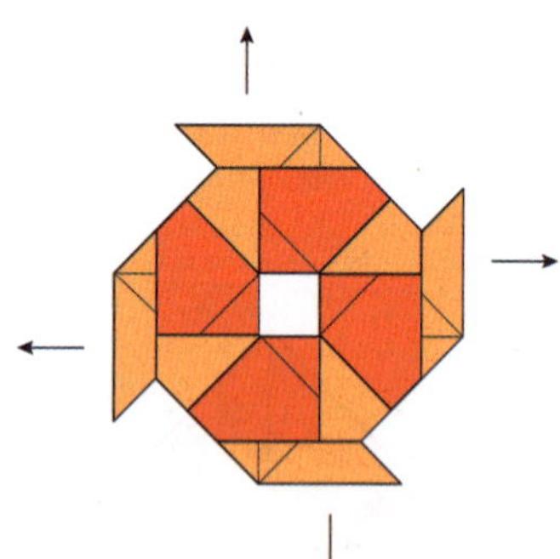

Pull outward on two opposite pieces until it reverts to the original untransformed state. Repeat steps to transform again and again.

INFINITY CUBE

There are many methods to make an origami infinity cube. The version shown here uses no sticky tape and more paper. You will need 48 x ((3.1 x 3.1in (8 x 8cm)) squares, and 16 x ((2.4 x 2.4in (6 x 6cm)) squares.

1

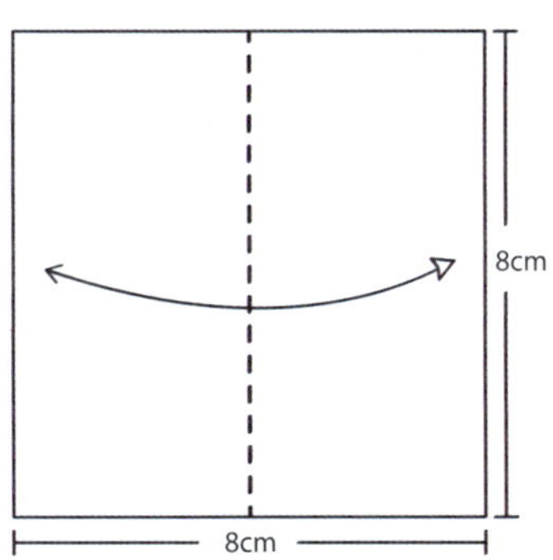

Begin with an a 3.1 x 3.1in (8 x 8cm) sheet. Book fold & unfold.

2

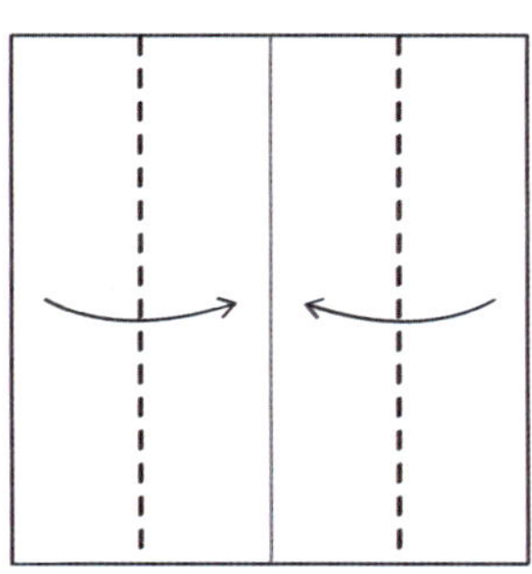

Cupboard fold and unfold.

3

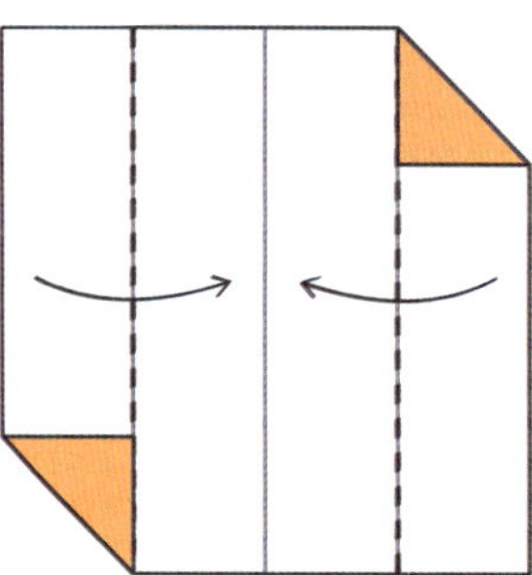

Fold top right and bottom left corners diagonally, into the existing creases.

4

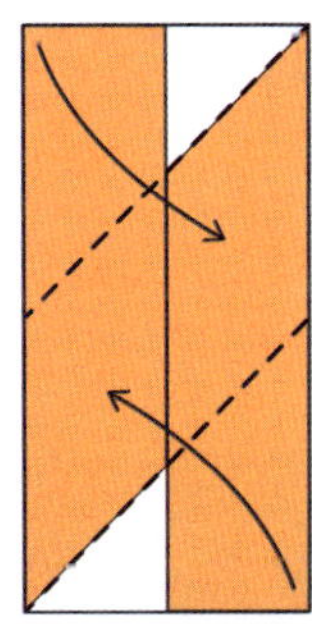

Cupboard fold again, on existing creases.

5

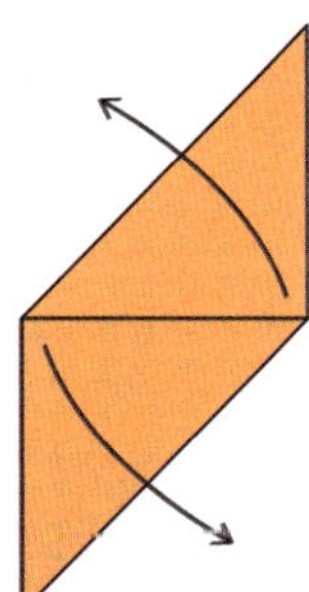

Fold bottom right and top left corners diagonally. Unfold.

6

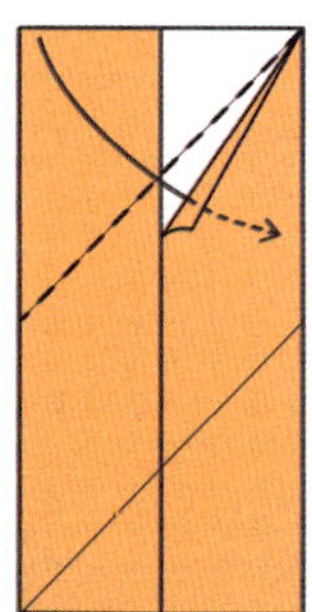

Fold top right corner back in diagonally on existing crease and tuck under cupboard fold.

7

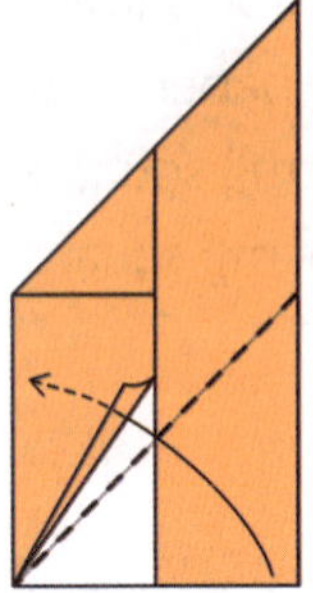

Repeat with bottom right corner.

8

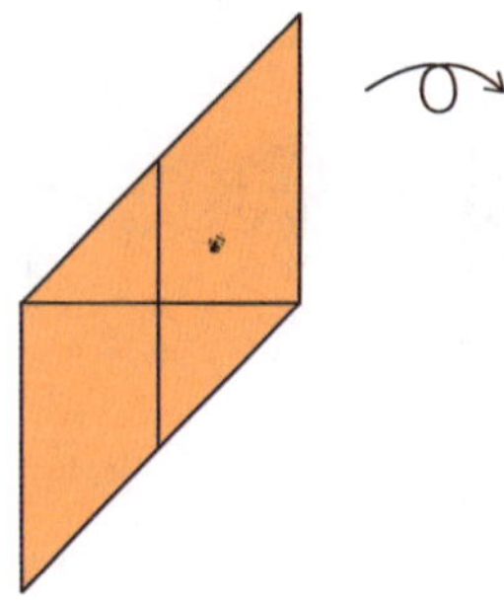

Flip over. Your completed unit should be in the shape of a parallelogram.

9

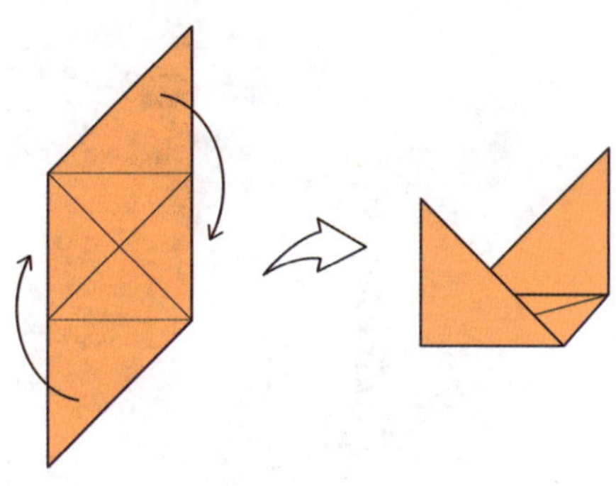

Fold 2 long corners in to make square face.

10

Repeat 5 times, to make the 6 units for a cube module.

11

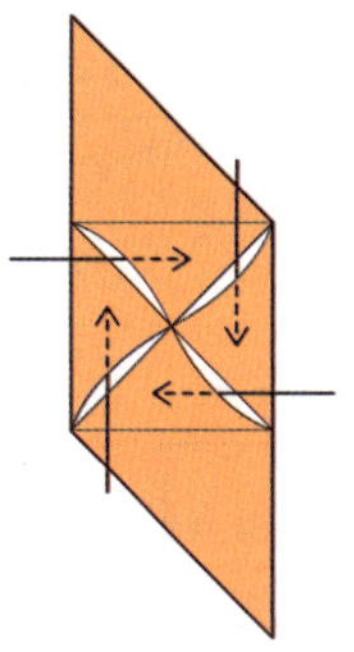

Each module will have 2 hands and 4 pockets.

12

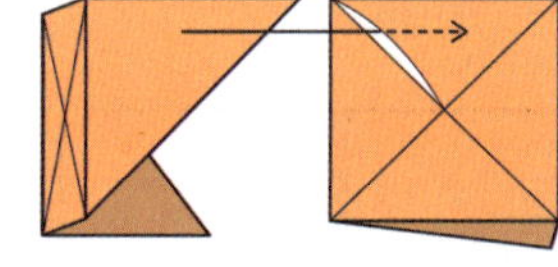

Hold one unit horizontally and another vertically. Insert the hand into the pocket.

13

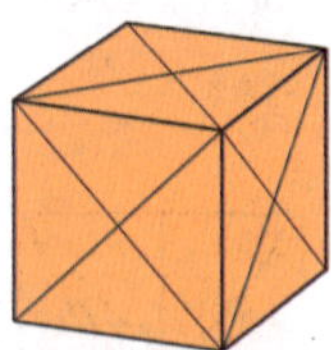

Continue inserting hands into pockets until you have a completed cube.

14

Repeat steps 1-13 to make 7 more cubes and lay out in a 2 x 4 grid.

15

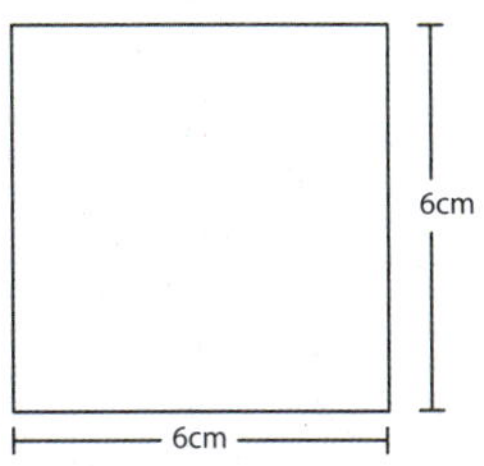

To make the connecting pieces, begin with a 2.4 x 2.4in (6 x 6cm) piece of paper.

16

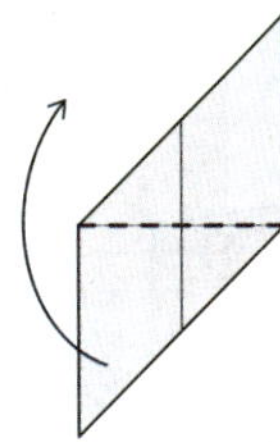

Repeat steps 1-8.

17

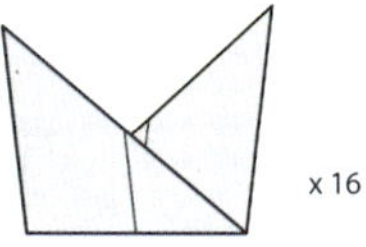

Fold the unit in half, so that there are two hands of equal length.

18

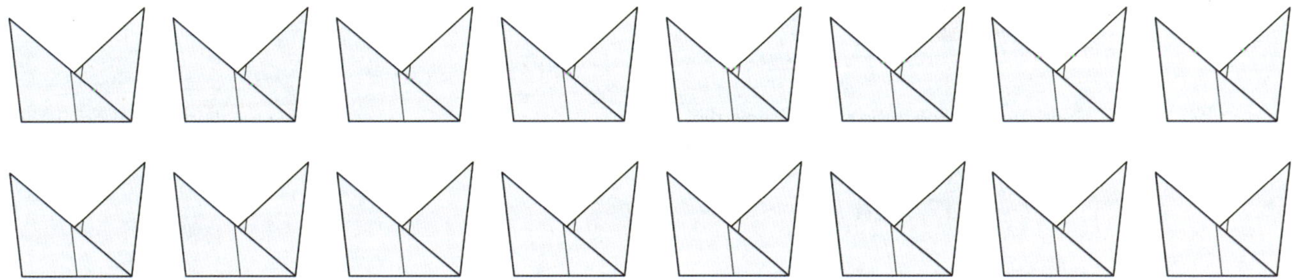

Repeat 15 times, for 16 units total.

19

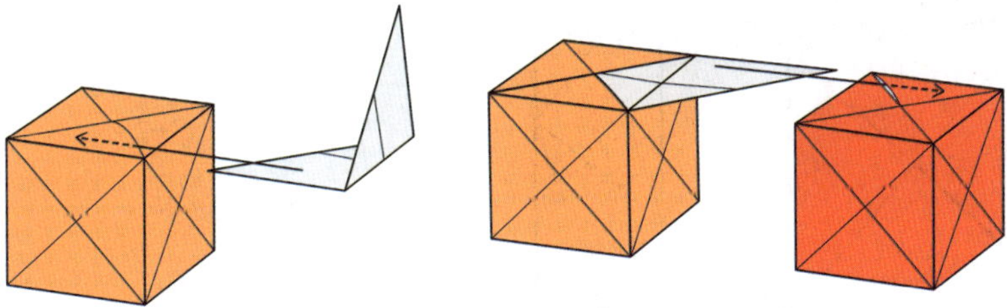

To connect the cubes, insert one hand of smaller unit into the side of cube module. Repeat for other hand with neighboring cube.

20

The two cubes are now connected.

21

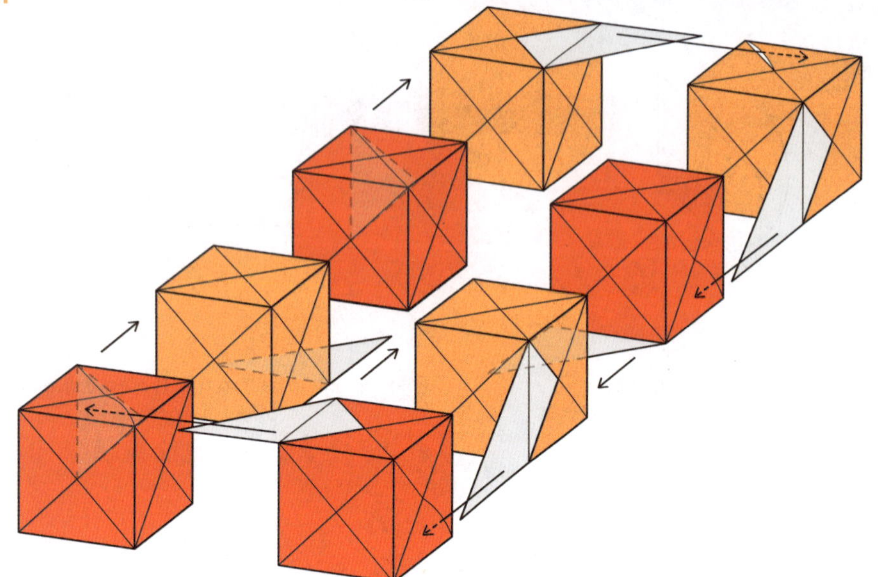

Continue to connect the cubes. Follow the diagram above to ensure all cube modules are connected correctly.

22

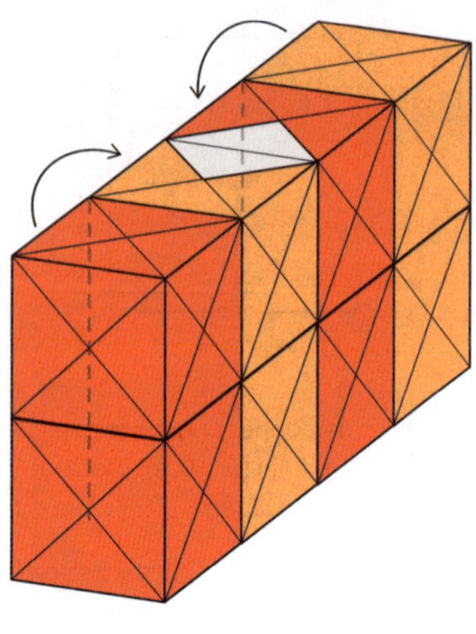

Have fun flipping the completed infinity cube.

MOVING FIREWORKS

This project uses 12 sheets with up to 6 varying colors. The only rule is to ensure each color is duplicated at least once. You can choose to use 2 x 6 colors (12 total), or 4 x 3, or 6 x 2.

1

Begin colored side up.
Fold and unfold diagonals.

2

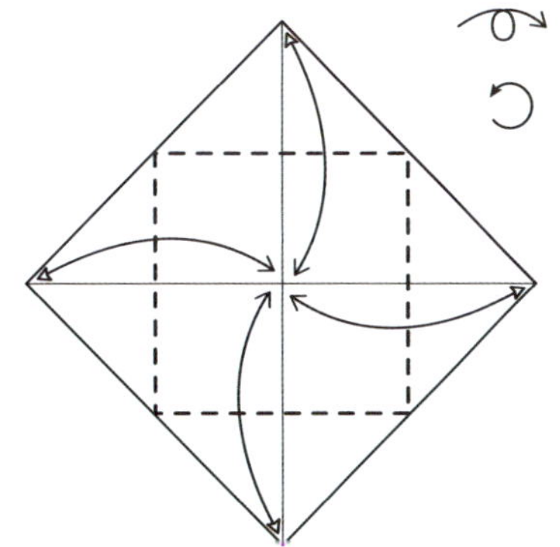

Blinz fold and unfold.
Turn over and rotate.

3

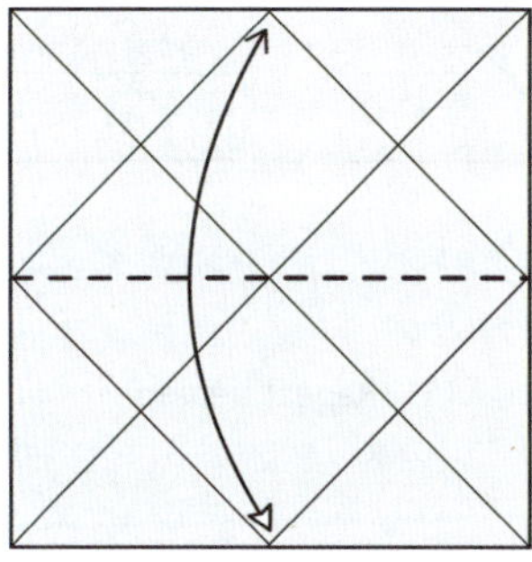

Book fold and unfold.

4

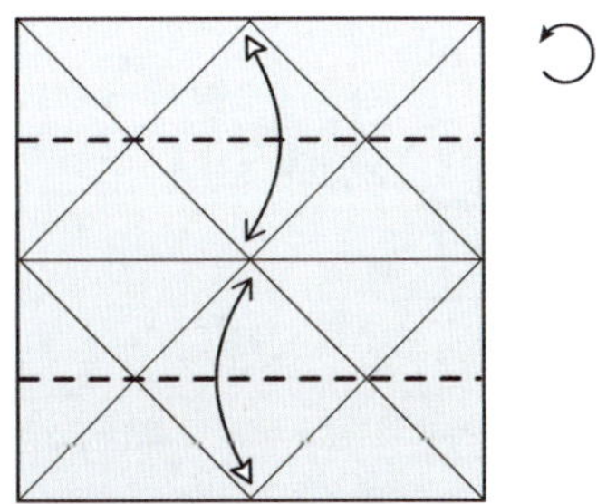

Cupboard fold and unfold. Rotate.

5

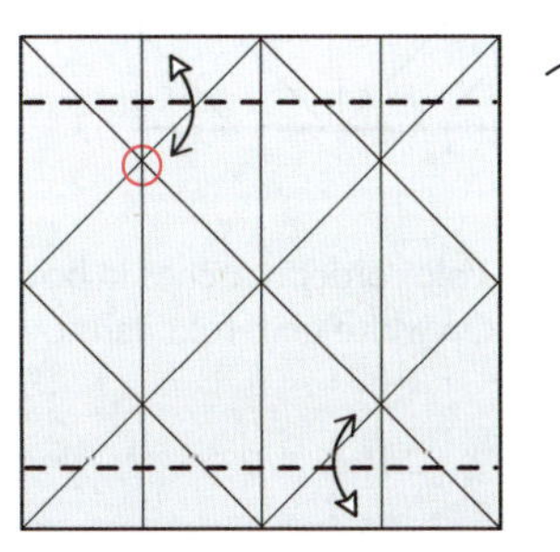

Valley fold and unfold. Turn over.

6

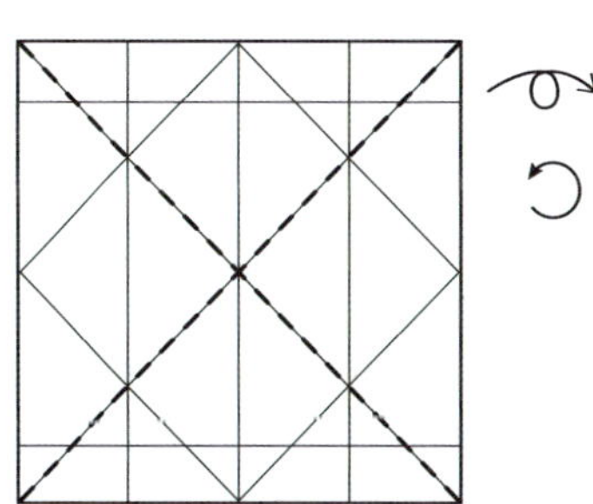

Fold diagonals along existing creases.
Turn over and rotate.

7

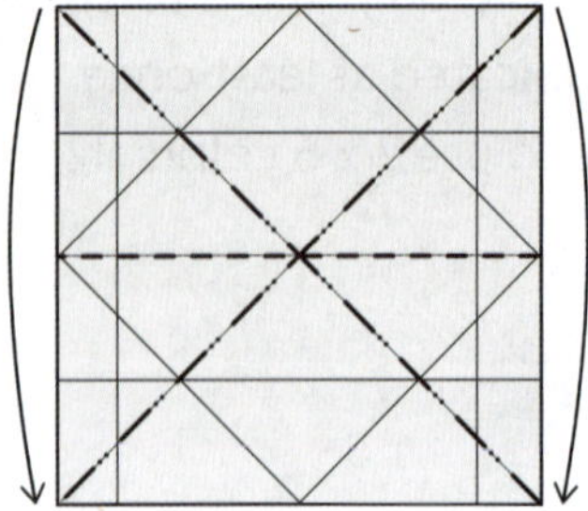

Collapse on existing creases.

8

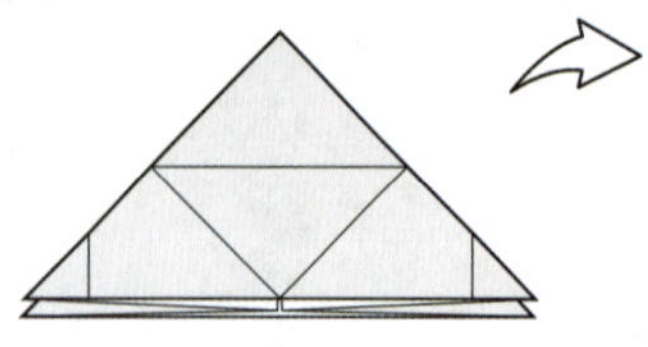

Completed waterbomb base.

9

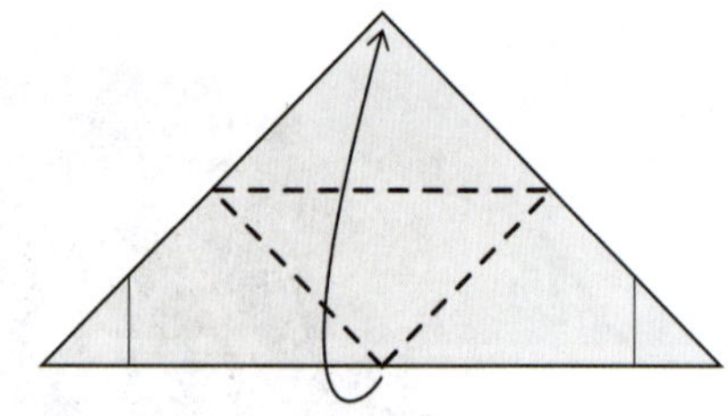

Squash fold using existing creases.

10

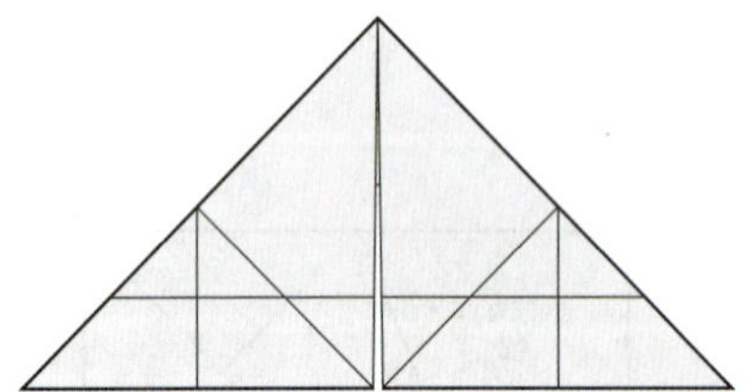

Repeat behind.

11

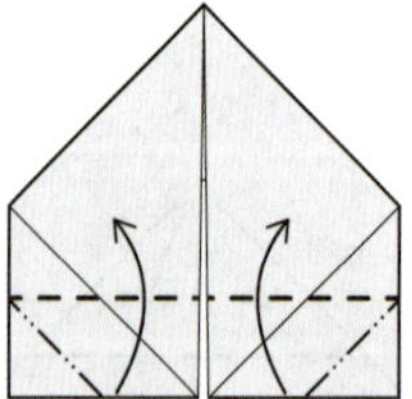

Squash fold on existing valley creases.

12

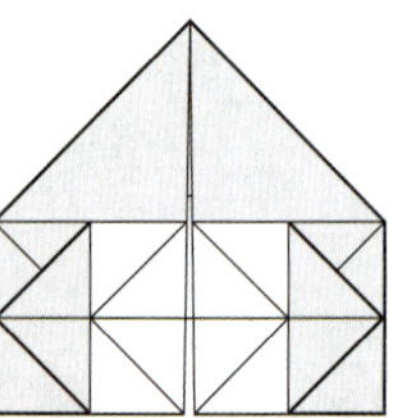

Unfold and repeat behind.

13

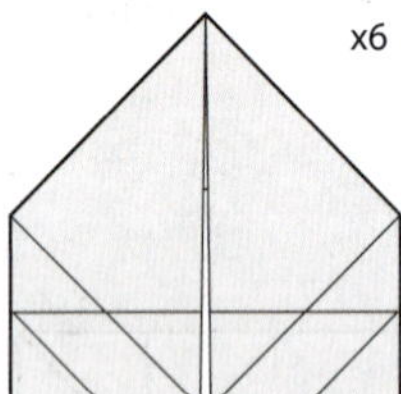

To make moving fireworks, you need twelve units. Repeat five times. Begin white side up and repeat another six times.

14

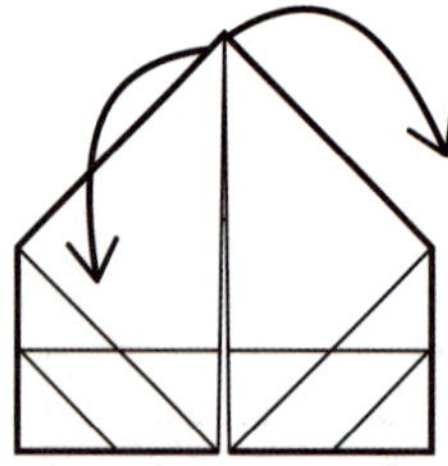

Ensure color order matches in both stacks. On white unit, fold flaps out.

15

HAND 1

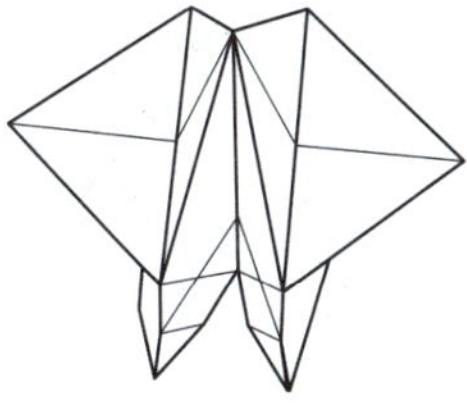

HAND 2

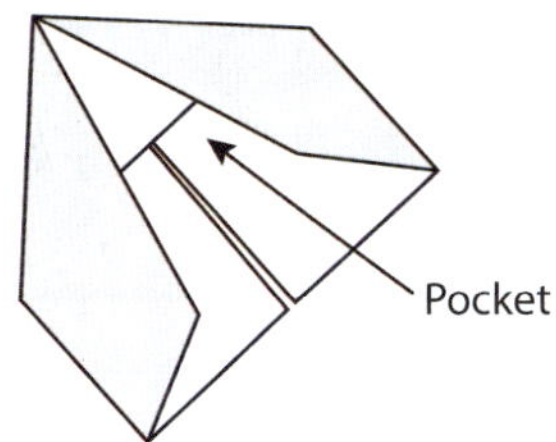

Completed units showing hands (white) and pockets (colored).

16

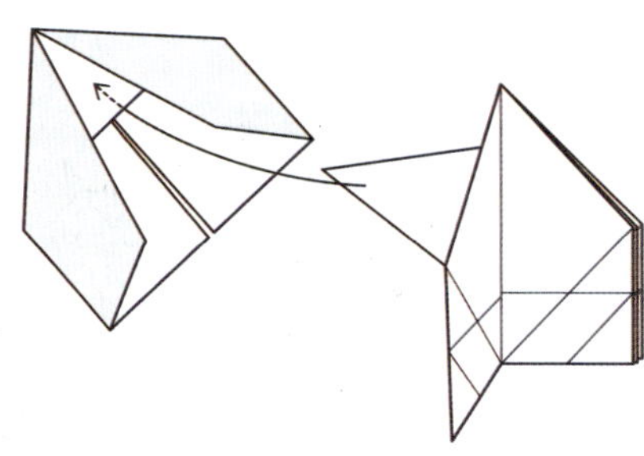

Pinch the right half of the white unit together and insert Hand 1 into pocket. The color inside the white unit should match the colored unit.

17

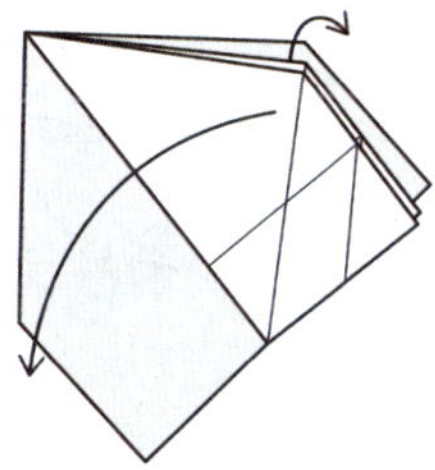

Open right half of the white unit to expose Hand 2.

18

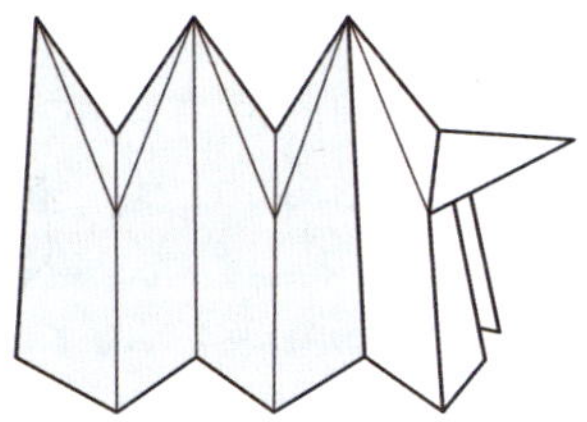

Side view of joined units.

19

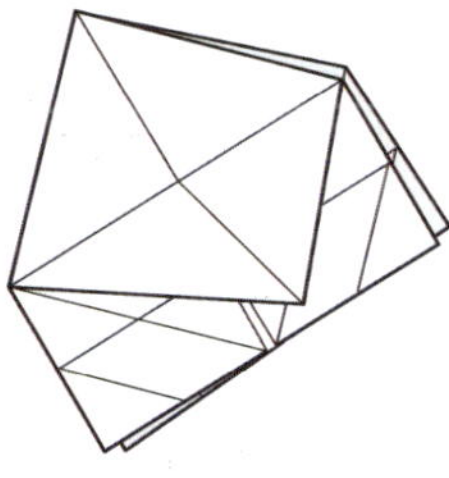

Insert Hand 2 from white unit into next color unit, and continue until all units are connected. Tap to ensure that bottoms are even. Rotate.

20

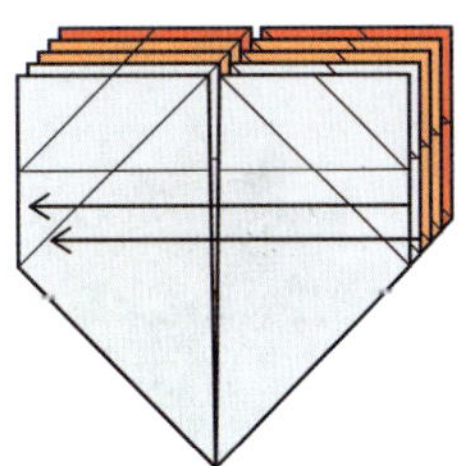

Lock units together by folding 2 flaps on the right side to the left.

21

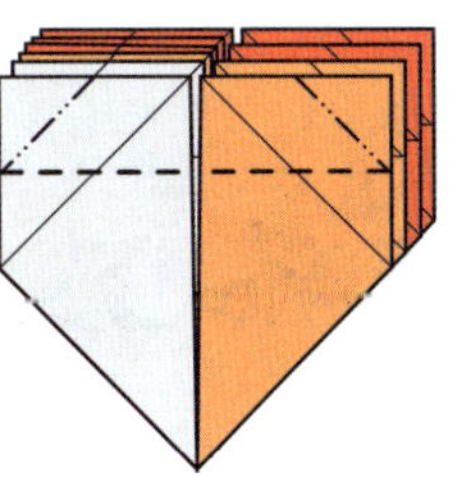

Use the lock creases (created in step 11) to secure.

22

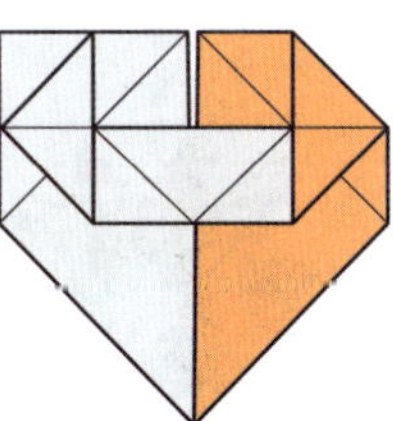

Finished lock. Continue to fold right flap to left and use lock creases to secure all units, skipping final white unit. Repeat on left side.

23

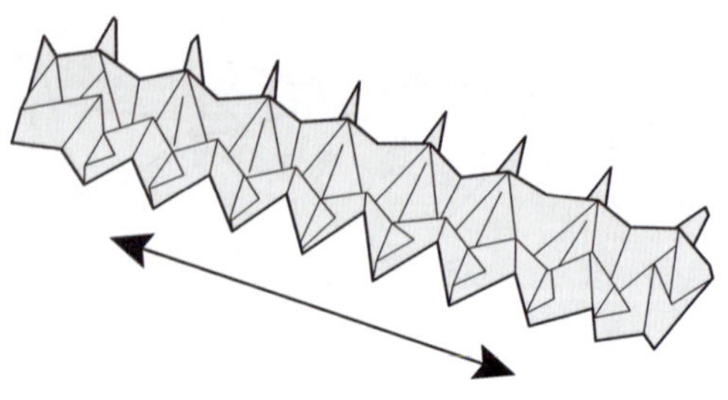

Stretch

24

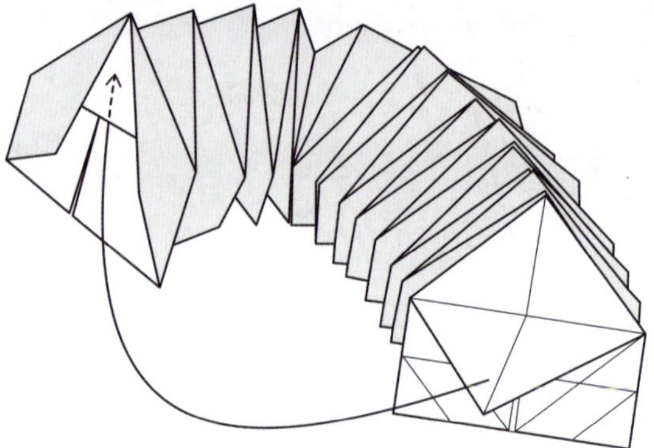

Insert remaining hand into pocket to close the loop.

25

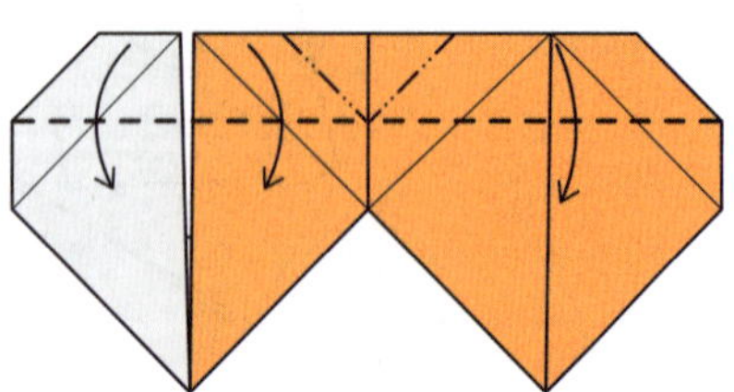

Secure the outer locks, then rotate model inside out to secure inner locks.

26

This is all twelve units fully connected. To transform, use both hands to rotate inside out.

27

Continue rotating for the full effect of the moving fireworks.

MAGIC BALL (DRAGON'S EGG)

This project is most easily completed using a rectangular sheet of paper with a ratio of 2:1. Letter sized printer paper or A4 paper cut in half lengthways works well. Note if using A4 paper, you will either need to trim it down a little or add an additional flap to then fan.

1

Start colored side up, with the long edge horizonal.

2

Diagonal fold bottom left corner to top edge.

3

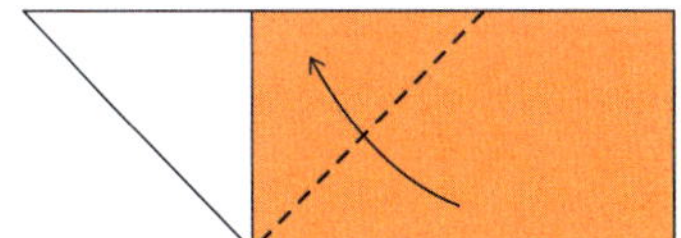

Book fold and unfold.

4

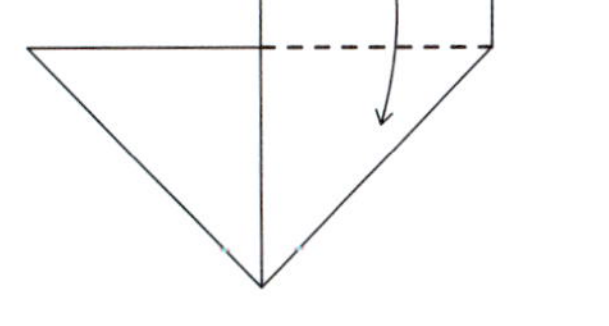

Turn over and fold flap down, in line with triangle edge.

5

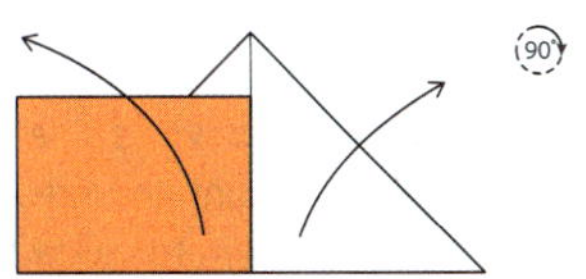

Unfold the diagonals, then rotate 90 degrees.

6

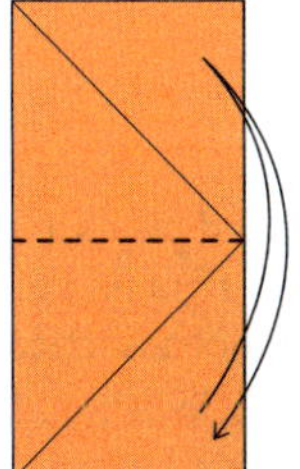

Book fold and unfold.

7

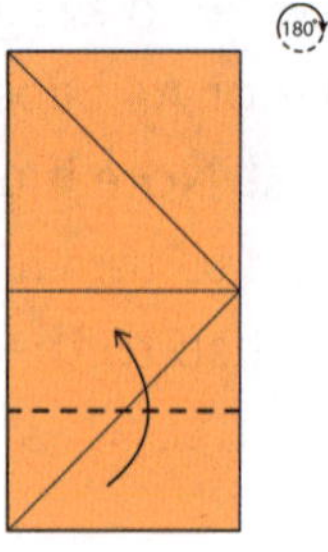

Fold bottom flap to middle crease.
Rotate.

8

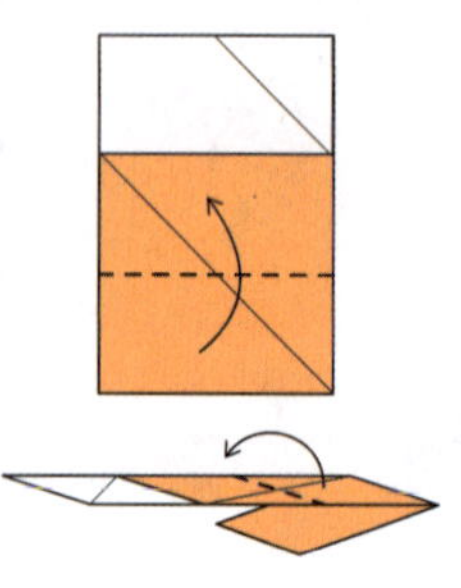

Fold bottom flap to middle crease.
The extra flap will swing out.

9

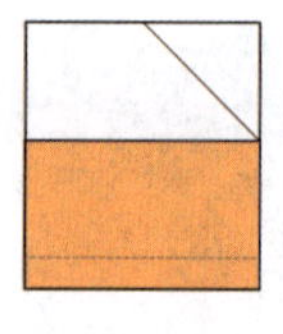

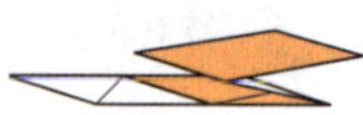

Your paper should now look like this.

10

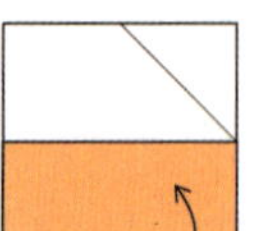

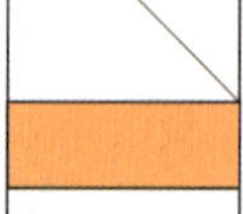

Fold edge of flap up, to align with bottom crease. Turn over.

11

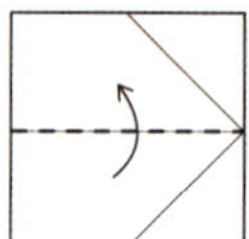

Fold in half, on existing crease.

12

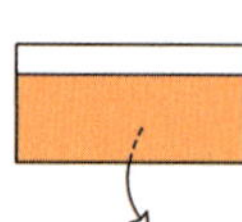

You should now have a folded fan.
Unfold.

13

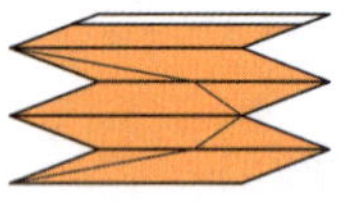

Side view of folded pleats. If using an A4 sheet of paper, add an extra fold to the next step to create an additional section in your paper.

14

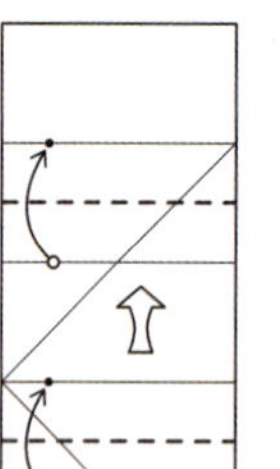

Turn over, so white side is up. Take the mountain folds, pinch and fold down to valley folds.

15

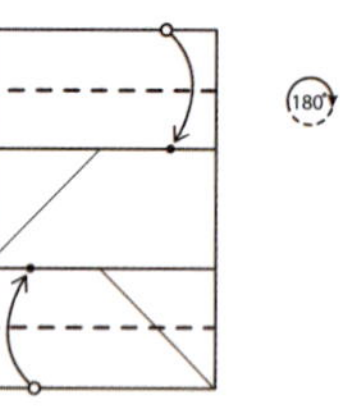

Fold both edges in, to the closest existing crease. Rotate.

16

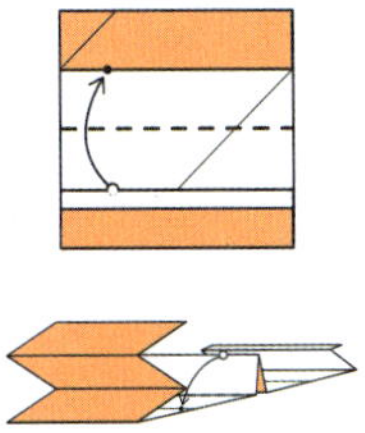

Take existing fold (from step 15) and fold in opposite direction, as though turning the page of a book.

17

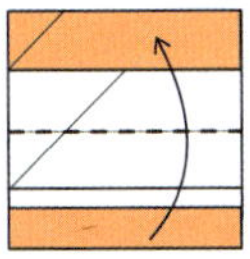

Fold in half on existing crease.

18

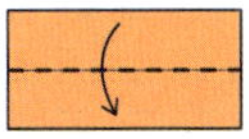

Fold top flap down to halve again, on existing creases.

19

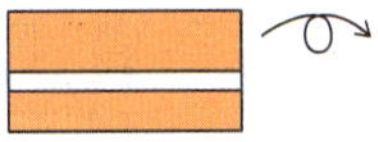

Turn over.

20

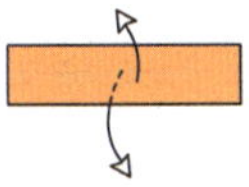

Repeat step 19 on this side.

21

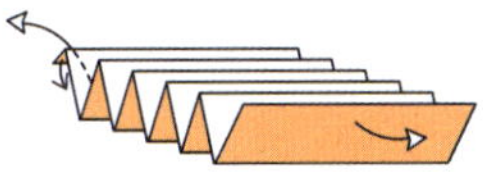

Fold flaps up. Spread out, white side facing up.

22

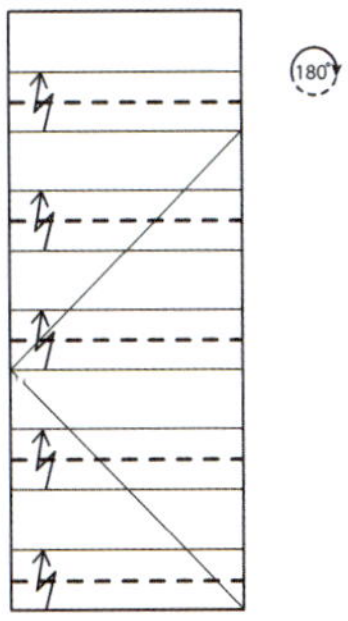

Take mountain folds, pinch and fold to closest valleys, working from top to bottom (or left to right). This includes the bottom edge. Rotate

23

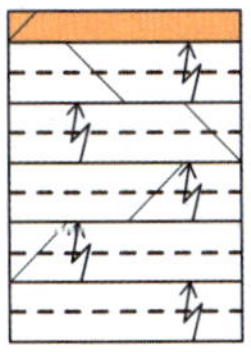

Take existing folds from previous step, and fold in opposite direction, as though turning the page of a book.

24

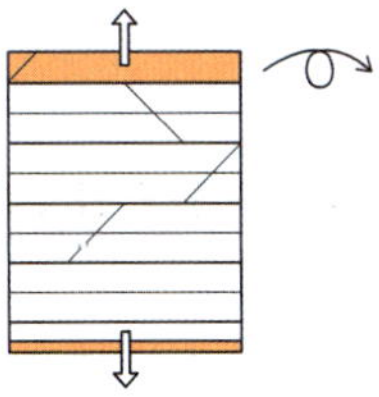

Fully unfold and turn over.

25

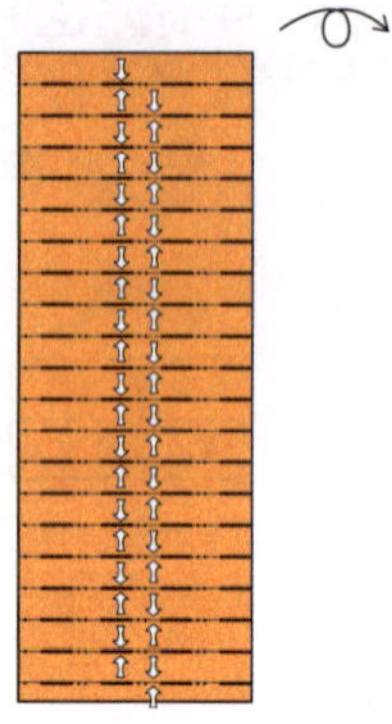

Colored side should now be up. All folds need to be refolded so that they are mountain folds. The paper will no longer lay completely flat. Turn over.

26

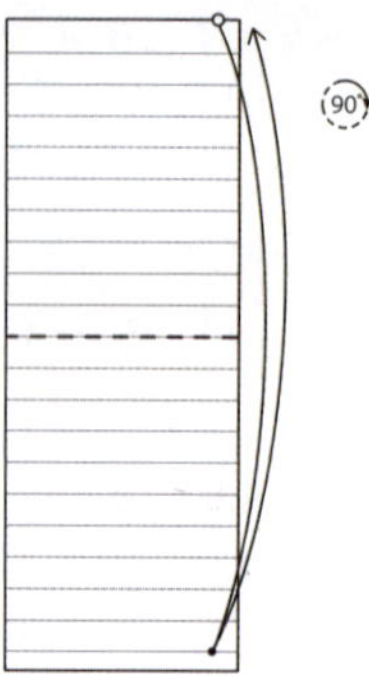

Fold in half. The sheet should only fold easily to the final crease, as there should be an odd number of sections. If there is an even number, chop one off. Unfold and rotate.

27

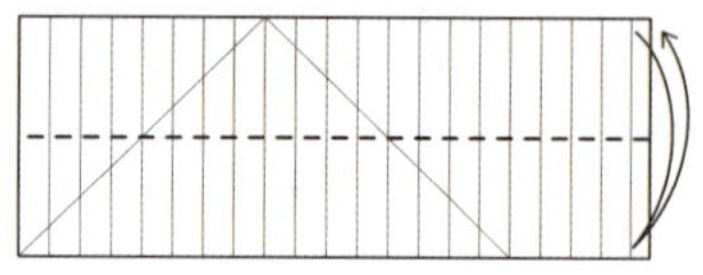

Book fold and unfold.

28

Cupboard fold and unfold. Turn over and rotate.

29

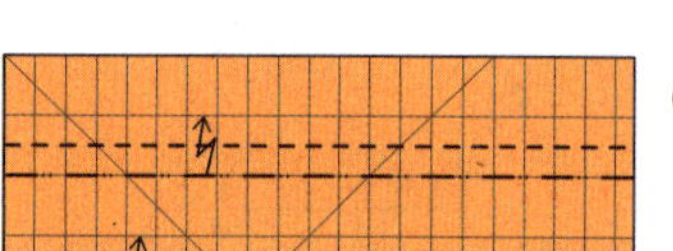

Take middle crease, pinch and fold up to closest existing crease. Repeat with bottom crease. Rotate.

30

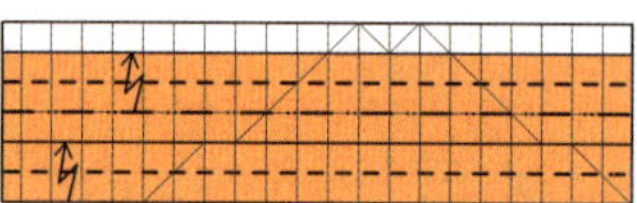

Pinch existing mountain fold from previous step, and fold in opposite direction, as though turning the page of a book. Fold bottom edge up.

31

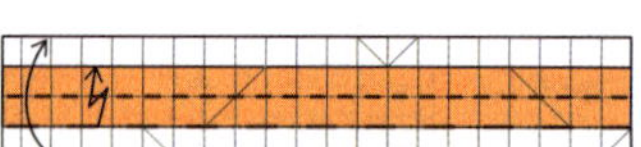

Fold in half.

32

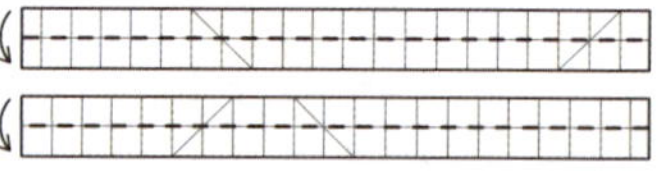

Fold outer flap down on existing crease. Turn over and repeat.

33

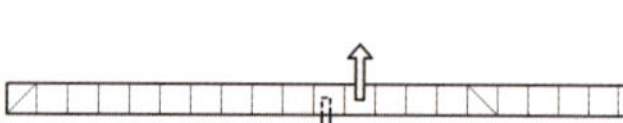

You should now have a fan shape. Unfold and rotate.

34

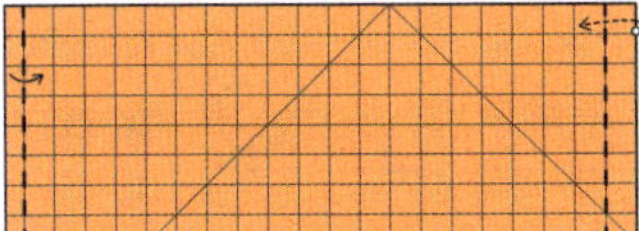

The colored side should be up. Fold edges in, left edge in front and right edge behind.

35

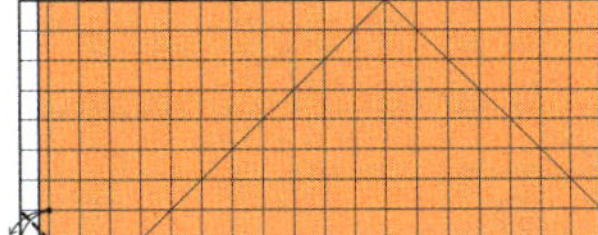

Fold bottom left corner diagonally to closest intersection of creases. Unfold.

36

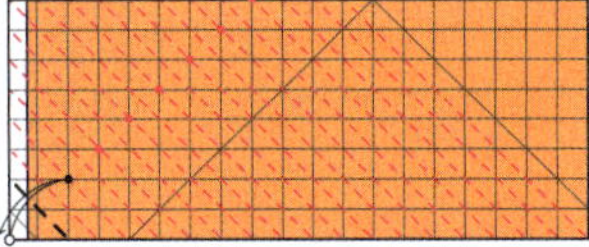

Fold to next intersection of creases. Unfold and repeat, moving up the sheet of paper.

37

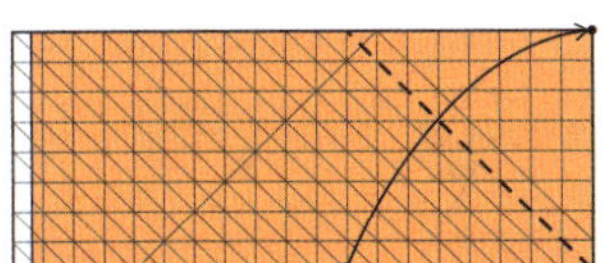

Once at the top edge, continue to fold to nearest crease (rather than intersection). Stop when you reach the bottom right corner.

38

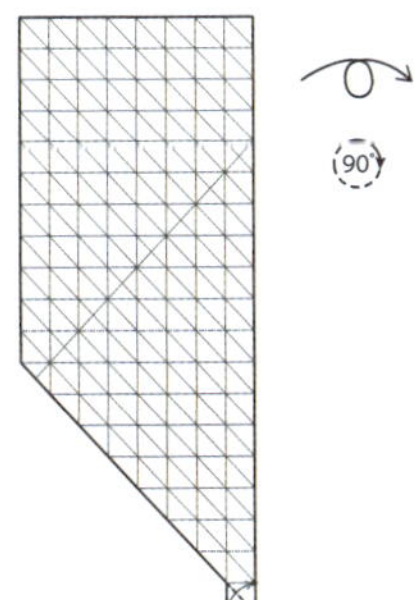

Your sheet will now look like this. Fold corner under, then turn over and rotate.

39

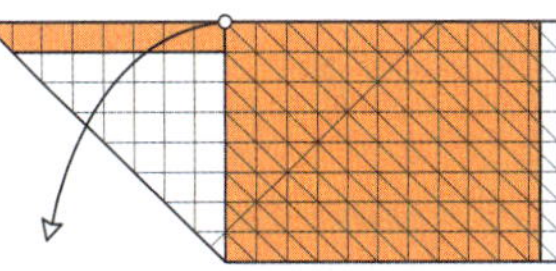

Starting at the last diagonal fold, unfold and fold diagonally to the closest crease intersection.

40

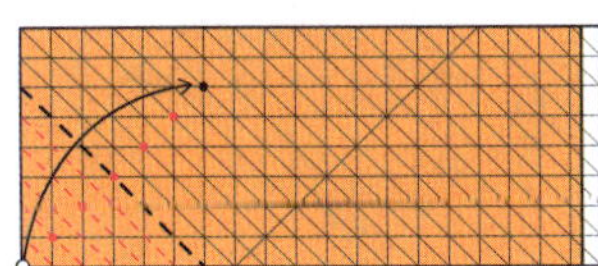

Repeat, moving down the sheet, until you reach the bottom corner.

41

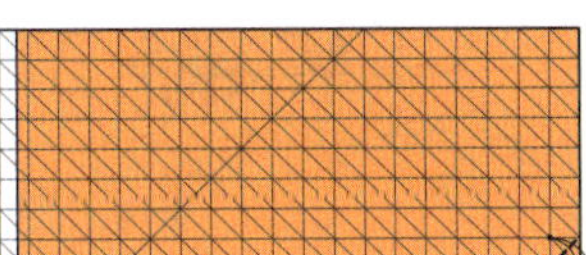

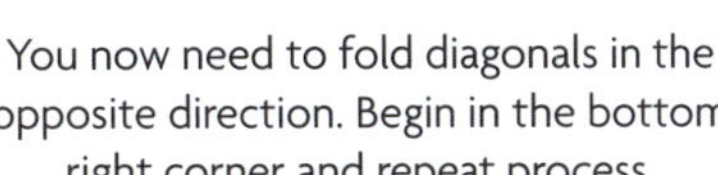

You now need to fold diagonals in the opposite direction. Begin in the bottom right corner and repeat process.

42

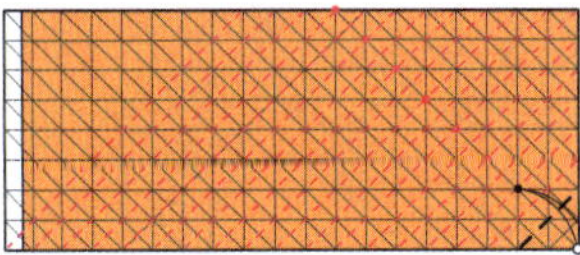

When the bottom left corner is reached, rotate and continue.

43

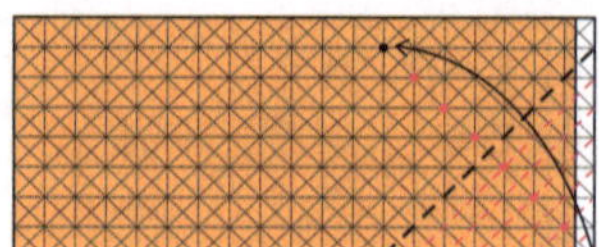

Repeat until full sheet has diagonal folds going in both directions.

44

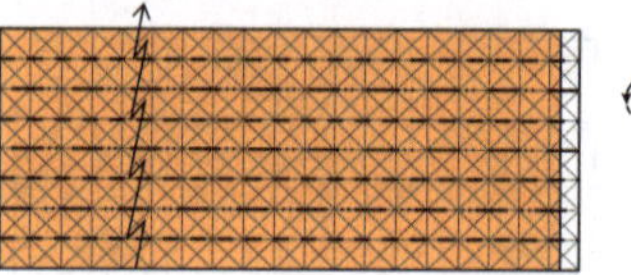

Re-fold the existing creased pleats to make a fan. Rotate

45

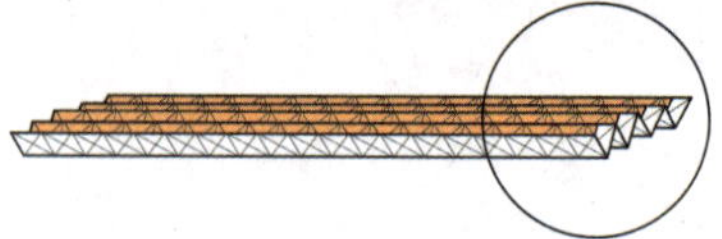

Reverse fold along existing creases at valley folds shown.

46

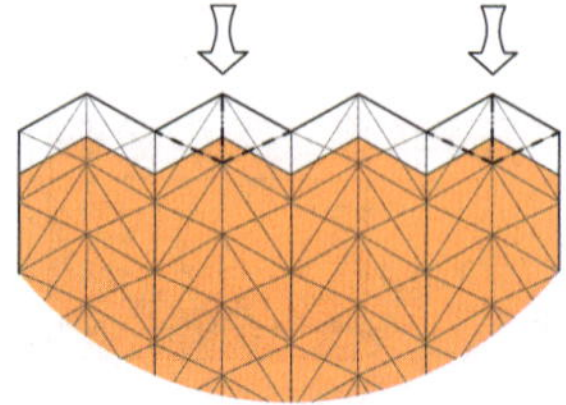

Open up the first valley fold and fold both corners in to make a triangle. Close fold and repeat.

47

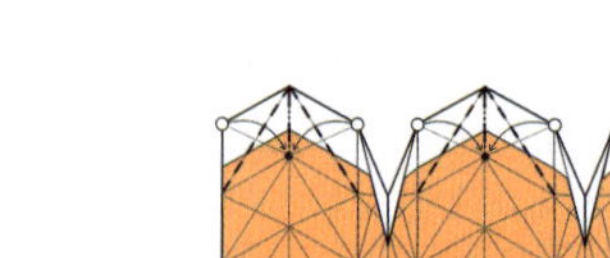

Turn over and rotate. Press in at point shown.

48

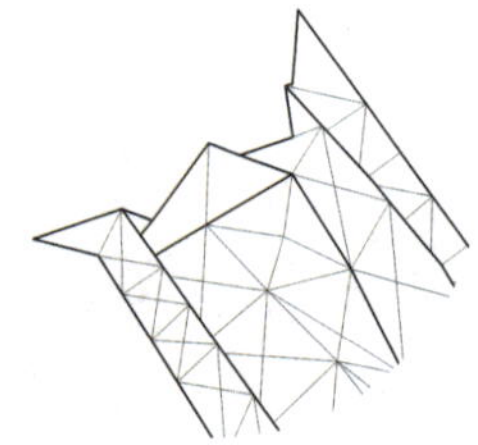

This creates a box shape that you can extend down the full row. Repeat on second point. Turn over.

49

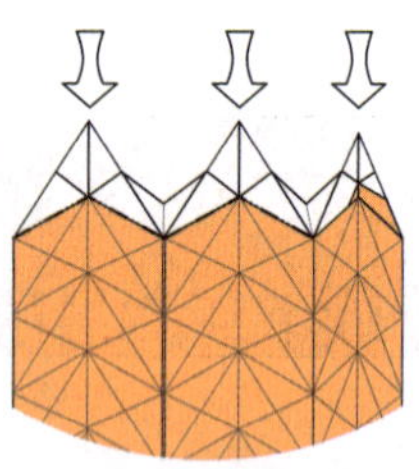

Pinch and push edges of boxes to collapse inwards.

50

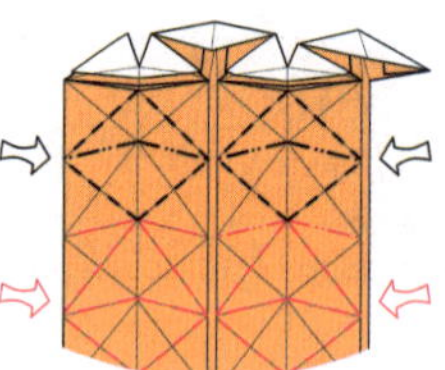

Open out and pinch at the creases shown. Push back together.

51

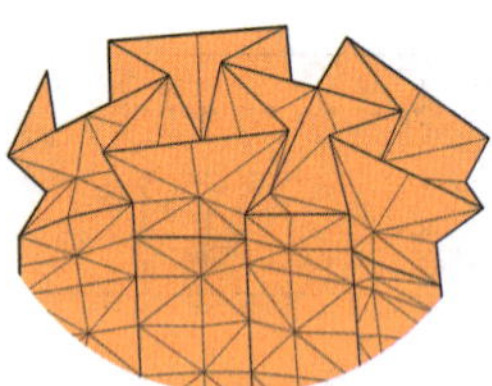

Pull apart again and repeat, alternating which columns are pinched and which are skipped each time.

52

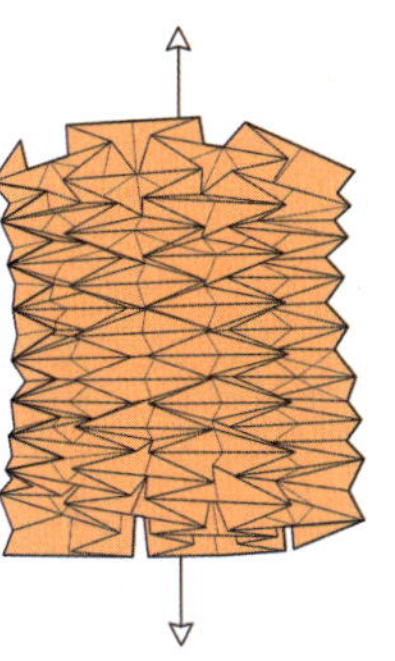

When complete, your sheet should look like this. Open out.

53

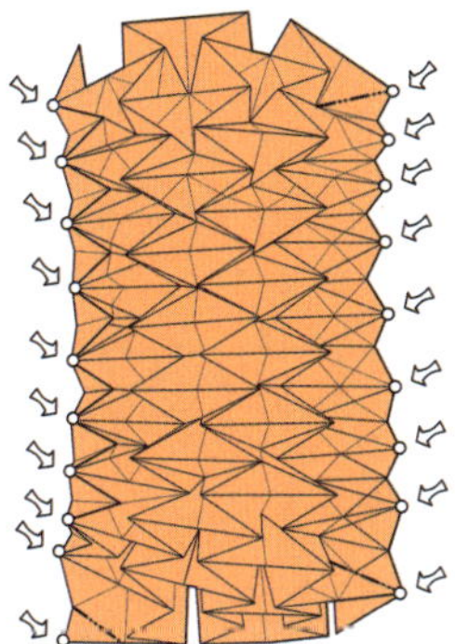

Reverse fold where shown along both edges.

54

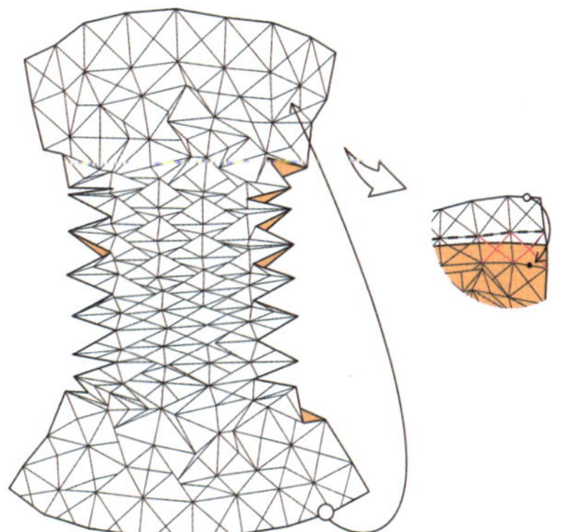

55

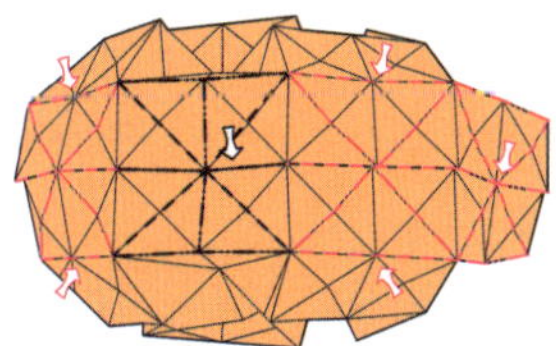

Pinch and push folds along edges, to recreate the folded pattern.

Unfold the corners and edges on both sides. With the white side up, bring the bottom edge up edge, ensuring the sheets line up on the sides. Fold a second time to secure. to the top crease. Fold top edge down, over the bottom.

56

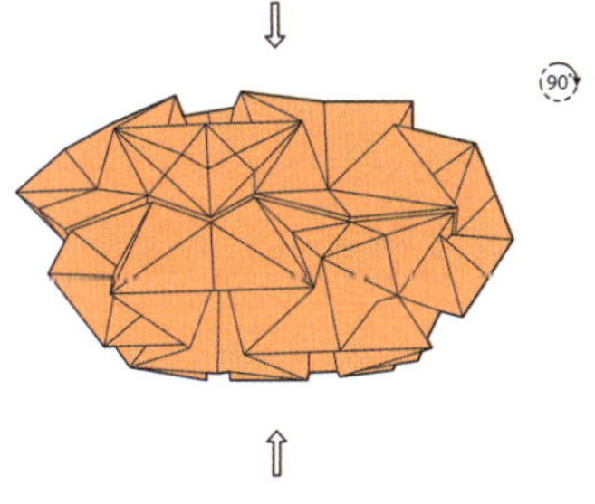

You should now have a completed magic ball. Push at the sides to fully deflate. Rotate.

57

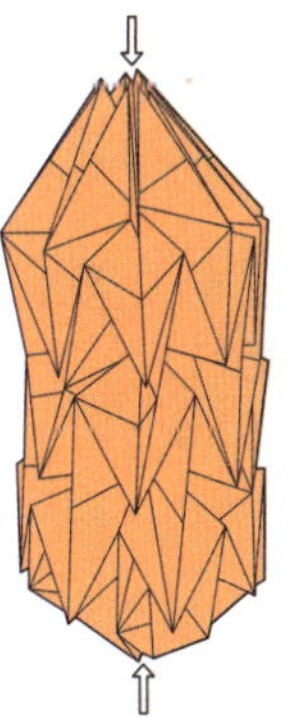

Push on top to inflate the ball.

58

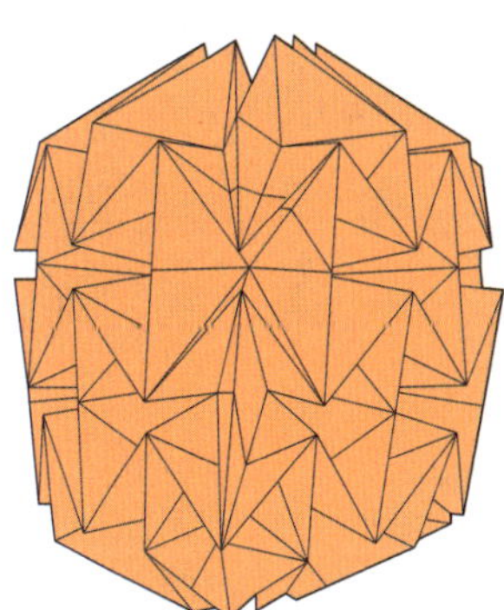

The inflated ball will look like this. Have fun deflating and reinflating!

ORIGAMI PAPERS

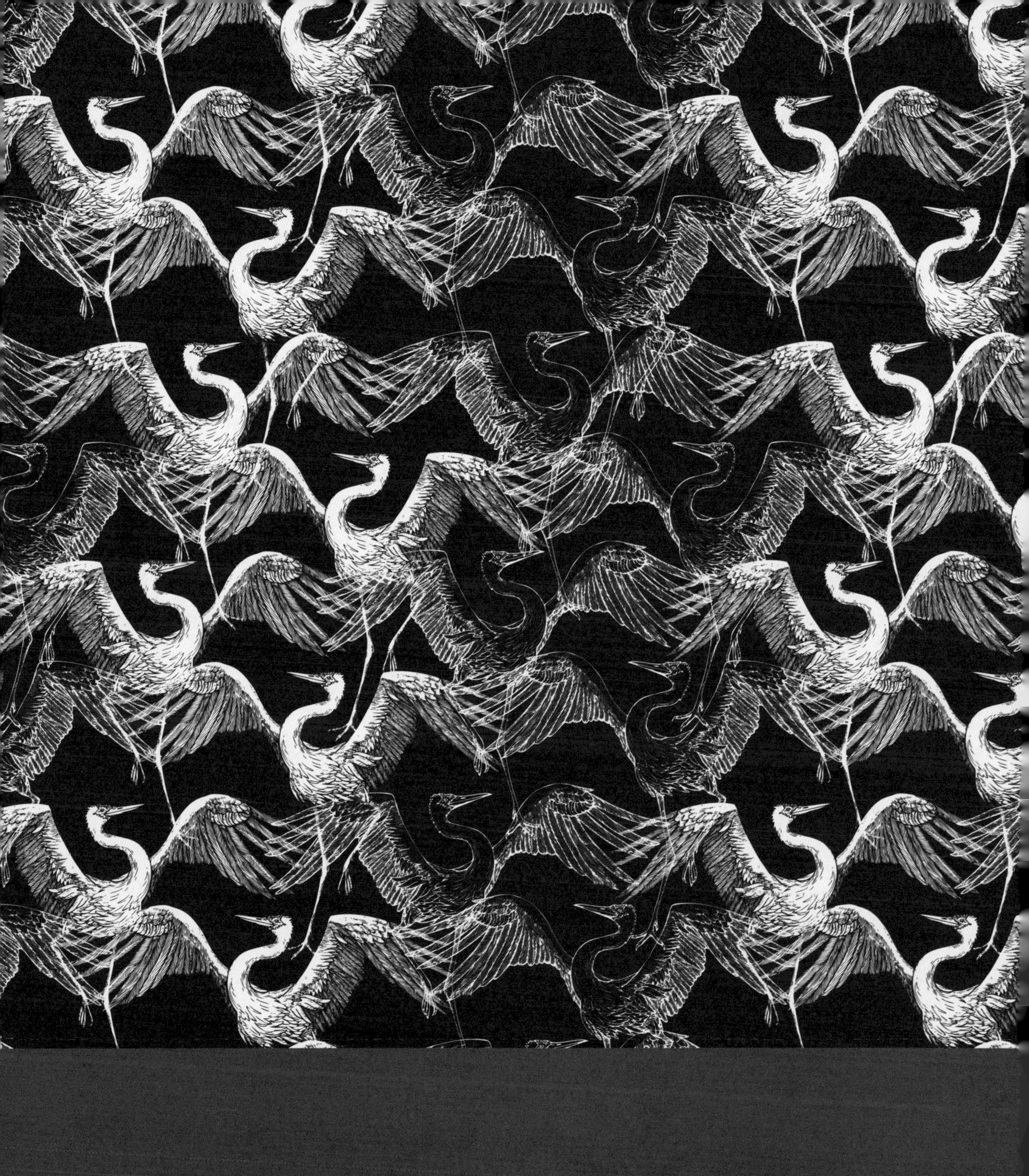

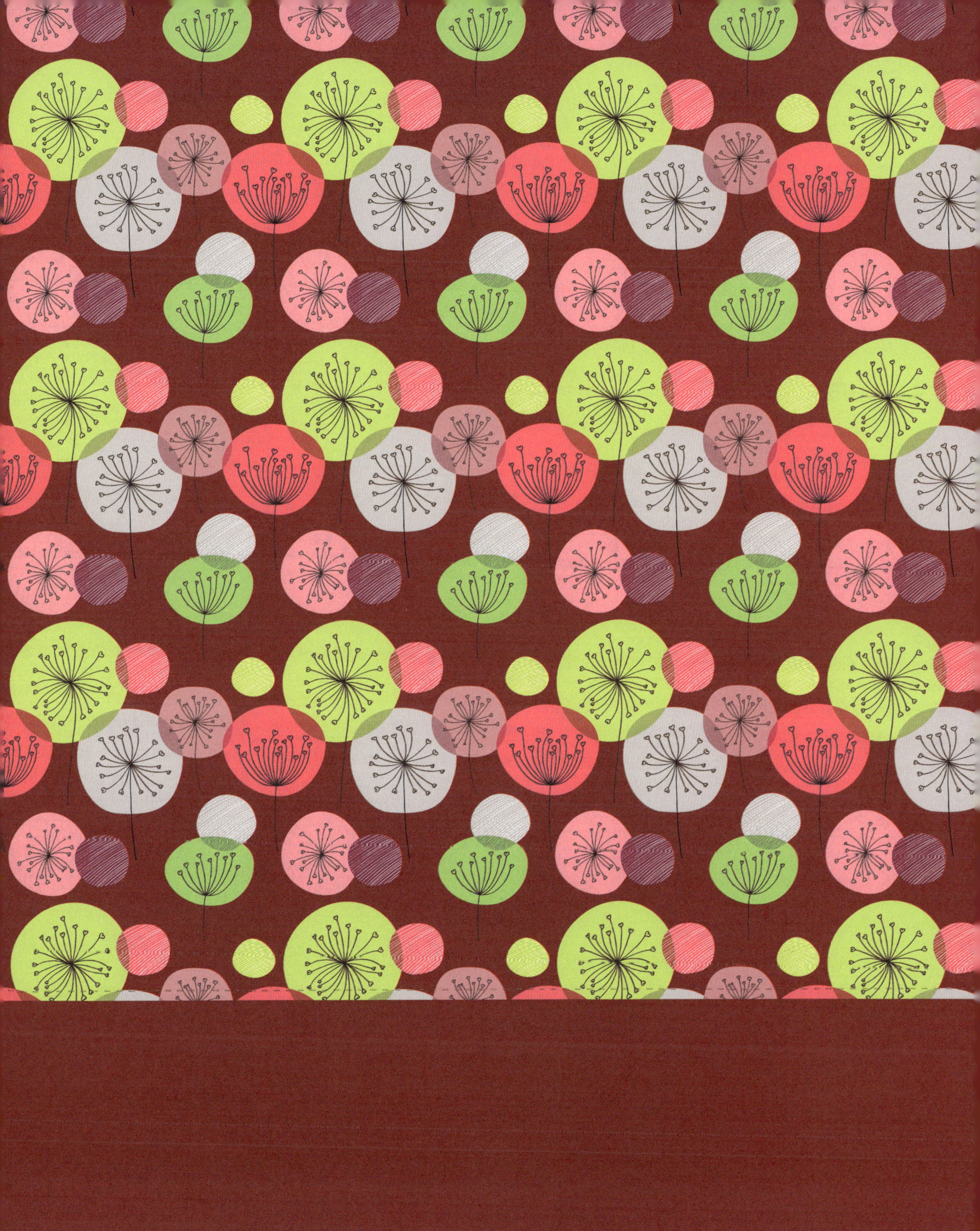